The Historical Consumer

The Historical Consumer

Consumption and Everyday Life in Japan, 1850–2000

Edited by

Penelope Francks
Honorary Lecturer in Japanese Studies, University of Leeds, UK

and

Janet Hunter
*Saji Professor of Japanese Economic History,
London School of Economics and Political Science, UK*

palgrave
macmillan

First published 2012 by
PALGRAVE MACMILLAN

Palgrave Macmillan in the UK is an imprint of Macmillan Publishers Limited, registered in England, company number 785998, of Houndmills, Basingstoke, Hampshire RG21 6XS.

Palgrave Macmillan in the US is a division of St Martin's Press LLC, 175 Fifth Avenue, New York, NY 10010.

Palgrave Macmillan is the global academic imprint of the above companies and has companies and representatives throughout the world.

Palgrave® and Macmillan® are registered trademarks in the United States, the United Kingdom, Europe and other countries.

ISBN: 978–0–230–27366–5

This book is printed on paper suitable for recycling and made from fully managed and sustained forest sources. Logging, pulping and manufacturing processes are expected to conform to the environmental regulations of the country of origin.

A catalogue record for this book is available from the British Library.

A catalog record for this book is available from the Library of Congress.

10 9 8 7 6 5 4 3 2 1
21 20 19 18 17 16 15 14 13 12

Printed and bound in Great Britain by
CPI Antony Rowe, Chippenham and Eastbourne

Contents

Tables

Illustrations

Map

Figures

Acknowledgements

The project out of which this book arose was generously funded by a grant made jointly by the British Association for Japanese Studies and the Daiwa Anglo-Japanese Foundation. This made possible a workshop for contributors, held in London in July 2010, and we are grateful to all the contributors for their active and positive participation. In addition Martin Dusinberre of the University of Newcastle and Christopher Gerteis of the School of Oriental and African Studies (SOAS) in London acted as discussants, and their contributions highlighted the interconnections among papers and greatly helped us to frame the introduction. The Department of Economic History at the London School of Economics (LSE) provided logistical support and our thanks go to Linda Sampson and Tracy Keefe for administrative support throughout. Michael Andrews gave valuable assistance with the organisation of the workshop and Steven Ivings with preparation of the final manuscript. Finally, thanks of course to Richard and Stephen for resolving computing crises, buying supplies and much else.

Contributors

Penelope Francks Honorary Lecturer in Japanese Studies, University of Leeds; Research Associate, School of Oriental and African Studies, University of London

Tomoko Futaya Part-time Lecturer, Nagoya Keizai University, Inuyama, Aichi, Japan

Andrew Gordon Lee and Juliet Folger Fund Professor of History, Department of History, Harvard University

Janet Hunter Saji Professor of Japanese Economic History, London School of Economics

Barak Kushner University Senior Lecturer in Modern Japanese History, Faculty of Middle Eastern and Asian Studies, University of Cambridge

Beverly Lemire Professor of History and Henry Marshall Tory Chair, Department of History and Classics and Department of Human Ecology, University of Alberta

Angus Lockyer Lecturer in the History of Japan, Department of History, School of Oriental and African Studies, University of London

Helen Macnaughtan Lecturer in International Business and Management (Japan), Department of Financial and Management Studies, School of Oriental and African Studies, University of London

Isamu Mitsuzono JSPS Fellow, Graduate School of Humanities and Sociology, University of Tokyo

Naofumi Nakamura Professor of Business History, Institute of Social Science, University of Tokyo

Satoru Nakanishi Professor, Graduate School of Economics, Nagoya University

Masayuki Tanimoto Professor of Economic History, Graduate School of Economics, University of Tokyo

Maki Umemura Sasakawa Lecturer in Japanese Studies, Cardiff Business School, Cardiff University

Note on Transliteration

Japanese names and words are romanised according to the modified Hepburn system. Long vowels are indicated by the use of macrons, which are omitted in the case of Tokyo, Osaka and Kyoto. Japanese names are given in line with the Japanese practice of family name preceding given name, with the exception of Japanese authors writing in English.

1

Introduction: Japan's Consumption History in Comparative Perspective

Penelope Francks and Janet Hunter

Introduction: defining consumption in the Japanese historical context

Over recent decades, we have become ever more familiar with consumer goods that originate in Japan, while the Japanese consumer, dressed in the latest fashion, exercising gourmet taste in food and drink and weighed down by the latest gadgets, has become an accepted part of the image Japan conveys at home and abroad. On the other hand, we are also well aware that Japanese households have demonstrated a phenomenal capacity to save and have appeared reluctant to spend their way out of the recent economic stagnation, suggesting an approach to consumption perhaps different from that typically associated with the spendthrift West. Nonetheless, we are far from familiar with the history that might help to explain the often distinctive features of Japan's consumption practice. While historians of Europe and North America have been busily discovering the long development path of the consumer, the consumption history of countries beyond the heartlands of Western capitalist industrialisation, such as Japan, has rarely been explored. Indeed, scholars such as Stearns (2001) seem to suggest that these regions have little consumption history of their own.

This assumption is now being challenged, as scholars of regions as diverse as China, India, Latin America and the Ottoman Empire begin the process of discovering the various histories of the 'non-Western' consumer. Their research demonstrates that these histories are long ones, seeming to confirm Kenneth Pomeranz's persuasive argument that the Great Divergence in the economic fortunes of West and East did not pre-date the Industrial Revolution (Pomeranz, 2000). It has also opened up the possibility of a comparative consumption history, and global historians of shopping, fashion and taste are beginning to be able to spread their net beyond Europe and North America.

Nonetheless, in the case of Japan, despite obvious evidence of consumer activity from the early-modern period onwards, and the global significance of the country's rapid industrialisation and modernisation from the second half of the nineteenth century, economic historians have remained reluctant to recognise the role of consumption. This contrasts with more extensive analysis of Japanese material life by cultural and art historians, and by sociologists and anthropologists. The difficulty of incorporating 'culture' into rigorous social science analysis has perhaps impeded a recognition that this work has much to offer economic history, while the area-oriented focus that characterises Japanese Studies, and the all too frequent institutionalised disciplinary divides, often pose a barrier to knowledge passing the other way. While this volume retains an economic emphasis in its approach to consumption, it also seeks to build on a wide range of historical literature and historical approaches, with a view to making a contribution to scholarship beyond a narrow economic-history audience.

The question of what actually constitutes consumption does not have a straightforward answer, and the authors of the chapters in this volume have taken a range of approaches to address that question. We have not sought to impose a uniform definition on them, rather asking them to justify their own choices in the context of their research questions, methodology and arguments. It is nevertheless important to acknowledge the difficulties associated with defining consumption and reconciling the very obvious differences of interpretation that exist even amongst economists and economic historians. Mainstream economics tends to treat consumption as denoting only the final purchase of goods and services by individuals, but broader definitions are also widely used, in both scholarly and popular works, and can imply all expenditure directed towards the satisfaction of individual needs and wants, even via the production of other goods. In both cases, however, consumption is likely to be regarded, for analytical purposes, as a one-off, final act involving the purchase of a particular good or service at a particular point in time, whether or not this is then used for some purpose other than final consumption. From a historical perspective, this focus on final purchase would seem to make it more difficult to understand the dynamic of consumption – for instance the links between goods within what Jan de Vries has termed 'consumption clusters' (de Vries, 2008) – and the complex ways in which any purchase was decided on, mediated and carried out. Moreover, if we are to understand the role of consumption in Japan's economic history, it is not just its volume and composition that matter, but also, following Douglass North (North, 1990; 2010), the formal and informal institutions through which it takes place.

Consumption as a one-off, final purchase has also frequently been placed in binary opposition to the act of production. Adam Smith's statement that all production was ultimately for the purpose of consumption has been used to some effect in justifying recent research on the importance of the 'consumer revolution' for European economic development (for example Berg, 2005). However the distinction between production and consumption is often an indistinct one, particularly in pre-industrial and industrialising economies in which both consumption and production activities are located mainly in the household and associated with a high degree of unpaid family labour. Japan was such a developing economy through to the 1960s, and the sewing machines discussed in Gordon's chapter in this volume, for example, were often utilised both for income earning (production) and as final use goods (consumption) for the personal enjoyment of the purchaser. It would therefore seem to make little sense to consider consumption completely separately from production; producers may have decided how best to make and sell their goods, but they did so in a context in which they had to be aware of and respond to the imperatives and desires of their consumers, albeit perhaps increasingly trying to shape those desires at the same time (for examples, see the chapters by Gordon, Francks and Kushner). For the historical analysis in this book, therefore, we believe that it makes more sense to consider consumption as part of the dynamic cycle of production, exchange and utilisation that characterises the everyday economic activities not just of individuals, but of all groups in a society.

Ambivalent consumers? The historiography of consumption in Japan

Japan's modern economic history has overwhelmingly been portrayed as a story of the growth of production, in which the government, private firms and other producers were the key to the successful manufacture and, increasingly, export of an ever-expanding range of goods. The consumption boom of the 1980s has frequently been interpreted as a 'new' stage in Japan's development, when it at last embraced consumerism and became a consumer society (see, for example, Clammer, 1997). Notwithstanding the existence of a consensus among a majority of economic historians of Japan that it was the domestic market, rather than exports, that was the main driver of the growth in production for most of the period since the late nineteenth century, a serious imbalance has emerged between our knowledge of the supply side and our knowledge of consumption.[1] Even as interpretations of Japan's transformation from the 'pre-modern', 'feudal' society of the early nineteenth century to the 'Asian giant' of the late twentieth century have evolved, the absence of a significant role for consumption and the consumer has remained a consistent feature of analysis of Japan's economic and, to a large extent, social history.

While neglect of consumption is indeed a common feature of work on the economic history of the non-Western world in general, specific aspects of the historiography of Japan also contributed to it in this particular case. The Marxist frameworks that dominated the historical analysis of Japan's economy in the inter-war years and into the post-war period were premised on ideas of rural over-population and oppressive landlord–tenant relations, forces which, it was argued, limited the possibilities for growth in the incomes and purchasing power of the rural and urban working classes. The presumed 'narrowness' of the Japanese domestic market was taken up by non-Marxist historians, and frequently seen as the major factor driving Japanese businesses to seek markets overseas, first in the Empire and later in the rest of the world.[2] Although the Marxist theory that once explained it has now been largely abandoned, rural poverty – hence an everyday life focused on 'necessities' rather than any consumerist 'luxuries' – remains a trope running through most accounts of pre-war life, whether academic or more popular.

As the post-war years progressed, 'modern economics' gradually came to dominate analysis of the history of Japan's economy, and the questions being asked about Japanese development were inevitably different ones. As analysts began to look to the past to help explain the phenomenal economic growth going on around them, they naturally came to focus on the historical roots of the technologies, institutions and government and business practices that appeared to be capable of generating the dramatic expansion in production represented by the 'economic miracle' of the 1960s. Hence, although the bulk of the increase

[1] A similar imbalance has existed in scholarship on regions such as South Asia and the Ottoman Empire.

[2] A line of thought that continues through to analysis of the late twentieth-century economy. See for example Katz, 1998.

in the output of Japanese industry has always been directed towards the domestic market, and everyday life was clearly transformed by the ability of the mass of households to acquire many more, and different, consumer goods, Japanese economic growth continued to be viewed as essentially a top-down, supply-side phenomenon.[3]

This approach has become increasingly at odds with developments in economic and social history more broadly. With the rise of the Annales school foregrounding historical research into everyday life, and the 'discovery' of the 'consumer revolution' of eighteenth-century England, work on the acquisition and use of consumer goods in pre-industrial and industrialising Europe boomed, to the extent that it has now become impossible to analyse the Industrial Revolution without reference to the growth in the demand for goods that preceded and accompanied it.[4] As suggested above, this excitement over research into retail, fashion and home decoration has been much slower to spread to those working on areas beyond the industrialised West, including Asia. However, the debate over the Great Divergence focused new attention on comparative living standards and consumption levels on the eastern side of the divide, and scholars of China in particular began to describe the early modern stirrings of the consumer, both elite and ordinary (Clunas, 1991; Brook, 1999; Adshead, 1997). More recently, those working on other parts of the world – the Ottoman Empire (Quataert, 2000), South Asia (Haynes et al., 2010), Latin America (Bauer, 2001) – have also begun the process of delineating consumption history as a legitimate field of study in their areas.

It would be misleading, of course, to claim that the consumer has been entirely absent from the work of economic and social historians of Japan. Scholars of the urban culture of the Tokugawa period have long recognised that the theatre, the production of books and prints, and the whole spatial and social environment of the great cities reflect their nature as centres of consumption (for example, Shively, 1991; Berry, 2006). The history of everyday life, as instantiated in 'folk' and craft objects, has consistently held a fascination for Japanese scholars, museum curators and ordinary people, and the 'Edo Boom' associated with the construction of the Edo-Tokyo Museum was fuelled by a new

[3] This applies both to classic economic analyses, such as Lockwood, 1968 and Ohkawa & Rosovsky, 1961, and to the more institutional literature that followed Johnson's seminal study of the Ministry of International Trade and Industry (Johnson, 1982).

[4] For a useful survey of the earlier 'consumer revolution' literature, see Glennie, 1995.

wave of nostalgia for past ways of life (Sand, 2006). In recent years, increasing interest in issues of 'modernity' in pre-war Japan has produced a number of studies of the ways in which the urban middle-class lifestyle evolved, with department stores and women's magazines taking centre-stage as the mediators of modernising influences (for example Sand, 2003; Sato, 2003). For the post-war period, Simon Partner's pioneering study (Partner, 1999) incorporated the role of the market into analysis of the rise of the electrical-goods industry, but his approach has not been followed up by mainstream economic historians, despite the explosion of interest in contemporary consumerism among anthropologists and sociologists.

What we find, therefore, is that few existing studies tackle the issues with which the consumption history of the pre-industrial and industrial West has been concerned, and evidence of the actual practice of day-to-day consumption is often hard to discern. By contrast, saving – often regarded as the obverse of consumer spending – has become an increasingly well-researched topic. Thanks to the work of scholars such as Sheldon Garon and Charles Horioka, we now know a great deal about the efforts made by the state to encourage habits of saving and the emergence in Japan by the second half of the twentieth century of significantly higher levels of household saving than those achieved in most other industrialised economies (see for example Garon, 2000; Horioka, 2006). The place of consumption within this literature is limited to the 'rational' use of 'modern' goods, within the context of the particular 'ambivalence' of Japanese people towards the desirability and appropriateness of consumption, at least until the latter part of the twentieth century.[5] Moreover in Japan, as elsewhere, the rhetoric has often juxtaposed saving and spending in a binary divide, according to which an increase in the one automatically meant a decrease in the other. Although work such as that of Horioka largely refutes such a proposition, it has been widely assumed that, if Japanese people saved a lot, they could not be prolific purchasers and consumers – perhaps a further justification for bestowing less attention on analysis of consumption activities.

However, recent research, together with many of the chapters in this volume, suggests that savings and consumption were indeed far from being two sides of a zero-sum game (see for instance Gordon, 2006). Furthermore, Scott O'Bryan has shown how increased personal consumption expenditure, especially on consumer durables, was central

[5] For a case study, see Partner, 2001.

to the policy discourse surrounding the adoption of economic growth as post-war Japan's primary goal, even as pre-war savings promotion continued (O'Bryan, 2009). Many Japanese were both spenders and savers, and exercised choices within the constraints that they faced. They carefully guarded what surplus they might have available, making use of institutions such as the post office savings system, but they also engaged in the disciplined practice of certain kinds of consumption, of both goods and services. Saving and consuming can therefore be seen as aspects of a cycle, whereby individuals and households engaged in a dynamic decision-making process regarding the allocation of their time, their effort and their money, with a view to maximising their utility and satisfying their wants and needs. That the outcome of this decision making may have been different from patterns of savings and consumption in other economies was in large part due to the institutions of the household and of consumption more broadly, and the general context within which spending and saving took place.

The present collection represents an attempt to build on and expand the scope of research into Japanese consumption history, with a view to enabling Japan to take its place within the comparative framework that is emerging from work on the industrialised West. It is also surely the case that the inclusion of Japan, as the first non-Western society to achieve modern economic development and industrialisation, might alter that framework and raise new issues within the emerging history of the non-Western consumer.

Consumption and its historical origins in Japan

Despite the limitations of existing research on consumption, it is nonetheless clear that, in Japan, as in other regions of Asia, the production and consumption of marketed goods, for purposes related to status, fashion and enjoyment that go well beyond basic subsistence, long predate modern industrialisation and the growing contact with the West from the mid-nineteenth century. In Edo (later Tokyo), Osaka and Kyoto, eighteenth-century Japan possessed some of the world's largest cities, with permanent and transitory populations dependent on the market for their food, clothing and leisure activity. As output grew and incomes increased through the long period of peace and stability under the rule of the Tokugawa Shoguns (1600–1868), those who could afford to do so, from among the feudal ruling class and the commercial sector that supplied them, were able to follow fashion in kimono and clothing accessories, eat out at a wide range of restaurants, accumulate beautifully crafted ceramics, lacquer-ware and decorative art, and purchase entertainment in the theatre or the pleasure quarters. At the same time, the enjoyment of consumption was by no means confined to the well-off; cheaper versions of everything – from street food and sake in a bar to accessories and knick-knacks bought from pedlars, to gambling, story-telling and many other pleasures – were widely available in the neighbourhoods of the great cities.

The vast majority of the goods that fed the growth in urban consumption into the early nineteenth century were produced not in the towns, but in the countryside. From early on in the most commercialised areas, then gradually throughout the country, networks of local producers grew up to manufacture processed food products, textiles, ceramics and an enormous range of differentiated household and leisure goods, typically utilising the spare labour time of households simultaneously engaged in agricultural production of food and raw materials.[6] The resulting growth in output generated rising incomes, not so much for the ruling class of samurai and feudal lords, who struggled to raise their income from tax revenues in line with the expansion in commercial activity going on around them, but rather for an emerging rural elite who combined farming and landlord activities with business pursuits. There is now significant evidence that this elite was increasingly acquiring and adapting the consumption tastes of the cities, if on a somewhat more modest scale, as they up-graded their houses, ate and dressed more elaborately, and engaged in sophisticated leisure pursuits and their associated expenditures (for examples, see Pratt, 1999; Platt, 2000).

Moreover, despite the 'traditional' picture of peasant immiseration during the Tokugawa period, the desire for a wider range of commercial goods does not appear to have been confined to the countryside elite. One major means of dissemination of urban consumption tastes was the so-called *sankin kōtai* (alternate attendance) system, whereby local feudal lords were obliged by the Shogun to house their families in Edo, and themselves spend every other year there, travelling from their domains with suitable retinues of samurai and servants. In much the same way as with the London Season, a significant proportion of the rural population, both high and low, thereby spent time in the city and in transit, acquiring new tastes, buying presents and souvenirs, and discovering new ways of living (Vaporis, 1997). As travel became in general more common, the ordinary consumer goods of the

[6] For a survey of this process, see Shimbo & Hasegawa, 2004.

cities – processed food products such as confectionery and soy sauce; clothing accessories such as hair-ties and fans; ceramics, paper products and all manner of small but useful or decorative household goods – began to appear in village shops (for examples, see Hanley and Yamamura, 1977; Hanley, 1997). A succession of sumptuary laws at the national and local levels attest to the obvious – and unstoppable – spread of high-status consumption goods, such as silk clothing, to the urban and rural commercial elite (Shively, 1964–65), while superior travellers, just like their European counterparts, continued to lament that distinctions in status were no longer reflected in distinctions in dress. Saitō Osamu concludes from his exhaustive study of early-modern comparative incomes and living standards that not only was the level and growth of income in pre-industrial Japan equivalent to that observed in many parts of Europe, but also that this income was more equally distributed in Japan (Saitō, 2008). This is clearly reflected and confirmed in the mounting evidence of the spread of consumer goods and their enjoyment in Tokugawa Japan.

This expansion of consumption was supported and promoted by a widening network of distribution and financial activities. In the first half of the Tokugawa period, this mainly took the form of the development of specialist traders and financiers, based in the cities, supplying regionally produced goods to the big-city market. Product lines ranged from relatively mass-market items such as sake and textiles, though both in highly differentiated forms, to all kinds of specialities from *tabi* socks and patent medicines to swords and funeral equipment (McClain, 1999). Such traders were able to supply not only locally produced goods but also, despite the trade restrictions in operation under the Tokugawa system, imported ones, such as Chinese medicines. With the growth of production in the countryside, however, trading networks based in rural areas increasingly sprang up, bypassing the city trading houses and linking rural producers directly with their markets. In the cities, retail facilities ranging from large-scale draperies and markets for fresh produce to corner shops and street sellers were already becoming well established by the middle of the Tokugawa period; later on pedlars and other types of travelling sales-people, as well as small-town and village shops, increasingly brought consumer goods to rural households.

As a result of these developments, by the middle of the nineteenth century, when Japan was 'opened up' to greater contact with the West and the Tokugawa regime was overthrown, many of the features that have come to delineate the emergence of 'pre-industrial' consumption in Europe were already in place, including the spreading demand for textiles, processed and household goods; the growth of local networks of small-scale manufacturing; and the development of distribution and retail systems reaching out from the towns and cities. The subsequent development of the consumer in Japan must therefore be understood as an interaction between the evolving pattern of 'indigenous' consumption and the new goods, technologies, practices and ideas that greater contact with the industrialised world inevitably brought.

By the early decades of the twentieth century, as urbanisation and modern industrialisation speeded up, the emerging middle classes in the cities confronted head-on the forces of global modernity, debating and experimenting with the ways in which 'modern' goods could and should be incorporated into Japanese life (Najita and Harootunian, 1988). Their solutions were eclectic: men wore suits in public, while women wore kimono in Western-inspired designs produced with synthetic dyes; main meals followed the Japanese-style rice-based format, while sugary snacks could be Western-style; 'modern' department stores sold high-fashion kimono alongside Western-style furniture adapted to Japanese rooms, while small shops and door-to-door sales-people supplied everyday items. In such ways, they created the outlines of the consumer lifestyle that the post-Second World War economic miracle was to make possible for many more of the 'middle masses'.

As this process proceeded, consumption became an increasingly fraught and politicised issue. 'Excessive spending', especially by women, came in for growing criticism, as the country struggled to cope with the financial crises that led up to the world-wide depression of the 1930s. In response, women's organisations focussed attention on the key role of the housewife as the manager of the household's expenditure and carved out a political niche for themselves in the promotion of 'modern', 'rational' consumption and saving practice, which their post-war successors continued to develop into a consumer movement largely driven by housewives. At the same time, the fact that the emerging 'rational', middle-class lifestyle involved Western-style elements – from arm-chairs and double-beds to cinema and baseball – that originated in the United States and other countries with which Japan was coming into conflict in Asia became increasingly problematic. The search for a modern, industrial, but nonetheless Japanese pattern of consumption became embedded in the political, and eventually military confrontation with the Western powers, even as ordinary consumers were setting about devising their own ways of enjoying the fashions, gadgets and treats that the West had to offer, alongside the Japanese-style foods and furnishings with which they remained most comfortable.

Once the war and its privations were past, the conflicts of the pre-war period began to resolve themselves, as the housewife, now firmly ensconced in her role as household manager, set the path determining the utilisation of the abundance of goods, Japanese- and Western-style, opened up by the economic miracle. By the late twentieth century, Japan, as a rich, highly developed and 'internationalised' society, had become part of the world of global consumerism, in terms of both the penetration of Western-style goods into the domestic market and the external diffusion of Japanese-style goods (for case studies, see Tobin, 1992). Nonetheless, the historical conditioning of the pattern of consumption, of both 'indigenous' and originally imported goods, was never far from the surface: golf, for example, was incorporated into the structure of Japanese business life in ways never envisaged by its Scottish progenitors. This historical conditioning is demonstrated in a number of interlocking interpretive issues running through the chapters in this volume, to which we now turn.

JP adopted western + traditional JP consumption patterns & emerge with something unique

Traditional and modern, Japanese and Western

The dichotomy between 'traditional' and 'modern', usually, in the case of Japan, mapped on to that between 'Japanese-style' and 'Western-style', has often been the leitmotif of such historical work as exists on everyday life and attitudes to consumption in Japan. Edward Seidensticker, who pioneered the English-language historical and literary study of urbanising and modernising Japan, coined the term 'double life' (*nijū seikatsu*) to describe the way in which intellectuals and others dealt with the possibilities created by modern, Western-style goods and ideas, switching as appropriate between a suit-wearing, meat-eating, Western-style persona and a kimono-wearing, rice-eating and increasingly nostalgic Japanese soul (Seidensticker, 1993, ch. 3). Modern, Western-style goods are thus often portrayed as alien imports, grafted on to a static traditional way of life; for post-war economic historians they could simply be classified as 'luxuries', in contrast to the 'necessities' of Japanese-style consumption (Horioka, 1993, pp. 278–79).

double life consumption

A similar discourse has permeated the wider field of comparative consumption history, as it has attempted to reach beyond the countries of Europe into their colonies and peripheries. Many accounts concern themselves with the diffusion of Western-style industrial products and implicitly assume that no 'pre-industrial consumers' existed before contact with the West. The 'birth of the consumer' is thus treated as intrinsically tied to the form of capitalist industrialisation that emerged in Europe, implying that consumption as a 'modern' activity was diffused to the rest of world through the globalising forces of Euro-centric trade and imperialism.[7] In Japan and elsewhere, the growth of consumption is measured in terms of the spread of Western-style clothing, the use of Western-style household goods, the establishment of modern retailing institutions such as the department store, and nowadays the appearance of McDonald's and Starbucks.

In recent years, the first steps towards a history of 'non-Western' consumption have significantly complicated this picture, and the chapters in this volume contribute to this in a number of ways. It is clear in the Japanese case that consumer goods were being produced and acquired in significant quantities prior to the 'opening to the West' in the mid-nineteenth century, and that many features of the consumer society – fashion, a developed retail system, even advertising – pre-date the Western impact. The patterns of consumption that emerged as the commercial economy expanded during the Tokugawa period undoubtedly persisted through the subsequent years of modernisation and industrialisation, but they can no longer be bracketed off as static and traditional. On the demand side, rising incomes enabled a wider range of consumers to enjoy the richer and more diversified diet that had once been the prerogative of the Tokugawa urban elite; commercialised versions of traditional food products – sake, soy sauce, cakes and sweets – appeared to cater to the expanding market. Nakanishi and Futaya's chapter provides evidence of how rural households came to consume a widening range of goods, gradually including the new elements made possible by imported techniques and tastes. Much consumer demand continued to be met by small-scale, traditional producers, but a combination of a growing market and the potential of newly available inputs and technology produced development and differentiation in response to the tastes and fashions of the domestic market. The 'traditional Japanese lifestyle' that inter-war and even late-twentieth-century commentators lamented emerges from this story as a crystallised and commodified version of what was, in fact, a continually evolving indigenous consumption pattern (see Creighton, 1998; Sand, 2006).

The 'social life of things' traced in a number of the chapters in this volume demonstrates how the traditional/modern and Japanese/Western dichotomies can in practice break down in the face of detailed historical analysis. The combination of a widening market, new technologies and design motifs, and modern marketing techniques

[7] For a critique of this approach, see Clunas, 1999.

meant that the fashionable kimono of the inter-war period discussed by Francks were dramatically different from their nineteenth-century predecessors. As Umemura shows, traditional Chinese medicinal products, once sold by travelling salesmen to poorer consumers as substitutes for Western medicines, became mass-produced, stylishly packaged and marketed answers to late-twentieth-century ills. Kushner's chapter describes how sugar, a domestically produced luxury during the Tokugawa period, became embedded into everyday consumption in both traditional and modern processed forms, to the extent of becoming a symbol of Japanese national and imperial life.

Like their Indian and Chinese counterparts, Japanese thinkers undoubtedly wrestled with the question of what might constitute an authentic Japanese way of life in the face of the globalising forces unleashed by Western industrialisation and imperialism.[8] However, the examples of the history of consumption and everyday life described here remind us that, on the ground, the traditional and modern, the indigenous and imported, interacted to produce a much more complex, changing and historically conditioned reality than such simple dichotomies suggest. This volume seeks to begin the process of showing how, in the Japanese case, that reality was shaped by the agency of the non-Western consumers that global and comparative history has too frequently neglected.

Households, time and gender

Although consumption may be regarded as a supremely individualistic activity, in practice, in developed and even more so in pre-industrial and industrialising societies, it is in large part determined and pursued within the household or family unit. Consumption history has therefore contributed to a shift of focus, in economic and social analysis, down to the household level. In this process it has in particular thrown new light on the changing roles of women, as workers, as shoppers and as managers of consumption within households.[9] For economic historians, the pioneer in this area has been Jan de Vries, whose model of the 'industrious revolution' treats the changing inter-relations between producing and consuming activities within the household as central

[8] For a Chinese comparison, see Gerth, 2003.

[9] For a useful survey of the changing theoretical approaches to consumption and gender, over the course of economic development, see de Grazia, 1996, pp. 11–24.

to the process of industrialisation.[10] For de Vries, the desire to acquire the increasingly attractive goods that the market can provide has to be recognised as a factor explaining the growth in participation in the market-based production activities – wage labour or proto-industrial manufacturing – that generate the cash required to purchase them. Hence the decisions of households in various parts of pre-industrial Europe to allocate more and more of their time to market-based work and less to subsistence production and housework, so as to be able to acquire commercially produced consumer goods, created the conditions whereby the resulting 'industrious' revolution paved the way for the 'industrial' one.

De Vries thus treats market-based labour and consumption as inter-linked substitutes for subsistence production and housework, with the shift from one to the other representing a major, household-level, driving force during the early stages of industrialisation. This contrasts with the pattern observed in the more advanced stages of industrialisation, according to which, as market-based incomes rise, women increasingly withdraw from the paid labour force in order to concentrate on the home-based activities – child-rearing, cleaning, food preparation – that characterise women's role in the 'breadwinner-homemaker' household model. In this case, increased consumption and time devoted to housework complement one another, within the context of the urban or suburban nuclear-family life made possible by rising incomes and industrialisation.

Tanimoto's ground-breaking chapter explores these same issues for Japan using inter-war empirical data on labour allocation within households. He shows how the allocation of time to housework was related to changing family structures and the availability of female labour – from family members or servants – within the household, but his results also imply that increasing consumption was linked to increased housework from early on in the process of economic development in Japan. Tanimoto's analysis, which is echoed in Gordon's chapter as well, thus suggests that the pattern of consumption that emerged in Japan, as incomes rose and the commercial and industrial economy grew, depended on growth and change in housework activities, particularly in forms of food processing and cooking, sewing and dress making. This opens up the possibility of a 'labour-intensive path of consumption growth' to parallel the supply-side 'labour-intensive path of industrialisation', now proposed for Japan and other parts of East Asia (see Sugihara, 2003).

---

[10] For the most recent presentation of the model, see de Vries, 2008.

By the later stages of Japan's economic development, these 'labour-intensive' housework activities were to take on a new role in generating the huge domestic market for household goods and gadgets on which many of the big names among Japanese electrical and electronic goods exporters initially depended. Debates persist over the extent to which modern household appliances were labour-saving or labour-using (Cowan, 1983; Lebergott, 1993), but the Japanese cases presented here – Gordon's study of the sewing machine and Macnaughtan's of the electric rice-cooker – suggest that the appeal of such goods to the consumer derived not only from practical convenience, but also from their role as tools whereby housewives could more easily create the particular kind of comfortable and respectable lifestyle that the 'middle masses' of post-war urban and suburban Japan aimed to achieve. Sewing machines were used to enable women to open up the world of Western-style fashion for themselves and their families by means of housework. Rice-cookers made it feasible, within the space and time constraints of modern urban life, to produce 'perfect' rice and the more diversified 'rice + side-dishes' menus that rising incomes and developments in food retailing made much more widely possible. These cases suggest that labour-saving household gadgets did not just free women's time for work or leisure activities outside the home, but raised the productivity of their housework time, enhancing their ability to produce the desired, historically conditioned, Japanese pattern of consumption.

Much work remains to be done on the relationship between consumption and the labour allocation decisions of Japanese households, but the fact that consumption patterns are clearly interrelated with changing household structures and time allocations seems indisputable. At the level of the household, as much as that of the local and national economy, decisions regarding consumption and production impinge on one another, through the distribution of labour time between the external labour market and household activities and through the relationship between housework and the desired pattern of consumption. The increased importance thus given to the internal operations of the household, and to the activities of women in particular within it, highlights the significance of consumption history for the wider field of gender. As Haynes and McGowan have cogently emphasised, consumption practices and attitudes towards them have been, and remain, major grounds on which gender has been constituted and re-constituted (Haynes and McGowan, 2010).

Three interrelated contextual shifts stand out as important for the gendering of consumption and the choices related to it over the period covered by the chapters in this volume. One, already mentioned, is the changing structure of the Japanese family and household. As indicated in Tanimoto's chapter, the multi-generational households widespread in pre-war Japan were able to rely on the household labour of more than one woman. The subsequent shift towards the dominance of the nuclear family impacted not only on the use of time, but on the household division of labour, and gendered participation in consumption and decisions relating to it. The decline in family size, with invariably just one woman undertaking housework tasks, was bound to influence the allocation of time and labour resources, and hence consumption decisions.

The second is the shift of productive activity out of the household. Research on the United States has suggested that a primary factor in increased consumer spending in the late nineteenth/early twentieth century was the transition away from home production (Lebergott, 1993, pp. 50–51). This shift was gradually taking place in Japan from the late nineteenth century, although it remained incomplete even into the latter part of the twentieth century. Its effect was to accelerate the existing trend away from consumer self-sufficiency; consumption that had taken place outside the market was shifted into it. As more women, as well as men, began to work outside the home, their potential ability to use at least some of their earnings on individual or household consumption grew. Hence, while many female earners in the pre-war years continued to see themselves as part of a family economy, there is also substantial evidence that women beyond just the elite and young urban workers played a role in increasing consumption. The fashionable, but relatively inexpensive, *meisen* kimono did not owe its popularity just to the patronage of the wealthy. Factory girls were increasingly able to spend surplus earnings on 'populuxe' goods such as cheap jewellery and cosmetics. From the economic-miracle period onwards, growth in the disposable income of unmarried females, and not just male-breadwinner families, has been well documented.

The third factor is the changing discourse on women's role in society. The growth in the importance of women for consumption decisions in the Meiji-Taishō years took place despite civil legislation that denied them autonomy and against a background of ongoing debates about the role of women in production, in the household and in society in general. The post-war years, and the rising incomes that they brought to male workers, underlined women's role as 'professional housewives' – full-time homemakers whose tasks included the making of major consumption decisions, up to, and including, those involving housing and children's education. Purchases of the rice cooker and the sewing machine have to be viewed in this context; they were not just sensible purchases or an insurance strategy at a time when resources were constrained, but also played a symbolic role in enabling the housewife to attain the 'ideal' standard. The attempts by the golf industry to attract female consumers, as described in Lockyer's chapter, show that discourses of gender continue to exercise a major influence on consumption patterns and attempts to change them.

Nor should we ignore the gendering of consumer items and tastes, which often interacts with the issue of 'Japanese versus Western' discussed above. The sweet treats described in Kushner's chapter have consistently been targeted at women, but during the Pacific War they were re-targeted at the male soldiers fighting for the nation. *Meisen* kimono were worn by women, but fashion was never a purely female thing. Why was it, moreover, that the shift to Western clothing styles for men (except on recreational and some formal occasions) had largely taken place by the 1930s, whereas the equivalent shift for women occurred much later? Here too, the interaction between economic, social and cultural factors cannot be disregarded.

Spaces and pathways of consumption

If we are to analyse the act of consumption as part of an ongoing dynamic rather than as a one-off purchase, the location of consumption itself and of the decisions surrounding it matters profoundly, as do the mechanisms and institutions that frame those decisions. The spatial aspect of consumption is played out in a number of ways in this collection beyond the already mentioned ones of the Japanese–Western dichotomy and the household. One involves the process of urbanisation. From the Edo period, towns and cities not only functioned as centres of consumption, but also played a crucial role in organising and disseminating patterns of demand. Along with urbanisation came an urban–rural divide prominent in political and economic discourse in Japan since before the Meiji period. There exists substantial statistical evidence to suggest persistent variation in urban–rural income levels, household structure and employment in modern Japan. Nakanishi and Futaya's small sample suggests some pointers towards the potential for rural–urban differences in consumption, while Tanimoto's chapter also draws attention to differences between rural and urban households in the inter-war period. Techniques such as mail order and the use of travelling sales-people, along with organisations such as the post office, may have helped to limit this disparity, but it remained in place until well into the second half of the twentieth century. As Simon Partner's work has indicated, persuading rural consumers to purchase electrical equipment was a considerably greater challenge than was selling to their urban counterparts (Partner, 2000; 2001).

Less often rehearsed in the English-language historiography is the significance of consumption in regional patterns of economic development. The importance of local and niche markets in the shaping of Japanese production and marketing systems has been well documented, but we often know little of the local consumers, or why demand for certain products evolved in particular places and at particular times. Existing patterns of local consumption could be both strengthened and weakened in the move to a more 'national' economy and greater market integration. While the origins of niche consumption have not been addressed here, it is clear that it represented a significant ongoing influence on how consumption took place, and how it was 'sold' to the public. Mitsuzono's mail-order firms shaped their sales to assumptions about local tastes and pushed consumption of identifiable 'regional' products. Nakamura's chapter shows how business use of the local railway system was important both for regional industrialisation and for its interaction with the industrial cores in Kansai and Kantō. While we have considerable evidence of long-distance marketing and sales in the Tokugawa period, it seems unlikely that consumption would have grown on the scale that it did in the twentieth century without the sophisticated physical and communications infrastructure that was developed from the latter part of the Meiji period. This infrastructure enhanced access to production sites and consumer markets, and disseminated information on products and how they might be acquired, as clearly demonstrated in the chapter by Nakanishi and Futaya.

The physical place of purchase was often a local retail shop or a department store, but it could also be the home or some other location. Medicines were largely acquired at doctors' surgeries, while railway travel was purchased at the station. Mail-order requests were despatched from the post office, one of a number of possible sites where consumption could be facilitated. Acts of consuming could not be divorced from the social spaces in which they took place. If we consider consumption as not just a one-off purchase, but as the utilisation of purchased goods and services, often over sustained periods of time, then the location of use was invariably different from that of acquisition. Individuals and families often identified a space within the home for any purchase, and that space was an indicator of the nature of its utilisation and its importance. The consumption of sweets by soldiers during war-time, as described by Kushner, took place in what might be called 'imperial' space, with all the nationalist connotations that that implied. Golf club membership, as Lockyer's chapter demonstrates, was less about playing golf than becoming a part of a particular social space, underlining the need to analyse consumption as an element in an ongoing socio-economic process.

Many locations of consumption, whether in the sense of consumer decision making, actual acts of purchase or subsequent use, thereby became crucial pathways through which notions relating to the acquisition of a range of goods and services, and to the goods themselves, became embedded in the daily life of Japanese people. A post office was not just a space in which actual transactions could be undertaken; it was a crucial intermediary institution bringing together a range of services that enabled the whole savings and spending cycle to operate. Mail order made use of those services, as well as of expanding transport systems such as the railway. The state, one of the main progenitors of these developments, became just one of many mediators in the consumption cycle. A range of organisations and individuals constituted other levels of mediation, but because consumption was essentially a social act, and not just an economic decision, the role of individual human intermediaries in the consumption process takes on a particular importance, and this is demonstrated in a number of the chapters in this volume.

Even in pre-industrial times consumption was rarely a straightforward two-way transaction between producer and consumer. Purchasers were largely dependent on retailers, itinerant merchants and salesmen or small-scale pedlars for access to many goods. As market transactions became more complex, more monetised and more long-distance, the likelihood of face-to-face producer–consumer interaction became even lower. The high transaction costs so often associated with imperfect markets in developing economies attracted intermediaries who sought to capitalise on those high costs, while producers and consumers were at the same time trying to minimise them. Over time such intermediation took on particular forms and often persisted through a degree of path dependence. Intermediary individuals ended up in a 'top-down' position in relation to the actual consumer, and hence exercised a strong influence over acts of consumption by others.

Some of this intermediation was essentially informal and is difficult to pin down. The American GIs in Kushner's chapter who distributed chocolates and sweets in Occupation Japan were not seeking financial return, but they were nevertheless important agents in the consumption process. Local gossip or advice from friends or family was of universal importance. A salesman or pedlar with a persuasive tongue and/or a genuine expertise was always likely to influence purchasers' decisions. In a conventionally hierarchical society such as late-nineteenth-century Japan, the chance of consumption 'advice' being taken from those regarded as socially superior and better educated, such as a local postmaster, was perhaps particularly great. Such 'advice' could easily become institutionalised. The 'entrusted choice' discussed in Mitsuzono's chapter allowed department store employees to decide what mail-order purchasers would actually acquire. This assumes a degree of trust between consumer and intermediary, a reliance on the intermediary's knowledge and expertise not dissimilar to the more universal reliance on physicians' recommendations for medication. In Japan, where doctors not only prescribe, but also reap economic benefits from the sale of medicines, a complex incentive system for the intermediary has shaped the pattern of consumption. Doctors and department store officials thus became proxy consumers. Where consumption is analysed as a one-off purchase, the decisions of these proxy consumers become identified with those of the actual purchaser, but a more in-depth historical analysis of the consumption dynamic surely requires us to pay more attention to the institutions of consumer decision making.

Notwithstanding diversity of approach and subject matter, the chapters in this volume seek to use the history of consumption, broadly defined, as a lens through which to view the complex interactions of individuals, institutions and social structures that have determined the changing pattern of everyday life in Japan. In so doing, they aim to make a contribution towards redressing the neglect of the consumer in the study of Japan's economic past, and to broaden the comparative framework within which global consumption history can be analysed. Much work remains to be done, and undertaking this research is a major challenge for economic historians. As Daniel Roche noted in his seminal work, in trying to analyse the history of material civilisation, the historian 'has to combine two approaches – that of the economy and its interpretation, in order to understand how societies function and the relation between consumption and production, and that of social and cultural analysis, which takes account of the imperatives of private and public life, the norms which manifest themselves in the choices of material culture' (Roche, 2000, p. 16). This volume represents a first attempt to take up that challenge, in relation to Japan, as one of the great, but neglected, consuming nations of the contemporary world.

References

Adshead, S. A. M. (1997) *Material Culture in Europe and China, 1400–1800: The Rise of Consumerism*, Basingstoke: Palgrave Macmillan.

Bauer, A. J. (2001) *Goods, Power, History: Latin America's Material Culture*, Cambridge: Cambridge University Press.

Berg, M. (2005) *Luxury and Pleasure in Eighteenth-Century Britain*, Oxford: Oxford University Press.

Berry, M. (2006) *Japan in Print: Information and Nation in the Early Modern Period*, Berkeley: University of California Press.

Brook, T. (1999) *The Confusions of Pleasure: Commerce and Culture in Ming China*, Berkeley: University of California Press.

Clammer, J. (1997) *Contemporary Urban Japan*, Oxford: Blackwell.

Clunas, C. (1991) *Superfluous Things: Material Culture and Social Status in Early Modern China*, Cambridge: Polity Press.

Clunas, C. (1999) 'Modernity Global and Local: Consumption and the Rise of the West', *American Historical Review* 104(5): 1497–1511.

Cowan, R. (1983) *More Work for Mother: The Ironies of Household Technology from the Open Hearth to the Microwave*, New York: Basic Books.

Creighton, M. (1998) 'Pre-industrial Dreaming in Post-industrial Japan: Department Stores and the Commoditization of Community Values', *Japan Forum* 10: 127–49.

De Grazia, V. (1996) 'Introduction' in de Grazia, V. and Furlough, E. (eds), *The Sex of Things: Gender and Consumption in Historical Perspective*, Berkeley: University of California Press, 11–24.

De Vries, J. (2008) *The Industrious Revolution: Consumer Behavior and the Household Economy, 1650 to the Present*, New York: Cambridge University Press.

Garon, S. (2000) 'Luxury is the Enemy: Mobilizing Savings and Popularizing Thrift in Wartime Japan', *Journal of Japanese Studies* 26: 41–78.

Garon, S. & Maclachlan, P. (eds), *The Ambivalent Consumer*, Ithaca, NY: Cornell University Press.

Gerth, K. (2003) *China Made: Consumer Culture and the Creation of the Nation*. Cambridge, MA: Harvard University Press.

Glennie, P. (1995) 'Consumption within Historical Studies' in Miller, D. (ed.), *Acknowledging Consumption*, London: Routledge, 164–203.

Gordon, A. (2006) 'From Singer to Shinpan: Consumer Credit in Modern Japan' in Garon, S. & Maclachlan, P. (eds), 137–62.

Hanley, S. B. (1997) *Everyday Things in Premodern Japan: The Hidden Legacy of Material Culture*, Berkeley: University of California Press.

Hanley, S. & Yamamura, K. (1977) *Economic and Demographic Change in Preindustrial Japan, 1600–1868*, Princeton, NJ: Princeton University Press

Haynes, D. & McGowan, A. (2010) 'Introduction' in Haynes et al. (eds) 1–25.

Haynes, D., McGowan, A., Roy, T. & Yanagisawa, H. (eds) (2010) *Towards a History of Consumption in South Asia*, New Delhi: Oxford University Press.

Horioka, C. (1993) 'Consuming and Saving' in Gordon, A. (ed.), *Postwar Japan as History*, Berkeley: University of California Press, 259–92.

Horioka, C. (2006) 'Are the Japanese Unique? An Analysis of Consumption and Saving Behavior' in Garon, S. & Maclachlan, P. (eds), 113–36.

Johnson, C. (1982) *MITI and the Japanese Miracle*, Stanford: Stanford University Press.

Katz, R. (1998) *Japan: The System That Soured*, New York: M.E.Sharpe.

Lebergott, S. (1993) *Pursuing Happiness: American Consumers in the Twentieth Century*, Princeton, NJ: Princeton University Press.

Lockwood, W. (1968) *The Economic Development of Japan*, 2nd edn, Princeton, NJ: Princeton University Press.

McClain, J. (1999) 'Space, Power, Wealth and Status In Seventeenth-century Osaka' in McClain, J. & Wakita, O. (eds) *Osaka: The Merchants' Capital of Early Modern Japan*, Ithaca, NY: Cornell University Press, pp. 44–79.

Najita, T. & Harootunian, H. (1988) 'Japanese Revolt against the West: Political and Cultural Criticism in the Twentieth Century' in Duus, P. (ed.) *The Cambridge History of Japan VI: The Twentieth Century*, Cambridge: Cambridge University Press, 711–74.

North, D. C. (1990) *Institutions, Institutional Change and Economic Performance*, Cambridge: Cambridge University Press.

North, D. C. (2010) *Understanding the Process of Economic Change*, New Haven, CT: Princeton University Press.

O'Bryan, S. (2009) *The Growth Idea: Purpose and Prosperity in Postwar Japan*. Honolulu: University of Hawai'i Press.

Ohkawa, K. & Rosovsky, H. (1973) *Japanese Economic Growth*. Stanford: Stanford University Press.

Partner, S. (1999) *Assembled in Japan*, Berkeley: University of California Press.

Partner, S. (2000) 'Brightening Country Lives: Selling Electrical Goods in the Japanese Countryside', *Enterprise and Society*, 1(4) December: 762–84.

Partner, S. (2001) 'Taming the Wilderness: The Lifestyle Improvement Movement in Rural Japan, 1925–1965', *Monumenta Nipponica* 56(4) Winter: 487–520.

Platt, B. (2000) 'Elegance, Prosperity, Crisis: Three Generations of Tokugawa Village Elites', *Monumenta Nipponica* 55(1) Spring: 45–81.

Pomeranz, K. (2000) *The Great Divergence: China, Europe and the Making of the Modern World Economy*, Princeton, NJ: Princeton University Press.

Pratt, E. (1999) *Japan's Rural Elite: The Economic Foundations of the Gōnō*. Cambridge, MA: Harvard University Asia Center.

Quataert, D. (ed.) (2000) *Consumption Studies and the History of the Ottoman Empire: An Introduction*. Albany, NY: SUNY Press.

Roche, D. (2000) *A History of Everyday Things: The Birth of Consumption in France, 1600–1800*, Cambridge: Cambridge University Press.

Saitō, O. (2008) *Hikaku Keizai Hatten Ron* (Comparative Economic Development), Tokyo: Iwanami Shoten.

Sand, J. (2003) *House and Home in Modern Japan*, Cambridge, MA: Harvard University Press.

Sand, J. (2006) 'The Ambivalence of the New Breed: Nostalgic Consumerism in 1980s and 1990s Japan' in Garon, S. & Maclachlan, P. (eds), 85–198.

Sato, B. H. (2003) *The New Japanese Woman: Modernity, Media and Women in Interwar Japan*, Durham,NC: Duke University Press.

Seidensticker, E. (1983) *Low City, High City*. London: Allen Lane.

Shimbo, H. & Hasegawa, A. (2004) 'The Dynamics of Market Economy and Production' in Hayami, A., Saitō, O. & Toby, R. (eds) *Emergence of Economic Society in Japan 1600–1859*, Oxford: Oxford University Press, 159–91.

Shively, D (1964–65) 'Sumptuary Regulation and Status in Early Tokugawa Japan', *Harvard Journal of Asiatic Studies* 25: 123–64.

Shively, D. (1991) 'Popular Culture' in Jansen, M. (ed.) *The Cambridge History of Japan V: The Nineteenth Century*, Cambridge: Cambridge University Press, pp. 706–70.
Stearns, P. (2001) *Consumerism in World History: The Global Transformation of Desire*, Abingdon: Routledge.
Sugihara, K. (2003) 'The East Asian Path of Development' in Arrighi, G., Hamashita, T., & Seldon, M. (eds) *The Resurgence of East Asia*, London: Routledge: 78–123.
Tobin, J. (ed.) (1992) *Re-Made in Japan: Everyday Life and Consumer Taste in a Changing Society*, New Haven: Yale University Press.
Vaporis, C. (1997) 'To Edo and Back: Alternate Attendance and Japanese Culture in the Early Modern Period', *Journal of Japanese Studies* 23(1) Winter: 25–68.

Part I

Gender, the Household and Consumption

2

The Role of Housework in Everyday Life: Another Aspect of Consumption in Modern Japan

Masayuki Tanimoto

Introduction

What determines the level of utility that people derive from their everyday lives? There is no doubt that the consumption of goods – necessities and luxuries – is primary in considering the utility level of ordinary people. However, tangible goods are not the only objects consumed. Various kinds of 'services' also have a great influence on the level of individual utility. Specifically, before the 'contemporary' age, services delivered inside the household made up an important part of the overall consumption. These services have mainly been provided by means of 'housework' in a broad sense. The purpose of this chapter is to shed light on the practice of housework in modern Japan from the point of view of consumption history.[1]

Gary Becker's seminal argument provides us with the basic framework for considering the relationship between 'goods' and 'housework' within the household (Becker, 1965). In this framework, the household is assumed to combine time and market goods to produce more basic commodities that directly enter their utility functions. These commodities are called Z-commodities and written as,

$$Z_i = f_i (x_i, T_i) \tag{1}$$

[1] Though the analysis of discourse related to housework is not uncommon in the literature, there is not much research investigating actual housework from a historical perspective. Shinada (2007, ch. 3) discusses the role of actual housework, though briefly, from the 1930s.

where x_i is a vector of market goods and T_i a vector of time inputs used in producing the *i*th commodity. On the other hand, the household must be under the constraint of 'time'.[2]

$$T = T_w + T_c + T_r \qquad (2)$$

where T is a vector denoting total time available in a household and is divided into three major categories: T_w, T_c, and T_r. Each household allocates the time of its members among these categories: labour to acquire the money income needed to purchase goods (T_w); labour retained within the household to transform purchased goods into Z-commodities (T_c); and leisure, which includes the time to actually consume the commodities (T_r). This formulation offers an explicit way of incorporating the role of 'non-working time', which has usually been recognised merely as 'leisure' or a residual in discussing the household economy. More specifically, the introduction of category T_c clearly indicates the indispensable role of housework in the production function of Z-commodities as shown in equation (1).

In fact, making use of this framework, Jan de Vries has provided us with a frame of reference in terms of the historical relation between consumption and housework (de Vries, 2008). De Vries discusses the historical changes in the time (labour) allocation behaviour of households in early-modern Europe, from the production of self-sufficient goods to the production of saleable goods and the provision of the household workforce to the external labour market. He also points out the emergence, during the nineteenth century, of the breadwinner–homemaker household, within which housework recovered its importance in the labour-allocation process. This is one of the most systematic accounts of the changing role of housework in the historical setting of the early-modern and modern periods.

However, we should consider carefully both the theoretical and factual aspects of the account given by de Vries before applying it to the consumption history of Japan. As de Vries pointed out, the household's decision to allocate its time (T_w) towards labour to acquire monetary income for the purchase of goods was ultimately based on revisions in the mix of desired Z-commodities in the direction of those produced by more goods-intensive consumption 'technology'. This implies, in other words, that the birth of consumer society was accompanied by the

[2] The formulation (2) is based on the exposition given by de Vries (de Vries, 2008, pp. 26–27).

reduction of housework. On the other hand, the Beckerian framework assumes that the choices available to households in the allocation of time depend on the alternative consumption technologies available to secure desired Z-commodities and the degree of substitutability between goods and time that they offer. Therefore, in theory, the exploitation of goods-intensive consumption technology was not the only way to increase the consumption level of households in modern Japan. Given the alternative availability of other consumption technologies and substitutability, other choices, such as housework-intensive technology, might be exploited in a certain historical context. This chapter tries to explore this question by focussing its observations on the practice of housework in inter-war Japan.

It is also worth reconsidering the applicability of the image, in de Vries's argument, of the representative household shifting from a multi-occupied labourer household to a breadwinner household. Making use of a figure which demonstrates the correlation between the self-employment ratio and the real per capita gross domestic product (GDP) in a sample of 15 countries from the 1930s to ca. 1970, I have shown elsewhere (Tanimoto, forthcoming) how the proportion of households engaged in self-employed occupations differed significantly among countries.[3] In general, there existed a negative correlation between real per capita GDP and the self-employment ratio. This implies that economic growth, expressed by the rise of per capita real GDP, entails an increase in the number of 'employed workers', typically in large factories and workshops. However, we should also note that the horizontal range of the self-employment ratio was rather wide in this figure, which implies that significant differences existed in the absolute self-employed ratios among countries with similar real per capita GDP. The locus for the UK, whose self-employment ratio has consistently fallen below 15 per cent, forms one extreme in this figure. The US, Sweden and Germany (West Germany during the post-war period) appear to follow the UK as the second group. The ratios were higher in the case of France and Italy, but they did not reach Japan's level. The locus for Japan represents an extreme opposite to that of the UK, and the absolute ratio is consistently four times as high as that of the UK and twice as high

[3] The sample countries included the UK, France, Germany, Italy, Sweden, Belgium, Czechoslovakia, Hungary, Portugal, the US, Mexico, Australia, Thailand and Japan.

as that of the second group.[4] Thus, the self-employment ratio not only reflects the degree of economic development, but also mirrors a specific employment pattern in each country. Japan's locus in the figure reveals the vital role of self-employed households in the twentieth-century, as they co-existed with households of employed workers ranging from multi-occupied labourers to breadwinner white-collar employees.[5]

This variety of household types resulted in the diverse roles of female members in Japan's households. In fact, population census data reveal that wives in farming households, as well as those in urban, self-employed households, showed higher labour force participation rates than wives in the households of employed workers, even in the midst of the post-war rapid growth era.[6] It is also notable that, judging from their working hours, their work style was not necessarily the same as that of 'full-time' employed workers. According to Figure 2.1, nearly half of female family workers in urban self-employed households allocated less than 34 hours per week to activities that related to their family business. A similar situation can be seen in the case of family workers in farming households during the agricultural off-season. Assuming eight hours per day as full-time working hours, these female family workers should be classified as part-time workers.[7] This suggests that ways of coping with domestic matters might differ among household types. This chapter will utilise these existing differences as a means of defining the nature of housework in Japan.

In the light of this, the next section ('The role of housework in farming households') focusses on farming households, which were the single largest type of household during the inter-war period. The main sources for the quantitative analysis are two kinds of 'Economic Survey of Farming Households' (*Nōka Keizai Chōsa*), which provide us with the housework hours of each household surveyed. The third section of

[4] The combination of the self-employment rate and real per capita GDP of Japan and the UK are as follows: Japan, 1930, 67.6 per cent, $1,780 at 1990 prices; 1970, 34.9 per cent, $9,448; UK, 1931, 13.7 per cent, $5,198; 1970, 7.1 per cent, $10,694. The data on real per capita GDP are obtained from Maddison, 1995.

[5] For a detailed discussion on the role of self-employed workers in Japan, see Tanimoto, 2006 and Tanimoto, forthcoming.

[6] In 1965, the labour participation rate of wives in households engaged in self-employment-based non-agricultural occupations was 60.5 per cent, while that of wives in households of employed workers was 39.6 per cent (Sōrifu Tōkeikyoku, 1970).

[7] Using the oral history method, Kurashiki (2007) provides us with real descriptions of married women working in multi-occupied rural households in the 1960s.

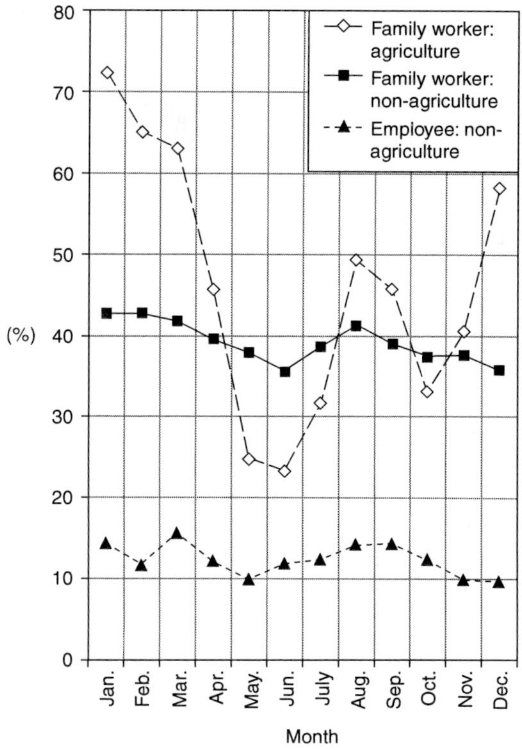

Figure 2.1 Proportion of female workers engaged in 34 hours or less per week, 1955

Source: Sōrifu Tōkeikyoku ed. *Kokusei chōsa Tokubetsu-shūkei, Setai oyobi Kazoku*, 1970.

the chapter ('Housework in urban households') discusses housework in non-agricultural households. Data surveys on domestic servants will help us to analyse housework in urban settings, despite the absence of source materials as rich as the surveys of farming households. The fourth section concludes the chapter.

The role of housework in farming households

Time allocation among household members

We can first consider the time allocation behaviour of farming households by means of the *Yojō Rōryoku Chōsa Jirei* (*Case Study of Surplus Labour*), edited by the Ministry of Agriculture and Commerce

(Nōshōmushō).[8] The household in question was located in Tottori prefecture on the Japan Sea coast, and the survey was carried out in 1918. Judging from the fact that the head of the household was a member of the village assembly, this household could probably have been classified as that of an upper-class farmer in the village. However, the household's area of cultivation, about one *chō* (1 hectare) of paddy land for rice and about five *tan* (0.5 hectare) of dry field for barley, was around the average level in this village, and its labour force was limited to the lineal family, as neither collateral family members nor employed workers were working that year. Therefore, the farmer chosen here was not an exceptional case, but represented some common features of an owner-farming household in that period. Cultivation occupied more than 60 per cent of the household's total working hours, alongside other manufacturing work such as *tatami*-mat production.

Table 2.1 shows the working hours of individual family members. The household head, his wife and his father devoted more than three-quarters of their working hours to 'production work', such as cultivation, and to 'industrial work', such as manufacturing *tatami*-mats or straw products and cocoon breeding. These three members were apparently mainly engaged in income-earning work in a broad sense (hereafter 'producing labour'). On the other hand, the household head's mother devoted more than 80 per cent of her hours (per year) to housework. The household head's older daughter spent 60 per cent of her total hours on producing labour and 40 per cent on housework. The second daughter, who was a student at that time, devoted around 1,000 hours to housework.

It is worth noticing that female labour played a significant role in cultivation as well as in the other sideline work defined in this survey as 'industrial work'. In this sense, it is not appropriate to say that there existed a clear division of labour between males and females in the field of producing labour. However, it is also clear that housework (except firewood making) was mainly done by females, not males. We can also observe a division of labour within the field of housework among female members. In other words, the housework demands in this household were fulfilled by multiple female members, and the total housework hours (6,854 hours) recorded in the table far exceeded the annual working hours of any single person.

This survey also provides us with information on what constituted housework. According to the second part of Table 2.1, cooking accounted

[8] The argument in this section is based on Tanimoto, 2003.

Table 2.1 Allocation of labour and housework within a farming household in Tottori Prefecture, 1918 (working hours per year)

			Agriculture and industry				
Position in the family	**Age**	**Total**	**Total**	**Agricultural work**	**Others**	**Housework**	**Others**
Household head	44	3,156	2,564	1,618	946	437	155
Wife	40	3,278	2,456	1,006	1,450	822	
Father	71	1,982	1,672	1,140	532	275	35
Mother	67	3,921	803	265	538	3,118	
Daughter	18	3,399	2,082	1,160	922	1,317	
Daughter	15	1,020	135	80	55	885	
Son	9						
Son	2						190
Total		16,756	9,712	5,269	4,443	6,854	380

Table 2.1(1) Breakdown of housework (working hours per year)

	A	B	C	D	E	F	G	H	I
Household head				270		25			142
Wife	80		100	140	180	25		240	57
Father				90		90			95
Mother	1,820	719				144	270		165
Daughter	292		790		200	25			10
Daughter		885							
Son									
Son									
Total	2,192	1,604	890	500	380	309	270	240	469

Note: A = Cooking, B = Childcare, C = Needlework, D = Making firewood, E = Weaving F = Cleaning, G = Heating the bath, H = Washing, I = Other tasks.

Source: Nōshōmushō (ed.) Yojō Rōryoku Chōsajirei (Kokusansha, 1921).

for the largest part of the housework, occupying on average around 6 hours per day. It is also noticeable that needlework, in third place behind child-care, accounted for 890 hours per year.[9] In contrast, the

[9] See also Gordon's chapter (Chapter 3) for a discussion of the significance of sewing among women's household activities.

hours devoted to cleaning and washing were rather limited. Thus, the main tasks constituting housework in farming households in those days seem to have been the preparation of food and clothing. Significantly, these tasks also conform to the original image of the production of Z-commodities, as cooking is the combination of food-stuff and cooking work, and needlework constituted working on textiles to tailor or repair clothes. In other words, the consumption of goods in this household was closely related to the housework provided by the female members of the family.

Since this is so far the only case that gives us a breakdown of housework hours, the above discussion on the content of housework should be recognised as tentative. However comparative research based on social surveys of housework hours around the year 2000, conducted in the UK, the Netherlands and Japan, reveals that the average cooking hours of women in Japan were relatively longer than those in the other two countries.[10] Together these results may suggest, therefore, that the long cooking hours shown in Table 2.1 reflect something specific to the nature of housework in Japanese households.[11]

Who carried out the housework?

The fact that the burden of housework was shared by plural female household members, clearly revealed through the case above, is worth further examination. We can confirm and generalise this finding by observing the data shown in the individual sheets of the *Nōka Keizai Chōsa* (Economic Survey of Farming Households), conducted by Kyoto Imperial University during the inter-war period.[12]

Tables 2.2 and 2.3 bring together data from the annual surveys of 44 different households conducted in 1927, 1928 and 1931. Although housework was on average carried out by 2.84 women and 2.30 men

---

[10] The average time spent cooking was 82, 83 and 151 minutes per day for women and 112, 112 and 156 per day for each household in the Netherlands, the UK and Japan respectively (Shinada, 2007, pp. 88–89).

[11] Another distinctive feature of the data in Table 2.1 is that even though the wife of the household head was the mother of a son aged two, she devoted considerable time to agriculture and other productive and domestic work but apparently none to child care. This sort of time allocation behaviour can also be observed in farming households of the 1960s (Kurashiki, 2007). It seems that, to the extent that there were other female members in the household, a household head's wife of an age appropriate for manual work was regarded as an income-earning worker within the Japanese farming community.

[12] These surveys are reproduced by Fuji Shuppansha in the form of a DVD. This chapter has so far utilised only a part of these surveys.

per household, few men did more than 1,000 hours of housework per year, and women performed 82.5 per cent of the total housework hours. Thus, it is clear that housework was disproportionately allocated to female members and that each household had on average more than one female member performing housework. The average number of women engaged in more than 1,000 hours of housework (1.34) reveals that there was often more than one key person doing housework, and that they were additionally complemented by women engaged in housework for relatively shorter hours. As is shown in the bottom part of Table 2.2, the proportion of total housework hours accounted for by the person who devoted the longest time to housework was on average only around 50 per cent. This observation seems to be consistent with the fact discussed above, namely that several women were carrying out the housework in each household.

Table 2.3 shows the attributes of household members engaged in housework. According to the simple average numbers in the first column, the household head's wife played a central role in housekeeping

Table 2.2 Average housework patterns across 44 farming households

Housework per household	
Housework hours	3,982 hours
Female proportion	82.5%
No. of persons engaged in housework	
Female	2.84
Male	2.30
No. of persons engaged in over 1,000 hours	
Female	1.34
Male	0.07
Proportion of total housework hours accounted for by the person who devoted the most hours to housework (%)	
Average	52.4
Maximum	95.9
Minimum	15.4

Note: Of the 44 households included in the sample, 33 were from Kyoto, 8 from Osaka and 3 from Nara prefecture. Twenty-seven were surveyed between March 1927 and February 1928, 15 between March 1928 and February 1929 and the remaining 2 between March 1931 and February 1932.

Source: Kyoto Teikoku Daigaku (ed.) *Nōka Keizaichōsabo*, 1927–33 (reproduced by Fuji Shuppansha as a DVD).

Table 2.3 Attributes of household members engaged in housework

	Average hours across the households in the survey	Average hours when present in the survey	No. of appearances of category in the survey
Female			
Wife	1,461	1,531	42
Mother	950	1,393	30
Wife of first son	201	1,265	7
Daughter	418	1,022	18
Other lineal relatives	15	322	2
Collateral relatives	254	933	12
Male			
Household head	260	266	43
Father	123	319	17
Son	157	300	23
Other lineal relatives	0.11	3	2
Collateral relatives	5	43	5
Employee	30	95	14

Source: As for Table 2.2.

and was the only one whose contribution exceeded 1,000 hours of housework. However, if we take into account the number of instances of each category (out of 44) given in the third column, we can see from the second column that, where the household head's mother did undertake housework, the hours devoted to it reached almost the same level as those of the household head's wife. The first son's wife (*yome*) also exceeded 1,000 hours, and the same was true of the head's daughter. It is also noticeable that the longest hours in the second column were less than 1,600. So, if we take into account the total working hours of the individual members in Table 2.1, even the household head's wife cannot be regarded as a full-time housewife, and yet the total housework hours per household shown in this table reached approximately 4,000, almost equivalent to the full-time working hours of one person. Thus women in farming households combined housework with other tasks, while fulfilling housework demands equivalent to those carried out by a full-time housewife.

The determinants of housework hours – a quantitative analysis

The discussion thus far reveals that the supply of housework was related to the existence of female members in the household. We now need to observe the demand side of housework and consider how demand and supply determined the level of housekeeping in farming households. In this section, we will approach these questions by analysing the data sets in the *Nōka Keizai Chōsa* (Economic Survey of Farming Households) conducted by the Ministry of Agriculture and Commerce from the mid-1920s to the early 1930s. Unlike the similar surveys conducted by Kyoto Imperial University utilised in the previous section, the individual sheets of this survey are not easy to access, though the annually published reports of the survey contain large tables showing a part of the data for individual households. Using these data sets, we will analyse the determinants of housework hours in order to consider the role of housework in the context of consumption.

Table 2.4 shows the descriptive statistics calculated during the surveys of 1929 and 1930. The statistics are aggregated by type of household defined by tenure status: owner, owner-tenant and tenant. According to the table, all the measures show significant differences by type of household. Nearly all the average numbers for both years are largest for owner households and smallest for tenant households. This suggests that owner-farmer households devoted the longest hours to housework and spent the largest amount of money. In so far as tenure status may correlate with income level, it seems that the degree of affluence positively influenced the housework hours and the scale of expenditure. However, if we take note of the variation in the number of members among household types, it is also plausible that family size itself caused the difference, as large families may be expected to require longer housework hours and incur larger expenses. In addition, we have to consider the diversity among households within the same category. The coefficient of variation shown in the table, which reached a maximum of over 0.5 in the highest case, suggests that the features of the household cannot be summarised by tenure status alone.

To confirm the possible influence of each factor on housework hours, we therefore need to conduct a multiple regression analysis. Annual housework hours per household are set as the dependent variable, and this variable is regressed on various explanatory variables such as family size, household expenses and income. Dummy variables for the year

Table 2.4 Descriptive statistics of farming households in Economic Survey of Farming Households, 1929 and 1930

	Type of tenure							
	1929				1930			
	Total	**Owner**	**Owner-tenant**	**Tenant**	**Total**	**Owner**	**Owner-tenant**	**Tenant**
No. of farming households	217	87	72	58	219	87	76	56
Average								
No. of family members	7.32	7.72	7.14	6.95	7.30	7.63	7.18	6.93
No. of family members engaged in work	4.24	4.54	4.04	4.03	4.11	4.32	3.96	3.98
Annual household expenses (yen)	1,073.9	1,267.7	999.2	875.9	802.3	919.5	768.0	667.0
Annual household income (yen)	1,155.3	1,368.1	1,124.5	874.3	723.4	837.2	698.8	579.7
Annual housework hours	4,380.2	4,768.5	4,136.3	4,100.7	3,968.6	4,398.6	3,697.9	3,668.1
Coefficient of variation								
Annual household expenses (yen)	0.40	0.36	0.39	0.33	0.39	0.35	0.43	0.30
Annual household income (yen)	0.44	0.41	0.43	0.32	0.43	0.35	0.47	0.40
Annual housework hours	0.53	0.50	0.56	0.56	0.46	0.48	0.46	0.38

Source: Nōrinshō ed., *Nōka Keizai Chōsa, Shōwa 4 and Shōwa 5.*

(1929 dummy) and for tenure status (tenant dummy and owner-tenant dummy) are put into the equation to absorb the specific effect of these factors. The dependent variable is converted into a logarithm, so that some of the coefficients, whose explanatory variables are also converted into logarithms, can be interpreted as the elasticity of each variable. Table 2.5 shows a summary of the results.

Table 2.5 Determinants of housework hours (results of multiple regression analysis, OLS)

Dependent variable	Housework hours per household (Log)		Household expenses (Log)
Model	(1)	(2)	(3)
Year	1929–1930	1929–1930	1929–1930
y axis-intercept	5.826*** (14.658)	5.064*** (11.325)	2.804*** (13.398)
No. of family members under 8	0.079*** (3.500)	0.068*** (3.099)	0.019 (1.620)
No. of female family members 15 and over	0.169*** (6.658)	0.152*** (5.955)	0.060*** (4.498)
No. of family members other than the above	0.036** (2.113)	0.021 (1.207)	0.045*** (5.074)
Income per household (Log)	0.268*** (4.359)		0.544*** (16.802)
Expenses per household (Log)		0.393*** (5.592)	
1929 dummy	–0.069 (–1.272)	–0.053 (–1.145)	0.035 (1.220)
Tenant dummy	0.016 (0.254)	0.259 (0.433)	–0.077** (–2.377)
Owner-tenant dummy	–0.077 (–1.421)	–0.053 (–0.992)	–0.083*** (–2.893)
R^2(adjusted)	0.220	0.241	0.637
No. of samples	436	436	436

Note: Coefficient in upper line and t-value below and in parenthesis. *** significant at one per cent level, ** significant at five per cent level. 'Log' refers to Logarithm.

Source: Nōrinshō ed. *Nōka Keizai Chōsa, Shōwa 4 and Shōwa 5.*

We can first consider two variables that might be expected to be relevant to the demand side of housework: income and expenses. The prevalence of production for subsistence use amongst farming households means that records made in money terms can be problematic. However, the income and expenses data in this survey can be relied on for our purposes, as they systematically evaluated the monetary value of subsistence production using the appropriate market prices at the time.

Model (1) and model (2) in Table 2.5 show that income and expenses positively correlate with housework hours, as each coefficient of income and expenses shows a plus sign and statistical significance at the one per cent level. Looking at the coefficients in each model, however, we can observe that the value of the coefficient for expenses is much higher than that for income. This implies that the influence of expenses on housework hours exceeds that of income. On the other hand, model (3) clearly shows that income, as well as the number of family members other than children under the age of eight, determine the value of expenses in each household. These findings imply that it is the household expenses that directly influence the length of housework hours, while the effect of income on it is rather indirect, functioning as one of the determinants of household expenses. Although there exists a general understanding that high income allows households to spare relatively long hours for housework, this is not what is suggested by these results. According to the value of the coefficient, a one per cent increase in expenses causes a 0.39 per cent increase in housework hours. If expenses are treated as a proxy for the acquisition of goods, it may be suggested that there was a complementary rather than substitutive relation between consuming goods and doing housework.

Secondly, we can consider the explanatory variables relevant to the number of family members. The number of male family members aged eight and over, shown in the fourth line of explanatory variables, can be seen as a proxy variable indicating the size of the demand for housework.[13] Making use of model (2) on the basis of the discussion above, we can see that the coefficient of this explanatory variable shows the smallest value among the three relevant variables given in lines two to four, and is statistically insignificant. This implies that, if we control for the other factors embodied in the various explanatory variables, housework hours did not necessarily rise along with increase in family size,

[13] This figure in fact includes female household members aged between 8 and 15. The reason for excluding female family members over 15 here is explained in the discussion in the next paragraph.

even though the descriptive statistics shown in Table 2.4 appear to suggest the influence of family size. This result is readily comprehensible if we recall that cooking for two people may require the same number of hours as cooking for four people. However, the implication of this result is not trivial. Since it indicates that the per capita cooking time for four people is smaller than that for two people, it implies that economies of scale certainly functioned within the household in terms of housework, or at least cooking. This significant feature of housework, the economy of scale, can be regarded as an essential factor in any understanding of the relation between household size and housework.

In contrast, the coefficient of the number of female family members aged 15 and over, given in the third line, shows a plus sign and is statistically significant. An increase in the supply of labour within the household thus seems to result in longer housework hours per household. The value of this coefficient is the largest of the three relevant variables, indicating that the addition of one person results in an increase of housework hours of 15.2 per cent. This finding allows us to assume the existence of strategic labour allocation behaviour in the household, with the female members being disproportionately allocated to housework. In other words, female members are strategically important for any increase in housework hours carried out within the household. On the other hand, the existence of small children might increase the demand for housework, as a child needs to be taken care of. This supposition can be confirmed by noting that the coefficient of the number of family members under the age of eight is also positive and statistically significant. Interestingly, the coefficient of this variable is insignificant in model (3). This finding, while revealing the time-consuming nature of child-care work, suggests that child care did not require extra expenses. In other words, the existence of the strong positive correlation between expenses and housework hours discussed above suggests the significance, in those days, of certain kinds of housework other than child care.

The analysis in this section thus reveals that the demand for housework was influenced by the amount of household expenditure, which in turn corresponded to a level of consumption of goods. On the other hand, the number of female workers determined the level of housework supplied. In sum, the length of housework hours per household depended on the level of consumption of goods and the endowment of family labour in each household. This suggests that there was a complementary relationship between goods and housework in the context of consumption.

Housework in urban households

Time-use survey

In contrast to farming households, there are few materials available to help us analyse the housework hours of non-farming households in the pre-war period. The first time-use survey by NHK (Nihon Hōsō Kyōkai [Japan Broadcasting Association] 1941) is almost the only source providing systematic information on housework hours. The survey aggregated women according to the occupation in which the household head was engaged, and collected information on how they used their time. The results are shown in the four graphs in Figure 2.2. Three occupations correspond to non-farming households: salaried worker, factory worker and retailer. The women in the two former household types (shown in Figure 2.2-(1) and 2.2-(2)) were almost full-time housewives, spending 600 to 700 minutes per day in 'housework' and 'needlework'. By contrast, women in the retailer households (shown in Figure 2.2-(3)) devoted around 300 minutes of their time to paid work, most likely in the family business as family workers. The profile in Figure 2.2-(3) seems to be much closer to that of Figure 2.2-(4), which denotes farming households, than to those of Figure 2.2-(1) or 2.2-(2).

Can we then conclude that the households of urban salaried or wage workers devoted more time to housework than farming households? Can we regard the household of the retailer, engaged in one of the most representative occupations of non-agricultural, self-employed workers, as a miniature version of a farming household in terms of housework issues? Before jumping to such conclusions, we have to scrutinise several points.

In particular, the sample bias of this survey in terms of household type needs to be reconsidered. First, the breadwinner household taken to correspond to the type described in Figure 2.2-(1) and 2.2-(2) may be over weighted. Not only was the number of salaried workers rather limited in those days, but also factory workers were often multi-occupied and had their earnings supplemented by the earnings of female family members, so it is not realistic to assume that Figure 2.2-(2) represents the majority of factory workers' households. On the other hand, data on the industrial status of workers in the population censuses demonstrate that 'workers on own account' (*gyōshu*), which can be a proxy for the self-employed, occupied a significant part of the gainfully occupied work-force (Tanimoto, 2002, 2003). There were many other sectors of manufacturing and commerce besides retailing containing a large number of self-employed workers. In that sense, the fact that NHK targeted only retailers and not those employed in other occupations biased the profile of households at that time.

Figure 2.2 Distribution of housework hours in various types of household, 1941

Figure 2.2(1) Average working hours of a woman per day in households of salaried workers (November 1941)

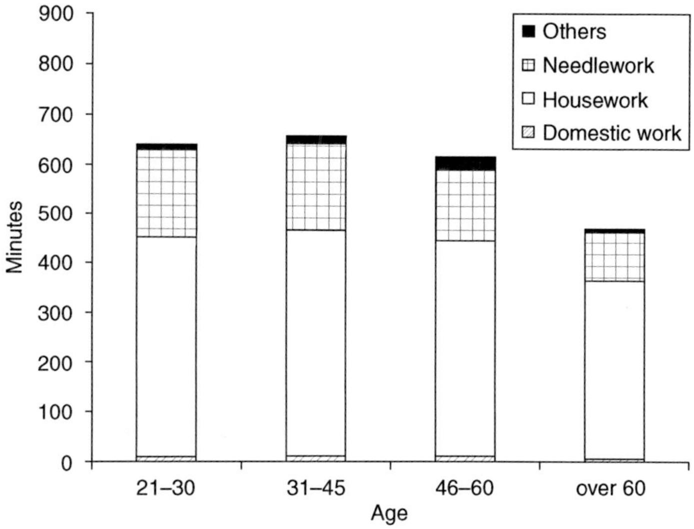

Figure 2.2(2) Average working hours of a woman per day in households of factory workers (November 1941)

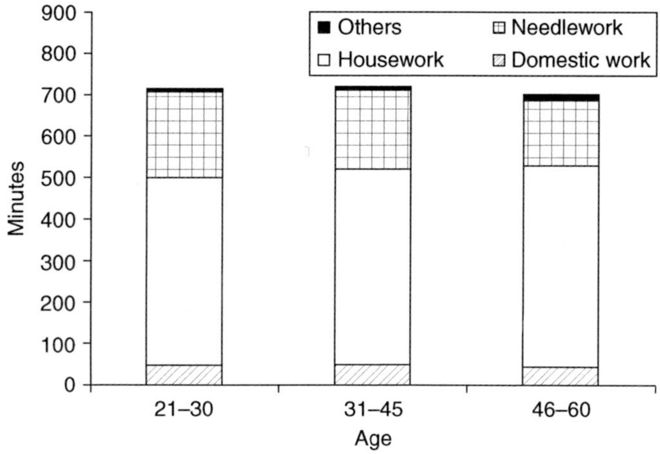

Figure 2.2(3) Average working hours of a woman per day in households of retailers (November 1941)

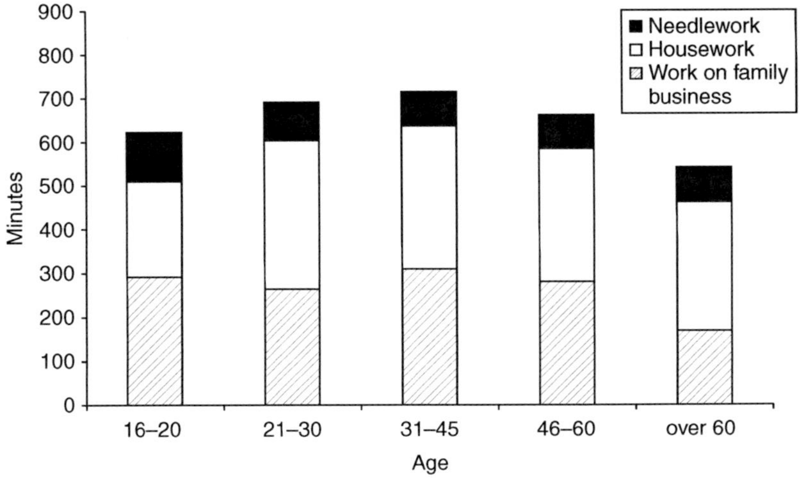

Figure 2.2(4) Average working hours of a woman per day in farming households (November 1941)

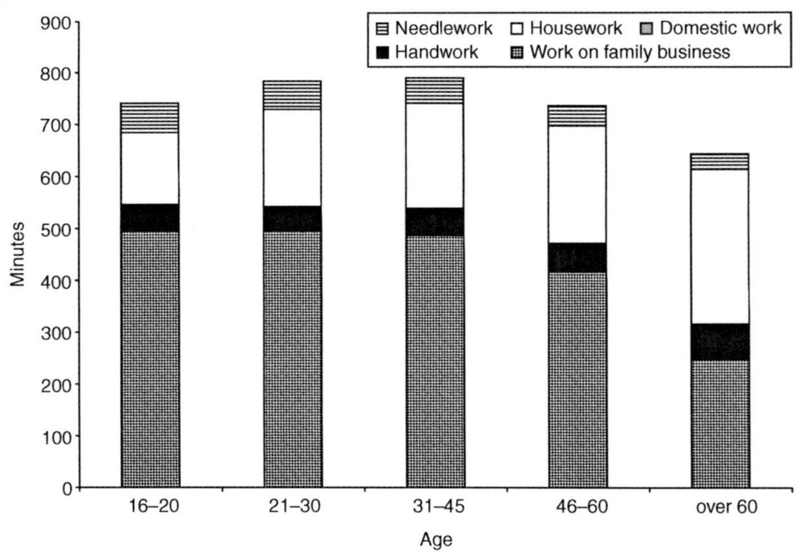

More importantly, we have to be aware that the data shown in Figure 2.2 were aggregated on an individual basis, rather than on a household basis. It is true that the working hours of women in farming households (Figure 2.2-(4)), who combined agricultural work with housework and needlework on an individual basis, coincide well with the findings outlined in the previous section. However, one important point made in that section was that housework was typically carried out by several members of the household, and not by a single person. Therefore, though the average individual housework hours amounted to fewer than 2,000 hours per year, the sum of housework hours per household was equivalent to, if not greater than, the number of hours done by a single full-time housewife. Thus, a naïve acceptance of the individual-based NHK survey might mislead us in terms of understanding the quantity of housework actually carried out in the household.

Domestic servants

Under these circumstances, information on domestic servants, who may be assumed to have played a significant role in housekeeping, offers clues as to how to approach the demand and supply of housework within the household unit.[14] In fact, the number of female domestic servants in inter-war Japan reached more than 700,000, and domestic service was the largest occupation among female employees, with numbers exceeding even those of textile factory workers.[15] Table 2.6 gives the aggregate number of domestic servants in 1920 according to the industry and employment status of their employer. Though the numbers of households categorised in this way are not available, the number of married men aged from 15 to 59 can be utilised as an approximation.

First, we can observe that the number of domestic servants per 100 gainfully occupied and married men aged 15 to 59, which we will hereafter call the domestic servant 'employment rate', differs significantly by employment status. 'Workers on own account' show the highest employment rate of domestic servants, closely followed by 'salaried workers'. By contrast, the domestic servant employment rate of 'wage workers' was far lower. If we consider the absolute number of households in each status, we find that it was the households of self-employed workers that employed the highest number of domestic servants.

---

[14] Nomoto (2001) gives a concise overview of the relationship between domestic servants and housewives in pre-war Japan.

[15] For the interaction between textile workers and domestic servants within the female labour market, see Odaka, 1995.

Table 2.6 Number of domestic servants per 100 households, 1920 (approximation)

	Total	Self-employed	Salaried workers	Wage workers
Tokyo City	20.85	29.73	27.91	0.76
Total number	75,874	55,272	19,788	814
Breakdown by industry				
Agriculture	8.47	10.61	57.80	0.44
Manufacturing	10.40	16.99	22.57	*0.62*
Commerce	26.37	28.34	28.34	*1.92*
Transportation	5.81	9.87	15.69	0.51
Public service and freelance professions	33.51	47.74	32.50	1.13
Whole country	4.18	8.39	7.90	0.20
Total number	634,882	556,367	63,180	15,335
Breakdown by industry				
Agriculture	3.63	4.61	6.34	0.12
Manufacturing	5.51	11.11	8.04	*0.60*
Commerce	13.75	15.20	12.72	*1.51*
Transportation	3.05	5.73	5.58	0.56
Public service and freelance professions	15.72	37.43	6.89	2.21

Note: Number of gainfully occupied and married men aged 15 to 59 is used as a proxy for the number of households.

Gainfully occupied men are classified by employment status and industry.

Source: Kokusei chōsa, 1920; Tokyo-shi Shisei Tōkei Genpyō, 1920.

Second, it is noteworthy that differences in the industries in which employers worked also matter in terms of the employment rate of domestic servants. The importance of the 'new middle class' can be observed from the large number of domestic servants employed by 'public service and freelance professionals'. On the other hand, agriculture shows the second smallest employment rate of domestic servants in both the upper and lower halves of this table, corresponding to Tokyo City and the whole country respectively. This implies that the high employment rate of domestic servants by self-employed households occurred in non-agricultural, urban households, and not in farming households.

These findings are consistent with the fact that domestic servant employment rates in Tokyo City were around four times higher than the averages for the whole of Japan, suggesting that employing servants was more of an urban phenomenon involving two major types of employer: the 'new middle class', including salaried and professional workers, and the 'old middle class', composed of self-employed households engaged in non-agricultural industries. If the domestic servant employment rate of 17 (16.99) per cent among the 'workers on own account' in the manufacturing sector, as shown in Table 2.6, can be taken as a proxy for the rate among the total number of manufacturing workshops, then we can assume that a certain number of workshops with capital of less than 5,000 yen employed domestic servants, as seems justifiable in the light of the findings of an industrial survey conducted in Tokyo in the early 1930s (Tokyo Shiyakusho, 1934).[16] Workshops of this size were, on average, based on family labour supplemented by an apprentice and an adult worker at the most.

We can draw two conclusions from these findings for our understanding of the demand and supply of housework within the household. Taking into consideration the relatively small numbers and superior position of salaried workers in pre-war Japan, it is natural to assume that the level of income operated as a decisive factor in determining the employment rate of domestic servants. Specifically, the big difference between salaried workers and wage workers – both groups of employees working under strict constraints in terms of place and times of work – suggests the importance of the ability to afford domestic servants. In other words, though the multi-occupied households of wage-workers potentially demanded a person who could make up for the shortage of family members doing housework, they could not afford to employ one. In fact, a report on the living conditions of married female textile workers in a weaving factory reveals that their limited time for housework resulted in less time spent cooking and unsanitary, untidy conditions in their homes (Rōdōshō Fujin Shōnen Kyoku, 1955, pp. 19–20). It is also noticeable that the high employment rate of domestic servants in the breadwinner households of the 'new middle class' did not necessarily result in the withdrawal of family members from housework. It is often

[16] This survey classified 82,508 manufacturing workshops operating in Tokyo City in 1932 into 10 categories according to the value of their capital. The number of workshops whose capital exceeded 5,000 yen represented 12.3 per cent of the total, which is less than the 17 per cent mentioned in the text. Hence a certain proportion of domestic servants must have been employed by workshops smaller than those with capital of 5,000 yen or more.

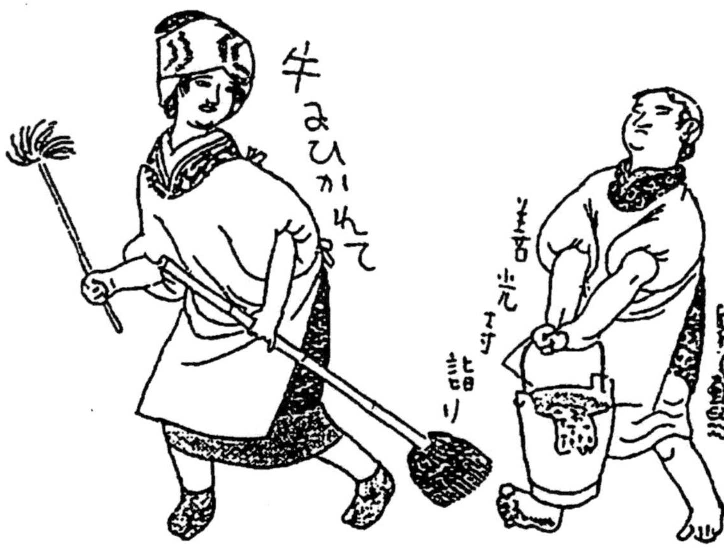

Figure 2.3 A housewife (left) working with a domestic servant (right), c .1930
Source: Shimizu (2004), p. 64.

reported that housework in the breadwinner household was executed as full-time work by the housewife, with the assistance of a young girl employed as a domestic servant (see Figure 2.3).[17] The employment of a domestic servant seems to have resulted in an increase in the supply of housework per household, and it may show households' preference for a better standard of living achieved by increasing the total housework hours.

On the other hand, it is possible that the high domestic servant employment rate in the households of 'workers on own account' reflects labour demand for work other than housework in the household. As we noticed in Figure 2.2-(3), female members in retailing households allocated a part of their working time to their family business, just as the females in farming households shared agricultural work with the males. What, then, is the reason for the sharp contrast in employment rates, high and low, between the urban and rural self-employment-based households? A clue is provided in Table 2.7. According to this table, the average family size of owners of small- and medium-sized factories or commercial workshops was slightly larger than that of salaried and

[17] For details of the actual activities of servants, see Shimizu, 2004, ch. 1.

Table 2.7 Family composition by employment status, Tokyo City, 1934

		Proportion by family types (%)		
	Average no. of family members	**Married couple or single parent with children**	**As column to the left plus husband's relatives**	**Others**
Total	6.22	76.4	17.6	6.1
Salaried worker and freelanced profession	6.20	72.7	19.4	7.9
Owner of small and medium scale enterprises	6.35	73.3	20.5	6.2
Agriculture, forestry, fishery	7.60	46.6	48.2	5.2
Factory	6.39	73.8	19.7	6.4
Commerce	6.24	75.2	18.7	6.2
Wage worker	6.09	82.9	12.5	4.6

Source: Tokyo Shiyakusho ed. *Kazoku Tōkei* (1935).

wage workers, but significantly smaller, by 1.25 persons, than that of families occupied in agriculture and forestry. The difference can largely be explained by the composition of the family, that is to say, whether the household included both lineal and collateral relatives of the household head. As discussed in previous sections, female family members, especially the household head's mother, played a significant role in the housework of farming households. The families employed in agriculture and forestry included a high proportion (48.2 per cent) in which the household head's relatives contributed to the family labour force. By contrast, non-agricultural self-employment-based households often lacked family labour resources, as only 20.5 per cent of the 'owners of small- and medium-scale enterprises' included both lineal and collateral relatives in their households. In other words, the lack of female members to share the burden of housework necessitated the recruitment of additional labour for housework, and a certain proportion of the urban self-employment-based households brought in domestic servants from outside. This interpretation is consistent with the differences in the age distribution of domestic servants according to the industry of the household head shown in Table 2.8. The high proportion of domestic servants

Table 2.8 Domestic servants by industry and age, 1920

Occupation of the household head in households employing domestic servants	Number of female domestic servants	Proportion of female servants (%)	Age group of female domestic servants (%)		
			0–14	15–59	60–
Total	634,882	90.2	37.4	58.4	4.2
Agriculture	164,369	85.5	72.2	24.0	3.8
Industry	106,994	93.4	30.2	66.0	3.8
Commerce	170,998	95.4	25.7	71.3	3.0
Public service and freelance profession	92,917	86.0	24.2	68.8	7.0

Source: Population Census, 1920.

under 15 in the agricultural sector indicates that the labour demand in this sector was largely for babysitting (*komori*), while other sectors demanded domestic servants old enough to be able to cope with various kinds of housework. In contrast to the case of the 'new middle class', in which domestic servants were additional to family labour, we could say that these self-employment-based households were compensating for the lack of labour supply within the family. From the viewpoint of consumption history, this suggests that the higher employment rate of domestic servants by 'workers on own account' could reflect a desire to maintain a certain standard of living which the multi-occupied workers discussed above might have given up trying to achieve.

Brief comparisons by country and period

It is also interesting that the number of domestic servants differed by country and by period, as shown in Figure 2.4.[18] The figure brings together data for two types of comparison: regional comparison between Japan and the UK (England and Wales) and a comparison between Tokyo and London. In each case the two are compared across the pre-war and post-war periods. The expected diversity caused by differences in the development stage of the economy is controlled by setting the per capita real GDP as the horizontal axis.

[18] The sources for this figure are the population censuses of each country. Higgs (1983) has noted that the number of domestic servants in the England and Wales censuses is somewhat problematic, especially in the mid–late nineteenth century, so the data shown in this figure should be seen as a first step towards the comparative study of domestic servants in Britain and Japan.

Figure 2.4 Numbers of domestic servants by GDP, Japan and the UK compared

Figure 2.4(1) Number of domestic servants by GDP, Japan, England and Wales (Japan: 1920–1965, England and Wales: 1851–1961)
(J = Japan, EW = England and Wales)

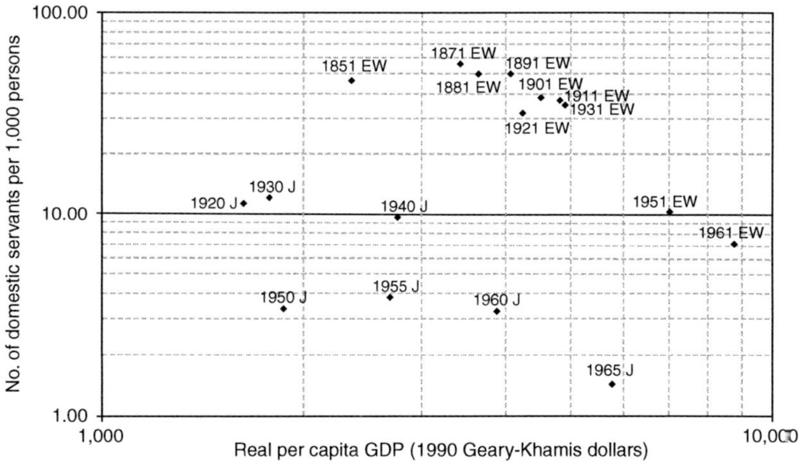

Figure 2.4(2) Number of domestic servants by GDP, Tokyo and London (Tokyo: 19(8–1965, London: 1851–1921)
(T = Tokyo, TC = Tokyo City, L = London)

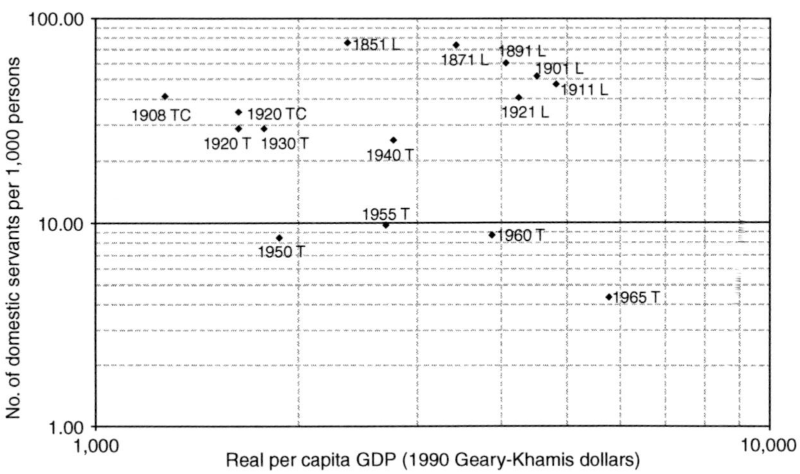

Source: Population censuses in Japan and England/Wales, Maddison (1995).

Table 2.9 Number of domestic servants per 1,000 persons, Japan and the UK

	1851	1901	1920–21	1930
Japan	–	–	11.34	12.12
England and Wales	46.24	38.15	32.00	–
Tokyo	–	–	28.92	28.92
London	76.19	52.27	40.81	–

Source: Population censuses in Japan and England/Wales.

We can clearly identify three separate groups in the figure: pre-war Japan (Tokyo), nineteenth–twentieth century England and Wales (London) and post-war Japan (Tokyo). Roughly speaking, all groups show a common tendency for increases in per capita GDP to exert a negative effect on the number of domestic servants. However, if we look at the absolute number of servants relative to population shown in Table 2.9, we see that there were significant differences among the three. In 1920, England and Wales had three times as many domestic servants relative to population as Japan, and London 1.5 times as many as Tokyo. Even larger disparities could probably be observed if we extrapolated from the numbers for England and Wales and London to the left of the table.

So, what could have caused the difference? Although this awaits further analysis, it seems likely that housework was disproportionately allocated to family members in Japan. This assumption seems to be consistent with the fact that the number of domestic servants was rather small in farming households in which lineal family members remained within the household. This line of discussion may reveal the relation between the supply of housework and the family system from a comparative point of view.

The amount of housework is a separate but relevant point to be scrutinised. At first glance, a large number of domestic servants seems to suggest an ample supply of housework to the household. However, if servants were employed so as to enable family members to withdraw from housework, the relatively large number of domestic servants was not necessarily equivalent to an abundant supply of housework.[19] An

[19] Kawamura (2010) summarises the recent literature on housework in nineteenth- and early twentieth-century Britain, and suggests that work done by domestic servants tended to replace the housework formerly carried out by family members. Confirmation of this interesting statement requires more detailed research.

empirical comparison of actual housework is needed to answer these questions.

In addition, it is also noticeable that the absolute number of domestic servants in Japan declined significantly after the Second World War. It is not appropriate to attribute this to the rising income level in the post-war period, as the development stage of the economy is controlled by the estimated real per capita GDP in the figure. Structural changes in housework therefore need to be analysed, to provide clues to understanding the relation between housework and consumption in post-war Japan.[20]

Concluding remarks

Lastly, we return to the two major findings of this chapter. The first is the complementary relationship between housework and the consumption of goods in Japanese households. This is suggested by the positive correlation between household expenses and housework hours, and offers an image of housework inconsistent with the interpretation of de Vries, who assumes a change over time from goods-intensive consumption to service-intensive (housework-intensive) consumption. In contrast, it seems that the consumption of goods in Japan was more closely related to housework even before the emergence of the breadwinner household. This discrepancy might suggest the possible hypothesis that this pattern can be formulated as a labour-intensive path of consumption growth, though this would have to be tested through further comparative studies of the role of housework in people's material lives.[21] Second, we considered the supply side of housework by measuring the contribution of both family members and domestic servants. The plurality of family members engaged in housework in Japan implies the existence of a kind of household remote from the breadwinner household model.

[20] The chapters by Gordon (Chapter 3) and Macnaughtan (Chapter 4) in this volume address this question through analysis of the introduction of new technology into post-war households. They show how the new technology embodied in the sewing machine and the rice-cooker impacted on the practice of housework in the specific fields of needlework and cooking.

[21] The role of housework in improving material lives in the West also merits discussion. Cowan (1983) indicates the role of cooking in farmers' households in eighteenth- and nineteenth-century North America, and Bourke (1994) insists on the positive value of home-made necessities for working class households in nineteenth-century England. In the light of information on actual housework carried out in the nineteenth century, the validity of de Vries' formulation for the West mentioned here should also be scrutinised.

It also suggests a link between housework and the family system, or more interestingly, a relation between the family system and consumption. To sum up, the chapter showed the determinants of housework among diverse households and tried to suggest that housework was one of the major fields through which the consumption behaviour of ordinary people in modern Japan can be evaluated.

This chapter has not considered how housework affected the actual level, style and pattern of consumption. The informative descriptions by Furushima Toshio tell us how closely housework can be related to the pattern of consuming goods (Furushima, 1996). Not only did an increase in housework enable a certain consumption style – cooking rice for three meals per day, for example – but equally the forced saving of housework in urban self-employment-based households might have created a consumption pattern dependent on outside catering and eating out, resulting in the creation of a certain urban eating culture. The incorporation of information and data on actual housework represents a further indispensable task to complement the quantitative approach undertaken in this chapter.

References

Becker, G. (1965) 'A Theory of the Allocation of Time', *Economic Journal*, vol.75 no.299, pp. 493–517.

Bourke, J (1994) 'Housewifery in Working-class England 1860–1914', *Past and Present*, no.143, pp. 167–97.

Cowan, R. S. (1983) *More Work for Mother*, New York: Basic Books.

de Vries, J. (2008) *The Industrious Revolution: Consumer Behavior and the Household Economy, 1650 to the Present*, New York: Cambridge University Press.

Furushima, T. (1996) *Daidokoro Yōgu no Kindaishi* (A Modern History of Kitchen Utensils), Tokyo: Yūhikaku.

Higgs, E. (1983) 'Domestic Servants and Households in Victorian England', *Social History*, vol.8, no.2, pp. 201–10.

Kawamura, S. (2010) 'igirisu no Kajihōkō no Rekishi to sono Shūhen' (On the History of British Domestic Servants and Related Matters), *Rekishi Hyōron*, no.722, June 2010, pp. 4–18.

Kurashiki, N. (2007) 'Kindai Kazoku Kihan Juyō no Jūsōsei (The Multi-layered Features of Adopting the Norm of the Modern Family)', *Nenpō Nihon Gendaishi*, no.12, May 2007, pp. 201–35.

Maddison, A. (1995) *Monitoring the World Economy 1820–1992*, Paris: OECD.

Nomoto, K. (2001) 'Kaji Rōdō o Meguru "Shufu" to "Jochū" (Housewives and Domestic Servants in Relation to Housework)' in Ōguchi, Y. (ed.) *Onna no Shakaishi: Ie to Jendā o Kangaeru*, Tokyo: Yamakawa Shuppansha, pp. 311–32.

Nihon Hōsō Kyōkai (ed.) (1941) *Seikatsu Jikan Chōsa* (Living Time Survey).

Odaka, K. (1995) 'Redundancy Utilized: The Economics of Female Domestic Servants in Pre-War Japan' in Hunter, J. (ed.) *Japanese Women Working*, London: Routledge.

Rōdōshō Fujin Shōnen Kyoku (ed.) (1955) *Fujin Rōdōsha no Seisan Katsudō to Kaji narabi ni Bosei Katsudō ni Kan suru Chōsa Kenkyū* (Research Report on Female Workers' Productive Work and their Housework and Child-rearing Activities).

Shimizu, M. (2004) *'Jochū' Imeeji no Katei Bunkashi* (Image of Domestic Servants and the Cultural History of the Home), Kyoto: Sekai Shisōsha.

Shinada, T. (2007) *Kaji to Kazoku no Nichijō Seikatsu* (Housework and the Everyday Life of the Family), Tokyo: Gakubunsha.

Sōrifu Tōkeikyoku (ed.) (1970) *Kokusei Chōsa Tokubetsu-shūkei, Setai oyobi Kazoku* (National Census Special Aggregation on Households and Families).

Tanimoto, M. (2002) 'Kindai Nihon no Toshi Shōkeiei' (Small Urban Businesses in Modern Japan) in Nakamura, T. (ed.) *Toshika to Zairai Sangyō*, Tokyo: Nihon Keizai Hyōronsha, pp. 3–49.

Tanimoto, M. (2003) 'Kindai Nihon no Josei Rōdō to "Shōkeiei"' (Women's Labour and Small Business in Modern Japan) in Ujiie, M., Sakurai, Y., Tanimoto, M. & Nagano, H. (eds) *Nihon Kindai Kokka no Seiritsu to Jendā* (Gender and the Formation of the Modern Japanese Nation State), Tokyo: Kashiwa Shobō, pp. 144–87.

Tanimoto, M. (2006) 'The Role of Tradition in Japan's Industrialization: Another Path to Industrialization' in Tanimoto, M. (ed.), *The Role of Tradition in Japan's Industrialization*, Oxford: Oxford University Press, pp. 3–44.

Tanimoto, M. (forthcoming) 'From Peasant Economy to Urban Agglomeration: the Transformation of "Labour-Intensive Industrialization" in Modern Japan' in Austin, G. & Sugihara, K. (eds), *Labour-intensive Industrialization in Historical Perspective*, London: Routledge.

Tokyo Shiyakusho (ed.) (1934) *Tōkyō-shi Kōgyō Chōsa-sho* (Industrial Survey of Tokyo City), Tokyo: Tokyo Shiyakusho.

3

Like Bamboo Shoots after the Rain: The Growth of a Nation of Dressmakers and Consumers

Andrew Gordon

Introduction

The female consumer stands – in advertisements quite literally – as one of the most prominent symbols of Japan's astonishing post-war economic rise to global prominence. Even in the impoverished aftermath of war, her smiling figure beckoned to her compatriots to share in the 'bright life' enabled by purchase of the fruits of modern industry. One of the goods she bought and used with greatest intensity – whether measured in the rate of diffusion or the daily hours of use – was the sewing machine. Perhaps because of the difficulty of neatly defining its economic or social character, the sewing machine is a product often overlooked in standard accounts of Japan's post-war consumer revolution. It was at once an object of consumer desire and a producer good used to make clothing not only for the family but also for the commercial market. But for this very reason I see the extraordinary spread of the sewing machine as both a harbinger and an example of a broader story: the heroines of Japan's post-war consumer revolution brought to the task of managing the household and filling it with all manner of goods a professional spirit not unlike that of their male counterparts, the 'salarymen' who designed, made and sold these products in Japan and around the world.

Even before the Second World War, as many as one in ten families owned a sewing machine. It had a distinctive profile of use: mainly in the home, mainly by women, in ways that positioned it as both a consumer and producer good and as a possession connected to a Western-oriented modern life. Its greatest selling point beyond speed was the ability to produce tight-locked stitches. This made it poorly suited to fabrication of traditional Japanese garments whose outer and inner pieces had to be loosely chain-stitched so they could easily be taken apart for laundering. Instead, from early in the twentieth century, women used the sewing machine to make Western-style clothes both for family members and, in some cases, for sale to neighbours or on piece-work consignment.

From this solid pre-war foundation, domestic purchase of sewing machines soared in the first two post-war decades. As early as 1953, according to estimates by the Ministry of International Trade and Industry, annual domestic sales reached 800,000 units, while dress shops and sewing schools sprouted 'like bamboo shoots after the rain' (*Mishin Kōgyō*, 1954, p. 25; Koizumi, 2000, p. 42). As Penelope Francks' chapter (Chapter 7) in this volume makes clear, the adoption of Western dress for women had been limited until the 1930s, and this had inhibited the spread of the sewing machine. Before the Second World War, the diffusion rate in Japan lagged noticeably compared to places with considerably lower per capita incomes (Gordon, 2011, ch. 2). But in the 1950s and 1960s, the bottleneck was broken; the near universal turn of women in Japan to Western dress both caused and resulted from the sewing machine's diffusion. The good became a key link in a feedback loop connecting home sewing, new fashion trends, and the consuming household. Its story opens a window to the era when the consumer became a truly dominant figure in the practice and the self-understanding of Japanese life, and women became truly entrenched as the managers of consumer life.

Long hours of sewing: the time allocation of the professional housewife

The sewing machine can be a tool for historical study of consumer and family life worldwide, but it is particularly useful for such an inquiry in relation to Japan because of the unusually long hours that Japanese women devoted to sewing. Several surveys of the early 1950s, both community studies and national samples, found that urban married women in both working- and middle-class families typically devoted *nearly three hours each day* to home sewing (Kawasaki Rōdō Shi Hensan Iinkai, 1987, p. 200; Rōdōshō, Fujin Shōnenkyoku, 1952). As a comparative point of reference, surveys from the United States find that already by the 1920s women averaged only one hour a day of needlework. French women in the immediate post-war years stood somewhere between: according to a 1948 survey, they devoted between 60 and 90 minutes daily to 'sewing, mending, knitting, and wardrobe management' (a more capacious definition than that used in Japanese surveys) (Vanek, 1973; Stoetzel, 1948, pp. 52–56). A 1949 study of 'working class wives in London' found an average of merely 20 minutes per day given over to 'sewing' (Mason, 1949, p. 372). These totals in all cases excluded home-based commercial sewing. Other surveys make it clear that home-based women in Japan – as elsewhere – also undertook considerable sewing for the market. In the two decades following the war, for various purposes but for many hours, all over the nation women sewed.

Some of this needlework was certainly done by hand, but home-sewing became an increasingly mechanised undertaking as millions of women bought sewing machines. Whether by hand or machine, women in Japan were sewing so very much due to a dynamic interaction of local and global practice. Although rigorous comparison based on time studies is not possible, it seems certain that in pre-modern times the need to unstitch and re-stitch garments in order to wash them was already making home-sewing a particularly time-intensive activity in Japan. From the Meiji period through the 1950s, as the practice of dress and sewing shifted from Japanese to Western modes, the efforts of salesmen, the exhortations of civilian reformers and state officials, and the needs and desires of millions of women would together reinforce the time-consuming practice of fabricating dress at home with sewing machines.

Insofar as one understands consumption in modern societies as an act that offers pleasure and satisfies wants as well as basic material needs, it is noteworthy that a 1959 survey revealed that, in addition to performing needlework under the rubric of 'household work', women in Japan ranked sewing their third most popular 'free time' activity after reading and listening to the radio. Asked how they used their average of two hours of free time daily, about half of the women said they read, just over one quarter listened to the radio, and another one quarter sewed. Playing with children was the primary activity of only 13 per cent (Rōdōshō, Fujin Shōnenkyoku, 1959, pp. 2–19).[1] During the years of the take-off in mass consumption of branded industrial goods, as they stitched both for family consumption and for the market, both as 'housework' and for pleasure, Japanese women in the 1950s and 1960s constituted a nation of seamstresses and dressmakers.

This activity was part of the daily routine of the 'professional housewife' in her heyday. She was the Japanese incarnation of the full-time

[1] Multiple answers were accepted so the total exceeded 100 per cent.

housewife who emerged to prominence in capitalist societies around the world in the mid-twentieth century. This label is at first glance an oxymoron. Professionals are those who work for pay, while the labour of the female household manager is unpaid. But I use it, following others such as Suzanne Vogel, because it better renders the Japanese-language expression *sengyō shufu* than the usual translation of 'full-time housewife' (Vogel, 1978, pp. 16–43). The character for *gyō* conveys the sense of occupation or job, and the term *sengyō* means 'specialised enterprise or occupation'. A *sengyō shufu* not only works 'full-time' but does so with a professional commitment to being a housewife on a par with the workplace professionalism of her salaried husband.

The concept and the social role of housewife (*shufu*) came into being from the late nineteenth century through wartime. The term carried to a mass audience the sense of the good wife and wise mother constructed in the ideology of late Meiji times. This understanding of the housewife was given wide currency in the inter-war era through monthly magazines, most famously *Shufu no Tomo* (*The Housewife's Companion*). The term 'professional housewife' came into common use only after the Second World War; through the era of recovery and high-speed growth, it came to be understood as the ideal role for a married woman (Kunihiro, 2001, pp. 4–6; Ochiai, 1994). The housewife's vocational training and obligations extended more widely than ever, from the management of home finances – and sometimes a stint supplementing family income as a home-worker – to housework, child rearing and education management. It included 'care for the physical, emotional, and developmental needs of the family' through tasks such as cooking and sewing (Vogel, 1978, p. 17). By examining the ways in which the sewing machine became the everyday tool of Japan's every-woman, we gain insight into the life of the 'professional' housewife and the dynamics of her endurance as a national ideal at the centre of the consumer economy.

What women wore: the end to the two-layered life

In 1957 the prominent cultural critic, Ōya Sōichi, declared in a newspaper column that a 'dress revolution' had brought an end to Japan's 'two-layered life' ('Nihonjin', *Asahi Shimbun* 13 January 1957, cited in Nakayama, 1987, p. 462). This term had come into wide use in the 1920s to describe and usually to lament a society in which daily life was torn between modes of housing, clothing and cooking identified as 'Japanese' and those defined as 'Western' (*washitsu/yōshitsu; wafuku/yōfuku, washoku/yōshoku* and so on).[2]

Because the sewing machine had long been understood as a tool suited only for the fabrication of Western clothing, the swift post-war shift to this mode of dress unleashed a flood of demand for it. By 1960, as many as 72 per cent of Japan's 20 million households possessed one, making it the second most widely owned consumer machine, after the radio at 89 per cent (and well ahead of the television at 55 per cent) (Nihon Mishin Kyōkai, 1961, p. 7).

Of course, this revolution in consumer life did not come immediately with the war's end. For at least a year, the dress options of city women were constrained by scarcity and rationing, and they continued to wear the trousers called *monpe*, adopted during wartime through a complex process of government and civic promotion mixed with improvisation on the ground. Only from 1949, with the recovery of domestic textile production, did significant supplies of fabric become available, and fabric rationing did not end until 1951 (Nakayama, 1987, pp. 455–56; Yoshimoto, 2004a, p. 30). But even in the face of scarce fabric and rationing, change in clothing practice was already underway in the form of a rush by women to put on Western dress. As one compelling retrospective essay described the situation:

> [At first] the situation for clothing, food, shelter, was beyond impossible. I believe it was around the start of summer the year after the defeat when it became possible to survive, still with extreme difficulty, first with food, then shelter and clothing. Because, as it started to get hot, women changed from *monpe* to skirts.... By 1948, it was clear that women's fashion [in Tokyo] had turned to the skirt, blouse, and some dabs of rouge. (Yoshida, 1955, pp. 140–42)

Kon Wajirō, a renowned ethnographer of Japan's modern daily life since the 1920s, wrote that, in the summer of 1950, 'I travelled through farm villages from Kansai to Tōhoku. What surprised me was that in whatever remote mountain valley, the women who gathered were almost all in Western dress.' Even the agricultural cooperatives were selling fabrics for Western wear such as simple blouses, skirts, and one-piece dresses, and new sewing schools had already appeared (Inoue, 2001,

[2] Penelope Francks' chapter (Chapter 7) on 'Kimono fashion' for this volume persuasively demonstrates the resilience and significance of the 'Japanese' side of this two-layered life in pre-war times.

pp. 239–40; Kon, 1967, p. 130). Kon exaggerated the speed and scope of the shift. During the summer of his farm visits, the *Yomiuri* newspaper conducted a nationwide poll and found that 61 per cent of respondents still wore both Western and Japanese dress, while 29 per cent had turned completely to Western wear. But even these totals represented a sharp change from pre-war or wartime surveys.

The sources of new fashions in city, town, and country, for women of all ages, were various. They included patterns featured in the ever-popular women's magazines, as well as the outfits worn by the 'pan-pan' (girlfriends or prostitutes to American GIs). As early as 1946, 'stylebooks' featuring patterns and instructions on how to make Western wear began to sell in great numbers, presenting eager readers with the latest in American trends. They conveyed a complicated mix of desire and defensiveness, and a non-linear course of change. The August 1947 founding issue of one of them, *Amerikan Fasshon* (*American Fashion*), acknowledged that 'with new fabrics or accessories so difficult to obtain, we must resign ourselves for some time to the need to make do and improvise with whatever we have at hand.' In addition, fashion writers faced a tension between Western styles and Japanese bodies. A certain skirt was said to 'be a problem for Japanese to wear'. A certain chemise dress was 'a look very difficult for Japanese to achieve, but what a free and easy way of dressing it is!' The magazine admitted frankly to readers that they were selling naught but dreams: 'wearing this sort of bold dress to a dinner or dance in today's Japan is unimaginable, but even the fantasy offers pleasure' (Nakayama, 1987, pp. 456–57).

Nonetheless, within a few years, large numbers of women were able to act out their fashion fantasies. Introduced via the United States, Christian Dior's 'New Look' long skirts of 1947 took off in Japan in 1948. From 1953, French designers, led by Dior, began to introduce their new spring lines in person in Tokyo, and over the following years trends in women's wear in Japan were integrated into a global world of fashion. As this happened, the path from Paris to the Tokyo cat-walk, and then into the wardrobes of millions of women, ran less through garment factories and stores with racks of ready-made dress than through the hands of home-based family sewers and dressmakers. This path is reflected in the results of a 1953 survey conducted by researchers at Chūō University, which asked 'how do you learn of the latest fashions?' Almost nobody mentioned department stores. A clear plurality, 33 per cent, replied 'from stylebooks'. These women were either making the clothes themselves or bringing the patterns to a dressmaker. In a literate nation of voracious readers, the role of print media was huge: second to stylebooks stood fashion magazines, the source for

25 per cent of the women, followed by newspapers at 15 per cent (Nakayama, 1987, pp. 458–59). Underlying and enabling this rapid change of clothes was the spread on the one hand of new materials, especially nylon and other synthetic fabrics, and on the other of a machine which at the same time moved from object of desire to familiar tool for millions of women sewing at home, whether for themselves and their family or for neighbours and strangers.

In sum, despite periodic 'kimono revivals' much celebrated by nostalgic commentators,[3] women did not return to a life centred on *wafuku* (Japanese-style clothing) after the Second World War. They moved from *monpe* through second-hand American surplus goods to their own fabrication of Western dress. Through the mediation of *monpe,* they had in fact begun to wear trousers earlier than women in the West (Nakayama, 1987, p. 456). The reasons for the triumph of Western dress were several and related. It had already been gaining adherents at a rapid pace in the 1930s. During wartime, the dynamics of officially promoted dress reform and the decisions of women to adopt *monpe* eroded the ground on which post-war advocates of a reformed Japanese dress might have stood (Gordon, 2011, chs 5–6). In addition, as Japan's mainly American occupiers proved themselves for the most part not the demonic figures of wartime propaganda, and as they brought attractive promises of democracy and peace, the appeal was profound of cultural forms – dress included – which had long been associated in Japan with America and modern life.

In these ways, the early post-war years put in place a feedback loop between home-sewing, new fashion trends, and the consuming and producing household. New domestic producers and new modes of women's dress made the sewing machine both available and indispensable, while mastery of this good reinforced the place of women as managers of post-war consumer life. A boom in sewing education, built on pre-war and wartime foundations, spread advanced skills at sewing and dressmaking to a remarkably high proportion of women. Often pursued and understood as a form of bridal training, these skills fostered the ascendance of the professional housewife in society and culture.

Training a nation of dressmakers

As women moved from *monpe* to the 'one-piece' dress, sewing education became a big business, and young women were its primary consumers.

[3] These included a revival of the pre-war *meisen* kimono described by Francks in this volume.

Some studied so they could fashion their own clothes from stylebooks, but at the same time purchases of order-made wear supported a burgeoning population of 'Western dress shops' that relied on a growing mass of dressmakers. In Tokyo, the number of such stores rose from 1,300 in 1943 to 15,000 in 1955, meaning the city boasted a density of one dress shop for every 120 households (Nihon Tōkei Kyōkai, 1987, p. 172). This total of dress shops in Tokyo alone was roughly the same as the number of post offices in the entire country. Ninety per cent of those who sewed for these stores were women working on contract from their homes or in the small workshops attached to some stores. The commercial production and sale of women's wear in the 1950s relied more on such dispersed networks of women sewing at home than on specialised centres of garment production. The latter existed, to be sure, but concentrated centres of small-to-medium scale garment producers in districts of Tokyo, Osaka, Gifu, Nagoya, Niigata, Kanazawa and Kyoto for the most part produced work clothes and children's and men's wear. By the end of the decade, garments in these categories were being assembled in such factories and sold ready-made to the majority of the population. But, in a persistently different pattern, most dress for women continued to be made at home (Nakayama, 1987, p. 461).

This situation contrasted sharply with that in the United States, much to the frustration of Itō Mohei. In 1929 he had founded a successful sewing school, which in the post-war era became a leader in training dress designers for the garment industry. In a 1960 piece in *Fujin Kōron* (*Lady's Forum*) entitled 'On the long wait for ready-made', he lamented that whereas the United States led the way, with 95 per cent of women's wear purchased ready-made, followed by Europe at 90 per cent, Japan lagged behind at a mere 40 per cent. A full 60 per cent of women's clothing was made to order. How could it be, he asked, that in a poor country, the majority of women chose the more expensive option? His convincing answer rested on the fact that Japan possessed a new abundance of dressmaking capacity. A vast pool of newly trained, home-based dressmakers and seamstresses yielded a balance of quality and cost in the production of ready-made and order-made dress which favoured the practice of sewing in the home (Itō, 1960, p. 62).

The home economics classrooms of the public school system did not offer sufficient hours or depth of instruction to impart more than a basic familiarity with machine sewing, so the primary providers of this expertise were dressmaking schools. The leading institutions had been founded in the 1920s; the most famous was Bunka Fukusō Gakuin (Cultural Dress Academy), abbreviated as Bunka. After the war, these schools, together with newly founded competitors, expanded at a pace that astonished observers. An extraordinary number and proportion of Japanese women learned to sew in their classrooms, whether to pursue a proper lady's hobby, or to acquire skills useful for a future career as household manager, seamstress, dressmaker, or sewing teacher in her own right. In 1958 the phenomenon inspired Ōya Sōichi to make the exuberant claim that 'no foreigner who observes Japan's Western sewing boom is unsurprised; ... there is no place in the world where schools for Western sewing are as popular as in Japan' (Ōya, 1958, p. 36).[4] Such training was part of the nurturing of the full-time, 'professional' housewife of post-war Japan.

This schooling boom was built figuratively, and in some cases literally, upon wartime ruins. In 1946, after a one-year hiatus, Bunka was able to recruit a full house of 3,000 students within several days of announcing that it was re-opening. With classes running in morning, afternoon, and evening shifts to make the best use of cramped facilities, enrolment doubled to 6,000 in 1947. By 1955, it had reached 10,000 students, now accommodated at a brand new Tokyo campus, at a time when the largest sewing school in the United States was said to enrol no more than 500 (Onuma, 1963, pp. 150–64; Nakayama, 1987, p. 462; Ōya, 1958, p. 36). Nationwide, by 1947, 400 sewing schools were already enrolling 45,000 students; these totals soared to 2,400 schools and 360,000 students in 1951, and as many as 7,000 schools with 500,000 enrolled by the mid-to-late 1950s. Roughly 900,000 girls were graduating from middle school in each of these years; about one-third of them went on to high school. It is clear that attending sewing schools for a time upon graduation from either middle or high school was a post-graduation course that virtually all young women must have thought about and as many as one half actually followed (Ōya, 1958, p. 37; Sōrifu Tōkeikyoku, 1957, pp. 436, 438–39).

Whether fabricating for themselves, their family or the market, the mass of students who graduated with relatively strong skills brought to their home-sewing a quasi-professional commitment. Ōya brilliantly captured this pragmatic spirit in his 1957 column in the *Asahi* newspaper titled 'The Japanese' (*Nihonjin*), in which he discussed the 'goals

---

4 Ōya's comparative claim is confirmed indirectly by several of the contributions to Burman, 1999, which stress the primary role of apprenticeship, home-based instruction, or home economics classes in ordinary (rather than commercial) schools as the route by which British or American women learned to sew in the twentieth century. In particular, see the contribution by Helventson and Bubolz, 1999, pp. 304–5, 309–11.

of entrants to Western sewing schools'. The energy of the entering students 'is focused not only on the desire to wear fine clothes and look beautiful, nor is it a mindset of faddish imitation of others'. The many young women who saw their studies as a 'pre-wed' course in bridal training had a sober self-understanding. Some saw the acquisition of sewing skills from one of these schools as a way to move up in the marriage market 'from the prospective bride of a low-ranked clerk in a provincial government office to the spouse of a supervisor or section chief'. Others calculated that their tuition fees would be offset by the ability to fabricate the clothes for a trousseau in the classroom. Still others felt that no self-respecting future wife should let her husband buy his suits off the rack: 'I want to make him a suit myself.' Many others, aiming to work as dressmakers or open their own shops, saw their studies in the pre-war spirit of 'self-sufficiency', as a step towards economic independence. Ōya concluded that a spirit ranging from realism, practicality, or independence to feminine affection and innocent dreams 'cannot be pigeon-holed as either hardboiled or sentimental. The sound of the sewing machines pedalled by the daughters of Japan is dynamic and complex' ('Nihonjin', *Asahi Shimbun*, 13 January, 1957, cited in Nakayama, 1987, pp. 463–64).

Pre-war sewing schools had enrolled both students seeking marketable skills and those looking for a bridal 'finishing' course and household management abilities. The occupational track had dominated, and given the relatively modest skills demanded by the industry at the time, one was employable after a short course of study. Over the post-war years, standards for Western dress and the corresponding skill requirements rose. Without further training, the many women who undertook only the short basic courses at these sewing schools were not prepared for careers as professional dressmakers or designers; for these women, sewing schools served more as bridal than vocational training, especially as skill in Western rather than Japanese sewing came to be seen in conventional morality as the incubator of feminine virtue (Nakayama, 1987, p. 464). But even these women had built a foundation for the acquisition of further skills if needed or desired. With a bit more practice or study, they could fabricate clothes for themselves and their children, demonstrating love of family and saving money into the bargain over the cost of either ready-made or order-made wear. And the significant minority who pursued longer-term, more advanced courses of study indeed graduated with the ability to sew professionally, whether from the home, in a dress shop, or as a factory-based seamstress (Yoshimoto, 2004a, p. 31).

This education of masses of women skilled in Western machine-sewing and interested in putting these skills to use furnishes a key part of the answer to Itō Mohei's frustrated question: why did the production of order-made clothing continue to dominate the domestic market for women's wear as the 1960s began? He answered his question by recognising that the cost differential in Japan was relatively small. In the United States, he wrote, even a cheap order-made outfit cost nearly four times as much as a dress off the rack. In Japan, it was only 30 per cent more costly. For Itō, whose school hoped to place graduates in jobs as designers of ready-made wear, the low mark-up resulted from self-exploitation by Western-style dressmakers who 'simply cannot afford to lose to ready-made clothing, so they make unreasonable efforts to sell cheaply. They live in poverty, and their products are too cheap. If they don't sell cheap, they can't get orders. This is after all a country with excess population and too many competitors' (Itō, 1960, p. 62).

There is a kernel of truth to his complaint, but it does not sufficiently consider two aspects of the production system. On the side of industrial producers, ready-made dress had not yet shaken off its reputation for poor quality; those wearing clothes off the rack were dismissed as *tsurushinbo*, a derogatory term with connotations similar to a racial slur.[5] On the side of the custom producers, the realm of dressmaking and the ownership of dress shops rested in the hands of women, based in the home, who were highly skilled, but who viewed their earnings as supplemental to family income. By combining skilled productive labour with the reproductive work of home management, they were led, or forced, to work so 'cheaply' that they could outdo the ready-made producers on quality for a modest premium in cost.

Sewing for the market

These dressmakers and seamstresses were among the many women who contributed to a counterintuitive post-war social trend. That thousands of war widows and other survivors desperately sought to make ends meet through home-work in the immediate post-war years is hardly surprising. Less expected is that such home-based production expanded significantly during the era of high-speed growth and surging consumption of the 1950s and 1960s, even as increased numbers of home-workers

[5] *Tsurushi* or 'hang' referred to clothes hanging on racks. The -nbo suffix was a derogatory reference to the person wearing such clothes, also used in ethnic or racial slurs at the time.

defined themselves and were viewed as members of the middle class. To make sense of these trends, rather than seeking to separate the daily routine of home-workers into practices that were *either* consumption *or* production, we should understand these women as engaged in practices that integrated consuming *and* producing roles, with the latter dimension relatively hidden as it took place in the home.

The Labour Ministry's Bureau of Women and Children took the lead in documenting this trend. Usefully for our purposes, its surveys defined home-workers expansively to include those who – so long as they did not maintain a storefront – themselves purchased the necessary materials, fabricated the good at home, and sold it directly to a consumer. Surveys of Osaka and Tokyo from the mid-1950s showed that at least one member was engaged in home-work at any one time in six to ten per cent of households (Rōdōshō, Fujin Shōnenkyoku, 1955b, pp. 1–3). A more broadly based survey covering most of the nation in 1968 found at least one person undertaking home-work in 12 per cent of all households, with at least one person in another 12 per cent of homes indicating a desire to do such work. In 9 per cent of the households surveyed, at least one person not engaged in home-work at that moment had undertaken it at some point in the previous five years (Rōdōshō, Fujin Shōnenkyoku, 1968, pp. 5–6). Put differently, in one out of five Japanese households at least one person had been a home-worker for some portion of the span from 1964 through 1968. Throughout Japan, home-workers supplementing family income numbered roughly 700,000 through most of the 1960s. This figure jumped suddenly and significantly at the end of the decade, to nearly 1.3 million in 1969 and 1.6 million in 1970, reaching a peak in 1973 of 1.63 million home-workers. Only in the following years did their ranks gradually decline (Rōdōshō, Fujin Shōnenkyoku, 1976, pp. 2–5).

Needlework was by far the most common form of home-work for women throughout these two decades. In Tokyo in 1954, 'Western sewing' accounted for 16.5 per cent and 'Japanese sewing' for 13.2 per cent of home-workers. These workers, plus those doing piecework for shoes, underwear, hats, gloves, knitting, embroidery and other miscellaneous tasks using sewing machines, accounted for 47 per cent of all home-workers, and the proportion engaged in one or another sort of needlework had increased to 61 per cent by 1968 (Rōdōshō, Fujin shōnenkyoku, 1968, pp. 3, 13).

The women in all these surveys were predominantly wives and mothers who combined home-work with other responsibilities of childcare and household management. In contrast to inter-war surveys, they reveal that a significant minority of these home-workers consisted of women in middle-class families. In Tokyo in 1954, a full one-third (34 per cent) of home-worker families were headed by a husband whose occupation was either 'company employee' (21.4 per cent), 'public employee' (6.7) or 'other salaried person' (5.9). Only 12 per cent of the male 'household heads' were factory workers and nine per cent were self-employed. Fourteen per cent of household heads were women, either the home-worker herself or her mother. The 1968 survey aggregated the data differently, but the middle-class proportion appears to have been comparable or increased (Rōdōshō, Fujin Shōnenkyoku, 1955b, p. 3; 1955a, p. 2; 1968, pp. 8–9).

In sum, over the two post-war decades of rapid economic growth, the overall numbers of home-workers increased, and these women provided an important supplement to family incomes. Home-work was never the monopoly of the poor; already in the inter-war era, a modest group of aspiring middle-class families had been engaged in home-work, alongside a larger proportion from the working class (Gordon, 2011, chs 3, 5). During the high-growth era, the relative weight of lower-middle and middle-class home-workers increased, and their activities most often involved needlework and the sewing machine.

Narratives left by home-workers, as memoirs but also in women's magazines, which delighted in presenting what they called 'true tales' of the economic and social strivings of women, nicely reveal how the roles of consumer and producer overlapped and reinforced each other. The war cast its shadow in one way or another over virtually every home-worker's story, and the Japan Association of War-Bereaved has preserved valuable traces of the self-understanding of such women. In 1963 it published a volume of accounts by 'survivors of the war dead' (Nihon Izokukai, 1963).[6] Typical was Matsuda Kazuko's tale. Her struggle began with her father's death in Sumatra in January 1945, when she was seven. In 1950 her mother used a government loan available to survivors of the war dead to purchase a sewing machine and cutting table and rent a room, so that she could start up as a dressmaker. Crossing the gender line, she learned to tailor men's clothes, but her earnings were hardly enough to support the family. She writes that it was hard to keep up with changing styles and customer taste, and difficult to manage housework at the same time. In 1953, Kazuko, herself now 15, began to study Western sewing at a sewing school. She helped her mother's business when she could, but they relied

[6] The Association has become internationally (in)famous in more recent times for its political role in controversies over the appropriate way for politicians and ordinary survivors to mourn the war dead.

on welfare payments to survive. Eventually, however, they succeeded in building a small home of their own, thanks to the survivor pension (Nihon Izokukai, 1963, pp. 92–98). Sotozaki Yae's tale of 'Twenty years of difficulties' ended somewhat better. Her husband died in 1939 in China. During the war she worked at home, sewing Japanese-style clothes, lonely and desperate, crying all the time. A friend suggested that she try to support herself with Western sewing, and the local authorities arranged for her to attend sewing school. She was later apprenticed to a local clothing store, given jobs by the sympathetic owner. But eventually she opened her own shop and prospered (Nihon Izokukai, 1963, pp. 253–57).

Comparable narratives appeared frequently in women's magazines of the 1950s, most notably in *The Housewife's Companion*. These read more like Sotozaki's account than Matsuda's darker story. T. S. from Kyūshū, just returned from overseas, with a husband working in a hospital, bought a sewing machine with a lump sum of compensation for luggage lost en route home, and offers a typical account. To satisfy her customers, she needed to keep up with fashion trends in women's magazines and department stores, and she took care to undercut the order-made prices of the latter by about 30 to 40 per cent. In the end, she happily supplemented her family income to the tune of 2,000–3,000 yen per month, sewing part-time while doing housework (Yoshimoto, 2004b, pp. 59–61).

Such stories were a staple of women's magazines of the time. In addition to such 'true tales', *Fujin Kurabu* (*Lady's Club*), the most popular competitor to *The Housewife's Companion*, ran advice columns on 'Home-work in the major cities' or 'How to seek and choose home-work', as well as numerous ads for sewing schools and sewing machines. These of course noted the opportunity to earn through home-working as an important reason to learn to sew or buy a machine. The sewing-machine sellers similarly filled their in-house magazines for the sales force, as well as glossier publications aimed at customers, with stories such as that of one Kawaguchi Kinuko who 'managed to save the sum of one million yen simply doing Western sewing home-work' with her reliable Janome machine ('Tatta sanzen en no shihon de dekiru yōsai naishoku no tebiki', *Janome Mōdo*, Spring 1962, p. 6). And Japan's national broadcaster, NHK, offered a semi-fictional version of these 'true tales' in the 1986 edition of its long-running morning drama, *Miyako no Kaze* (Breeze of the Old Capital). Such narratives represent tips of an iceberg of home-based needlework, and the editors or producers hoping to sell magazines or win viewers had reason to tilt towards tales of success. The mass of home-workers often laboured in more difficult circumstances, paying a price for their earnings with their health or their time for family or other pursuits. The willingness of so many of these women, dispersed in their homes and carrying out domestic labours as well, to work long hours for modest profits resulted in the abundant supply of order-made dress at a quality level and cost sufficient to outsell the producers of ready-made women's wear which so frustrated Itō Mohei.

Nonetheless, to cast these home-based commercial needle-workers as an immiserated underclass of producers is to misread their story. They included both survivors and upwardly mobile strivers. The era of high economic growth coincided with a sharp rise in the numbers of home-workers, and the causal links ran two ways. Certainly Japan's 'economic miracle' was in part fuelled by the low-paid labour of these women. But their stories reveal them to be in touch with a world of fashion and glamour; to succeed as a dressmaker one had to read women's magazines and follow the latest style trends. These women worked both to fulfil their customers' dreams of a bright new consumer life and in the hope of securing this life for themselves and their children.

Sewing for the home

However important was the role of home-based commercial sewers in supplying order-made clothes for the masses, the majority of sewing machine users stitched for themselves and their families. The best statistical evidence of their prominence is provided by the time studies of the 1950s and 1960s. Surveys which found women sewing for two to three hours each day made a point of noting that commercial sewing was categorised separately. Averaged across all households, the commitment of women to home-based commercial sewing was a modest fraction of the time spent on family sewing.

This allocation of daily time was reflected in a long-term shift in the reasons why most women enrolled in sewing school. Acquisition of the skills needed for a future as housewife and home manager came to outweigh vocational training as the motive for enrolment (Nakayama, 1987, p. 464). The Yokohama Western Sewing Vocational School was founded in 1927 and renamed after the war for its founder, Iwasaki Haruko, as the Iwasaki Academy. Under her guidance, it became the city's most important sewing school. Ōtsuki Toshiko and Takayama Kazuko were two of Iwasaki's veteran teachers, handpicked from among the most talented young students in 1940 and 1948. Decades later, these women recalled that in the late 1940s all the students attended in order to learn a skill whereby they could earn money for themselves or their families. Takayama noted that many were widows with children, and they were desperate. Ōtsuki added 'the students were truly committed and serious. They had a spirit, a resolve born of desperation that was not there before or after. I can never forget those students.' They would start doing home-work while still students, taking home their class projects and selling them, remaking and reselling old clothes, and passing on their lessons to others at home. Such students were common as well in the 1950s, in their recollection, but in the 1960s and 1970s students on the pre-wedding track came to dominate. The latter opted for a six-month 'short course' which allowed them to cycle through similar courses in cooking, and perhaps flower arranging or tea ceremony, as they or their parents looked for a mate (Author's interview with Ōtsuki and Takayama, 2003).

Monthly magazines and the daily papers played to these graduates in ways that both expanded this swiftly growing audience of domestic sewers at the time and left signs to posterity of their importance. In the 'Family' or 'Women's' pages of daily newspapers, and in monthly magazines for women, patterns and instructions for dresses, blouses and skirts for women, along with all manner of outfits for boys and girls, outnumbered the frequent accounts of home-based sewing for independence and income. The *Yomiuri* newspaper in late 1952 inaugurated a five-year run of a column devoted to 'Western sewing lessons' (*yōsai ka*), placed prominently on the paper's 'Women's Page' every two or three days – precisely 581 lessons in all. A sidebar to the first column, 'On the opening of our Western sewing classes', pledged to offer both basic knowledge and the latest fashions for the 'edification of ordinary women with interest in Western sewing' ('Yōsaika Kaisetsu ni Tsuite', *Yomiuri Shinbun*, 1 November 1952, p. 5). This feature ended in June, 1957. A more elaborate but less frequent 'This month's Western sewing' ran 67 half-page features from January 1960 through August 1965, followed by a weekly 'Yomiuri Western sewing' column from January 1967 through August 1975 (see Figure 3.1). After this, regular sewing columns disappeared from the paper.

This press support for home-sewing reflected and reinforced the emergence of Western sewing over Japanese *wasai* as both a practical skill and a pre-eminent feminine virtue. As noted above, the 1959 survey of 'free time' made it clear that, for as many as one in four housewives, sewing was not so much work as a 'leisure' activity. Put differently, one might say that many Japanese women approached their leisure in a remarkably practical or professional spirit. A survey undertaken three years earlier by what the Janome sewing machine company called 'an authoritative research institute in Tokyo' offers nice insight into the self-understanding of home-sewers. The survey looked at what it called 'the psychology of

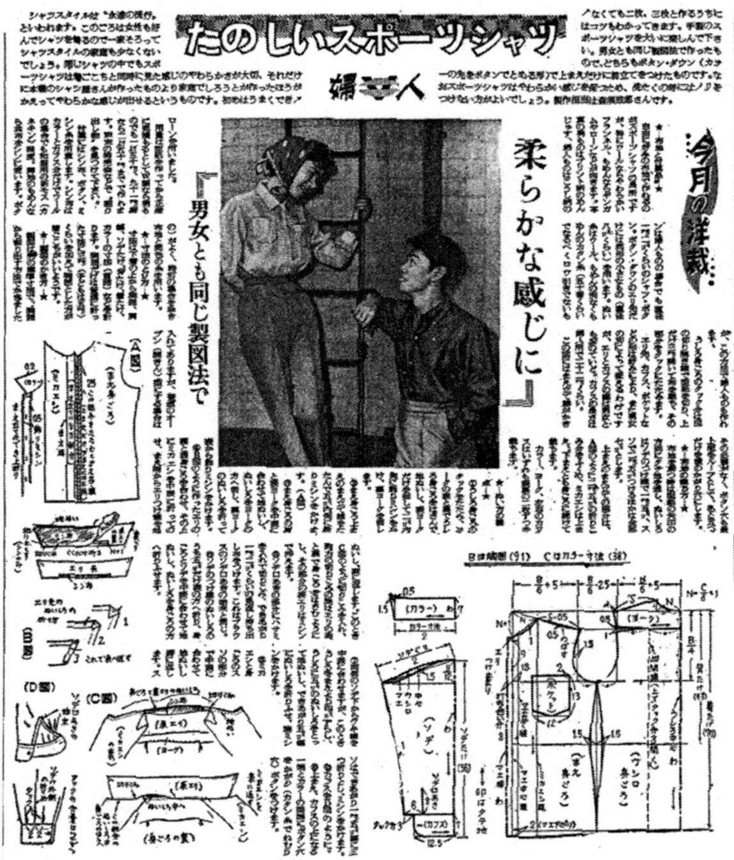
たのしいスポーツシャツ

婦人

今月の洋裁

柔らかな感じに

男女とも同じ製図法で

Figure 3.1 Newspaper sewing column
Source: Yomiuri Shinbun 27 February 1960.

buying' to answer the question 'what does a lady want to buy?', with focus on the relative attraction of various 'household cultural goods' ('Gofujin gata wa Nani o Kaitai ka', in Janome *Shanai hō*, 1956, p. 11).

The respondents were asked to ponder the following story: 'Akiko desperately wants to buy household cultural goods. She has saved 30,000 yen for this. She goes with this money to a department store and looks around at various goods. An electric washing machine is 25,000 yen. A sewing machine is 26,000 yen. A TV is 80,000, and a mixer is 12,000. What does Akiko most want to buy, and why?' The goal of framing the survey in this fashion, it would seem, was to posit a person who owned none of these goods in order to induce the respondent to state her own preference among items she already owned as well as those she did not yet possess. Just over half of the women surveyed (51 per cent) believed that Akiko's greatest desire would be to buy a sewing machine, followed by a washing machine at 41 per cent, and an electric mixer at 4 per cent. Only 2 per cent of the sample made the television Akiko's first choice.

The survey interestingly divided these replies into groups of respondents who actually owned particular clusters of goods. Of those who already possessed both sewing and washing machines (19 per cent of all), 49 per cent had Akiko buy a sewing machine and 37 per cent had her buy a washing machine, but of those who did not yet own either of these goods, 69 per cent had her buy a sewing machine, while just 22 per cent had her buy a washing machine. It seems reasonable to see this difference as a measure of the power of marketing and peer pressure to generate desire for the sewing machine. The lower priority given to it by those who already owned it suggests that a number of buyers were disillusioned once they actually owned a sewing machine; they had probably ended up not using it as much as they expected and with greater difficulty than promised, so they had Akiko opt for a washing machine. Even so, this is only a relative diminution of desire; the preference for the sewing machine over all the other 'cultural goods' is indeed impressive.

The respondents were also asked why Akiko made her particular choice. Among those who had her buy the sewing machine, the vast majority (91 per cent) gave 'usefulness, necessity' as the most important reason, followed by 'preparation for the future' (6 per cent). The remaining handful noted 'just because she wants it' or 'no particular reason'. The investigators probed further into what women meant by 'usefulness' and 'necessity'. The most frequent elaborations were 'it has a greater use value than other household goods' (18 per cent), 'because I can do Western sewing and home-work myself' (17 per cent), and 'it is the most needed item for a woman in family life' (10 per cent). The first and last of these comments represented a plurality who saw the *mishin* as useful primarily in its contribution to family and home life (28 per cent), while the second defined 'useful' as a combination of value directly to the family and indirectly through home-work wages ('Gofujin gata wa Nani o Kaitai ka', in Janome *Shanai hō*, 1956, p. 11).

The sewing machine overall offered to such women, and to those who in 1959 told government surveyors that they saw machine sewing as a leisure activity, a powerful combination of pleasure and practicality.

A woman saved money by sewing for the family rather than buying clothes order-made or ready-made. She took pride at the pleasure shown by children or a husband in their dress. She could make herself attractive as well.

The home-based sewers of early post-war Japan gained satisfaction at their mastery of a skill understood to define feminine virtue and validate a woman as a competent, responsible household manager. The fact that women throughout Japan possessed this high level of skill as part of their 'professional' competence helps explain an intriguing puzzle in their behaviour: their reluctance to embrace paper patterns. The American publishers of sewing patterns, Simplicity and McCall, entered the Japanese market with high hopes in the early 1960s, at first glance with good reasons. As Ōya Sōichi had noted a few years before, Japan boasted a reputation as the world leader in both sewing machines per household and, by an even greater margin, the number of students enrolled in sewing schools (Ōya, 1958, p. 36). What could be more promising for sellers of paper patterns that promised easy fabrication of the latest fashions for women and children? Yet, despite this seemingly huge pool of ready customers, Simplicity and McCall fared poorly. By the early 1970s, at a point when 600,000 women were graduating annually from Western sewing schools, the two companies were selling only several million patterns a year compared to 400 million in the United States ('Hōmu Yōsai Jidai Kitaru to iu keredo…', 1973, p. 163; Emery, 1999, pp. 235–53).

The logic and hopes of Simplicity and McCall had failed to take account of the skills and professionalism of the sewing housewife or her young adult daughter. As Ōtsuki and Takayama of the Iwasaki Sewing Academy explained, their students saw these patterns as a short-cut beneath the dignity fostered by their training and skills. It was not that the graduates of sewing schools never used paper patterns. They simply had no need to buy them from Simplicity. Projecting from small-scale drawings, with arithmetic skills and the ability to take their own measurements or those of a child or a customer, they were well able to make their own paper patterns. Only the widespread possession of this ability can explain why mass-circulation dailies would devote precious space several days each week to the sort of small-scale drawings shown in the illustration above. Indeed, teaching the skills to do this was at the heart of the sewing-school curriculum. Ōtsuki and Takayama stressed the professional consciousness of home-sewers: they considered it a source of pleasure and pride to create clothing from their own materials and ideas (Author's interview with Ōtsuki and Takayama, 2003).

Conclusion: the era of dressmakers and consumers

Whether used for home-work or family wardrobes, the sewing machine in post-war Japan (and elsewhere as well, I suspect) was not a tool which primarily immiserated its users, as described and predicted by Karl Marx; nor was it a means to protect local traditions and live a simple life, as claimed by Mahatma Gandhi (Marx, 1921, pp. 516–18; Gandhi, 1960, ch. 7). Rather it connected women and families to the modern consumer world. It offered them hopes of climbing the social ladder as the economy surged. It was a tool of class integration more than division, as it helped build the cultural hegemony of middle-class life-ways in the high-growth era. And, as women moved between the roles of home-worker/housewife and full-time housewife, it linked their identity as income earners to that as responsible consumers and professional home managers.

The lifespan of the regular sewing column in the *Yomiuri* ran from 1952 to 1975. These years mark the rough chronological bounds of two related eras: the time of Japan as a nation of dressmakers and the time when the professional housewife reigned most securely as the ideal for women. Her position as the natural exemplar of adult womanhood was never unchallenged; periodic 'housewife debates' erupted in public life across these years, and we can be sure many private conversations offered diverse answers to the question of how women might best lead their lives (Ueno, 1982; Fujii, 2002, pp. 15–22). Even so, a trans-war social and cultural formation runs from the 1920s across the war and through the high-growth era. It was marked, in terms of women's roles, first by the prominence of the pre-war-to-wartime 'housewife' (*shufu*) unmodified, and then by the 'professional housewife', defined in part according to well-honed skills in organising and fabricating the family wardrobe, as well as managing the family as consumer of mass-produced goods of all kinds.

In the area of dress, this era ended with the ascendance of ready-made women's wear. The practice of women sewing at home for their family members began to decline in the 1960s (Nihon Hōsō Kyōkai, 1970, pp. 11–12, 1172). From an all-time peak in 1969, the domestic sale of sewing machines began a long, slow decline. Articles began to appear in the press in the early 1970s lamenting that so many sewing machines sat unused at home. All told, from the 1970s onward, the place of sewing in the daily routines of women diminished greatly. In the realm of cooking a similar shift took place, a bit later and more gradually, towards reliance on prepared foods. Although most married women, including the increasing numbers who worked outside the home, retained the role of household manager, they acted less as the fabricators or processors of that which the family consumed and more as the purchasing agents who managed the acquisition of all manner of goods and services. In the realm of family and daily life, this shift marks the end of an era.

Even so, the professional housewife has had a remarkably long afterlife. Throughout the second half of the twentieth century and into the early twenty-first, Japan ranked just after South Korea at the top of the industrial capitalist world in the depth of its 'M-curve', the graphic representation of the proportion of women who leave the job market during years of childbirth and childrearing (Brinton, 1993, p. 29).[7] In explaining the endurance of the full-time housewife both as social ideal and in experience, negative incentives, such as an income tax system which penalised families that had two full-time wage earners, are important to note. But to understand this endurance fully, one must also recognise the positive social validation of the work of the 'professional' housewife, including her management of the family wardrobe. Of course she was not created purely and simply by the sewing machine and its associated skills, but sewing was significant among the several realms of endeavour that brought a wider consumer economy and culture intimately into the home, offering a powerful connection to that wider world and affirming her role in managing those links.

References

Brinton, M. (1993) *Women and the Economic Miracle: Gender and Work in Postwar Japan,* Berkeley: University of California Press.

Burman, B. (1999) *The Culture of Sewing: Gender, Consumption, and Home Dressmaking,* Oxford: Berg.

Emery, J. S. (1999) 'Dreams on Paper: A Story of the Commercial Pattern Industry', in Burman, B. (ed.) *The Culture of Sewing: Gender, Consumption, and Home Dressmaking,* Oxford: Berg.

Fujii, H. (2002) *Sengyō Shufu wa Ima: Tayōka to Koseika no naka de* (Full-time Housewives of Today amidst Diversification and Individualization), Tokyo: Mineruba Shobō.

Gandhi, M. (1960) *All Men are Brothers: Life and Thoughts of Mahatma Gandhi as Told in His Own Words,* Kripalani, K. (ed.) Navajivan Mudranalaya, Ahemadabad: Jitendra T. Desai, accessed on 10 June 2010 at: http://www.mkgandhi.org/amabrothers/amabrothers.htm

'Gofujin gata wa Nani o Kaitai ka' (What would the Lady Like to Purchase?) (1956) in Janome *Shanai hō,* vol. 1, no. 2, p. 11.

---

[7] For more recent comparative data, see the category of 'labour force statistics by sex and age' at http://stats.oecd.org/index.aspx. Accessed 10 August 2009.

Gordon, A. (2011) *Fabricating Consumers: The Sewing Machine in Modern Japan*, Berkeley: University of California Press.

Helventson, S. & Bubolz, M. M. (1999) 'Home Economics and Home Sewing in the United States, 1870–1940', in Burman, B. (ed.) *The Culture of Sewing: Gender, Consumption, and Home Dressmaking*, Oxford: Berg.

'Hōmu Yōsai Jidai Kitaru to iu keredo...' (They say the Age of Home Dressmaking has come but...), *Josei Jishin*, 24 March 1973, p. 163.

Inoue, M. (2001) *Yōfuku to Nihonjin: Kokumin fuku to iu Mōdo* (Western Clothing and the Japanese: Fashion of the Nation's People), Tokyo: Kōsaidō Shuppan.

Itō, M. (1960) 'Redi Meedo Taibō Ron' (On Ready-Made Style), *Fujin Kōron*, 20 May.

Kawasaki Rōdō Shi Hensan Iinkai (1987) *Kawasaki Rōdō Shi* (A History of Kawasaki Labour), Kawasaki.

Koizumi, K. (2000) *Shōwa no Kurashi Hakubutsukan* (The Museum of Shōwa Life), Tokyo: Kawade Shobō.

Kon, W. (1967) *Janpā o Kite 40 nen* (40 Years of Wearing Jumpers), Tokyo: Bunka Fukusō Gakuin Shuppankyoku.

Kunihiro, Y. (2001) *Shufu to Jendā* (Housewives and Gender), Tokyo: Shōgakusha.

Marx, K. (1921) *Capital*, volume 1, chapter 15, section 8e, New York: Charles H. Kerr and Co.

Mason, C. A. (1949) 'Le Budget-temps de la Femme à Londres dans les Classes Laborieuses', *Population* (French edition), vol. 4, no. 2, p. 372.

Mishin Kōgyō (Apr.1954) 'Mishin no Fukyū Jōkyō to Kongo no Juyō ni kansuru Hito Kōsatsu' (Observation on the Diffusion of Sewing Machines and Future Demand), No. 52.

Nakayama, C. (1987) *Nihon Fujin Yōsō Shi* (A History of Japanese Women's Dress), Tokyo: Yoshikawa Kōbunkan.

Nihon Hōsō Kyōkai (ed.) (1970) *Kokumin Seikatsu Jikan Chōsa* (Investigation into the Lifestyle and Time Use of the Nation's People), Tokyo: Nihon Hōsō Kyōkai.

Nihon Izokukai (ed.) (1963) *Ishizue: Senbotsusha Izoku no Taiken Kiroku* (Cornerstone: A Record of the Experience of Families of the War-Dead), Tokyo: Nihon Hōsō Kyōkai.

Nihon Mishin Kyōkai (ed.) (1961) *Nihon Mishin Sangyō Shi* (A History of the Japanese Sewing Machine Industry), Tokyo: Nihon Mishin Kyōkai.

Nihon Tōkei Kyōkai (ed.) (1987) *Nihon Chōki Tōkei Sōran* (Long Term Statistics of Japan Vol.1), Tokyo: Nihon Tōkei Kyōkai.

Ochiai, E. (1994) *21 Seiki Kazoku e: Kazoku no Sengo Taisei no Mikata, Koekata* (Towards the 21st Century Family: Interpreting and Transcending the Post-war Structure of the Family), Tokyo: Yūhikaku.

Ōnuma, J. (1963) *Bunka Fukusō Gakuin Yonjūnen no Ayumi* (Forty Years of the Bunka Fashion College), Tokyo: Bunka Fukusō Gakuin.

Ōya, S. (1958) 'Nihon no Kigyō: Doreme' (Japan's Enterprises: Doreme), *Shūkan Asahi*, vol. 63, no. 4.

Rōdōshō Fujin Shōnenkyoku (1952) *Kōjō Rōdōsha Seikatsu no Chōsa* (Investigation into the Lifestyle of Factory Workers), Tokyo: Rōdōshō Fujin Shōnenkyoku.

Rōdōshō Fujin Shōnenkyoku (1955a) *Katei Naishoku no Jitsujō: Ōsaka shi Chūkan Hōkoku* (Actual Conditions of Work within the Home: Report on Osaka city), Tokyo: Rōdōshō Fujin Shōnenkyoku.

Rōdōshō Fujin Shōnenkyoku (1955b) *Katei Naishoku no Jitsujō: Tokyo 23-ku* (Actual Conditions of Work within the Home: Tokyo's 23 Wards), Tokyo: Rōdōshō Fujin Shōnenkyoku.
Rōdōshō Fujin Shōnenkyoku, ed. (1959) *Shufu no Jiyū Jikan ni kansuru Ishiki Chōsa* (Survey of Housewives' Attitudes towards Free Time), Tokyo: Rōdōshō Fujin Shōnenkyoku.
Rōdōshō Fujin Shōnenkyoku (1968) *Naishoku Shūgyō Kihon Chōsa Hōkoku* (Report on Basic Investigations into Employment and Working from Home), Tokyo: Rōdōshō Fujin Shōnenkyoku.
Rōdōshō Rōdō Kijunkyoku (Sept. 1976) *Kanai Rōdō no Genjō* (The Present State of Work within the Home), Tokyo: Rōdōshō Fujin Shōnenkyoku.
Sōrifu Tōkeikyoku (ed.) (1957) *Nihon Tōkei Nenkan 1957* (Japan Statistical Yearbook 1957), Tokyo: Nihon Tōkei Kyōkai.
Stoetzel, J. (1948) 'Une étude du Budget Time de la Femme dans les Agglomerations Urbaines', *Population* vol. 3, no. 1, 52–56.
'Tatta Sanzen'en no Shihon de Dekiru Yōsai Naishoku no Tebiki' (A Guide to dressmaking as a Home Side-job with only Three Thousand yen in Capital) (Spring 1962) *Janome Mōdo.*
Ueno, C. (1982) *Shufu Ronsō o Yomu* (Reading the Housewife Controversy), Tokyo: Keisō Shobō.
Vanek, J. (1973) 'Keeping Busy: Time Spent in Housework, United States, 1920–1970', University of Michigan: PhD dissertation in Sociology.
Vogel, S. (1978) 'The Professional Housewife: The Career of Urban Middle Class Japanese Women', *Japan Interpreter* vol. 12, no. 1, pp. 16–43.
Yoshida, K. (Extra issue of Mar. 1955) '*Monpe* kara A line made: Fukusō Fūzoku no Sengo 10-nen' (From the *Monpe* to the A-line: Dress and Manners in the Decade since the War), *Bungei Shunjū*, pp. 140–42.
Yoshimoto, Y. (2004a) 'Hanabiraku Yōsai Gakkō' (The Hanabiraku Dressmaking School), in Koizumi, K. (ed.) *Yōsai no Jidai* (The Age of Dressmaking), Tokyo: OM Shuppan.
Yoshimoto, Y. (2004b) 'Onna no Jiritsu o Sasaeta Yōsai' (Dressmaking and Women's Independence), in Koizumi, K. (ed.) *Yōsai no Jidai* (The Age of Dressmaking), Tokyo: OM Shuppan.

4

Building up Steam as Consumers: Women, Rice Cookers and the Consumption of Everyday Household Goods in Japan

Helen Macnaughtan

Introduction

Consumption in Japan, as elsewhere, is strongly gendered. While patterns of consumption have evolved a great deal since the mid-nineteenth century, the role of women and gender in consumption has remained a central issue, particularly in the context of the rise of the housewife and breadwinner-homemaker model. Scholars have analysed women's association with consumption, and why women across the globe have become the main shoppers and consumers (de Grazia, 1996; de Vries, 2008). Research on gender and consumption in regions such as the United States and Europe has highlighted the relationship between production and consumption. With the separation of home and work over the course of industrial development came a gendered division of labour, within which men's roles and responsibilities became defined by the public domain and by productive work, while women's roles and responsibilities became defined by the private domain and by 'non-work' activities, mainly comprising housework, childrearing, maintaining family life, leisure and consumption (Costa, 1994). Francks (2009b, pp. 140–41) notes that in Japan '... growth in consumption in the forms that it took could not be divorced from the shifting patterns of work and family organization and, in particular, from changes in the role of women within the household and the labor force.' This development has earlier origins, but occurred in Japan most markedly from the 1950s.

In post-war Japan, the ideal womanly role of full-time housewife (*shufu*) has often contrasted sharply with increasing rates of female participation in the labour market, as Japanese women, particularly the older, married cohorts, have entered the paid economy in growing numbers (Macnaughtan, 2006). Japan has also been at the forefront of development in electrical household appliances, involving a distinct growth in time-saving (and time-using) appliances, in these post-war decades. The growing production in this sector of manufacturing has had a major effect on domestic consumption by Japanese households since the 1950s.

This chapter discusses the increasingly important role played by women as everyday consumers in post-war Japan, focussing on their consumption of household and kitchen appliances, specifically the electric rice cooker. Two key areas are explored. First, I investigate the development, production and consumption of this appliance. The electric rice cooker was developed by Japanese manufacturers from the mid-1950s and was at the time unique to the Japanese manufacturing sector and the Japanese consumer market. It rapidly achieved significant sales, both at home and abroad.[1] Its success in the Japanese market during the post-war years demonstrates the key role of everyday household appliances in the history of gender and consumption in Japan, as they impacted on women's roles inside and outside the home. The chapter will show that although the rice cooker was in many ways a humble product, it had a revolutionary impact on Japanese women's primary role as housewives.

Second, the chapter places the rice cooker within a broader context, discussing the role played by Japanese women as key consumers of household appliances and as a gendered consumer group. It explores the significance of housewives as consumers in Japan during the post-war decades, the associated gendering of consumer practices, and the extent to which housewives, as holders of the purse-strings within the Japanese nuclear household, were empowered by the establishment of the breadwinner-homemaker model.

The importance of rice

The development of the electric rice cooker was in many ways a product of the history and significance of rice in the Japanese diet and cuisine. In Japanese cuisine, rice is eaten plain and separately, with a preference for sticky rice that is steamed and takes time to cook. Rice was still viewed as the staple food in the immediate aftermath of the Second World War,

[1] For a discussion of the impact of the electric rice cooker in Asian markets, see Nakano, 2009.

when it was often unobtainable. While Japan's rice crop was (at least in theory) controlled by the Food Agency and marketed at controlled prices by state-authorised dealers, Japanese consumers commonly used black market channels to buy rice and other basic commodities. It fell primarily upon women to undertake the everyday struggle to feed and clothe families in this challenging environment, helping to validate their role as household managers and controllers of consumption (Francks, 2009a, pp. 148, 152).

Over time, particularly from the mid-1960s, there was some diversification in the Japanese diet involving the inclusion of Western-style ingredients – notably the consumption of bread for breakfast (promoted by the convenience of new electric toasters) and sandwiches for lunch. However, the format of 'rice plus side dishes' persisted as the basic pattern for most proper meals in the Japanese household. Rice remained central to the Japanese diet and to the image of the Japanese housewife. The Japanese Housewives' Association (*Shufuren*), established in 1948 and probably the most important consumer group in post-war Japan, adopted the rice paddle (*shamoji*) as its symbol.

Rice had long been cooked in Japan using *kamado*, earthenware (later also metal) cooking pots placed directly over open fires. Cooking rice in a *kamado* involved much skill and some mystique, and characterised a woman as a good wife. The first experiments with the use of electricity to cook rice, using what were described as 'simple tubs with heating coils attached', took place in the mid-1920s (Toshiba Corporation, 2009). In the late 1940s, Mitsubishi Electric, Matsushita and Sony produced this kind of electric rice cooker, but, like earthenware and metal *kamado*, they were labour-intensive, requiring total attention while cooking. The use of traditional *kamado* thus remained prevalent across Japan.

However, in 1955, the first automatic electric rice cooker was launched. The development of this innovative product was a reflection of both the importance of rice and the association of women with the cooking of rice in Japan, and it quickly gained a key position among the electrical appliances being produced and consumed in Japan at this time.

The development of the Japanese electric rice cooker – the Toshiba story[2]

The rice cooker was developed specifically for the market in Japan, where meals were focussed around rice and the housewife needed to cook rice

[2] Several sources have been used for this chapter courtesy of Toshiba, including in particular *Firsts of Their Kind*, cited here as Toshiba Corporation 2009. These can be accessed at http://museum.toshiba.co.jp/history/1goki/1955rice.

daily. The appliance remains an essential and ubiquitous item in Japanese households today. Many studies have charted the rise of the Japanese electrical and household appliance industry, but few have focussed on the production and demand for the rice cooker, or on the role Japanese housewives played in its development as a key household appliance. Nakano (2009) describes the development of the Japanese rice cooker abroad, analysing its adaptation and advance via Hong Kong into the rest of the Asian market, but the importance of the electric rice cooker for the Japanese domestic market remains largely unexplored, despite its significance for everyday lives, particularly those of women. Nakano (2009, p. 1) suggests that the launch and success of the electric rice cooker in the 1950s was immediately 'overshadowed by that of the "Three Sacred Treasures" – the television, washing machine and refrigerator – that were considered the true icons of modern Japanese living. In comparison, the rice cooker was seen as a minor, though useful, appliance targeted at housewives (*okusan-yōhin*)'. This highlights the crucial fact that the cooking of rice had long been considered routine women's work, though the end product was consumed by all members of the family. The three 'Sacred Treasure' appliances, particularly the television, seemed much more exciting in terms of physical arrival, impact, size and presence in the Japanese house. This chapter argues that the more subtle presence of the rice cooker in the Japanese home should not lead us to overlook its impact, or its success as a product.

Toshiba Corporation was the first to develop an automated electric rice cooker. The company records that it took on the challenge of developing the electric rice cooker around 1950, 'certain that Japan would fully enter the era of electric home appliances in the near future' (Toshiba Corporation, 2009, pp. 33–34). Yamada Shōgo, then the Development Department Manager in Toshiba's Home Appliances Division, took the lead. The development story was captured in one episode of the NHK *Project X: Challengers* series,[3] which has been used here

---

html. Toshiba was also kind enough to provide, via email communication and one informal interview, answers to the direct questions I posed, as well as illustrations, production data and marketing slogans.

[3] *Project X: Challengers* was a weekly documentary series produced by NHK. A total of 177 episodes were aired between March 2000 and December 2005, documenting post-war technological innovations in Japan and telling the 'forgotten stories of organisations and people' behind them. The origins of these innovations were meticulously researched by NHK, which makes the programme an interesting historical source. It was also a highly popular series in terms of audience ratings in Japan. The programme on the origins of the first automated electric rice cooker, used as a source for this chapter, was programme No. 42 of the series, aired in 2002.

as a source, together with Toshiba records. In the *Project X* documentary, the development of the rice cooker is told as a story of Yamada, the 'silver-tongued' Toshiba salesman, and his collaboration with Minami Yoshitada, manager of a small, family-run factory in the Ōta ward of Tokyo, which was on the brink of bankruptcy. Together Yamada, Minami, and Minami's wife and six children turned the family home into an 'engineering laboratory' to develop the first electric rice cooker for Toshiba and for the Japanese market. This development is described repeatedly in the programme and in Toshiba documentation as a 'revolution for the Japanese kitchen'.

The *Project X* story begins in 1951, with Allied Occupation troops and their families beginning to pull out of Japan. The programme records that Americans living in Japan were 'rich', and had been ordering many appliances, such as washing machines and refrigerators. Their withdrawal was therefore a big blow to small neighbourhood factories acting as subcontractors to the larger Japanese manufacturers. Minami's small factory had supplied electric water heaters to the occupying forces, but orders had dried up and he faced imminent bankruptcy.

Yamada is introduced in the *Project X* story as a 'famous salesman', who entertained audiences around Shinbashi Station with his self-made *kamishibai* (paper card theatre). Toshiba had already launched the electric washing machine, which Yamada demonstrated and sold, telling housewives that each year they were washing by hand the weight of an elephant. From his meetings with housewives all over Japan, Yamada learnt that cooking rice was actually their hardest chore. They began the day at 5:00, sitting in front of the *kamado,* and were regarded as 'failed housewives' if they could not control the fire properly. Yamada was also told that having to cook rice three times a day meant insufficient sleep.

Nonetheless, Yamada's idea of developing an automated electric rice cooker did not initially find favour with his superiors at Toshiba. Alternatives to the *kamado* already existed in the form of the rice cookers with electric-coils, as well as others for use on gas hobs, and both Mitsubishi and Matsushita had already failed in their attempts to develop an automatic electric version. The *Project X* documentary also records that Yamada's superiors somewhat 'chauvinistically' believed that a woman who wanted to sleep rather than cook rice was a failure as a wife. As a result, Yamada was unable to secure a development budget.

Hence, when Minami subsequently came to Toshiba begging for subcontracting work, and Yamada heard that Minami's factory produced electric water heaters and had extensive knowledge of heating systems, he suggested to Minami that he try to develop an automatic electric rice cooker. Having no knowledge of rice cookers, Minami reportedly hesitated at first, but on reflection thought that it might help him out of his difficulties, and when he got home he asked his wife Fumiko to help him. He borrowed money for the project, using his house as security, and started to work on the development in 1953.

At this point the story really becomes Fumiko's, as it describes her lengthy struggle to research the heat levels and temperature changes involved in the successful cooking of rice. The programme reports how she sat for hours in front of her open-fire *kamado* and experimented with existing (non-automated) electric rice cookers, attempting with her husband to solve the biggest challenges of all: when and how to adjust the temperature of the cooker so that the rice would not burn, and how to create a cooker that would not only cook rice successfully, but also switch off automatically after 20 minutes of boiling.[4] Yamada and a technician from Toshiba assisted with the project, supplying Minami with a bi-metallic strip which would bend at high temperature, cutting off the switch automatically. Yamada's suggestion that the rice cooker had to work in any climate, including the cold winter of Hokkaidō and the hot summer of Kyūshū, meant that Fumiko had to test the cooker for endurance over a period of many months, experimenting outside on chilly winter mornings, on the roof of the family house in the scorching sun, next to a steaming bathroom and inside a *kotatsu*.[5] Minami tried making many prototypes of cooker using aluminium and glass, but the heat always escaped from the cooker in cold conditions. When Fumiko became ill testing the prototypes in cold winter weather, the rest of the family pitched in to help. Chikashi, the third son, commented in the programme: 'my mother used to say, if we succeed with this development, Japanese women will not need to cook rice three times a day. They could do something else for three hours a day. With an automatic rice cooker, they could go to work as men do.'

By 1955 Minami was despondent and financially on the brink of losing his house and factory. Yamada then pointed out how, in Hokkaidō, he had seen cooking pots covered with tin and asbestos to keep the heat in during winter, and Minami and one of his sons thought it might

[4] The programme records how the many trial-and-error experiments required a tonne of rice, which the Minamis managed to acquire through a contact who used the black market.

[5] A *kotatsu* is a low table covered by a quilt, with heating built in underneath, so that the lower body under the quilt is kept warm.

be possible to cover the cooker with a triple-layered iron exterior. This final prototype was tested in an ice warehouse at minus 10 degrees and proved successful. The *Project X* documentary notes this moment as 'the birth of the world's first automatic electric rice cooker'.

Determined to make the product a success, after the huge personal sacrifices of the Minami family, Yamada attempted to sell the convenience of this first automated rice cooker to housewives in northeast Japan, but the response was slow. The device was priced at 3,200 yen, at a time when the average basic monthly salary was around 10,000 yen. Housewives said it was too expensive, and that they could cook rice in the old way, even though it was time-consuming. However, when Yamada showed them that the cooker could also produce *takikomi gohan* (rice mixed with soy sauce), which was very difficult to cook in a traditional *kamado* as the soy sauce was prone to burning, the housewives were reportedly very surprised and applauded the demonstration. Yamada's report on this demonstration led to the manufacture of 700 completed units, and on 10 December 1955 Toshiba began to sell this first electric rice cooker nationwide. Within two years Minami's small factory was operating three shifts day and night and had produced more than 10,000 rice cookers.

Selling the electric rice cooker in the Japanese market

The new electric rice cooker rapidly revolutionised the process of cooking rice in Japan. Matsushita (now Panasonic) launched its own model the year after Toshiba, and a shaky start was followed by huge commercial success. Within the first year, Toshiba was producing some 200,000 rice cookers per month, and by 1960 automatic rice cookers could be found in half of all Japanese households. The company's 'award-winning design remained unchanged for nine years', and by 1970 Toshiba was recording an annual output of 12.35 million rice cookers. Over the high-growth decades, the three big electrical appliance producers – Toshiba, Matsushita and Hitachi – together with other niche players such as Zōjirushi and Tiger corporations, further developed the technology of their electric rice cookers for consumption on the Japanese domestic market. Matsushita (Panasonic) commented that the 'electric automatic rice cooker streamlined housework, causing a sudden increase in demand for automatic rice cookers, unlike that for any other home appliance, which led to what was called the "rice cooker boom" of 1957' (Panasonic Corporation, 2011). The electric rice cooker was therefore a product that had a sudden and significant impact on the consumer market in Japan.

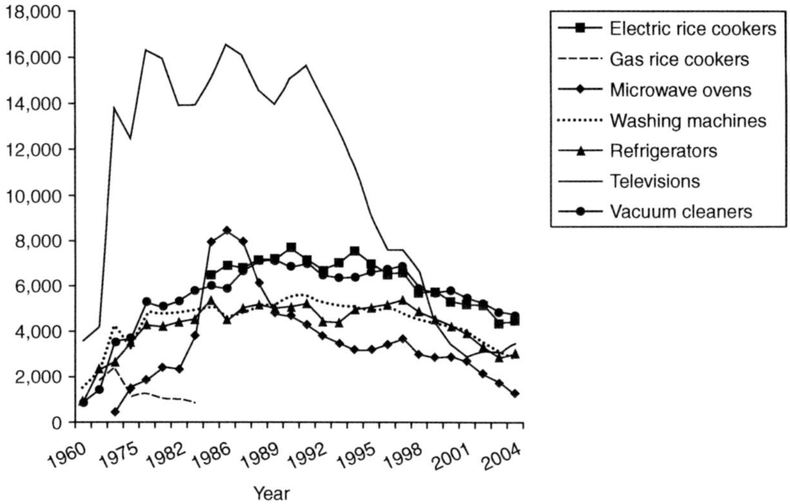

Figure 4.1 Production of selected home appliances, 1960–2004 (1,000 units)
Source: Statistics and Research Bureau, Ministry of Economy, Trade and Industry (METI).

Historical trends in the production and diffusion of electric rice cookers after 1955 are somewhat difficult to establish, and data on electric rice cooker production are omitted from official manufacturing statistics before 1985.[6] This is not the case for other household and kitchen appliances; TVs, washing machines, refrigerators, vacuum cleaners, sewing machines and even *kotatsu* are all included in MITI/METI statistics from the 1950s.[7] Figure 4.1 shows that the production of gas rice cookers declined between 1965 and 1983 in the face of competition from their electric counterparts. For the period 1985–2004, for which data exist, we find that the volume of production of electric rice cookers displays a trend of declining annual production similar to that of other key appliances, but the relatively high volume of production compared to many other electrical goods suggests an ongoing and

[6] These statistics were compiled by MITI, the Ministry of International Trade and Industry (now METI). Accessed at: http://www.stat.go.jp/english/data/chouki/08.htm

[7] A contact at Toshiba Corporation was surprised when I mentioned this omission in the statistics. When I informally asked why he thought these data were not recorded, he commented that maybe it was because the rice cooker was a 'women's product'. I was unable to pursue the omission of this data with METI.

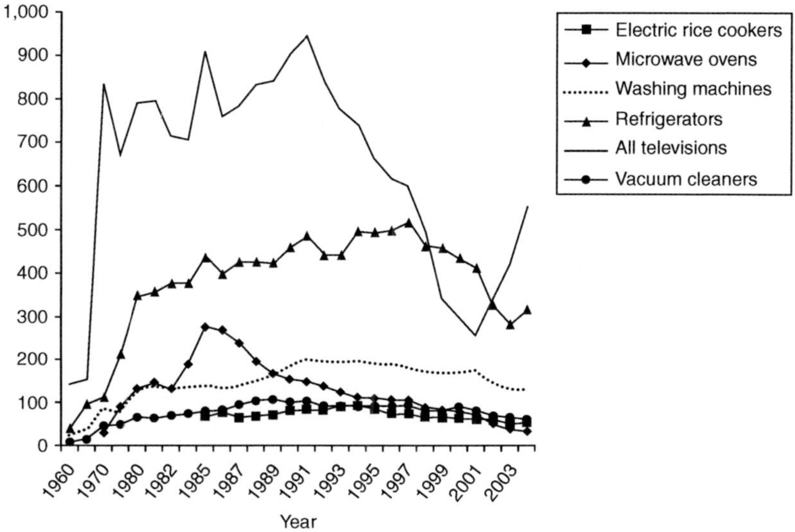

Figure 4.2 Value of selected home appliances production, 1960–2004 (¥ billion)
Source: Statistics and Research Bureau, Ministry of Economy, Trade and Industry (METI).

stable consumer market for this product.[8] Figure 4.2 shows that the value of electric rice cooker production was, not surprisingly, much lower than that of the larger, more expensive appliances, but comparable to those of similar size and durability, such as microwave ovens and vacuum cleaners.

That production volume was much higher in the early years (late 1950s onwards), when the electric rice cooker was a newly available and innovative product on the market, is confirmed by comparing the available METI data (1985–2004) with data from Toshiba (Figure 4.3). Toshiba's 1970 output of 12.35 million electric rice cookers is comparable to METI's figure for TV production the same year (13.78 million). It therefore seems likely that the inclusion of electric rice cooker production from other companies would make it one of the most significant appliances on the domestic market at the time, and potentially the largest in terms of annual domestic production.

[8] These data cover domestic production (and may include production for export as well as domestic consumption). Overseas production of electrical appliances by Japanese producers grew rapidly from the 1980s, resulting in the 'hollowing out' of Japanese manufacturing.

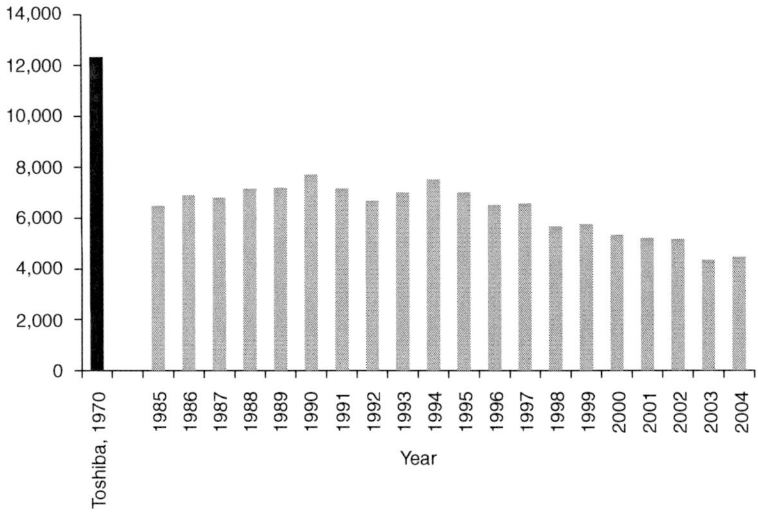

Figure 4.3 Production of electric rice cookers, 1970 and 1985–2004 (1,000 units)

Source: 1970 data: Toshiba Corporation (2009); 1985–2004 data: Statistics and Research Bureau, METI.

Over time the electric rice cooker has seen continual technological development, as newer and better models have been launched on to the domestic market. The technological characteristics developed by producers reflected the ways in which Japanese consumers cooked and ate rice as part of their daily lives. The initial impact of the automatic 'one switch' function out of which further technologies evolved cannot be overemphasised. In the early 1960s, some manufacturers introduced a function that could keep rice warm after cooking until it was served, as well as some models with a timer switch, for setting cooking times in advance. Figure 4.4 shows successive new rice cooker models developed by Toshiba since its pioneering original model of 1955.

The initial two models prior to 1978 were simple 'rice boiling' models that allowed for rice to be cooked at the touch of a button, with, from 1968, a glass lid that enabled the cook to view the progress of the rice. The 1978 model was described as more 'oven-' or 'kitchen stove-' like in style; it had a colourful 1970s vibe, and allowed for easy transportation by means of a handle at the top. From 1982, the rice cooker became electronic, with microcomputer technology enabling a range of automation settings and options. Later models focussed on induction heat-

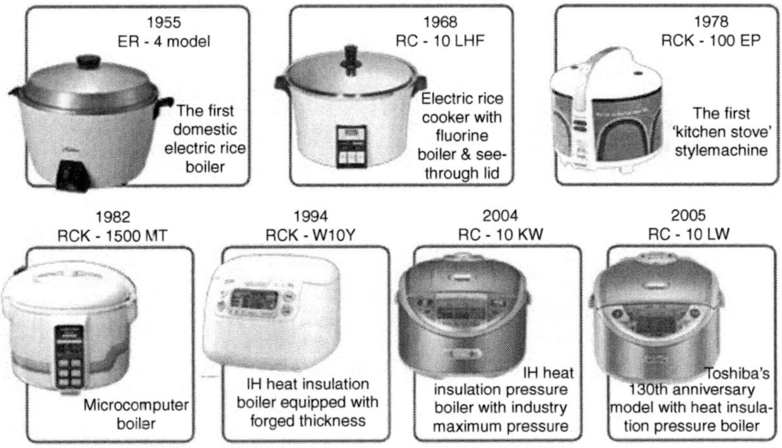

Figure 4.4 Development of the electric rice cooker by Toshiba, 1955–2005

Note: Author's translations of original Japanese captions supplied by Toshiba.

Source: Courtesy of Toshiba.

ing (IH), heating insulation, and pressure steaming technologies. Over time, therefore, Japanese consumers could buy newer, more efficient models reflecting their desire both to keep up with the latest gadgetry and to produce even more efficiently cooked and better tasting rice on an everyday basis.

The consumption of electrical household appliances in Japan

The production of consumer durables, including household and kitchen appliances, in post-war Japan, was, of course, a significant sector of the Japanese economy (Partner, 1999). Growth in the domestic demand for electrical household appliances went hand-in-hand with growth in the production of these goods in Japan (alongside rapid expansion and investment in electric power from 1951). The large and growing market allowed Japanese manufacturers to test their new technologies and products and enhance their designs before moving into export markets. How domestic producers tested, marketed and sold their products to Japanese consumers and households is therefore an important area of investigation. From the perspective of consumption, we need to ask why Japanese households were buying these appliances, who was making the decision to buy, and what impact home electrical goods, particularly kitchen appliances, had on the lives of Japanese women in terms of their primary role as 'home-makers'.

The growth in the number of household appliances had a major impact on the Japanese kitchen. The kitchen (*daidokoro*) has always been a focal point of the Japanese household (Kosuge, 1991), and Sand (2003) has suggested that, from the late nineteenth century onwards, the kitchen was evolving to become the 'housewife's laboratory', where women were expected not just to cook but to practise the new field of home economics, focussing on such issues as nutrition, hygiene and budgets. From around 1890 the introduction of Western-style cooking and kitchen equipment (designed to be used while standing) meant that gradually the floor in the Japanese home ceased to be used for food preparation or serving meals (Yamaguchi, 1988; Yamaguchi, 2008), but Partner suggests that kitchens in much of rural Japan until the late 1950s were 'miserable places' where women still squatted on earth floors to carry out most food preparation, and campaigns to improve rural kitchens became part of a broader 'lifestyle improvement' process (Partner, 2001, pp. 492–93). Kitchens gradually became more linear and 'set' in terms of layout and style, encouraging a process more akin to an assembly line.

From around 1956, the kitchens of housing complexes built by the Japan Housing Corporation had set kitchens in sparkling stainless steel, with typically a gas cooker, kitchen counter and sink arranged in a linear design. By the 1960s, it had become customary to display cooking utensils, lining them up on shelves or hanging them along the wall above the counter, but Japanese household magazines soon began to criticise this practice as a sign of a disorderly kitchen and poor domestic management, and set-kitchens started to include drawers and cupboards (Yamaguchi, 2008). Into the new and evolving space of the compact dining-kitchen (DK) came a growing range of Japanese- and Western-style kitchen equipment and appliances. The electric toaster appeared in 1953, followed by the electric rice cooker in 1955, the electric refrigerator, the microwave oven and, by the early 1970s, induction-heating devices, particularly in rice cookers (Yamaguchi 2008). Appliances ranged from the large-scale – refrigerator and washing machine – to smaller-scale and uniquely Japanese appliances such as the electric *kotatsu*, electric rice cooker and electric vacuum jugs (*potto*) for storing and dispensing hot water for green tea preparation. With consumption boosted by the modish slogan of *mai hōmu* ('my home'), these appliances changed both the concept and environment of cooking within the Japanese household and the time spent by women on the preparation and production of food.

Research on the world-wide development and diffusion of electric household appliances has identified them as falling into two distinct classifications: 'time-saving' goods, such as electric washing machines and vacuum cleaners, and 'time-using' goods, which required the use of discretionary time, such as radios and TVs (Bowden and Offer, 1994). In many countries the diffusion of time-using goods as items of consumption appears to have been much faster than that of time-saving goods, and this was also true in Japan, where the TV was the key 'Sacred Treasure' item in terms of production and diffusion. However, it was suggested above that the electric rice cooker may have surpassed the TV in production and diffusion during the 1960s and 1970s. It may have been a 'humble appliance targeted at housewives' (Nakano, 2009, p. 1) but its impact in the market was enormous.

Women as the target market for electric rice cookers

The emergence of the urban, middle-class, nuclear Japanese family from the 1950s and 1960s was associated with an ideal 'model' of men commuting to long hours of work, and women, even those who had paid employment, being primarily responsible for the everyday management of the household. That responsibility included making decisions regarding allocation of expenditure within the family budget, especially relating to day-to-day shopping and cooking for the family. Japanese women, or rather Japanese 'housewives', were thus viewed as the key target consumers for the new electric rice cookers from the mid–late 1950s. As housewives, they were the most likely to decide to purchase the product, and were (correctly) assumed to be the ones who would use it in the home. The image of the modern Japanese housewife was widely used by companies marketing the electric rice cooker and other household appliances.

The advertisement in Figure 4.5, with its modern-style Japanese woman opening the cooker lid, records the launch of Toshiba's first electric rice cooker.

It includes several interesting slogans:

> 'Releasing housewives from the vigil of the stove' (*kamado no ban kara shufu o kaihō*)
>
> 'Giving housewives time for sleep' (*hajimari wa shufutachi ni suimin jikan o*)
>
> 'With one switch anyone can easily cook rice' (*suitchi hitotsu de dare ni demo kantan ni gohan ga takeru*)

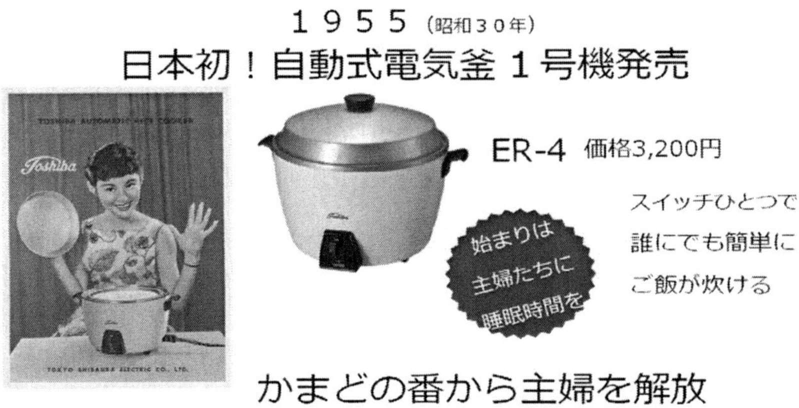

Figure 4.5 Toshiba advertising their first electric rice cooker, 1955
Source: Images courtesy of Toshiba.

The slogans reveal something of the meaning of the electric rice cooker within Japanese households. Housewives would be liberated from the task of standing or squatting at the *kamado*, constantly keeping an eye on the rice, so women's burdens would be reduced. Japanese women could now sleep more in the morning, instead of getting up to prepare rice for breakfast; during the day, they could perhaps take a cat-nap while the rice for the evening meal was bubbling. The electric rice cooker was therefore clearly a 'time-saving' device for women, in terms of everyday routine and hours spent on rice cooking. However, Toshiba's marketing slogans also imply that although the appliance may have made it easier for the housewife to carry out her rice-cooking duties, it did not free her up for anything significantly more productive than some rest or down-time. The third slogan subtly suggests that anyone, and not just women or housewives, could now easily perform the task of cooking rice, though who those others may be is not indicated. It seems unlikely that the intention was to suggest that rice cooking could now be a man's daily task too; rather it seems to imply that *any* housewife could now produce perfectly steamed rice, no longer needing to acquire the skill from her mother-in-law (and being unfavourably compared to her).

In 1956, Toshiba enlisted the electric power companies to help distribute the new electric rice cooker and win the trust of consumers made suspicious by the failure of earlier electric rice cooker models in the late 1940s. In those early days, Toshiba and Matsushita took their product

Figure 4.6 Toshiba selling their first electric rice cooker in a Japanese department store, c. 1955/56

Source: Images courtesy of Toshiba.

directly to the consumer, with employees going from home to home to demonstrate this first automated model and holding appliance and cooking demonstrations in public spaces and in new apartment complexes (for example, Senri New Town in Osaka in the case of Matsushita) (Nakano, 2009). Toshiba also held demonstration sales within department stores and later in its own electrical appliance retail stores. One Toshiba manager recounted that Toshiba-franchised small electrical stores were the key sites for retail sales in the Japanese domestic market until the 1990s, when they were replaced by larger-scale electrical stores not affiliated to any one company. Figure 4.6 shows the first Toshiba model on sale in a Japanese department store. In the first photograph a group of male customers is gathered around the new rice cooker, while the sales assistant is a woman.

Women also helped to popularise and sell these appliances directly. By the early 1960s, Matsushita employed female retailers in their 'Mom and Pop stores' to sell household appliances including the rice cooker, centrally providing them with training and the means to keep up-to-date with new products (Nakano, 2009). Women were eventually also involved in the design and engineering of rice cookers. Nakano (2009) describes how, until the 1970s, Matsushita used all-male teams of engineers to research and design the appliances, an assignment regarded as 'disappointing' by male engineers who would have preferred to work in the higher-tech divisions within the company. However, in 1979, Matsushita hired a 'female rice specialist' with a Master's Degree in Home Economics, who went on to make subtle yet successful advances in the technology required to regulate the temperature inside the cooker, so as to enhance cooking and flavour and produce 'perfectly steamed rice'. The company's rice cooker division then began to hire female engineers, who became informally known as the 'rice ladies' (Nakano, 2009, pp. 132–36), as well as recruiting women into their marketing teams. One of the early R&D 'rice ladies' went on to become director of Matsushita's Cooking Appliances Business Unit and has described how the Japanese 'obsession with perfectly steamed rice' has meant that the market for rice cookers in Japan developed very differently from that in other parts of Asia; Japanese consumers have come to view the rice cooker as only to be used for 'steaming white rice and refuse to cook anything else in the pot', whereas in other parts of Asia it has to be a 'versatile multi-cooker' in order to sell to consumers (Nakano, 2009, p. 155).

By implication, this means that Japanese consumers have been more willing to spend money on an appliance the function of which is only to 'perfectly steam rice'. Hence, for Japanese housewives still reluctant to do anything that might damage the taste of future batches of steamed rice, the production of 'perfect rice' requires a dedicated appliance, and the cultural implications of this have significantly influenced the design, marketing and consumption of the rice cooker in the Japanese domestic market. However, it has also meant that, in the domestic market, the electric rice cooker has remained a somewhat humble, minor and housewife-oriented appliance compared to its more 'elevated' status elsewhere in Asia (Nakano, 2009, p. 176).

Given the focal role of rice cooking in women's housework duties and the skill required to make good rice, the arrival of the electric rice cooker in the mid-1950s revolutionised food preparation, cooking routines and meal preparation hours for Japanese women, and its impact on the market was immediate and significant. Sazae-*san*, the central housewife character in a highly successful comic-strip and, as one Japanese academic has commented, a lens through which to view the life of ordinary Japanese during the early post-war decades (Tamaki, 2003), started using a Toshiba electric rice cooker in 1960 (Goo, 2005), suggesting that just four years after its product launch the automatic rice cooker was on its way to becoming an essential everyday item in Japanese households.

It is debatable how far appliances like the electric rice cooker were really time-saving in freeing up Japanese women to spend time on other activities, such as paid employment or leisure activities, and how far these appliances simply enabled women to divert their attention to other household tasks, further creating or enhancing the image of the 'modern' Japanese housewife and the 'modern' Japanese home. Women who were full-time housewives may simply have devoted more time to other housework and the preparation of more elaborate side-dishes to accompany their perfectly steamed rice. However, it is certainly possible to argue that key appliances, including the electric rice cooker, at the very least helped to free housewives from formerly time-consuming daily routines and enabled them to enter paid part-time employment. The new 'bundle' of time-saving household appliances increasingly owned by the average family meant that women could perform daily housework and food preparation in less time than previously. With rising demand for female labour, especially part-time (*pāto*), from Japanese employers seeking to maintain a workforce under the conditions of rapid economic growth (Macnaughtan, 2005), these key home appliances added to the 'supply side' conditions enabling married women to enter paid employment while still fulfilling their key 'housewife' role.

As her son Chikashi mentions in the *Project X* documentary, Fumiko had considered the possibility of freeing women from rice-cooking duties to go out to work like men, as she experimented with the development of Toshiba's first automatic rice cooker. Chikashi also comments in the programme that 'leading manufacturers had failed to develop a successful electric rice cooker since the end of the Taishō era. I think the reason why ours was successful was because women and families participated in the development' (NHK, 2002). In Japan (and in Western markets) from the 1960s, manufacturers and advertisers gradually came to realise that products like the electric rice cooker, targeted at or destined for consumption by women, benefited from having women involved in both development and marketing.

The role of Japanese women as consumers

Through the 1950s and 1960s, as they fulfilled their central role as housewives, Japanese women established themselves as arbiters of the new urban household's image, taste, fashion and consumption. Department stores sold new appliances that aimed to 'rationalise housework' and 'project the housewife as a household expert and domestic manager' (Young, 1999, p. 65). Through this role, women, especially housewives, came to be associated with a high level of consumer awareness and consumer behaviour, first as holders of the purse-strings within the Japanese household, and second as key players within community consumer groups. Since its inception in 1948, Japan's *Shufuren* (Housewives' Association) has played a leading part in the post-war consumer movement, demonstrating the importance of a gender perspective in bringing government and producers to task over consumer concerns. Japanese women, particularly housewives, were increasingly viewed as knowledgeable and responsible consumers, aware of environmental issues, strong players in the development of consumer rights, and in themselves an active, identifiable, consumer group in the domestic market. From the 1970s, there were two distinct female-consumer categories for advertisers and market researchers: working women (predominantly young, single women) and housewives (older, married women). Assmann (2003) describes how women's magazines in Japan have reinforced notions of gender roles and gender groups, emphasising the divide between working and home-making women. Implicit in her argument is that magazines are also the delineators of detailed 'rules' or 'instructions' on what certain groups of Japanese women should buy.

This categorisation of Japanese women into identifiable consumer groups has continued. A 1997 market report identified four key consumer types: (1) *Silver* (persons aged 50+), (2) *Active Singles* (unmarried working persons aged 20–39 years), (3) *Youngsters* (persons aged 10–24 years) and (4) *Influencing Women* (working women and housewives aged 20–49 years). This last category was made up of two sub groups, 'internalist housewives' and 'materialists', together comprising 21.4 per cent of the Japanese population. Internalist housewives were focussed on their personal lifestyles, communities and the environment and were the primary target group for a range of 'home-use products'. 'Materialist women' valued material goods and money as key drivers of happiness, and were 'clinging to the attitudes of the bubble period' through their propensity to buy luxury, fashion and branded goods (TrendScope,

1997, pp. 10, 16–17). A more recent consumer trend report by Yomiuri in 2008 identified 'ladies aged around 40' as one of the four key consumer profile categories in the Japanese market. These women had entered the working world during the bubble economy and were described as having 'lived in the lap of luxury... active, energetic women who continue to work after marriage... noted as a group with stable spending habits' (Yomiuri, 2008). Whether homemaker or working, these women, mostly married and over 30 years of age, have been the obvious consumer target group for products such as household and kitchen appliances.

This targeting was tied to the prevailing consensus that such women hold a substantial level of power in the Japanese household. They are responsible for the family budget, balancing income and expenditure and favour stability and limiting debt, while projecting the image of an orderly, 'middle-class' home. A survey by the Japan External Trade Organization (JETRO) in 1981 found that 43.0 per cent of married women took sole responsibility for the budget, and 40.7 per cent shared the responsibility with their husbands. Only 16.3 per cent of women responded that their husband ruled the family purse (JETRO, 1981, p. 10). In the same survey, 59.1 per cent of women responded that they were solely responsible for the purchase of domestic appliances, while 37.2 per cent said they shared the purchase decision with their husband. Only 1.8 per cent responded that their husband was solely responsible for the purchase of a domestic appliance, compared to 32.7 per cent for an audio or TV purchase, and 44.2 per cent for a car.

The 1981 JETRO study also noted that consumer purchases were primarily of domestically produced products, but as purchasing power increased, so would the desire to purchase imported goods. It also commented that 'the Japanese market is changing and it is not entirely coincidental that the Japanese woman – consumer and housewife – is also going through a process of evolution' (JETRO, 1981, p. 1).

While demand for foreign or international products, particularly in the areas of leisure, food and fashion, including luxury brands, did grow over the post-war decades, such products had to compete in price and quality within the forceful domestic market. When the Japan Market Research Bureau polled over 1,000 women in the Tokyo/Yokohama area in 1978, only 15 per cent agreed with the statement that 'most foreign products are of better quality than Japanese ones' (quoted in JETRO, 1981, p. 18). Moreover, consumer products had to demonstrate that they were appropriate to, or could be absorbed into, the Japanese lifestyle. As Japanese homes and rooms were on average smaller than in the West and were often multi-purpose, there was a need for flexibility, compactness and durability (JETRO, 1981, p. 13), particularly apparent in relation to the consumption of home-ware, kitchen and electronic goods. Few Japanese housewives wanted to purchase a Western-style dinner service, for example, preferring to have an array of smaller plates and a variety of mix-and-match tableware products (JETRO, 1981, p. 14). Japanese kitchens could not usually accommodate Western-size refrigerators or ovens, so domestically produced products dominated the market. Domestically produced electric rice cookers offered Japanese women the opportunity to cook rice in an efficient and compact appliance that took up little space in the kitchen and was easily transported from one room to another for serving purposes.

The electric rice cooker therefore developed as it did because of the importance of rice in Japanese daily meals, the centrality of rice-cooking to the (real or symbolic) role of the Japanese housewife, and as part of the technologically driven growth in Japanese manufacturing. As consumers, Japanese women, particularly married ones, influenced what was produced through their need or desire to maintain their housewife role within the context of 'modern' life. The electric rice cooker offered the perfect adaptation of 'modern' technology to urban middle-class meal patterns and the lives that women were leading in their new urban housing.

The impact of the electric rice cooker

In an attempt to add some consumer 'voices' to this chapter, I conducted a survey on the purchase and use of rice cookers.[9] The primary target respondents were Japanese women who had purchased and used rice cookers. Although the survey is not comprehensive in terms of the number of respondents, nor conclusively representative of the Japanese domestic market for this product, the responses can throw light on

---

[9] This was an online survey via www.surveygizmo.com that ran for three months from October 2010 to January 2011. A total of 135 completed responses were collected for analysis (117 responses were either abandoned by respondents or only partially completed and not suitable for analysis). All the respondents were Japanese nationals (88 per cent living in Japan, the remaining 12 per cent currently living outside Japan). The percentage of female respondents was 97.4, with the majority married and aged in their 30s and 40s (breakdown by age: 4.3 per cent were 25–29 years; 41 per cent in their 30s; 41 per cent in their 40s; 10.3 per cent in their 50s; and 3.5 per cent in their 60s; breakdown by marital status: 62.3 per cent were married; 25.4 per cent single, 7.0 per cent divorced, 2.6 per cent cohabiting and 2.6 per cent widowed).

some of the topics explored in this chapter, particularly the key issue of gendered consumption of the electric rice cooker. The survey reinforced the suggestion that it is women who are the key consumers of rice cookers in Japan. Of all female survey respondents, 93 per cent had purchased a rice cooker for themselves, while 54 per cent had received a rice cooker bought for them. Of those who had received a rice cooker as a 'gift', 81 per cent said it had been purchased by another female, with the majority (55 per cent) receiving one from their mother (although 18 per cent of recipients said they had received one from their husband). When questioned as to whether they remembered, as children, their family purchasing an electric rice cooker, 54.3 per cent responded that they did, and of those, 83.5 per cent said that their mother had been the person who decided on the purchase (compared to only 9.6 per cent who remembered their father as the purchaser of this appliance).

When questioned on their own purchasing decisions, a majority said they made their purchase choice based on technology (45.8 per cent), compared to price (18.3 per cent), size (7.5 per cent), design (5.8 per cent) and brand loyalty (1.7 per cent). Only 34.7 per cent of all respondents said they were influenced by any form of advertising. A majority of respondents (72.5 per cent) had purchased a rice cooker more than once; 11.1 per cent of this group had purchased one within the past 12 months, 45.3 per cent during the past 1–5 years, 29.1 per cent during the past 5–10 years and 14.5 per cent more than 10 years earlier. Of those who had purchased more than one appliance, 45.3 per cent had purchased to replace a damaged model and 25.6 per cent to upgrade to a newer-technology model. The percentage of respondents who used their rice cooker at least once a day was 49.3, and 21 per cent on average 3–4 times per week.

When asked about the 'impact' of the electric rice cooker on the 'everyday lives of Japanese women' (including their mothers and grandmothers), 48.4 per cent responded that the appliance had had a 'very important impact', 35.2 per cent an 'important impact' and 13.1 per cent 'some impact'; only 3.3 per cent felt it had had 'little impact' or 'no impact'. When asked to comment freely on rice cookers more broadly, many respondents commented on the 'time-saving' nature of the appliance, stating how its simplicity, efficiency and reliability gave them more 'time' that could be used 'freely' and 'efficiently'. Many stated that the technology in modern rice cookers was crucial to this, particularly the 'automatic timer' function and the 'keep warm' function that allowed for hot rice to be served at any time, enabling family members to eat separately if necessary. Many respondents also wrote that the appliance 'reduced the burden' or 'shortened the time' required for housework or household chores.

While many women commented that it was relatively simple to cook rice using a *donabe* (earthenware pot) or pan over gas, most of them regularly used their rice cooker to cook plain, steamed rice. A few commented that the transition from gas cooking with a *donabe* saved some time and the need to be physically present, but the gains were less than those involved in the transition from cooking rice with a traditional fire *kamado*. As one woman commented, 'it is impossible to imagine how difficult this was 70 years ago.' One respondent wrote: 'my grandmother could not move away from the *kamado*, as she often needed to adjust the level of direct flame while she cooked the rice,' and another commented: 'my mother's family used to cook rice for their large family using a *kamado* with firewood outside the house in the very early morning. It must have been hard work to prepare even two other side dishes. My grandmother was a teacher, and I cannot imagine how she combined work and being a housewife.' Several respondents commented that the electric rice cooker was a 'must have' or 'necessity' item.

Several respondents also made comments such as 'it is important that the rice is delicious because it is our staple food', and emphasised how rice is embedded in the 'culture' of the Japanese. One respondent felt the appliance had 'protected the Japanese food culture that is centred on rice', and another commented: 'both my mother and I have a strong insistence on rice, and we have rice every day. I choose to buy delicious rice even if it costs more. We don't like to throw away left-over rice, so our main priorities are the ability to cook delicious rice and the "keep-warm" function of a rice cooker.'

It may be that the rice cooker has reached a mature point in its product life-cycle. One respondent commented that, while 'there must be no family without a rice cooker in Japanese society, its impact is nowadays reduced. Microwaves are more influential.'Another said: 'with the spread of *musenmai* [no-rinse rice], I find it sad that more and more people do not rinse rice and also cook rice without rice cookers.' Several respondents also commented on the continuing technology that keeps Japanese companies rolling out advanced models. One respondent wrote: 'some expensive rice cookers are sold nowadays, but I think that the modest-priced rice cookers can still cook rice deliciously with their advanced technology', while another commented that 'recent rice cookers have too many functions. I think it's enough with minimum functions. The price is getting too high.' Other respondents wrote: 'if I compare the rice cookers of my mother's generation (they were simple so there were not many parts to get worn out, and they lasted over 20 years), I think that rice cookers using rubber parts last only 7–8 years nowadays', and 'I see TV adverts with many high-tech rice cookers, but I don't understand the difference between IH [induction heating], *maikon* [microcomputer] and *kamado*-style cooking-method appliances. I am happy when a rice cooker can cook rice; I have a simple one.' Several respondents did, however, comment on how rice tasted better cooked in a traditional *kamado*, and this issue of taste no doubt influenced producers to develop different models and technologies, including so-called *kamado*-style rice cookers that attempt to reproduce the taste of the 'traditional'.

Some responded more positively to the advancing technology: 'rice cookers are getting more convenient recently – you can rinse rice without scratching the inner bowl. They are also evolving, for example, there are products which avoid steam coming out upwards.' Another commented: 'I have tried a lot of rice cookers and I like the one I am currently using. There are quite big differences in the taste of rice cooked by different rice cookers. As long as the rice is delicious, any side dishes can be delicious, too!' One woman wrote: 'I feel that the role of the rice cooker has moved from its initial role, which was to free women from housework, to that of enabling them to cook delicious rice. This shows in the fact that expensive rice cookers costing around 100,000 yen sell well'. Another stated: 'as a nation of rice eaters, rice cookers are absolutely indispensable for our lives. Now we have expensive models, with high-tech ability to cook the best rice (not too soft, not too hard, glossy as crystal, and moderately sticky). They can cost as much as 100,000 yen or more. But we do not hesitate to purchase such a device, because we would like to enjoy great rice every day at home. The problem is that the models change too rapidly. We are sure the newest one is the best, so we try hard to resist its charm and not to purchase one after another. Actually, my mother (who is 74 years old) has a dozen rice cookers at home and evaluates which one is best. Ridiculous!'

The comments of some respondents linked technology, history and the importance of rice, for example: 'it seems that people move like a pendulum in time. Rice cookers have evolved from gas to electric ones, with modern timer and "keep-warm" functions. However, user feedback has suggested that rice cooked by gas or fire is better than that cooked by electric means (it might be a childhood memory of taste). In response to those users who are concerned about the old fire method of cooking, manufacturers have introduced pot and firepower functions into their electric rice cookers.' One woman commented that 'when my family first bought a rice cooker, it was a gas rice cooker. But my family was getting large, and I think that the electric rice cooker became necessary for my mother to cope with the preparation of lunch boxes and different meal times every day. The performance of modern rice cookers bears no comparison to the old ones. Previously, the rice became yellowish in colour and got hard when you left it in a "keep-warm" function, but nowadays the rice remains soft and delicious and there are functions other than for cooking rice. At the same time, however, frozen foods and microwave technology mean we can have delicious rice without sticking to freshly cooked rice. I think that the functions sought after by those in the 1970s and 1980s are quite different from the demands of the current generation. I think that [the rice cooker] was a great influence for women's housework life and time in the 1970s and 1980s, but now I feel it is different.'

Overall there is a sense from the survey respondents that the electric rice cooker played a key role in enabling women to go out to work and still easily produce an evening meal based around rice. One woman in her 50s said: 'for my generation, rice cookers with a timer setting... were available, so we set the timer in the morning and we could go to work.' Another commented: 'the number of working women is increasing. When we have to prepare breakfast in the early morning and dinner after work, using an electric rice cooker means the rice is ready to eat. I think this makes women feel more free. I feel it gives them the ability not only to cook rice, but to breathe and face other things while it's cooking.' Other respondents wrote: 'as rice cooking has become easier, I think women can work more easily' and 'I think that rice cookers greatly contributed to women's freedom to work in our society, especially since the timer setting became available.'

Concluding comments

In focussing on the history of the automated electric rice cooker since its development, inception and launch on to the Japanese domestic market in the 1950s, this chapter has tried to integrate the manufacturing side of the story, with specific reference to Toshiba, and the consumer side of the story, in particular the role of women as consumers. After 55 years, the cooker remains important. A Toshiba manager commented to me that the electric rice cooker remains a core product within the company's kitchen and household appliance division, and that 'the importance of the product is high, as it is the product that boils the staple food for the Japanese people.'

This 'modest' appliance in many ways helped to 'revolutionise' the life of the average Japanese woman. Sadly, Fumiko, the original female consumer of this product, does not appear in the *Project X* documentary programme. She died, aged only 45, in 1959, just as the rice-cooker boom was hitting Japan, but not before reportedly receiving in hospital letters from housewives all over the country, recording how thankful they were to be released from the hard work of daily rice cooking and how they now enjoyed more relaxing mornings and evenings. I like to think she would be pleased that this impact has continued. As one of my survey respondents commented, 'it was a good experience to think about the rice cooker as I have never really thought about this. I am 34 years old, so electric rice cookers have existed since I was born. I hadn't thought about its impact on women and how it helps to reduce time and effort.'

References

Assmann, S. (2003) 'Japanese Women's Magazines: Inspiration and Commodity', in *Electronic Journal of Contemporary Japanese Studies*, Discussion Paper 6.

Bowden, S. & Avner, O. (1994) 'Household Appliances and the Use of Time: The United States and Britain since the 1920s', *Economic History Review*, 47, 4, pp. 725–48.

Costa, J. ed., (1994) *Gender Issues and Consumer Behaviour*, London: Sage Publications.

de Grazia, V. (ed.) (1996) *The Sex of Things: Gender and Consumption in Historical Perspective*, Berkeley CA: University of California Press.

de Vries, J. (2008) *The Industrious Revolution*, Cambridge: Cambridge University Press.

Francks, P. (2009a) *The Japanese Consumer: An Alternative Economic History of Modern Japan*, Cambridge: Cambridge University Press.

Francks, P. (2009b) 'Inconspicuous Consumption: Sake, Beer, and the Birth of the Consumer in Japan', *The Journal of Asian Studies*, 68, 1, February, pp. 135–64.

Goo (2005) *Kyō no Koto Arekore to...: Toshiba ga Denkigama o Hatsubai Shita Hi* (This and That on this Day...: the Day Toshiba Launched the Electric Rice Cooker), Online Blog accessed on 10 December 2005 at: http://blog.goo.ne.jp/yousan02/e/b30cf4698e2c3b76afa1f1ebb6dd2057?st=1

JETRO (1981) *The Female Factor in Japan's Import Market: A Survey of the Purchasing Attitudes and Experience of 687 Women*, Tokyo: Japan External Trade Organization (JETRO).

Kosuge, K. (1991) *Nippon Daidokoro Bunkashi* (Cultural History of the Japanese Kitchen), Tokyo: Yūzankaku Shuppan.

Macnaughtan, H. (2005) *Women, Work and the Japanese Economic Miracle: the case of the Cotton Textile Industry, 1945–75*, London: Routledge Curzon.

Macnaughtan, H. (2006) 'From "Post-war" to "Post-bubble": Contemporary Issues for Japanese Working Women' in Matanle, P. & Lunsing, W. (eds) *Work, Employment, and Society in Contemporary Japan*, Basingstoke: Palgrave Macmillan.

Nakano, Y. (2009) *Where There Are Asians, There are Rice Cookers: How " 'National' " Went Global via Hong Kong*, Hong Kong: Hong Kong University Press.
NHK (2002) *Project X: Challengers*, Documentary No. 42.
Panasonic Corporation (2011) *Panasonic Corporate History: Innovative Products, 1956, Automatic Rice Cooker*, accessed at: http://panasonic.net/history/corporate/products/inp1956.html
Partner, S. (1999) *Assembled in Japan: Electrical Goods and the Making of the Japanese Consumer*, Berkeley, CA: University of California Press.
Partner, S. (2001) 'Taming the Wilderness: The Lifestyle Improvement Movement in Rural Japan', *Monumenta Nipponica* 56, 4, Winter, pp. 487–520.
Sand, J. (2003) *House and Home in Modern Japan: Architecture, Domestic Space and Bourgeois Culture 1880–1930*, Cambridge, MA: Harvard University East Asia Center.
Tamaki, E. (2003) *Sazaesan ni miru Sengo Nihon no Kurashi* (The Lives of Post-war Japanese, as seen through 'Sazae-san'), Jissen Women's University, Faculty of Human Life Sciences.
Toshiba Corporation (2009) *Firsts of their Kind*, Toshiba Project Technology History accessed at http://museum.toshiba.co.jp/history/1goki/1955rice.html
TrendScope (1997) *Trend Watch: The New Consumer Trends in Japan*, TrendScope, August 1997, Tokyo.
Yamaguchi, M. (1988) *Daidokoro Kūkangaku: sono Genkei to Mirai* (A Study of Kitchen Space: The Prototype and the Future), Tokyo: Kenchiku Chishiki.
Yamaguchi, M. (2008) 'The Japanese Kitchen: Modern Era to Innovation', accessed at: http://1st-japanese-food.blogspot.com/search?q=yamaguchi
Yomiuri (2008) *About Japan: Consumer Trends*, Accessed at: http://adv.yomiuri.co.jp/m-data/english/market/about_japan2.html
Young, L. (1999). 'Marketing the Modern: Department Stores, Consumer Culture, and the New Middle Class in Interwar Japan', *International Labor and Working-Class History*, 55, Spring, pp. 52–70.

Part II

Tradition, Modernity and the Growth of Consumption

5

Japanese Modernisation and the Changing Everyday Life of the Consumer: Evidence from Household Accounts

Satoru Nakanishi and Tomoko Futaya

Introduction

In Japanese economic history circles in recent years attention has been shifting away from the production side and towards consumption. This perhaps reflects the growing concern, in the contemporary world, with the nature and quality, and not just the quantity, of consumption goods. However, research into Japan's consumption history is hampered by a lack of the kinds of surviving evidence, such as inventories and wills, which has been used to evaluate the historical accumulation of goods in Europe and North America. On the other hand, Japanese scholars have been able to access a number of collections of the account books frequently kept by landowning and business households in the past. These typically record the income and expenditure of the household under various categories, and can thus provide a valuable source of detailed information on the goods and services acquired by households engaging with the commercial economy in different parts of the country.

Consumption history was in fact a major theme of the series on the History of the Japanese Economy published by the University of Tokyo Press and completed in 2010. Volume 1 of this series, covering the late Tokugawa/early Meiji period, included our earlier study using historical household accounts to examine the consumption lives of well-to-do commercial and landowning households in the second half of the nineteenth century (Nakanishi, 2000). That paper mainly looked at the consumption patterns of two households during the Meiji period: one was the landowning Miyabayashi family in Toyama Prefecture and the other was the Hiromi family who were fertiliser merchants in Osaka Prefecture. In general, the Miyabayashis, living in a relatively remote area, continued to maintain a traditional lifestyle, purchasing Western-style goods only as expensive foreign luxuries acquired on their trips to distant big cities. The Hiromis, on the other hand, living on the outskirts of Osaka, began to experience elements of a Western lifestyle from relatively early on, using their employees' trips to the city as a means to acquire imported goods.

However, the two households were both similarly wealthy members of local upper-class society and comparisons based on class or locality were not pursued. Since household accounts have as yet been little used as sources in Japanese economic history,[1] and further case-studies of Japanese consumption history are needed if Japan is to be fitted into a global comparative framework, the present chapter uses two other sets of household accounts – those of family X, who owned a business brewing sake and soy sauce in Aichi Prefecture, and family K, who were farmers and landowners in Yamagata Prefecture – as the basis for a comparative examination of the ways in which consumption patterns were affected by class and occupation during the first stages of Japan's modernisation in the period of the late nineteenth and early twentieth centuries.[2]

In the kinds of nineteenth-century household account books utilised in this chapter, the division between family and business was far from complete, and the accounts therefore included the balance sheet for all income and expenditure, including that of any family business. For this reason it was the head of the household (the person responsible for management of the business) who usually had the responsibility for making records in the account books, and this was undertaken systematically from one generation to the next. The main objective was to control the balance of income and expenditure, and what was recorded was actually very simple. As we enter the modern period, however, the introduction of a modern tax system, including for example income tax, made it essential to differentiate between household income and expenditure and that of the family business, so account books gradually included more and more detail. This chapter therefore makes use of account books from around 1880, by which time the recording had become relatively clear. There were no instructions from public bodies

---

1 An exception to this is the work of a group led by Nakamura Takafusa. See Nakamura ed., 1993.

2 The families are referred to as X and K in order to maintain anonymity.

as to the organisation of the items to be included in household account books, so there are considerable variations according to family and time period, and any systematic arrangement is very difficult, but if we think of the account books as sources for internal use, and not as official documents, they can be regarded as relatively unembellished reflections of the actual situation.

The many aspects of everyday life can be classified for analytical purposes in a number of ways. An earlier study of home life in the Meiji period lists as appropriate categories: family relations, household economy, clothing and eating habits, housing, health, culture, home education, the education of girls, women's issues, and social welfare (Chūbu Kakei Keieigaku Kenkyūkai, ed.,1972). Here, our main concern is with the correlation between the lifestyle of the household and the social environment that surrounds it. We therefore roughly divide the domains of home life on the one hand into areas such as health, education and culture, where the influence of the social environment is strong, and on the other into areas such as food, clothing and shelter which specify the individual lifestyle of the household. Hence, in what follows, we will analyse expenditure on food and clothing as indicative of the everyday lifestyle of the household, and medical and educational expenditure as reflecting the boundary areas between the social environment and home life.

Our first case-study concerns the X family, a wealthy and prominent household which had managed a brewing business in the village of Kosugaya on the Chita peninsula in Aichi prefecture since the Tokugawa period, and also owned land in the area. During the Meiji period, the X family branched out into beer production and the bakery industry, diversifying their management interests on the basis of their original brewing activities. Shinoda Toshio has studied the records of this family in the Tokugawa period, and has shown that the development of their brewing business depended on their ability to take advantage of the expansion of the Edo market (Shinoda, 1983).

Our second case-study concerns the K family, who lived in the village of Saigo, about 10 km south of Yamagata city in Yamagata Prefecture. In the early Tokugawa period, the family owned and farmed an average-sized holding, but thereafter gradually expanded the area they managed, so that by the early twentieth century they had become a significant owner-farmer household. The basis for their success lay in their diversification into sericulture and silk-reeling, together with the production of and trade in Japanese paper as a further by-employment. Oba Masami has researched the farm management of the K family in detail, charting its progress from owner/tenant farm household to owner-farmer and eventually cultivating landlord (Oba, 1960). He shows how the agricultural income of the household increased sharply from the second half of the 1910s, as a result of the rapid growth in its cocoon sales. Other earlier work has also looked at the consumption expenditure of the K family from 1908 onwards (Gotō, 1978, 1979). On the basis of our own analysis of these two case-studies, the final section of the chapter will compare the consumption patterns of the two households and consider how they might have been conditioned by the local environments within which they operated.

For any analysis of household account books over a sustained period, we need to take into account changes in prices, and in modern Japan there were some quite substantial price changes from the 1870s–1880s through to the 1900s, and in the latter half of the 1910s. In the case of the X family, the main period covered in the analysis is from the late 1880s through to the 1900s, but even if price changes were taken into account it would be unlikely to affect the results of the analysis. There is no doubt that in the case of the K family price changes did have an influence in the context of rapid increases in levels of household expenditure during the 1920s. However, given that the focus of our analysis in this chapter is the composition of expenditure and relative changes in its breakdown, rather than changes in the actual amount of expenditure, a detailed consideration of the issue of price changes lies beyond the scope of our argument.

The case of the X family

Food and drink

The X family's household accounts record only the total amount and value of the staple grains – rice, together with wheat, barley, and so on – that formed the basis of their diet. However, expenditure on 'supplementary' food items is recorded in much more detail, and Table 5.1 presents the breakdown of expenditure on such items for the financial years 1879, 1884, 1889, 1894, 1899, 1904, and 1909.[3] Total expenditure on these items rose from 53 yen in 1879 to 287 yen in 1899 and 399 yen in 1909. Considering first fish and meat, expenditure on fish typically continued to represent the main item in the total up to 1904, but in

[3] All subsequent references to years in the X family accounts imply financial years (March to February or February to January). Since the K family produced their own rice and rarely purchased grain, the omission of the X family's grain expenditure also aids comparison.

Table 5.1 Food expenditure, X family (yen)

Item/Financial year	1879	1884	1889	1894	1899	1904	1909
Bean curd	3	8	4	17	12	5	11
Sake	1	0	4	3	37	131	94
Seasonings	4	10	3	14	65	60	71
Fish	29	107	38	88	65	94	54
Eggs	1	3	5	12	10	51	9
Milk	0	41	43	71	56	48	39
Total meat	0	7	9	7	23	55	71
of which chicken	0	7	5	6	0	28	53
Fruit & vegetables*	15	14	9	59	19	33	51
Sub total	53	189	115	271	287	477	399
Total household expenditure	1,861	2,552	1,739	4,673	5,011	6,929	9,580

*The types of fruit and vegetables consumed could vary from year to year. The main items were ginger, lotus root, *konnyaku*, aubergine, bamboo shoot, butterbur, carrot, Japanese radish, asparagus, squash, burdock, shiitake mushroom, taro, leek and wasabi. In addition to this a number of items appeared less often such as strawberry, watermelon, citron, plum, orange, potato, persimmon, Japanese medlar, orange, chestnut, pear, royal fern and sweet potato etc.

Source: Compiled from *Nyūyōkata-tozachō*, 1879, 1884, 1889, 1894; *Shonyūyō-no-chō*, 1899, 1904, 1909. X family documents deposited in Reikei Shiryōkan.

1909 it was overtaken by expenditure on meat. The family lived in a coastal area and had usually eaten fish. They did not buy any meat or poultry in 1879 and only a little in 1894. However, from 1899 onwards, they began to purchase it on a daily basis. Most of what they bought was chicken; they occasionally bought beef, but never pork. Chicken farming had taken root and developed in Aichi prefecture in the Meiji period, and the number of chicken-breeders in the family's local area began to increase rapidly from the early twentieth century (Tokoname-shi Shi Hensan Iinkai ed., 1976). The family's purchases of chicken were mainly from local retailers, and their expenditure on it, which was negligible in the nineteenth century, started to increase in the 1900s, reaching 53 yen in 1909. Similarly, expenditure on eggs was only 1 yen in 1879 but had risen to 51 yen by 1904.

The rapid growth in the family's expenditure on chicken would thus seem to have had a connection with the development of the chicken-farming business in the local area. That is to say, the X family, as influential local entrepreneurs, actively purchased chicken and eggs so as to support the development of a new local industry. In that sense, the family's buying behaviour represented an example of the practice of so-called *chisan-chishō* – 'local production-local consumption'.

The family also purchased vegetables such as ginger, lotus root, *konnyaku* (devil's tongue paste) and aubergine every year, and in 1909 for the first time bought napa cabbage (Chinese cabbage) and navel oranges. From the beginning of the twentieth century onwards, they were thus able to buy fruits and vegetables that had not been available in the nineteenth century. In that sense, the family's diet became more varied and abundant. That said, however, the key feature of their diet, looked at as a whole, was its strongly traditional character, dominated, as in the Tokugawa period, by fruit and vegetables, supplemented with chicken produced in the local area.

It seems likely that the strength of the traditional aspects of the X household's diet was related to the nature of their family business. That is, the family's eating habits embodied the traditional eating culture expected of a sake and soy sauce brewer who was also a leader of local industry and influential in the region. The family converted their business into a company in 1898, and thereafter purchased considerable amounts of sake, soy sauce and soybean paste from it. Although after the Restoration they had tried to expand the production of beer and wine, their venture into grape cultivation in the 1880s ended in failure, and the beer company that they established was eventually taken over by a large national beer company (Handa-shi shi Hensan Iinkai, ed., 1989). The result was that the X family was unable to adapt their family business to Western-style food culture. This was the context in which the family would seem to have made a conscious choice to maintain a strong traditional emphasis in their eating habits.

Clothing

Table 5.2 shows the breakdown of the X family's clothing expenditure. The family purchased a range of clothes from retailers in a number of different places and gradually the variety of their clothing increased. The amounts spent fluctuated from year to year, depending on the scale of purchases outside the local area in the large-scale kimono shops of cities such as Nagoya and Tokyo. The family purchased textile materials for processing into splashed cotton and dyed goods locally in the village. However, since Kosugaya was an isolated farming and fishing community, they also purchased textiles from towns in various parts of the Chita peninsula, such as Handa, Kowa, and Utsumi, and from the large-scale shops dealing in kimono material that were to develop into department stores, such as the Daimaru and Itō kimono stores in Nagoya.

Table 5.2 Clothing expenditure, X family (yen)

Item/Financial year	1879	1884	1889	1894	1899	1904	1909
Cotton/hemp products	18.0	22.0	8.9	12.2	13.8	6.4	48.5
Silk products	28.0	92.8	10.6	42.0	55.0	8.7	71.8
Textile materials	14.8	36.6	19.6	29.0	19.7	17.7	14.4
Processing wages	16.2	9.2	15.8	30.6	17.9	19.2	56.7
Western-style ready-made goods	1.1	0.9	5.4	2.0	91.1	19.0	71.7
Japanese-style fancy goods	49.2	41.3	8.7	20.9	52.5	11.5	23.4
Unspecified goods of which bought in:	257.9	212.0	79.7	147.5	160.6	135.2	377.5
Nagoya	255.0	109.3	74.0	86.2	21.9	17.4	161.8
Kyoto				9.6			43.5
Tokyo					98.6	62.0	
Total	385.3	509.6	148.7	286.6	426.0	217.8	663.9

Note: Western-style ready-made goods = shirts, hats, socks etc. Japanese-style fancy goods = *obi, tabi, haori-himo* etc. Unspecified goods = items recorded only as 'clothing' etc.
Source: as Table 5.1.

The X family, like the Hiromi family described in our earlier research, were clearly sending their employees to Osaka to buy kimono material and imported goods for them. Although the Chita peninsula was famous for cotton production, it specialised in basic white cotton, and the X family had to use the large-scale Nagoya dealers when they wanted to buy more highly processed and expensive kimono material. However, they were also able to buy various textiles in Handa, the communications hub of the Chita peninsula and the centre of the brewing industry, where a number of wealthy people lived. In addition, in 1889 they purchased flannel and Chichibu textiles through their relatives, the Nakano family, who lived in Handa.

With the advent of the railway, members of the family were often able to undertake business trips, when they could purchase kimono material, and the family began to travel frequently, both within Aichi prefecture and also more widely in the Kansai region (Nakanishi, 2006–7).[4] The household head bought kimono fabric not only in Nagoya, but also, in

[4] On the increasing use of rail travel by business households elsewhere in the country, see also Nakamura's chapter (Chapter 9) in this volume.

1909, in Kyoto, and when he travelled to Tokyo in 1899 and 1904, he purchased many Western-style clothes.

On the whole, the X family tended to buy silk fabrics, which were higher-class than the cotton and hemp fabrics used for ordinary clothing. As a result, they seldom bought the locally produced white cotton and, in the case of their clothing, did not pursue the 'local production-local consumption' policy that they followed in their eating habits. Moreover, it gradually became possible to obtain Western-style clothing items and imported textiles from local retailers. For example, in 1899, the family purchased a hat and a shirt, as well as some calico, from Hikojirō, a local retailer in Utsumi. As a result, purchases of Western-style ready-made articles from local retailers increased rapidly from then on.

Healthcare

Table 5.3 details the healthcare expenditure of the X family in 1879, 1889, 1899, and 1909. Looking at their expenditure on general practitioners, it seems that the family consulted several doctors every year. Dr. Itō appears to have attended them in 1879 and 1884 and Dr. Naitō in 1889 and 1894, while Dr. Watanabe Yaichirō was their family doctor in 1899, 1904 and 1909. All of them lived in the same village as the family. However, in 1909, a child in the family was treated by Dr. Tada, a paediatrician from Nagoya (Honda, ed., 1926). When the illness was outside the scope of the local general practitioners, the family took its children to Nagoya, the largest city in Aichi prefecture, to receive specialist paediatric treatment. They thus appear to have selected doctors according to patients' symptoms.

When a member of the family was hospitalised in 1909, the hospital charges amounted to 81 yen, which represented around 37 per cent of their total medical expenditure that year. They opted for hospital treatment when the family doctor was unable to cure an illness and were prepared to pay highly for this. Similarly, large costs were involved when the family started to receive dental care, and they paid about 40 yen in 1894 and 20 yen in 1899 to dentists. They also bought home medical supplies, such as clinical thermometers in 1894 and 1909 and a catheter in 1904, as Western technology came to be applied to their treatment at home.

Turning to their purchases of medication, during the cholera epidemic of 1879, the family distributed the traditional Japanese-Chinese medicine *goreisan* to those working in their warehouses in an attempt to ward off the disease. This medicine was meant to treat diarrhoea, acute gastroenteritis, heat exhaustion, headache, and swelling (Okazaki, 1976).

Table 5.3 Medical expenditure, X family (yen)

Item/Financial year	**1879**	**1884**	**1889**	**1894**	**1899**	**1904**	**1909**
General practitioner: Total	17.8	135.6	89.2	190.7	80.6	402.5	118.5
Itō	13.3	87.1	35.3	12.0	3.0	13.2	10.6
Osawa	2.0	40.5					
Naitō			52.7	110.2			
Oda			0.2				22.0
Suzuki (dentist)				39.0		32.3	
Watanabe				6.5	55.8	140.1	73.9
Sawa (dentist)					11.7	9.0	
Watanabe(dentist)					10.1		
Higuchi						205.0	
Sugihara (ENT specialist)						0.9	
Kanō (dermatologist)						0.8	
Tada							10.0
Others	2.5	8.0	1.0	23.0		1.2	2.0
Hospital						7.0	81.3
Herbal medicine	54.1	1.5	0.1	2.4	2.4	3.2	0.9
Patent medicine	4.0	4.7		0.1			18.0
Midwife				13.0			
Nursing		3.5		1.0		5.0	
Massage				12.6			
Medical supplies				12.8		4.6	1.3
Total	77.9	145.3	89.3	232.5	83.0	422.3	219.7

Source: as Table 5.1.

The family spent 54 yen on *goreisan*, around 70 per cent of their total medical expenditure for the year. However, it appears to have had little effect, and the family also purchased dilute sulphuric acid, a Western-style medicine thought at the time to aid against diarrhoea. This was despite a government recommendation in favour of the use of carbolic acid as an antiseptic, and it is clear that the family was trying to deal with the cholera outbreak through their own types of medication.

However, by 1899 the family was purchasing carbolic acid in order to try to prevent the occurrence of infectious diseases, such as dysentery, that were spreading at that time. Between 1879 and 1899, therefore, the family's understanding of infectious diseases had clearly changed. In 1909 they bought new patent medicine made from recently discovered modern materials. On the other hand, in both 1879 and 1909, they purchased Japanese-style plasters and ointments (*kōyaku*), and they were clearly using both traditional treatments and newly available patent medicines.

Education

In Kosugaya, where the X family lived, two schools for commoners had been set up at the end of the Tokugawa period. Modern schooling began with the establishment of the national educational system in 1872, and the Reikei elementary school was founded in the village in 1874 (Tokoname-shi Shi Hensan Iinkai ed., 1976). However, the establishment of a higher elementary school in Kosugaya was delayed, and the family, along with other volunteers, founded the private Reikei School in 1888, inviting Mizoguchi Kan to become its teacher.

Table 5.4 shows the family's education-related expenditure, the main items of which were tuition fees, books and stationery. The absence of expenditure on fees in 1879 and 1884 must be explained by the fact that

Table 5.4 Educational expenditure, X family (yen)

Item/Financial year	1879	1884	1889	1894	1899	1904	1909
Books	2.0	4.0	2.3	11.1	11.6	17.3	60.0
Tuition fees			14.1	15.0	13.3	24.5	51.9
Western-style stationery		1.7	0.5	0.1	4.6	16.0	13.3
Japanese-style stationery		0.2	0.3	0.1	0.0	8.7	0.3
Cost of studying away from home		11.9		11.8			1,022.2
Educational contributions						64.5	106.6
Others			1.0	0.1	0.2	0.0	0.9
Total	2.0	17.8	18.2	38.1	29.7	131.1	1,255.0

Note: Western-style stationery = erasers, pencils etc. Japanese-style stationery = writing brushes, ink sticks etc.
Source: as Table 5.1.

there were no children of elementary-school age in the family at that time. In the year following the founding of the private school in 1888, the family paid fees for children called Izō, Nobu, Heisuke, Kumakichi and Hansuke. Entries such as 'fees for Miss Nobu' on 10 January 1890 imply that Nobu was the daughter of the X family. On the other hand, entries for 'shop Izō', 'Heisuke from the store', and 'boy Kumakichi' suggest that Izō, Heisuke, and Kumakichi were apprentices or the children of employees. The X household thus sought to educate its workers and their families by paying their educational expenses. Given their role in the establishment of the Reikei School, it is clear that the family was enthusiastic about education and believed that modern schooling was necessary both for the family and its employees.

Purchases for Izō, Nobu, and Heisuke included Western-style paper, erasers, and pencils, and we can assume that the teaching carried out in the Reikei School was Western-style. Eventually, the private school was converted into a public higher elementary school, and by 1899 the family was no longer paying the fees of apprentice boys or the children of employees.

As the number of children in the X family increased, the outlay on tuition fees rose considerably. In addition to the cost of the usual public education, one son, Hikotarō, studied at the private Takagi School in Nagoya, and the family purchased stationery for him there. By 1910, the children of the family were entering university and girls' colleges, and education-related expenditure increased rapidly. Hikotarō, although registered at Kansai College, seems to have been receiving private tuition from a Mr. Maeda, with a view to going to study in Tokyo. Another son, Manji, took classes in English, and eventually both he and Hikotarō studied in Tokyo. The family laid out 504 yen as expenses for the two people studying in Tokyo; with the inclusion of the cost of Hikotarō's time at Kansai College, the total amounted to 725 yen, and accounted for the bulk of education-related expenditure in 1909.

The family also invested in the education of their daughters, and Yuki and Ito entered Kōbe Women's College. Expenditure related to the two daughters' studying in Kōbe amounted to 208 yen. In addition, it seems that the family made its daughters learn the *koto*, and another daughter, Ume, studied English. One son, Keizō, clearly liked tennis, and items such as 'cost of racket repair' and 'tennis necessities' also appear.

The case of the K family

The X family came from the influential and wealthy local elite. In order to analyse differences in consumption patterns between social classes, we can take the owner-farmer K family as a comparison. The household accounts of the K family exist for the period from 1880 to 1950 (Zaidan Hōjin Nōsei Chōsakai, 1955), and we will use them for the period from 1880 to the 1930s.

Food and drink

The K family lived in a valley area to the south of Yamagata City. The share of fish within their supplementary food expenditure was therefore lower than that of the X family (who lived on the coast), while the shares of alcohol and seasonings were larger (Table 5.5). They rarely bought meat, and only small amounts of fruit and vegetables, and it seems that until the beginning of the twentieth century their main sources of nutrition were rice, other cereals, and sake. The family bought only traditional vegetables that had been available in the Tokugawa period, such as burdock, aubergine, potatoes and traditional melons, and their diet does not appear to have had much variety. In addition they may have grown some vegetables for their own use, but it is likely that most of their non-irrigated land was used for growing mulberry to use in their side-line sericultural activities.

Table 5.5 Food expenditure, K family (yen)

Item/Financial year	1881	1892	1902	1909	1917	1925	1933
Bean curd	0.6	0.4	0.1	0.4	1.6	5.4	2.0
Sake	5.1	0.4	5.6	23.1	6.1	23.0	23.7
Seasonings	2.3	3.0	3.2	4.7	10.0	14.5	12.3
Fish	6.1	2.3	1.4	2.8	9.9	42.0	32.7
Eggs	0.1	0.8	0.2	0.5	0.0	5.6	3.5
Milk	0.0	0.0	0.0	0.5	1.0	19.0	4.2
Meat	0.0	0.0	0.0	0.2	0.0	0.0	0.0
Fruit/Vegetables*	2.2	2.1	1.1	1.8	1.1	7.2	4.7
Food sub-total	17.1	9.3	13.4	35.3	31.8	124.5	94.5
Total household expenditure	165.5	102.4	271.8	456.4	450.2	1,853.8	896.6

* The types of fruit and vegetables consumed could vary from year to year though less than was the case in the X family. The main items were burdock, aubergine, yam, gourd, bean sprouts and *konnyaku*. In addition to this a number of items appeared less often such as leek, persimmon, Japanese radish, orange, apple, chestnut, buckwheat, watermelon, edible wild plants, garlic, mushroom, watermelon, onion, plum, peach and pear etc.

Source: compiled from *Jisakunō Nōka Kakei ni kansuru Shokiroku* (Nōsei Chōsakai, 1955).

However, their dietary pattern changed markedly from the 1920s. Expenditure on fish increased, as did the range of fish consumed. This probably reflected the development of cold-storage transport technology and the expansion of the railway network (Ko, 2009). Up to the beginning of the twentieth century, the majority of the fish purchased by the family consisted of herring caught in Hokkaidō or nearby in Yamagata Prefecture. However, from the 1920s, the family began to buy many different kinds of fish, brought to them in refrigerated transport.

Furthermore, from the 1920s the family came to purchase much more milk. They also started to buy fruit and vegetables of Western origin introduced into cultivation after the Tokugawa period, including such things as spinach, onions and bananas, and as a result their expenditure on fruit and vegetables increased. On the other hand, they hardly ever purchased meat, and even by the 1930s the meat-eating habit had not been established in the K family. In this sense, their basic diet of fish and vegetable side-dishes did not change, although the diversification into a wider range of fish and vegetables from the 1920s clearly added variety.

Clothing

Table 5.6, showing the breakdown of the K family's clothing expenditure, reveals a big turning point at the beginning of the twentieth century. Before then, during the inflationary period from 1877 to around 1880, farmers' purchasing power had increased considerably, and the family's clothing-related expenditure in 1881 was higher than in 1892. In 1878, they spent 17 yen on clothing, but in 1892 and 1902 they spent very little, and spending on higher-quality silk goods was rare. In the meantime, they purchased materials such as cotton fabrics, which they must have been using to make their own clothes at home.

However, this self-supply of clothing changed greatly from around 1909, alongside growth in the household's total expenditure. In particular, purchases of silk goods increased significantly from 1909. Although the family continued to purchase textile materials, such as cotton, they no longer wove or sewed textiles, and instead paid out wages to those making up their clothes for them. Nonetheless, the family was not purchasing ready-made Western-style goods, such as shirts, in 1909, and only began to buy these items in the late 1910s. On the other hand, they purchased a great deal of Japanese-style underwear, such as long drawers, as well as many Japanese-style clothes and accessories, such as *tabi* and *yukata*, and their clothing culture remained firmly Japanese-style. With the considerable rise in their income in the 1920s, their clothing

Table 5.6 Clothing expenditure, K family (yen)

Item/Year	1881	1892	1902	1909	1917	1925	1933
Cotton and hemp products	5.3	2.2	0.4	1.8	0.2	10.4	7.0
Silk products	7.1			13.9	6.7	43.3	3.1
Textile materials	0.3	0.6	1.9	4.0	2.3	9.0	1.1
Processing wages	2.1			10.5	1.4	8.4	
Western-style ready-made goods					2.8	8.1	4.4
Japanese-style fancy goods	2.1	1.7	2.7	6.1	6.5	19.3	3.6
Kimono	11.4	1.9	3.3	2.3	3.7	6.9	1.7
Underwear	1.8	0.0	0.4	4.9	10.4	14.7	2.5
Purchase of cloth for kimonos				3.5			44.3
Other	0.1	0.0					
Total	30.1	6.3	8.8	47.0	33.9	120.0	67.6

Note: definitions as Table 5.2. Purchase of cloth for kimonos = expenditure on items apparently bought from non-local kimono shops.

Source: as Table 5.5.

expenditure also increased, but the most rapid growth was in high-class Japanese-style silk clothing, including *tsumugi* silk and *haori* jackets. Although they did purchase shirts and cotton flannel for Western-style clothing, they continued to buy Japanese-style underwear and kimono accessories, such as *obi* sashes and *han'eri* collars, and the majority of their purchases were of Japanese-style goods. The clothing culture of the K family thus remained Japanese-style.[5]

In 1933, however, their clothing culture at last began to change. For example, they purchased two items from the Igarashi kimono store, costing 39 yen, which were described as 'coats' (*uwagi*). This was a new term and it seems from their prices that these must have been Western-style overcoats. In various places it is clear that the family was buying goods that they had not obviously purchased up to the 1920s, such as, in 1933, children's hats. Moreover, these purchases were not made solely from the Igarashi kimono shop. In 1933 there were purchases

[5] Collars and other accessories are among the items mentioned in Francks' discussion of Japanese fashions in this volume.

from the Itō kimono shop, which developed into a department store, and it seems likely that these were made by mail order (for mail order purchases see Mitsuzono, 2009). Although there were no department stores in Saigo, where the family lived, they were able to use mail order to purchase modern goods from big-city department stores. Through diversification and change in the retail outlets and methods that they used, therefore, the first signs of Westernisation began to appear in the K family's clothing style in the 1930s.

Healthcare

Table 5.7 shows the K family's medical expenditures, and reveals that these were very small in 1878 and 1892, amounting to less than 1 yen per year. Most of their medical expenditure involved the purchase of herbal and patent medicines, reflecting the fact that at this time the family was trying to treat its illnesses itself. However, from the beginning of the twentieth century their payments to local general practitioners started to increase, and their total medical expenditure rose to 11 yen, as they started to use a family doctor. Judging from the amounts paid out and the periods of treatment, from the 1910s to the 1930s the family's doctor was Dr. Kobayashi. However, they still did not depend entirely on him, and although the share of doctor's fees in their medical expenditure rose, they continued to purchase medicines to treat themselves.

Later on, in 1920, a member of the family had to enter hospital in Yamagata city, not far from the family's home. As a result, their medical expenditure increased markedly, rising to 328 yen in 1920, with hospital charges making up about half of the total. Doctors' fees and the cost of medicines each came to more than 60 yen, and the family's medical expenditure that year was thus substantial.

Alongside the cost of doctors' fees and pharmaceuticals, new items were also entering the family's household expenditure, including, from 1914, eye lotions and eye wash, from 1917, acupuncture and massage, and from 1920 hot spring cures. In this way, from the 1910s at least, the family was able to expand its choice of medical treatment, as a result of its increasing income.

Education

The education-related expenditure of the K family was also quite small in the late nineteenth century (Table 5.8). By 1909, the family was beginning to spend more money on schooling, and educational expenditure

Table 5.7 Medical expenditure, K family (yen)

Item/Year	1878	1892	1906	1911	1914	1917	1920	1923	1926	1929	1933
General practitioner											
Total	0.1		10.0	10.6	12.2	7.5	82.4	43.7	39.1	9.4	11.7
Umezu	0.1			10.1	3.6	0.2	10.5				
Kobayashi				0.5	8.6	4.2	65.5	28.4	35.6	5.5	6.1
Asakura						2.0					
Sasaki						1.1	6.4				5.6
Nihonmatsu								7.8			
Others			10.0					7.5	3.5	3.9	
Hospital											
Total							156.0	7.2			
Shiseido							156.0				
Saiseikan								7.2			
Herbal medicine	0.1	0.4	0.1	0.4		0.1	63.4	4.6	6.1	12.4	4.4
Patent medicine		0.1				0.2	4.0	5.9	8.1	11.3	3.8
Medicine from peddlers						2.2	7.5		8.8		
Eye lotion					0.2	1.3	0.1	2.4		0.5	
Acupuncture/Massage						0.6	2.4	1.1	15.5	7.1	3.4
Hot springs							5.0	14.5	7.9	17.0	
Others							7.4	2.7	4.2		
Total	0.2	0.5	10.1	11.0	12.4	11.9	328.2	82.1	89.7	57.7	23.3

Note: Milk, eggs, and beef consumed for medicinal purposes were included in Table 5.5, and are therefore not included in this table.
Source: as Table 5.5.

Table 5.8 Educational expenditure, K family (yen)

Item/Year	1881	1892	1902	1909	1917	1925	1933
Books	0.2	0.1	2.9		1.1	15.8	0.2
Tuition fees	0.2	1.0	5.8	30.7	5.1	16.0	7.9
Stationery					0.8	2.6	0.9
Educational contributions				0.3	1.6		
Total	0.4	1.1	8.6	31.0	8.5	34.4	8.9

Source: as Table 5.5.

continued to increase as the children went on to higher elementary school. Thereafter, although the family's income was increasing, educational expenses fluctuated greatly year on year. This is explained by the fact that the scale of educational expenditure depended on the ages of the children in the household and so was not necessarily correlated with income. Similarly, medical expenditure fluctuated sharply, depending on whether family members fell sick.

In practice, the family laid out 11 yen in tuition fees to Kaminoyama School in 1925, with the result that its education-related expenditure that year was significantly higher than in 1917 or 1933 when they had no children enrolled in the school. However, since the family did not have the financial resources to enable it to send children to higher educational institutions away from home, its overall expenditure on education was considerably less than that of the X family.

Conclusion

Comparing the cases of the X and K families, as far as eating patterns are concerned, it is clear that both households retained traditional Tokugawa-period ways until the late nineteenth century. Their diets gradually began to alter from the beginning of the twentieth century, and in the 1920s in particular change was significant. The eating habits of both families became more varied and abundant, through diversification in the kinds of fish and vegetables that they consumed. The X family increased their purchases of chicken rapidly in the early twentieth century, but this was related to the development of local industry and may not necessarily have been because they particularly liked it. In fact they had purchased chicken from a travelling seller in 1889, but it seems that it was not much to the family's taste, and they did not purchase any chicken at all in 1899. Thereafter, once the local chicken-farming business started up at the beginning of the twentieth century, they regularly purchased chicken from local retailers.

As regards the purchase of clothing, neither in Saigo, where the K family lived, nor in Kosugaya, where the X family lived, were there modern shops or department stores dealing in kimono. However, from the beginning of the Meiji period, the X family was making shopping trips to Nagoya, and they had many opportunities to come into contact with Western-style clothing. In Nagoya and in Tokyo too, they purchased not only expensive kimono but also Western-style clothing, and it is clear that Western clothing culture had become part of the life of the X family from quite early on. However, at the same time, they continued to purchase many Japanese-style clothes, and it is probable that their everyday clothing culture remained largely Japanese-style.

On the other hand, the K family had almost no opportunity to come into contact with Western-style clothing culture until the 1930s, and till then their experience was limited to the occasional purchase of a shirt. However, by the 1930s the big-city department stores were in increasing competition with each other, and began to put more resources into door-to-door sales and mail order so as to increase sales in rural areas (Mitsuzono, 2009). As a result, the K family had more opportunity to encounter Western-style clothing, and they began to purchase Western-style coats and hats. In this way, Western clothing culture gradually came to permeate into rural areas remote from the big cities.

The similarities and differences in the families' healthcare can be observed in the changes in their medical expenditure. The owner-farmer K family began to receive treatment from general practitioners in the 1900s, but before that, as long as they thought they were dealing with a minor sickness, they diagnosed their own ailments, selected medicine and tried to make themselves well. That is to say, they mainly used self-medication, although the medicines they used for this did change over time. The members of the X family, on the other hand, were already receiving treatment from general practitioners in 1880, and even changed their family doctor several times in the 1880s and 1890s.

However, both families chose to use hospitals, the leading providers of medical services at that time, when a member was seriously ill, even though this cost them considerable sums. At the same time, the types of medical service that the families selected also reflected the difference in social class between wealthy families and farmers. The members of the K family underwent acupuncture, hot spring cures and bloodletting as treatment for the fatigue resulting from their heavy work schedule in farming and by-employments. Judging from their medical expenditure, no such kinds of treatment were required by the X family.

Education-related expenditure, like medical expenditure, fluctuated sharply year on year. In particular, the X family laid out large sums on education while their children were studying in higher educational institutions away from home. Although the K family, not having the financial scope to send their children to study away from home, had much smaller educational expenditures than the X family, they did lay out a certain amount in tuition fees when their children went on to higher elementary school. Nonetheless, it remained difficult for farming families to enable their children to achieve higher academic qualifications. In this sense, although the gap between the medical and educational expenditures of the two households was usually no more than could be explained by the income gap between them, when special situations arose, such as sickness in the family or the need to study away from home, a clear difference emerged between the two income brackets. Thus it appears that the income and price elasticities of medical and educational expenditures were higher than those of food- and clothes-related expenditure.

As mentioned above, in the consumer life of modern Japan, regional differences between urban and rural areas and differences between income groups and occupations were related to each other in complex ways, and elements of the Western lifestyle came to spread in a somewhat piecemeal fashion. Families such as the X family continued to lead a predominantly Japanese-style life, while expanding the range of items consumed as their income and circumstances changed and their options widened. Into their Japanese-style meal patterns came the chicken that they consumed (possibly reluctantly) in order to promote a local industry; as improvements to the transport infrastructure opened up the possibility of more trips to the kimono shops of the big cities, so also did Western-style items began to enter their wardrobes; when required, modern hospitals and doctors trained in Western medicine could be called in when traditional forms of treatment were inadequate.

For family K, the enjoyment of such options depended on the growth in their income, as they began to profit from the expanding market of industrialising Japan, but they too, if with a lag compared to the X family, were eventually able to incorporate both a wider range of Japanese-style items and the occasional new product into their diets and wardrobes, and to employ modern medical services in emergencies.

The families' surviving account books can thus help us to understand the details of the complex process of consumption growth, as it spread from town to country and from the well-off to the more average, in a modernising and industrialising society.

References

Chūbu Katei Keieigaku Kenkyūkai (ed.) (1972) *Meijiki Katei Seikatsu no Kenkyū* (Research on Daily Life in the Meiji Period), Tokyo: Domesu Shuppan.

Gotō, K. (1978–79) 'K-ke Kakei Kiroku no Seikatsushiteki Kenkyū' (Research on the History of Lifestyles from the Household Record of the K Family), pts 1–2, *Iwate Daigaku Kyōikugakubu Kenkyū Nenpō*, vols. 38–39, pp. 85–109 (pt 1), pp. 19–48 (pt 2).

Handa-shi Shi Hensan Iinkai (ed.) (1989) *Shinshū Handa-shi Shi* (A New Version of the History of Handa City), Handa City: Handa City Government.

Honda, R. (ed.) (1926) *Nihon Isekiroku* (Japan Doctor's List 2nd edition), Tokyo: Ijijironsha.

Ko, U. (2009) *Senkanki Nihon no Suisanbutsu Ryūtsū* (Distribution of Marine Products in Interwar Japan), Tokyo: Nihon Keizai Hyōronsha.

Mitsuzono, I (2009) 'Senzenki Nihon ni okeru Daitoshi Gofukukei Hyakkaten no Tsūshin Hanbai' (The Mail Order Business of the Big City Kimono Stores in Interwar Japan), *Keiei Shigaku*, vol.44, no.1, pp. 31–57.

Nakamura, T. (ed.) (1993), *Kakeibō kara mita Kindai Nihon Seikatsushi* (The History of Daily Life in Modern Japan through Household Accounts), Tokyo: University of Tokyo Press.

Nakanishi, S. (2000) 'Bunmei Kaika to Minshū Seikatsu' (Civilization and Enlightenment and People's Lives), in Ishii, K., Hara, A. & Takeda, H. (eds), *Nihon Keizaishi 1, Bakumatsu Ishinki* (Economic History of Japan, 1 The *Bakumatsu* and Restoration Period), Tokyo: University of Tokyo Press, pp. 217–81.

Nakanishi, S. (2006–07) 'Yusōmō no Kindaika to Tabibunka no Henyō' (Modernization of Transportation Network and Change of Travel Culture, pts 1–2), *Keizai Kagaku* (Nagoya University), vol. 54, nos 3–4, pp. 25–48 (pt 1), pp. 63–90 (pt 2).

Nōsei Chōsakai (1955) *Jisakunō Nōka Kakei ni kansuru Shokiroku* (Records relating to Household Accounts of Self-cultivating Farmers), Zaidan Hōjin Nōsei Chōsakai.

Oba, M. (1960) *Nōka Keiei no Shiteki Bunseki* (Historical Analysis of Farm Household Management), Tokyo: Nōgyō Sōgō Kenkyū Jo.

Okazaki, K. (1976) *Kusuri no Rekishi* (History of Pharmacy), Tokyo: Kōdansha.

Shinoda, T. (1983) 'Chitashu no Shijō' (The Market for Chita-zake), Toyota Kōgyō Kōtō Senmon Gakkō Kenkyū Kiyō, vol.16 *Senmon Gakkō Kenkyū Kiyō*, pp. 13–20.

Tokoname-shi Shi Hensan Iinkai (ed.) (1976) *Tokoname-shi Shi* (History of Tokoname City) Tokoname City: Tokoname City Government.

6

Sweetness and Empire: Sugar Consumption in Imperial Japan

Barak Kushner

Introduction

Sugar has featured strongly in analyses of the consumer revolutions in Europe and North America, with a growing literature looking at the ways in which industrialisation and the consequent changes in social and working lives conditioned the growth of sugar consumption (Mintz 1985; Mazumdar 1998; Akesaka 2002; Woloson 2002). In Japan, too, sugar consumption grew significantly over the course of industrialisation, and this chapter will consider some of the ways in which the sweetness of sugar increasingly came to be incorporated into the everyday lives of Japanese people, as an indicator of rising levels of 'modernity', and as a harbinger of Japan's arrival on the international imperial stage. Japan's mounting consumption of sweet things, from the Meiji era through to the post-war period, depended in part on technological progress in food manufacturing, but must also be explained as the result of the advertising of new treats processed with sugar, and the expansion of imperial possessions to be developed according to an 'industrial' agricultural policy. All these changes galvanised the gustatory interest in what were frequently deemed 'foreign' flavours and tastes.

The market for sugary products certainly predates the Meiji Restoration, but these developments forcefully opened up the previously rather closed world of Japanese dietary preferences, especially with the appearance of items such as chocolate, caramel, and sweetened 'health' drinks. My research considers how such products altered the concept of 'sweetness', as embodied in items processed with sugar, as an element in 'modern' food; it also considers how the consumption of sweet products operated in the economic and imagined cultural landscape. The images created assisted in raising the profile of sugar, and hence its consumption, and shifted the meaning of 'sweet' in modern Japan. I argue that although sugar was consumed as a luxury item in the early-modern period, in the early decades of the twentieth century, and especially during the war years, the consumption of sweets became inseparable from the idea of Japanese modernity, linked to the act of consumption within the sphere of Japanese empire.

My purpose in this chapter is therefore to examine the historical drivers of the growth in the consumption of sugar in Japan. This process began with Meiji-period changes in Japanese food culture, but the resulting market forces were combined with an influx of imported 'new' sugar from Taiwan from the late nineteenth century, as a prime means of 'assisting' the imperial economy. This created the opportunity for new Meiji- and Taishō-era businesses to ride a wave of mass culture and media by means of the development of new sugary imperial products to feed the nation. I define consumption broadly, along the lines suggested by de Grazia, in terms of 'processes of commodification, spectatorship, commercial exchanges, and social welfare reforms, processes that involve the desire for and sale, purchase and use of durable and non-durable goods, collective services and images' (de Grazia, 1996, p. 4). John Clammer further argues that studying consumption in this way can assist our historical understanding because 'consumption reveals cultural patterns and economic organization in a clearer light' (Clammer, 1997, p3). The rising national digestion of sweets also reflects the rise of consumerism, which Peter Stearns defines as characteristic of 'a society in which many people formulate their goals in life partly through acquiring goods that they clearly do not need for subsistence or for traditional display' (Stearns, 2001, p. ix).

Nonetheless, as Francks has pointed out, 'work on Japan's economic history has continued to concentrate, for the most part, on the supply side, and, insofar as it has considered final consumption, the question has remained "how much?" (very often with the underlying query "enough?"), rather than "what?" or "why?"' (Francks, 2009a, p. 136; see also Francks, 2009b). In what follows, I will attempt to address this lacuna by analysing the changing ways in which 'sweetness' was conceived in Japanese society and the manner in which sugary products were sold, thereby providing a basis for considering the 'why', as well as the 'how much' of sugar consumption in Japan.

Pre-Meiji roots

The history of sugar in modern Japan is the result of a nexus of changing consumer patterns, an expanding market culture and an imperial colonial policy able to feed consumer needs. However, sugar was not a product new to Meiji Japan; it had already been a prized commodity for centuries, originally introduced from China, Korea, and Okinawa, and was a staple feature of *wagashi*, traditional Japanese-style desserts served at court and during elite tea ceremonies. Eric Rath, in his analysis of Tokugawa-era treats, suggests that early-modern confections might not in fact have been particularly sweet, 'but they did hold other significance for the banquet participants' (Rath, 2008, pp. 45–46). The sweets served at shogunal gatherings typically remained true to the original definition of the Japanese word for them (*kashi*), meaning fruit, but the term was also used for items made with sugar, and the south of Japan was already home to many kinds of the saccharine elixir.

Hence, although sugar undoubtedly commanded a high price as a luxury product in Edo, by the later part of the Tokugawa era it was also starting to be made into various confections that were sold on the street to large numbers of the lower classes (Itō, 2008, p. 41). According to the historian Ujima Eishun, during the later Edo period the number of sweet-pedlars plying their trade in urban areas grew exponentially. Such individuals are picturesquely detailed in the *Morisada Mankō*, a collection of diaries and notes describing life and daily customs in late-Tokugawa Japan that specifically cites the proliferation of sweets for sale in Osaka, Kyoto and Edo (Kitagawa, 1992). Like other food pedlars, sellers of sweets would often perambulate with a portable shop strung between two poles, or set down a large barrel, unfurl an umbrella to keep the sweets from melting under the hot sun, and wait for passers-by to stop and purchase a treat (Ujima, 2009, p. 41). Constantine Vaporis analyses the impact of the alternate attendance (*sankin kōtai*) regulations that kept many on the highways during the Tokugawa era. These laws, at least in part, helped form the basis of modern Japanese culture, leading to the development of roads, markets and travel, and thereby creating 'an instant class of consumers' (Vaporis, 2008, p. 192).

Many of the new foodstuffs and foodways emerging in Tokugawa Japan had entered the country via Nagasaki, the portal to China and the Netherlands for much of the medieval and early-modern period, and this was reflected in the means of selling them, influenced by customs that could be imagined as 'foreign', even if not conforming to actual foreign practice. During the Edo period it was common for individuals to don what the Japanese considered 'Chinese' costume, and go out on to the streets to sell sweets. These salespeople became known as *tōjin* sweet-pedlars. *Tōjin* was originally an ancient term for 'Chinese', but the label had stuck, even some thousand years after the initial diplomatic missions to China. The pedlars often dressed in a Chinese style, and their drum-playing was accompanied by something called a *charumela*, from the Portuguese term for 'a little trumpet' (Ujima, 2009, p. 55). The peddlars' songs were often far from clear – many were just trying to imitate the Chinese language or what it sounded like to them – but what mattered was the exotic nature of the act of purchasing sweets. Such activities continued well into the late-Meiji period and reached all corners of the nation, as pre-Meiji practice continued to condition the forms of consumption within the newly industrialising and urbanising society that Japan was to become (Ujima, 2009, pp. 56–57).

Meiji developments[1]

In his evaluation of the radical shifts in the Japanese lifestyle from the mid-nineteenth to the early-twentieth century, the Japanese anthropologist Yanagita Kunio noted that what people ate became 'warmer, softer, and sweeter' (Yanagita, 1976, p. 60). The practice of taking tea breaks, often involving small meals, was beginning to develop, so that 'the spread of tea in the Meiji period led to an increased number of short resting periods in farming villages, and at times even people who were not working at all began to drink cup after cup out of boredom' (Yanagita, 1957, p. 44). This created a rising demand for snacks, and tea-cakes (*chagashi*) were increasingly consumed to accompany the beverage during the tea break. Although sugar was not widely used in traditional Japanese cuisine and average daily consumption of sugar in the nineteenth century was low in comparison to that in the West, Japan's subsequent imperial expansion into Taiwan and the development of new manufacturing technology enabled Meiji-era businessmen to produce, and imperial subjects to consume, new goods that raised the profile of sugar and greatly expanded the market for confectionery products. One of the biggest changes that allowed for this transformation was the

---

[1] I would like to thank Professor Satoru Nakanishi for correcting several of my misconceptions about the consumption of sugar in Meiji Japan. Unfortunately, space limitations have meant that I have been unable to incorporate many of his suggestions.

shift from the production of 'black' sugar from Japan's southern islands, including Okinawa, to the domestic processing of imported cane sugar from Taiwan into white sugar.

Nonetheless, although the Meiji Japanese liked sugary concoctions, they did not immediately take to foreign products based on tastes found in Europe and the United States. The 1871 Iwakura mission to the United States and Europe at one point stopped for a first taste of chocolate, while visiting a confectionery factory in France. The product was so unknown that no word had yet been created for it, so Chinese characters appropriate to the pronunciation were chosen, and pronounced *chokorēto*. However, the flavour was far from appreciated, since products that smelled of butter and milk were regarded as repellent (Nihon Chokorēto Kokoa Kyōkai, 1958, pp. 7–8). This was not an uncommon experience, and reports from personal travels and diplomatic and trade missions abound in complaints regarding Western dining fashions. Ambassador Shinmi Masaoki wrote in his diary that he could not stomach most of the banquets in America, ate little, and often waited until he had retired to his room so he could cook miso soup. Nonomura Tadazane recorded that the shipboard menu was no better, lamenting that 'the only thing I could eat was bread. I put some sugar on the bread so that I might not starve' (Katō 1975, p. 194; Finn n.d., p. 24).

However, as the Meiji era developed, sugar and sweets slowly became staples not only of Japanese entertainment and upper-class banqueting, but also of a broader popular culture, depicted in children's stories and consumed as part of daily life. What had once been unappreciated became over time something to be gobbled up by hungry children and adults, while worming its way into the subconsciousness of the society through literature, advertising, and commerce. A prominent *rakugo* comedy story that appears to have originated in the early modern era, the tale *Filial Sweets*, involves a stupid commoner named Yōtarō. The nature of the skit suggests the extent to which sweets were by this time part of everyday life (Yano, 2002, pp. 83–87 and see Figure 6.1). The proliferation of 'Chinese peddlers' who sold their sugary treats in urban neighbourhoods, shouting 'sweets for sale, sweets for sale', became an aural trope of the era and a source of amusement for audiences watching the routine performed live. The humour translates poorly into English so it is not worth repeating here, but the fact that comedy now hinged on stories surrounding sweets and their consumption reveals how commonplace they had become in Meiji-era popular culture.

Figure 6.1 A sweet-seller (top left) in Meiji-period Tokyo. He is of the sort described in the *rakugo* sketch, and is pictured here amongst other tradesmen. He is shown balancing a huge assortment of treats on a tray on his head.

Source: Hiraide, 1902, p. 46.

Sugar and Japanese imperialism

As the pace of industrialisation and urbanisation increased through the early twentieth century, Japanese people came to consume ever greater amounts of sugary products. Comparative and European historical research concerning the growth in personal consumption of luxury goods as an indicator of expanding national wealth suggests the need to look more closely at the situation in East Asia (Pomeranz, 2002; de Vries, 2008). Preliminary findings imply that sugar fitted easily into pre-existing domestic food consumption habits and then merged seamlessly into the mass culture generated by the birth of modern advertising. For these reasons, confectionery, as a subset of the range of sugar products, can be used as a case-study to demonstrate how nationalism, imperialism, and the idea of 'modernity' (embodied in such things as forms of packaging and an emphasis on hygiene) came to be used in campaigns that resulted in the promotion of sugar consumption.

The key factor in this process was Japan's acquisition of Taiwan in 1895. Taiwan was already a major locus of sugar production, as indicated in reports of contemporary observers. James W. Davidson, a member of the Peary Arctic expedition who stopped over on the island of Taiwan for a stay that coincided exactly with the start of the first Sino-Japanese War (1894–95), observed in his memoir that even prior to the initiation of Japanese colonial policy, the production of sugar engaged a large proportion of the people and land, and in terms of profit was surpassed only by tea plantations. In 1890, the British consular attaché, W. Wykeham Myers, reported that 'Formosa is exceptionally fortunate in possessing in Japan a large market to which it can gain entrance on more favourable terms than will probably ever be offered foreign sugar producing lands' (Davidson, 1988, p. 452).

Even before colonial imports of sugar began, many authors were already 'sugarcoating' Japanese imperialism through the medium of children's literature. Kyō no Warabe's story, *Momotarō Now*, published in April 1895, appeared just as Taiwan had come under Japanese control, but before formal colonial structures were implemented. Momotarō, the peach boy, is an iconic symbol of the Japanese nation in children's stories, and in this iteration of the story an old man and woman each receive peach-shaped sweets as souvenirs from Tokyo. They are amazed to find inside the first sweet a small bugle, in the second a Japanese flag, and in the third Momotarō (Henry, 2009, pp. 221–22). Momotarō is described as defeating the devils (*oni*) on 'devil island' (Onigashima), which is imagined in the story as Taiwan and depicted as the site of barbaric acts against Japan some time in the not-too-distant past (Fraleigh, 2010, pp. 43–66). In the surrender ceremony, the devil offers Momotarō a large cup filled with a sweet liquid made from the sugar cane that was one of the chief products of the island. The story then puns that the hero named the island 'Taiwan,' using the Chinese characters that mean 'big cup'. Literary scholar David Henry posits that the 'story framed colonialism as an adventure with sweet rewards for children that could be easily appreciated' (Henry, 2009, pp. 221–22).

Japanese sugar production did not get going immediately, but it did not take long. Taiwan was the site of the first imperial company set up abroad with Japanese national capital, so it was of prime importance for Japan's international image that it should succeed. According to historian Kubo Fumikatsu, it was recognised that if Japan could establish an effective sugar industry on the island, it would contribute significantly to the overall success of Japanese imperialism, but equally, if the venture failed, the effects would be quite damaging. In December 1900 the company began operations under Japanese oversight (Kubo, 1997, p. 30).

The perplexing issue nonetheless remains as to why, by the early twentieth century, the authorities believed they needed to supply so much sugar to Japan, given that it was not necessarily a native delicacy. The answer lies in part in the fact that sugar production fitted in with a colonial policy designed to create an economic showpiece of Taiwan, but it is clear that policy also had to take account of insatiable and growing consumer demand. According to estimates quoted by Mazumdar, annual per capita consumption of sugar in Japan had risen from 2.27 kg in 1888 to 4.55 kg in 1897, reaching 5.45 kg by 1903. Production in Japan's Ryūkyū islands was able to meet less than one-fifth of this growing domestic demand (Mazumdar, 1998, p. 375).

Through the Meiji era, therefore, not only was sugar becoming an increasingly popular additive to snacks, but confectionery treats were also turning into big business. However, this growth in consumption was not a foregone conclusion: as the next section ('The early twentieth-century confectionery boom') will show, it depended in significant ways on the means, particularly advertising, through which the public learned to appreciate sweetness and purchase sugar products.

The early twentieth-century confectionery boom

One feature frequently glossed over in historical studies of consumption is the linkage between the act of consuming and advertising. Yamamoto Taketoshi, the doyen of the modern history of advertising in Japan, has remarked that advertising should be regarded as an indispensable aspect of modern Japanese society, shaping and pulling it into new directions. Yet, despite its being an integral element of the 'consumption society', at least as far as pre- and early post-war Japan is concerned, most research has focused on the government's campaigns to resist 'excessive' consumption, and this tendency has shaded our historical understanding (Yamamoto, 1984, p. iii).

Yamamoto's research on the period from the first Sino-Japanese War through the Russo-Japanese War and into the First World War suggests that the commercialisation of newspapers and magazines continued to increase

(Yamamoto, 1984, p. 117). Revenues rose not only due to an expansion in readership, but also because the advertising fees collected by newspapers increased; these were invested in news production, producing a further boost in circulation. As changes in transport, commerce and the national diet speeded up, so too did the development of advertising. Tokugawa-period practices were not entirely abandoned, and many companies continued to employ *chindonya* – colourful street performers who used music to draw crowds – to boost sales or announce a new product. However, there is no doubt that a revolution was occurring, not only in the ways in which producers used advertising to entrance the public with their products, but also in the fundamental areas of product design and packaging.

References to new products and snacks were frequent in the expanded media. For example, a popular children's favourite publicised at the time was the mellifluously labelled 'Smash the Baltic Fleet Memorial Tōgō Marshmallow,' commemorating Admiral Tōgō Heihachirō's stupendous victory over the Russian fleet at the Battle of Tsushima in 1905 (Shōwa Joshi Daigaku Shokumotsu Kenkyūshitsu, 1971, p. 278). At the same time, newspapers were not only highlighting advertisements for sugary snacks, but also publishing pieces by gourmet writers, such as Murai Gensai, whose fictional accounts of fine dining in *Kuidōraku* (*The Gourmand*) were later published in book form and became a runaway bestseller, selling over 100,000 copies (Aoyama, 2003, p. 253. See also Aoyama, 2008).

Within this expanded promotional framework, readers/consumers of Meiji advertising campaigns for foreign candies, soaps and so on perused detailed advertisements that often had to include fairly long explanations of what the products were. Companies battled it out to gain a domestic following for Western-style treats such as chocolate and caramels, revolutionising advertising with the use of colour inserts and branding involving new national slogans (Yamamoto and Tsuganezawa, 1986, p. 196). An example of this is provided by the case of caramel, which interestingly (given its prevalence in Japanese convenience stores today) was not initially promoted successfully in Japan. At first, orders came mostly from foreigners living in Japan, while Japanese consumers failed to appreciate caramel products, finding the butter and milk smell too overpowering, even 30 years after the Iwakura Mission's first complaints (Yamamoto and Tsuganezawa, 1986, p. 199). Despite this, the charter of the Meiji Confectionery Company declared that the essential level of civilisation or barbarity of a nation could be measured by the amount of sugar or sweets consumed, emphasising the cultural push behind the idea of 'sweetness' in early twentieth-century Japan (Meiji Seika Shashi Henshū Iinkai, 1968, p. 40).

In 1899, on the cusp of the change in public eating habits, Morinaga Taichirō strode on to the national stage to start selling chocolate, caramel, marshmallows and banana-flavoured treats. Morinaga had gone to the United States at the age of 24, becoming a Christian and staying for over a decade. Many of his sweets were advertised bilingually on the label, with English words offering a certain frisson of foreignness to the consuming public. Nevertheless, few appreciative consumers came forward and a mass market for foreign sweets was slow to materialise. Even students, growing in number and eating out more at night, preferred the cheaper varieties of domestic sweets, such as *yōkan*, a sweetened bean paste, and the slivers of yams or sweet potatoes for sale on the streets (Inoue, 2010, p. 169).

The Morinaga Company therefore had its work cut out to convince more Japanese consumers that foreign sweets were tasty. Near the turn of the century, when per capita incomes were still too low to guarantee that most consumers would want or be able to buy packages or blocks of candy, Morinaga, like most other companies, sold its sweets as loose items. It subsequently pioneered the innovatory practice of placing a few items together in a bag and selling it for small change. In 1908, the company crafted a small tin in which several of its milk caramels could be carried about and eaten outside or while walking (Morinaga Seika Kabushikigaisha Henshū, 2000, p. 58). This hand-held carrying device allowed treats to be consumed in ways that were previously not available. Building on that success, the company started putting a few caramels in a small box with the slogan 'Get the sweet taste in your mouth – one bag, one *sen*' (Morinaga Seika Kabushikigaisha Henshū, 2000, p. 54). Yamamoto Taketoshi differs on the details of timing and price, claiming that the pocket-size box of caramels, with 20 in a box for 10 *sen*, was first launched as a product at the 1914 Tokyo Expo (Yamamoto and Tsuganezawa, 1986, p. 201), but it is clear that, whenever it appeared, the small tin box was not only new, but a harbinger of modernity, breaking with the past practice of selling sweets in the ways previously used by the 'Chinese' pedlars. People could now eat caramels wherever they wanted, for instance while attending one of the increasing number of cinemas that offered a new pastime for those living in urban areas.

Nonetheless, the manner in which sugary treats were sold did not change overnight. Not only did pedlars continue to sell their candies to children in the various villages and neighbourhoods, but traditional scrap dealers encouraged housewives and children to trade metal scraps for sweets, in the manner of recycling schemes nowadays (Ujima, 2009,

Figure 6.2 Sweet-sellers in colonial Korea
Source: Tōkanfu, 1910 (no page numbers).

p. 62). Ujima makes the case that pedlars' exaggerated costumes were not in fact Chinese but originally Korean, dating back to the numerous Korean missions that visited Japan, but these origins then became distorted in public memory. Certainly, from around the time of Korean annexation in 1910, numerous accounts of the activities of actual Korean sweet-pedlars were appearing in newspapers (see Figure 6.2). Koreans often worked in low-paying, strenuous jobs in mines, foundries and so on, and many went into the side-business of selling sweets as a means to earn extra money or to avoid backbreaking alternative forms of employment (Ujima, 2009, p. 121; see also Silverberg, 2006, pp. 206–12).

The competition was on, with a tussle for sales between traditional sweets and the more commercially produced and manufactured confections of modern companies. In this battle, Morinaga employed whatever new advertising opportunities were available, for example purchasing a truck, a rare sight at that time, and using the vehicle not only to deliver stock but as a form of advertising in itself. There were so few trucks in Japan then that the Morinaga truck license plate merely displayed the number 2. Morinaga sold modern candies in modern boxes and now transported them using the latest technology. After the success of the truck as a form of mobile advertising, Morinaga also started a band, made up of 17 people wearing smart uniforms, to publicise its products, building on the *chindonya* practice, and the company's concerted effort in design, product placement and packaging helped push sales upward. During the early era of imperialism, the Morinaga Company was not only selling domestically but also internationally, making forays into Korea, Taiwan and China to sell its products. Companies and factories were established in Hōten (Shenyang), Pyongyang, Taipei, and elsewhere. Morinaga candy stores grew popular throughout the empire, but also in peripheral locations such as Hong Kong (Morinaga Seika, 2000, pp. 112–13).

However, if Morinaga had established one of Japan's first confectionery manufacturers, it was the Meiji Confectionery Company that in 1916 beat him to the punch by making milk chocolate bars available for the first time in Japan. Confectionery products were growing in popularity due to the variety of ways in which the expanding Japanese repertoire of sugar-based products fulfilled functions within an emerging urban industrial society. Sugar on bread represented a quick and easy breakfast, at a time when it normally took two hours to cook rice, and this was further popularised as a sign of cultured living (*bunka seikatsu*) in Natsume Sōseki's novel *I am a Cat*.

The rise in sugar consumption also reflected the way in which, during the Meiji and Taishō eras, sugar had come to represent society's level of civilisation and understanding of nutrition. In fact, at the turn of the century, Tokyo Imperial University Professor Kawamoto Teisuke implored Japanese people to eat *more* sugar because he had calculated this was a less expensive way of acquiring calories at a time when staple food prices were rising.[2] Japan's imperial expansion, especially the colonisation of Taiwan and associated plans for sugar production, would provide the necessary imports for this transformation to be achieved. Estimates

---

[2] This was a common refrain. Nihon Hyōronsha (1926, p. 121) also published evidence that sugar offered needed calories. One could digest it during mountain climbing, and soldiers could carry it with them, making it a convenient form of nutrition. The report advised that, for its small weight and size, sugar provided a good-value source of the calories needed to feed the body.

by the Bank of Japan suggest that per capita sugar consumption more than tripled between the early twentieth century and the late 1930s, reaching a level of around 15 kg precisely at the time when Japan's war in China was heating up (Bank of Japan Statistics Department, 1966, table 129). Francks, employing data from Shinohara (1967), calculates that per capita expenditure on sugar had almost doubled in real terms between 1875 and 1935 (Francks, 2009a, pp. 148–50).

Not only was sugar increasingly consumed in home-cooking, chocolates and caramels, but, in addition, Taishō-era adventurer-cum-entrepreneur Mishima Kaiun was one of the first to consider making a drink product that was to revolutionise Japanese tastes. Sweet products developed in the late Meiji and Taishō eras often captured the public imagination with a blend of imperial adventure, exotic 'eastern' foreignness, and hypothetical health benefits. Mishima had always been a nationalist, wanting to do something for his country, and a strong Buddhist as well. Back in Japan, he attempted to replicate a tasty drink a fermented yoghurt concoction that he had enjoyed in Mongolia, but his initial campaigns came to nought (Karupisu Shokuhin Kōgyō, 1989, pp. 22–50). In frustration, Mishima gathered his employees together to brainstorm ways to create a new drink. Someone had taken one of the experimental drink products, added sugar and let it sit for a while on the sideboard. Two days later, when someone drank it, it was much tastier than the products of previous trials. Bent on improving the nation's health, Mishima realised that the drink needed a dose of something lacking in the daily Japanese diet – calcium, which Japanese scientists had already noted was in short supply in most people's everyday lifestyle (Karupisu Shokuhin Kōgyō, 1989, pp. 54–55). The resulting product, Calpis, was immensely popular due to the combination of sweet taste and nutritional benefits that it supposedly offered (Roberson, 2005, pp. 365–84). During the 1920s, an expanding coffee-house culture also saw sugar being placed on tables as a condiment to add to the beverage, while *ramune*, a sweet and fizzy lemonade, became a tasty treat for children.

In the 1920s nutrition became a watchword for a strong, healthy country, and sweets offered needed calories. In 1922 the Ministry of Education conducted the first national inquiry into school lunches, and this led to the movement to establish a 'nutritious nation', a phrase employed by politicians at the time (Hagiwara, 1987, p. 12). Sugar was thought of as part-and-parcel of this push to be healthy, not as an item to be avoided as it is today. By the time that Japan became further involved in Asia in the 1930s, the government had already pushed for the creation of a Ministry of Health and Welfare, and urged policies promoting a stronger population. Sport was obviously a key element in this venture, but so was eating nutritious and calorific meals.

Meanwhile, urbanisation was increasing the demand for pre-prepared meals, and sugar became more ubiquitous in processed Japanese food. In Europe, trends in state and society drove a growth in populist consumerism during the First World War, and similar changes were apparent in Japan. State planning led to the recognition of consumer interests and, as Frank Trentmann posits, 'the war thus placed new social, ethical and political responsibilities on the consumer, even or especially in producer-oriented national traditions' (Trentmann, 2006, p. 43). We only have to look at the growth in purchases of small boxes of caramels in the period around the First World War to find suggestions of a sea-change in the manner of Japanese snacking, and in preferences for previously disliked Western-style sweets. In 1914 Morinaga sold 11,363 kg of caramels, but by 1922 sales had exploded to 68,181 kg. The Meiji Confectionery Company placed particular emphasis on its chocolate, and in 1926 it was selling Meiji Milk Chocolate, branding it as a healthy and nutritious delight with a great taste (Yamamoto and Tsuganezawa, 1986, p. 197). By the later Taishō years, recipes in women's magazines were touting Western-style desserts as a way to keep the family healthy, expand the daily repertoire of food, and increase appetites at home (Murase, 2009, p. 65; Satō, 2002, pp. 20–25).

Japanese imperial concern, at both civilian and government levels, for the health of the nation led to a constant stream of 'daily life improvement movements' (*seikatsu kaizen undō*), campaigns for the improvement of living standards. A central feature common to most of these campaigns was a focus on increased levels of nutritional intake, standardisation of healthy meals, and improved personal and community hygiene (Minami, 1987, pp. 60–65). Meanwhile, it was not just confectionery products that Japanese consumers were getting used to, but sweeter food in general, as observed by Yanagita Kunio. For example, Katarzyna Cwiertka shows how, by the 1920s, the imperial Japanese military was providing its soldiers not only with doughnuts for dessert, but also with stews and curries containing meat that was often flavoured with sugar (Cwiertka, 2002, p. 9).

At the same time the research of Kawamoto Saburō demonstrates the continued linkages between Meiji sugar salesmen dressed as 'Chinese' foreigners and the later expansion of the market for sugary processed foods during the 1910s–1930s. Kawamoto analysed trends in Taishō-era Japanese literature, looking at the works of writers such as Nagai Kafū,

Tanizaki Junichirō and Satō Haruo, and detected a subconscious psychological split. Kawamoto argues that the Meiji reforms, along with Japan's growing military prestige and its involvement with the Allied side during the First World War, had produced a wealthier and, at least on the face of it, a more prosperous society. However, as Tanizaki saw it, anxiety lurked beneath the façade of 'Westernisation'. Many Japanese intellectuals during the 1920s began to feel that Japan had turned its collective head away from its past and had thus lost its true nature (Kawamoto, 2008, pp. 175–96; see also Rimer, 1990). In this manner, these intellectuals (and consumers) sought to replace what they believed had been lost by means of the purchase of exotic 'Chinese goods' or other foreign products. This suggests that the China consumer boom of the late 1920s and early 1930s, as well as the upsurge in the consumption of 'foreign' products from the southern islands, including Taiwan, reflected a desire to return to a cherished 'Asian' past. Kawamoto labels this social and consumer phenomenon the 'adoration for foreign lands'.

The evolution of this hybrid Taishō-era society, detested in part by some, enthralling to others, involved a mixing and matching of styles, high and low, that had by the late 1920s produced what Miriam Silverberg has labelled the 'grotesquerie of Japan's mass culture'. The carnival atmosphere of theatre, cinemas, shopping and temple worship, as witnessed in the playground of Asakusa in Tokyo, included 'the celebration of food'. This was where 'tourists "up from the country" prayed and bought trinkets at the Asakusa Kannon, factory workers on their days off went to the moving pictures, and where everyone, including the beggars, ate a panoply of foods from East and West' (Silverberg, 2006, p. 205). It was not only adults who played in the playgrounds of Tokyo and ate treats from all around the world; children, too, were engaged in consumer activities. *Kamishibai*, 'paper plays', in which a middle-aged man would flip panel cards from a box perched on a bicycle and perform exciting stories for the crowds of children who gathered round, served as one of children's greatest entertainment pleasures from the 1920s to the 1950s. *Kamishibai* performances were intricately linked to children's purchases of sweets from the man who performed, and hence to the consumption of treats (for details see Kushner, 2009, pp. 243–64).

The historical forces that brought sugar into the everyday Japanese diet, through snacks, treats and sugary beverages, were a direct outgrowth of colonial policy and the particular economic and social conditions that developed during the first few decades of the twentieth century. The manufacture of confectionery products, the infiltration of sugar into new

Japanese goods, the growing quotidian consumption of sweet items, and the relation between this consumption and Japanese advertisements of modernity pushed the average consumer towards a greater purchase of sweet products in the competitive marketplace for processed foods. The opportunity for Japanese confectionery companies to latch on to a popular foreign film star, or use the arrival of a favoured guest, continued the trend of using the foreign to market the increasing domestic consumption of sugary treats. On 14 May 1932 Charlie Chaplin, narrowly missing an assassination attempt, arrived in Japan to great fanfare (Silverberg, 2006, p. 1). The two major confectionery companies, Morinaga and Meiji, jumped on the bandwagon and offered their customers a special delicacy. Morinaga Chocolate created a special chocolate bar that was wrapped in a bilingual sheet of foil with the announcement, 'Welcome Charlie Chaplin'. The Meiji Company created a milk caramel box that featured an image of Chaplin and the poem 'Happiness Chaplin has arrived, Lots of fun this caramel' (Silverberg, 2006, p. 213).

Sweet war

Given what we know of the austere physical life of Japanese soldiers during wartime, we would not normally associate confectionery treats with Japan's experience of the Second World War. While we cannot deny the reality of the situation in the 1940s, this picture may stem from the fact that research often gives predominance to the Pacific-island wartime theatre as representative of Japan's entire wartime experience.[3] The historian Ichinose Tatsuya recommends revisiting this question, at least examining the evidence from earlier periods of the war. The cultural background of the period up to the Second World War may provide insight into the expansion of the consumption of sugar through the 1920s and into the war-time and post-war years as well. As Ichinose reveals, many soldiers wrote in their letters home that they were constantly hungry, and thus needed money to buy additional food and snacks at the local soldiers' canteen (Ichinose, 2004, p. 141; Lone, 2010, p. 88). Known as the *shuho* in Japanese, these small shops were often run by civilians, but with permission from the military authorities. They would stock and sell treats, snacks and alcohol, with which the soldiers could supplement their otherwise fairly stringent intake (Masuda, 2004, p. 33).

[3] See, for example, Fujiwara, 2001, which details the deaths of Japanese military personnel in the Pacific.

Japanese military men thus engaged in Japan's war on the Chinese continent, and then in the Pacific against the Western Allies, having consumed sugary and manufactured foods. The war itself was a long and tortured historical event, ultimately wreaking massive destruction on the country. Within the midst of such economic, psychological and physical dislocation, and, by the later 1930s, the increasingly severe rationing necessary to feed the military machine required to keep the enemy at bay, it might be expected that sweets would have quickly absented themselves from the market. In actuality, however, the situation was not so black-and-white. With confectionery already embedded in the Japanese diet, producing companies used the war as a means to further the consumption of their product, portraying its very manufacture and purchase as acts of patriotism. By the time that all-out war began in China in 1937, children and young women on the home front were not thinking twice about placing soft caramel chews in comfort bags (*imon bukuro*) to send to the battlefront. Japanese now considered confectionery products as part of the national landscape of consumption and, more importantly, consumed them with zeal. Sweets were in high demand among soldiers, especially, it seems, those in China. By September 1937, Japanese servicemen near the Shanghai front were experiencing unexpected wartime hardship, following the failure of their gamble that they would easily defeat the Chinese. They wrote of their plight in their diaries, complaining that 'the one thing you can't get a hold of on the battlefield are sweets. We have no sugar, so everyone is sucking on sorghum. Some went out to collect sorghum in the fields, but they got nailed by enemy fire and came back empty-handed' (Moore, 2006, p. 123–24).

Meanwhile, back in home-front Japan, confectionery sales continued to increase through the 1930s, as did promotional advertising. In June 1938 the Meiji Confectionery Company created an advertising car, replete with supplies of chocolate and caramel, which travelled around towns playing the company song over a sound system. The company later held contests for two songs, the 'Meiji Caramel Song' and the 'Meiji Chocolate Song', and pressed the winning tunes on to records (Meiji Seika Shashi, 1968, pp. 52–53). The Meiji Chocolate Song hints at the linkage, discussed by Kawamoto Saburō, between the consumption of sweets and the exotic image of the southern islands in the prewar Japanese psyche. The lyrics of the song are somewhat inane, but at one point read 'I am a young boy from the south, feeling the beautiful chocolate melt in my mouth'.

The Japanese home front was tied to the battle front by a well-known series of wartime journalistic reportages describing what the Japanese soldiers were enduring in China. Hino Ashihei was already a popular writer before the China war, but his embedded journalism developed into a semi-fictional genre during the war and resulted in several best-sellers that detailed the trials and tribulations of Japanese soldiers at the front. *Wheat and Soldiers* (*Mugi to Heitai*) (1938), *Dirt and Soldiers* (*Tsuchi to Heitai*) (1938) and *Flowers and Soldiers* (*Hana to Heitai*) (1939) sold in unprecedented numbers and launched Hino's career as a wartime literary force. The *Asahi Shimbun*, pleased to capture the adulation – and wallets – of adoring fans, sponsored a nationwide tour for Hino. The author said that during the war he was aware that many commercial companies were borrowing the style of his titles, adding the phrase 'and soldiers' to the names of their products as a means to tie into the militarisation of society. He even recalled that he was offered free beer for life if he penned a book entitled 'Beer and Soldiers' (Rosenfeld, 2002, p. 52).

Chocolate, again brought to the public by the Meiji Chocolate Company, also joined the bandwagon of the 'and soldiers' phenomenon, with the Tōhō film *Chocolate and Soldiers* (1938), a humanistic story of love and tragedy filmed by Satō Takeshi.[4] Through this film, the public's desire for chocolate as a sweet treat linked the home front to the battle front, not only through popular songs and 'comfort bags', but in the cinema as well. The movie centres on the story of a man, Saeki, who has a young son, Ichirō, and a daughter, and who works as a printer in a small village. Life is blissful until he is eventually conscripted to the Chinese front. In the early parts of the film, Ichirō has already told his father that he is saving up his chocolate-bar wrappers for a prize. Once he is mobilised to the front, Saeki starts collecting chocolate-bar wrappers from his fellow soldiers and sends a big packet of them back to his son at home. Ichirō is delighted and says he is going to use all the wrappers to claim a prize, but his mother suggests that, given his massive collection, he should send a letter to the chocolate company, in the hope that he might receive a bigger prize. Ichirō's letter moves a clerk to tears when she reads about Saeki's love for his son and how he collects wrappers at the front to send home. The company manager suggests that they should send a large 'comfort bag' to Saeki at the front, in recognition of his patriotism and familial love. Saeki

[4] This film is virtually unobtainable, and I thank Andrew Gordon for graciously offering me a reprint of his treasured copy.

continues to collect chocolate wrappers on the battle front in China and sends home an even larger packet a few weeks later. Unfortunately, his packet arrives in his village on the same day as a courier delivering a letter telling the family that Saeki has died in battle. Chocolate, or the chocolate company, has managed to unite the home front and battle front, as well as family and friends, across this small village and the empire. Moreover, so moved is the head of the chocolate company when he hears about the tragedy that has befallen Ichirō that he agrees to pay for his education (though no one mentions the future plight of Saeki's little daughter).

The tragic film's final scene is of Saeki's two smiling children, hand-in-hand and beaming toward the camera, as the chocolate company has now sent them gifts, and even though their beloved father has died in war, the future looks bright (High, 1995, pp. 171–72). A copy of the film had made it into American hands by the start of the Pacific War, and was dubbed for research purposes and shown to the film director Frank Capra and the anthropologist Ruth Benedict, as a means to help decode the Japanese wartime psyche. Famously, upon viewing this provocative wartime propaganda piece, Capra is supposed to have claimed that it was filled with pathos and more a tragedy than it was anti-American, so that from an American point of view it represented the most effective anti-war film (High, 1995, p. 172). On the Japanese side though, the movie was part-and-parcel of the wartime propaganda that galvanised the public, a slice of humanity that revealed the connective tissue bonding soldier and society together. *Chocolate and Soldiers* was also a hit song, pressed on to record (Meiji Seika Shashi, 1968, p. 54). So powerful was its story that it retained salience in the post-war period, emblematic of wartime sacrifice and tragedy (*Asahi Shinbun,* 14 August 1967).

This tenacious relationship between consumption and war, demonstrated through sweets, in part contradicts a certain suggestion among scholars of consumption, like Frank Trentmann and others, that 'in societies like early twentieth-century Japan, users or purchasers found it difficult to imagine themselves and agitate as consumers, being preoccupied instead with the imperative of strengthening themselves as a nation (*kokumin*). The resulting identity of producer and patriot – more than the negative cultural connotations of consumption (*shōhi*, referring to extinction and waste) – explains the historical weakness of Japanese consumer identity' (Trentmann, 2006, p. 51; see also Garon, 1998, pp. 312–34; Garon, 2000, pp. 41–78). How can we account for the continued war-time growth in the production and sale of various Japanese consumer products, if we treat militarisation of consumption, corresponding also to the militarisation of advertising, as something other than consumption (Wakabayashi, 2008; Nanba, 1998)? As Francks (2009a, p. 138) suggests, this blindness towards consumption 'may also reflect the long-term "official" or ideological view in Japan that consumption is bad and that frugality, saving, and self-sufficiency are good', but this view clearly did not appear to impede the sale of sweets or appreciably reduce the market for them. And the market continued to grow with vigour once the war was over.

Chocolate and Soldiers demonstrates that, despite state disapproval, consumption, and the advertising that promoted it, remained a powerful force within war-time society. In fact, it was flagrant consumption, not consumption in general, that worried the authorities, leaving war-time businesses to continue to portray consuming as a burden expected to be taken on by the people to promote the nation.

The post-war boom in sugar consumption

Once the war was over, and with the nation in poverty, sugary treats once again took on a patina of 'foreignness'. Even *kamishibai* performers had to make do with less. Kata Kōji, author of the immensely popular Golden Bat series, recalled in his post-war memoirs that most of the snacks performers could sell at first were scraps of flour fried in fish oil to look like flat crackers (*senbei*), and sweet potato slivers (Kushner, 2009, p. 261). Of course, during the Occupation, American soldiers tossing candy to hungry street urchins become a treasured, if not somewhat mythical, image of the benevolent victor, the physically large and gum-chewing American. This might have helped to assuage Japanese anxiety about the nature of the Occupation, but the Australian press, for example, was more critical of American post-war largesse in Japan. Japanese children from the era well remember American candy, but other Allied countries felt that their inability to deliver the same treats to occupied Japan put them at a post-war disadvantage. Australian media of the time noted: 'Our soldiers [Australians] do not give gum or candy and very few cigarettes in comparison with the Americans. Moreover, the Americans have a sentimentalism that makes them much easier and more friendly in manner to the Japanese' (Takemae, 2002, p. 73).

The very confectionery businesses that had helped ease the Japanese public down the path towards modernity and imperialism were also interested in regaining public trust through a renewed set of campaigns that once again placed their products at the centre of a resurgent Japan. In October 1947, the Food Products Section within the Food Control

Bureau of the Ministry of Agriculture and Forestry sent a missive to the National Confectioners' Association, noting that the Americans were releasing a ton of cocoa and asking what treats should be made with it (Morinaga Seika, 2000, p. 149). The Association consulted with confectioners at the Morinaga and Meiji companies and decided to make cocoa caramel treats from it. This required a large-scale effort, involving factories around Japan, but by August of the following year chocolate caramels were being distributed to heavy-industry workers and children throughout Japan, as a bonus and pick-me-up during difficult early post-war economic times.

Sugar, and more importantly the sweet products that derived from it, have held a long association with the exotic in early-modern and contemporary Japan, but over the past 150 years the taste and texture of sugary substances have embedded themselves in the domestic culture and seduced consumers. The consumption of sweet treats cannot simply be explained by unilaterally citing rising statistics on sugar imports and thus implying that the Japanese adopted Western practice. The links between advertising and empire proved key to shaping the ever-changing context in which Japanese consumers understood and appreciated these new tastes and processed foodstuffs. Confectionery goods tied in with Japanese colonialism as well as they did with Japan's war and the Occupation. This suggests that consumerism in Japan has already exceeded the narrative contours to which historians have previously confined their analysis.

The fact that in a society in which sugar was not thought to have been consumed outright in large quantities, sweets could play such a significant role in the formation of modern consumer preferences, suggests that we need to start examining the history of consumption in Japan along different lines, recognising its connection with empire and larger ideas of civilization. We also need to consider carefully the ways in which it demonstrates similarities with Western patterns, but also exhibits its own distinctive characteristics.

References

Akesaka, E. (2002) *Sugā Rōdo: Satō ga Deshima ni Yatte Kita* (Sugar Road: How Sugar Arrived in Deshima), Tokyo: Nagasaki shinbun shinsho.

Aoyama, T. (2003) 'Romancing Food: The Gastronomic Quest in Early Twentieth-Century Japanese Literature', *Japanese Studies*, December, pp. 251–64.

Aoyama, T. (2008) *Reading Food in Modern Japanese Literature*, Honolulu: University of Hawaii Press.

Bank of Japan Statistics Department (1966) *Hundred-Year Statistics of the Japanese Economy*, Tokyo: Bank of Japan.

Clammer, J. (1997) *Contemporary Urban Japan – Sociology of Consumption*, Oxford: Blackwell Publishers.

Cwiertka, K. J. (2002) 'Popularizing a Military Diet in Wartime and Postwar Japan', *Asian Anthropology*, 1, pp. 1–30.

Davidson, J. W. (1988) *The Island of Formosa: Past and Present: History, People, Resources, and Commercial Prospects*, Taipei: Southern Materials Center (reprint of 1903 publication).

De Grazia, V. (1996) *The Sex of Things: Gender and Consumption in Historical Perspective*, Berkeley, CA: University of California Press.

de Vries, J. (2008) *The Industrious Revolution: Consumer Behaviour and the Household Economy, 1650 to the Present*, Cambridge: Cambridge University Press.

Finn, D (no date given) 'Guests of the Nation: The Japanese Delegation to the Buchanan White House', *White House History* 12, 14–38.

Fraleigh, M. (2010) 'Japan's First War Reporter: Kishida Ginko and the Taiwan Expedition', *Japanese Studies* 30, 1, pp. 43–66.

Francks, P. (2009a) 'Inconspicuous Consumption: Sake, Beer, and the Birth of the Consumer in Japan', *Journal of Asian Studies*, 68, 1, February, 135–64.

Francks, P. (2009b) *The Japanese Consumer – An Alternative Economic History of Modern Japan*, Cambridge: Cambridge University Press.

Fujiwara, A. (2001) *Uejinishita Eireitachi* (War Dead who Died of Starvation), Tokyo: Aoki Shoten.

Garon, S. (1998) 'Fashioning a Culture of Diligence and Thrift: Savings and Frugality Campaigns in Japan, 1900–1931', in Minichiello, S. A. (ed.), *Japan's Competing Modernities: Issues in Culture and Democracy, 1900–1930*, Honolulu: University of Hawai'i Press, 312–34.

Garon, S. (2000) 'Luxury is the Enemy: Mobilizing Savings and Popularizing Thrift in Wartime Japan', *Journal of Japanese Studies* 26, 1, pp. 41–78.

Hagiwara, H. (1987) *Jissen Kōza Gakkō Kyūshoku, Dai Ikkan, Rekishi to Genjō* (Practical Lectures on School Lunches, vol. 1, History and the Current Situation), Tokyo: Meicho Henshūkai

Henry, D. (2009) 'Japanese Children's Literature as Allegory of Empire in Iwaya Sazanami's *Momotaro* (*The Peach Boy*)', *Children's Literature Association Quarterly* 34, 3, Fall, pp. 218–28.

High, P. B. (1995) *Teikoku no Ginmaku: Jūgonen Sensō to Nihon Eiga* (*The Empire's Silver Screen: the Fifteen Year War and Japanese Film*), Nagoya: Nagoya Daigaku Shuppan.

Hiraide, K. (1902) *Tōkyō Fūzokushi*, Jōkan (History of Tokyo Customs, vol. 1), Tokyo: Fuzanbō.

Ichinose, T. (2004) *Meiji Taishō Shōwa Guntai Manyuaru: Hito wa Naze Senjō e Itta no ka* (Meiji Taishō Shōwa Military Manuals: Why Did People Go to the Battlefield), Tokyo: Kōbun shinsho.

Inoue, Y. (2010) 'Wakamono no Yashoku wa Dō Kawatte Kita ka' (How Has the Evening Dining of Young People Evolved?), in Nishimura, H. (ed.) *Yashoku no Bunkashi* (Cultural History of Evening Dining), Tokyo: Seikyūsha, pp. 161–95.

Itō, H. (ed.) (2008) *Satō no Bunkashi: Nihonjin to Satō* (Cultural History of Sugar: The Japanese and Sugar), Tokyo: Yasaka Shobō.

Karupisu Shokuhin Kōgyō Kabushikigaisha Iinkai Henshū (ed.) (1989) *Nanajūnen no Ayumi* (Seventy Years of Progress), Tokyo: Karupisu Shokuhin Kōgyō.

Katō, H. (1975) 'America as Seen by Japanese Travelers', in Iriye, A. (ed.), *Mutual Images, Essays in American-Japanese Relations*, Cambridge, MA: Harvard University Press.

Kawamoto, S. (2008) *Taishō Genei* (Taishō Illusions), Tokyo: Iwanami Shoten.

Kitagawa, M. (ed.) (1992) *Morisada Mankō* (Morisada Record of Slow Travels), Tokyo: repr. Tokyodō Shuppan, 5 vols.

Kubo, F. (1997) *Shokuminchi Kigyō Keieishiron – Jun Kokusaku Kaisha no Jisshōteki Kenkyū* (Management History of Colonial Enterprises – Actual Research on Quasi-national Companies), Tokyo: Nihon Keizai Hyōronsha.

Kushner, B. (2009) 'Planes, Trains and Games – Selling Japan's War in Asia', in Purtle, J. and Thomsen, H. B. (eds), *Looking Modern: Taisho Japan and the Modern Era*, Chicago: University of Chicago Press, pp. 243–64.

Lone, S. (2010) *Provincial Life and the Military in Imperial Japan*, London: Routledge.

Masuda,Y. (2004) *Jūgun to Senchū Sengo*, (The Homefront During and After the War), Tokyo: Bungeisha.

Mazumdar, S. (1998) *Sugar and Society in China*, Cambridge, MA: Harvard University Press.

Meiji Seika Shashi Henshū Iinkai (ed.) (1968) *Meiji Seika no Ayumi, Sōritsu kara Gojūnen* (History of Meiji Confectionary Treats, 50 Years from the Start), Tokyo: Toppan Insatsu.

Minami, H. (1987) *Shōwa Bunka, 1925–1945* (Shōwa Culture, 1925–1945), Tokyo: Keisō Shobō.

Mintz, S. (1985) *Sweetness and Power: The Place of Sugar in Modern History*, New York: Viking.

Moore, A. W. (2006) 'The Peril of Self-Discipline: Chinese Nationalist, Japanese, and American Servicemen Record the Rise and Fall of the Japanese Empire, 1937–1945', PhD dissertation, Princeton University Department of East Asian Studies.

Morinaga Seika Kabushikigaisha Henshū (ed.) (2000) *Morinaga Seika Hyakunenshi* (Hundred-Year History of the Morinaga Confectionery Company), Tokyo: Toppan Insatsu.

Murase, K. (2009) 'Fujin Zasshi to Ryōri – Shoku Jōhō no Taishūka to Gōrakuka' (Women's Magazines and Cooking – Rationalization and Spread of Information on Cooking), *Vesta* 73, pp. 62–67.

Nanba, K. (1998) *Uchiteshiyaman: Taiheiyō Sensō to Kōkoku no Gijutsushatachi* (We Will Not Stop Fighting! Graphic Artists and the Pacific War), Tokyo: Kōdansha.

Nihon Chokorēto Kokoa Kyōkai (ed.) (1958) *Nihon Chokorēto Kōgyōshi* (History of the Chocolate Industry in Japan) Tokyo: Nihon Chokorēto Kokoa Kyōkai.

Pomeranz, K. (2002) 'Political Economy and Ecology on the Eve of Industrialization: Europe, China, and the Global Conjuncture', *The American Historical Review*, 107, 2, April, pp. 425–46.

Shōwa Joshi Daigaku Shokumotsu Kenkyūshitsu (eds) (1971) *Kindai Nihon Shokumotsushi* (History of Food in Early Modern Japan), Tokyo: Daibundō.

Nihon Hyōronsha (ed.) (1926) *Shakai Keizai Taikei* (Socio-economic System), Tokyo: Nihon Hyōronsha.

Rath, E. C. (2008) 'Banquets Against Boredom: Towards Understanding (Samurai) Cuisine in Early Modern Japan', *Early Modern Japan* 16, pp. 43–55.

Rimer, J. T. (ed.) (1990) *Culture and Identity: Japanese Intellectuals during the Interwar Years*, Princeton, NJ: Princeton University Press.
Roberson, J. (2005) 'Fight!! Ippatsu!!: 'Genki' Energy Drinks and the Marketing of Masculine Ideology in Japan', *Men and Masculinities*, 7, 4, pp. 365–84.
Rosenfeld, D. M. (2002) *Unhappy Soldier: Hino Ashihei and Japanese World War II Literature*, Oxford: Lexington Books.
Satō, T. (2002) *Kingu no Jidai – Kokumin Taishū Zasshi no Kokyōsei* (The King Era – People's Mass Magazines and their Public Nature), Tokyo: Iwanami Shoten.
Shinohara, M. (1967) *Kojin Shōhi Shishutsu, Chōki Keizai Tōkei* (Personal Consumption Expenditure: Long-Term Economic Statistics, Vol. 6), Tokyo: Tōyō Keizai Shinposha.
Silverberg, M. (2006) *Erotic, Grotesque Nonsense – The Mass Culture of Japanese Modern Times*, Berkeley, CA: University of California Press.
Stearns, P. N. (2001) *Consumerism in World History: The Global Transformation of Desire*, London: Routledge.
Takemae, E. (2002) (trans. Robert Ricketts) *The Allied Occupation of Japan*, New York: Continuum.
Tōkanfu (1910) *Dai Nihonteikoku Chōsen Shashinchō, Nikkan Heigō Kinen* (Imperial Japan's Collection of Photographs from Korea, Memorial of the Annexation), Tokyo: Ogawa Kazumasu Shuppanbu.
Trentmann, F. (2006) 'The Modern Genealogy of the Consumer – Meanings, Identities and Political Synapses', in Brewer, J. & Trentmann, F., *Consuming Cultures Global Perspectives: Historical Trajectories, Transnational Exchanges*, Oxford: Berg, pp. 19–69.
Ujima, E. (2009) *Ame to Ameuri no Bunkashi* (Cultural History of Sweets and the Selling of Sweets), Tokyo: Genshobō.
Vaporis, C. (2008) *Tour of Duty: Samurai, Military Service in Edo, and the Culture of Early Modern Japan*, Honolulu: University of Hawai'i Press.
Wakabayashi, T. (2008) *Tatakau Kōkoku: Zasshi Kōkoku ni miru Ajia Taiheiyō Sensō* (Fighting with Advertising: Asia's Pacific War as seen through Magazine Advertisements), Tokyo: Shōgakkan.
Woloson, W. A. (2002) *Refined Tastes: Sugar, Confectionery, and Consumers in Nineteenth-century America*, Baltimore: The Johns Hopkins University Press.
Yamamoto, T. (1984) *Kōkoku no Shakaishi* (Social History of Advertising), Tokyo: Hōsei daigaku shuppankyoku.
Yamamoto, T. & Tsuganezawa, T. (eds) (1986) *Nihon no Kōkoku* (Japanese Advertising), Tokyo: Nihon Keizai Shinbunsha.
Yanagita, K. (1957 edited and compiled) *Japanese Manners and Customs in the Meiji Era*, 4, Tokyo: Ōbunsha.
Yanagita, K. (1976) *Meiji Taishōshi Sesōshi* (History of Social Conditions in the Meiji and Taishō Eras), Tokyo: Kōdansha.
Yano, S. (2002) *Rakugo: Nagaya no Shiki no Aji* (Rakugo: Four Seasons of the Tenements), Tokyo: Bungei Shunjū.

7

Kimono Fashion: The Consumer and the Growth of the Textile Industry in Pre-War Japan

Penelope Francks

Introduction

'His nation had not changed its costume for over a thousand years', a Japanese official reportedly told a shipwrecked Spanish trader in 1609, going on to criticise the castaway's compatriots as, by contrast, 'so inconstant that they are dressed in a different way every two years'. This incident was famously quoted by Fernand Braudel in *The Structures of Everyday Life* to demonstrate the significance of clothing fashion as an indicator of the attitudes to tradition and change that stimulated the emergence of capitalism and industrialisation in Europe: 'the future was to belong to the societies fickle enough to care about changing the colours, materials and shapes of costume' (Braudel, 1981, p. 323). Braudel in fact went on to outline some of the more material links between the emergence of fashion as a determinant of clothing consumption and the growth of production and trade that was starting to transform key parts of the European economy. Nonetheless, for many years, his hints were largely forgotten, as supply-side analysis of technical and organisational change dominated approaches to the understanding of industrialisation. More recently, however, as research has begun to return the consumer to a central position in economic history, it has ceased to be possible to ignore clothing fashion as a factor in the 'consumer revolution' now regarded as a 'necessary analogue' to the industrial revolution itself.[1]

Hence, fashion can now be seen to have acted as 'a cultural catalyst to consumption' (Lemire, 2009, p. 206), spurring the growth in demand

[1] Terms coined by Neil McKendrick in his seminal paper (McKendrick, 1982).

for textiles that underpinned technical change and investment in what proved to be a key sector in industrialising economies. In eighteenth-century Europe, imports of exciting new cotton fabrics from India and elsewhere, later copied by domestic producers, encouraged innovations in dress and the more rapid turnover of styles that has been termed the 'fashion system'. While the better-off spent growing amounts of time and money keeping up with the latest fashions, members of the middle and even lower classes adopted and adapted their own new styles, through, for example, use of the second-hand market or the acquisition of 'populuxe' versions of the accessories sported by the fashionable elite (Lemire, 2005, ch. 5). The resulting demand for increasing quantities of textiles in an expanding and faster-changing range of qualities and designs fuelled the 'cotton revolution' and lay behind the technological and design innovations in fabric production that played such a central role in the industrial revolution itself.

The emergence of the fashion system has thus come to be seen as an inherent part of the development of industrial capitalism in Europe and North America. For Japan, on the other hand, the assumption that, up to the Second World War at least, incomes were too low to generate anything other than a 'narrow' domestic market has deflected attention away from any role for consumer demand in sustaining industrialisation. As regards clothing, a link between consumption, fashion and industrial growth has equally been excluded on the grounds that the majority of Japanese people, especially women, continued to wear Japanese-style garments. The fabrics for these were produced within the 'traditional' sector of the economy, where the supply-side forces assumed to have driven industrialisation – imported technology, business structures and products – were thought not to operate. At the same time, if fashion as we know it is inextricably tied up with the emergence of the Western-style industrial economy and the clothing in which it is dressed, it cannot have been operating, as Braudel's anecdote seeks to demonstrate, within the supposedly static, 'traditional' clothing systems inherited by the non-Western world.[2] The kimono-clad Japanese could not, therefore, have participated in the kind of fashion-driven growth in textile demand that played such a role in the industrialisation process elsewhere.

---

[2] The assumption that involvement in fashion depends on the adoption of Western-style dress appears to be widely held amongst those who study fashion (see for example Wilson, 2007 or, for a recent Japanese case, Slade, 2009), although Finnane, in her study of Chinese clothing history (Finnane, 2008), decisively refutes it.

This is to ignore the numerous ways in which Japanese-style clothing, for men but especially for women, changed over the period of economic development and industrialisation from the late Tokugawa period to the Second World War, and the existence in Japan, as elsewhere, of mechanisms that spread new fashions to ever wider sections of the population. Moreover, the 'traditional sector' of the economy, within which Japanese-style clothing materials were produced, is no longer seen as static and 'backward', so that a role for domestic textile demand in promoting and conditioning Japan's industrialisation becomes a possibility. In what follows, I seek to show that production for a domestic market dominated by Japanese-style clothing played a significant part, quantitatively and qualitatively, in the crucial stages of growth in the textile industry. The characteristics of 'traditional' Japanese-style clothes and the nature of the accelerating trends in their fashions are essential elements in any explanation of the pattern of economic and technological change in an industry central to Japan's modern development. Hence, the consumers of kimono fashion played their part too in determining the distinctive characteristics of Japanese industrial growth.

The textile industry and the domestic market

The production of textiles has long been recognised as having played a key role in the industrialisation process in pre-war Japan, as in many other industrialising countries. Textile output grew in real terms at an annual average rate of 6.6 per cent over the whole 1874–1940 period and at over 10 per cent up to 1900 (Ohkawa and Shinohara, 1979, table 5.4). The share of textiles in manufacturing output rose from around 20 per cent in the 1870s to almost 50 per cent at its peak in the 1890s, remaining at 30–40 per cent through to the mid-1930s (Table 7.1). The main focus of interest in this process has always lain with textiles produced for export: the raw silk reeled from domestic cocoons that provided Japan's major source of export revenue following the opening to trade in the 1850s; the cotton yarn, spun from imported raw cotton, that the first modern textile mills were successfully able to sell abroad from the 1890s; the woven cotton fabric competitively produced for export, once integrated spinning and weaving mills began to be set up around the turn of the century. Growth in these areas of textile production has been viewed as crucial to Japan's industrialisation, not just in terms of the expansion of output and exports, but also as driving the process of adoption of modern forms of technology and industrial organisation, with relatively large-scale textile mills pioneering mechanised methods and the development of a factory labour force.

Textiles drove early industrialisation
= ↑ output and exports
↑ technology innovation
∴ ↑ demand/development of new fabrics domestically

Table 7.1 Textiles and fabric production in the domestic economy (%)

	Share of textiles in manufacturing output	Exports* as a share of total textile output	Share of fabric in total textile output	Share of exports* in cotton fabric output	Share of exports* in silk fabric output
1875	22.3	14.9	44.8	0.1	0.2
1880	27.9	10.6	42.5	0.2	0.3
1885	28.4	18.3	40.8	1.0	0.5
1890	36.1	13.1	35.8	0.5	7.3
1895	47.3	19.7	37.5	3.7	19.2
1900	35.8	24.1	41.5	9.3	22.3
1905	31.9	37.3	35.0	16.1	50.1
1910	33.6	40.0	40.8	16.8	29.1
1915	33.1	40.7	39.5	21.1	35.5
1920	34.3	38.2	43.8	48.3	33.9
1925	39.4	45.2	37.4	56.1	28.3
1930	30.6	37.2	42.2	55.2	16.8
1935	29.1	37.2	44.2	61.2	13.4

*outside the Japanese empire.
Sources: LTES 10 (1972), tables 1 & 18; Bank of Japan Statistics Department (1966), table 116 (1); Ohkawa and Shinohara (1979), tables A19 and A26.

Nonetheless, production for export and the emergence of large-scale mills are far from representing the whole story of the role of the textile industry in Japan's economic history. Even at their high point in the 1910s and 1920s, exports still accounted for less than half of the value of textile output as a whole (Table 7.1). The domestic market for textiles continued to exert a major influence on producers in the industry, stimulating growth in both the 'modern' and 'traditional' sectors in forms that interconnected with and complemented the expansion of exports. In mechanised cotton-spinning, output increased more than 50-fold between the 1880s and the First World War, but exports were insignificant before the 1890s and still accounted for only a third of output in 1914 (Abe, 1990, table 2(3)-1). As large-scale cotton-spinning mills were established, a major part of their rapidly growing production therefore went to supply the domestic cotton-weaving industry. In raw silk production, the bulk of the expansion in output of the machine-reeled thread produced by larger-scale mills was exported, but still, by the inter-war period, 30–40 per cent of the raw silk produced in Japan was consumed by the domestic weaving industry. Most of this took the form of the lower-grade thread that came from hand-reelers or small-scale mills and was intended for use by weavers producing fabric for the domestic market (Matsumura, 2006, pp. 96–97).

The weaving sector, which produced around 40 per cent of the overall value of textile output throughout the pre-war period, therefore represented a major user of Japanese-made yarns, whether from large-scale modern mills or more 'traditional' establishments. Exports of woven cloth were negligible before the end of the nineteenth century, and although they subsequently increased to account for over half of cotton fabric production, they rarely constituted more than a third of woven silk output (Table 7.1). The domestic market for clothing materials thus remained central to the overall demand that Japanese textile producers – spinners and weavers – aimed to meet.

Moreover, that market was expanding fast: expenditure on clothing in real terms grew at an annual average rate of almost 5 per cent over 1874–1940, so that annual per capita expenditure on clothing multiplied ten-fold in real terms between the 1870s and the 1930s, and the share of clothing in total consumption expenditure rose from 3 per cent in the 1870s to 12 per cent in the 1930s (LTES 6, 1967, table 4; Ohkawa and Shinohara 1979, tables 8.3 and 8.6). Given that the relative price of clothing fell by two-thirds over the period, it must have been the case that Japanese people were coming to acquire a great many more, though cheaper, items of clothing, fuelling the growth in the domestic textile market.

This growth clearly had its origins, as elsewhere in the world, in the switch from home-made to purchased materials, especially cotton. By the later Tokugawa period, most urban consumers were buying their clothes, but in the countryside it was still only the better-off who had the cash incomes to purchase clothing material, new, second-hand or as thread to weave (Tanimoto, 1987, pp. 54–55). Thereafter, however, rural as well as urban consumers began to enter the market for cotton cloth in growing numbers and increasing amounts, as cash incomes rose and the price of clothing materials fell. Some of this expansion in demand was initially met by imported cotton broadcloth, so that, at their peak in the 1870s, imports accounted for around a third of domestic purchases of cotton cloth, while other imported materials, such as wool, also found their way on to the market. However, imported cloth was very different, in design and quality, from that produced by domestic weavers for use in Japanese-style dress and the share of imports soon fell off, as producers responded and consumer demand for 'traditional' clothing materials increased, in the process to be described in later sections (Tanimoto, 1987, pp. 60–63;

Saitō and Tanimoto, 2004, pp. 278–94). The domestic clothing market therefore remained, to a large extent, the province of those producers able to come through import competition and the temporary down-turn in the 1880s, and to tap into the widening network of textile dealers and retailers supplying the fast-growing, though competitive, market for the kinds of textiles that Japanese consumers demanded.

For reasons to be examined in detail below, these producers proved for the most part to be those manufacturing specialised, differentiated products on a relatively small scale. Uchida estimates that in the 1890s, before there was any significant production for export, about half of cotton cloth output consisted of the striped (*shima*) or splash-patterned (*kasuri*) yarn-dyed, narrow-width kimono fabrics associated with local weaving areas; the other half was largely made up of plain white cloth, which could, for certain uses, be factory made or even imported, but was still predominantly produced by small-scale weavers for use in 'traditional' clothing, either cloth-dyed, as for casual kimono (*yukata*), or undyed and bleached for linings, socks etc. (Uchida, 1988, pp. 159–61). The market for silk remained even more heavily dominated by the narrow-width fabrics, intended for kimono and their accessories, that were produced by small-scale, specialised weavers.

As a result, a division of labour emerged, with the large-scale integrated mills specialising in production for export, leaving the major part of the growing domestic market to small-scale producers. In cotton-weaving, the vast majority of weavers continued to work either on contract at home or in small-scale workshops (Tanimoto, 2006, pp. 12–13). Most in due course came to operate within local industrial districts – known as *sanchi* – specialising in particular types of cloth, and Abe and Saitō estimate that *sanchi* production accounted for 81 per cent of total cotton-cloth production in 1919 and still 64 per cent in 1929 (Abe and Saitō, 1988, p. 146). In weaving as a whole, through to 1940, around 90 per cent of plants with more than five workers were in the smallest 5–29-worker category (Minami, 1987, p. 215), and many continued to work in household enterprises with fewer than five workers. While larger-scale producers carved out for themselves a growing share of the overseas textile market and some *sanchi* producers did eventually succeed in becoming exporters,[3] the local weavers, dyers and finishers who made up the small-scale sector survived and developed for the most part as suppliers to the domestic market for Japanese-style clothing textiles.

[3] By the inter-war period, 40–50 per cent of cotton cloth exports were coming from *sanchi* (Abe, 1989, pp. 4–5).

As the growth in this market demonstrates, Japanese consumers proved no different from consumers elsewhere in desiring more clothes more often, as soon as they were able to afford them, and it was to the domestic weaving industry, dominated by small-scale producers, that they turned, as their spending power and desire for clothing grew. As a result, production for the domestic market in Japanese-style fabrics continued to represent a distinct and important element in the expanding textile industry of pre-war Japan. The next section ('Fashion and Japanese clothing') will argue that underlying this was the development of consumer demand for clothing along lines laid down by a predominantly indigenous fashion system. The subsequent section ('Demand and supply interact: fashion and the development of the textile industry') seeks to demonstrate that this in turn became a major factor determining the characteristics of the 'traditional' but far from static producers who responded to that demand.

Fashion and Japanese clothing

The silk and cotton fabrics that dominated the domestic textile market throughout the pre-Second World War period were designed to be made up into garments and accessories, the basic forms of which had become more-or-less fixed early on in the Tokugawa period. These included the full-length robes now known generically as kimono, together with the short unfitted jacket (*haori*) worn over kimono, and a huge range of accessories, from the *obi* sash that holds a kimono outfit together, through under-kimono, collars, ties and purses, to split-toed socks and sandals. Increasing contact with the West from the mid-nineteenth century brought with it knowledge of Western-style clothing, and a significant number of men, though by no means all, gradually adopted suits or uniforms for public activities, including white-collar work, although many continued to dress in Japanese style on more relaxed occasions. By the inter-war period, 'advanced' young women and urban sophisticates, together with those obliged to adopt 'modern' uniforms, were wearing Western-style outfits at least some of the time, while children were increasingly dressed in what were regarded as cheap and efficient Western forms of clothing. Nonetheless, the vast majority of women – rich or poor – continued to dress in Japanese fashion, so that into the inter-war years observers even in high-fashion spots such as the Ginza in Tokyo found almost all women to be wearing kimono.[4]

[4] One survey of the Ginza in 1925, for instance, found 67 per cent of men wearing Western-style clothes but no more than one per cent of women (Jō, 2007, p. 264).

The kimono is an unfitted garment, usually sold as a fixed length of cloth, to be cut and sewn at home or by a seamstress, and periodically taken apart for cleaning or alteration.[5] Historically, the kimono market divided into, on the one hand, an *haute couture* sector centring on individually dyed lengths produced to order on the basis of pattern books and, on the other, an off-the-shelf sector involving lengths of dyed and woven silk or cotton in stripes and other all-over patterns (Kiyoshi, 2006, p. 68). Both forms were sold in the draperies from which Japan's department stores were eventually to emerge, but also far and wide by travelling sales-people, and there has always been an active second-hand market. At the same time, until the late nineteenth century, many poorer households spun and/or wove their own clothing materials in hemp or cotton, according to traditional local designs.

The general assumption among experts in Western clothing systems has been that the decisive move in the emergence of fashion was the shift, beginning in medieval European cities, away from draped robes towards fitted and ultimately cut and tailored garments (Wilson, 2007, p. 16). Although it is possible to discern changes in, for example, the cut of kimono sleeves, this has not generally been the case with Japanese-style clothing, encouraging the belief that it has remained unchangingly 'traditional' and unsusceptible to fashion. In other respects too the kimono might seem a far-from-ideal vehicle for the kind of rapid turnover in clothing implied by the fashion system. Although there clearly were fashion trends operating in both male and female clothing during the Tokugawa period, the garments involved, especially when made of silk, were expensively hand-crafted and available only to the better-off. In general, kimono fabrics are produced in such a way as to be long-lasting and hard-wearing, but relatively expensive. Being unfitted or easily adjusted, they can be handed on from person to person, patched and repaired, and, if carefully stored and maintained, can last for generations. In some respects, they resemble investment goods or stores of value,

[5] Kimono were always hand sewn in ways that made them easy to disassemble. Hence, as Gordon demonstrates in Chapter 3, the sewing machine became associated only with Western-style dress-making. In pre-industrial England clothing was similarly purchased as cloth to be made up, and if needs be altered, but by the eighteenth century, the trade in ready-made clothes was emerging as a result of factors such as the growth in demand for military uniforms. See Lemire, 1997.

acquired through inheritance or dowry and easily pawned or cashed in through the second-hand market if necessary.[6]

Nonetheless, as the growth in expenditure on clothing through the pre-war period indicates, these features of Japanese dress did not stand in the way of consumers using their rising incomes to purchase more clothes, more often and more cheaply, and it is clearly possible to discern at work a number of the same forces as defined the operation of fashion in Europe, even if the persistence of the kimono dictated the form that fashion would take. As is now becoming increasingly clear, the adoption of cotton world-wide was driven as much by its fashion possibilities as by its cheapness and convenience, compared with linen and other alternatives (Styles, 2009). Inspired to compete with imported Indian fabrics, European producers developed clothing materials that were lighter and more easily washable, but also susceptible to manufacture in a wide range of more rapidly changing colours and designs. In Japan, high-quality cotton in elegant stripes had become fashion-wear among samurai and urban merchants by the early decades of the nineteenth century, competing with less expensive forms of silk for casual occasions (Tamura, 2004, pp. 302–7). Thereafter, Japan experienced its own 'cotton revolution', as clothing consumers, first in cities and towns but gradually also in the countryside, abandoned home-made cloth for the products of manufacturers weaving Japanese-style fabrics commercially for the domestic market.

This process is usually interpreted as driven by supply-side forces, such as the growing availability of paid work for women who would otherwise have spun and woven home-made clothes, but it is also the case that commercial producers, often making use of the labour of those same women, could offer a much wider range of colours and designs in fabrics that were of a more consistent quality and easier to care for and wear. Through the nineteenth century and beyond, such cotton fabrics typically appeared in the standard formats of woven stripes or *kasuri* (ikat/resist dyed) patterns – originally influenced, it is now argued, by Indian fabrics imported during the Tokugawa period (Fujita, 2009) – but in a growing range of regionally branded colours and designs. A new kimono-length in such a fabric was not particularly cheap: Uchida presents data suggesting that it would have cost the equivalent of about a month's wages (at day-wage rates) for a female spinner or weaver in the late Tokugawa period (Uchida, 1988, pp. 162–63). As elsewhere, therefore, the expanding market for cotton fabrics has to be explained, at

[6] On clothes as stores of value, see Ozeki, 2003.

least in part, by their role in the spread, if not of high fashion, at least of an appreciation of the possibilities of variation in colour and pattern in relatively everyday clothing.[7]

Nonetheless, in the Japanese context, the emergence of cotton as a fashion good could not undermine the historical cachet of silk as a kimono fabric. It did however mean that, if silk producers were to tap into the growth of the domestic clothing market, they had no choice but to seek to compete with cotton in the fashion stakes. They too, therefore, set about developing and designing cheaper but also more wearable and exciting fabrics intended to appeal to the expanding market of clothing consumers pursuing kimono fashion. Meanwhile, wool muslin, increasingly produced as a kimono fabric after the opening of the ports, also competed with silk for its feel and wearability and for the clear and bright colours in which it could be dyed or printed (Rosovsky and Nakagawa, 1963, pp. 64–65). Given the historically conditioned form of Japanese-style clothes, the focus would remain on the fabric, but success in the expanding clothing market depended on producing material that was distinctive in colour and design, wearable and not too expensive, but with the visual and sensual qualities that had defined luxury silk.

If being in fashion meant acquiring a whole new kimono length in an up-to-date fabric, then it would demand a relatively significant outlay, though, as prices fell, one that more and more clothing consumers were clearly able to make. However, at the same time, the flexibility and adaptability of Japanese-style clothing made it in many ways ideal territory for the operation of populuxe copying of elite fashions by means of alterations and accessories that also increased the demand for appropriate textiles in the domestic market. The periodic dismantling and cleaning of kimono provided an opportunity for a range of revamping – by the owner herself or a professional – with more up-to-date trimmings and decorations. The *obi* emerged as the most fashion-dependent element in women's clothes, offering wide scope for changing patterns and materials at less than the cost of a whole kimono (Tamura, 2001, p. 34). By the inter-war years, the detachable kimono collar (*han'eri*) had become a fashion battleground, available in a shifting range of colours and forms of

[7] According to Uchida (1988, p. 164), as a result of the spread of Japanese-style cotton fabrics, 'the ordinary Japanese people wore more colourful and more fashionable garments than the contemporary Western masses.' Certainly, in 1886, the British Vice-Consul was criticising British cotton exporters for making no attempt to meet Japanese people's 'taste for changing and fanciful patterns' (quoted in Sugiyama, 1988, pp. 293–94).

decoration (Nakamura, 2005, p. 76).[8] Accessories also provided a vehicle for the introduction of new materials and Western-style elements into kimono fashion, and from the opening of the ports onwards, shawls and bags, as well as collars and linings in soft and brightly coloured, newly introduced wool, were increasingly being utilised to add a 'modern' element to a kimono look.

At the same time, the long-term value of a kimono length, together with the fact that it could be made to fit anyone, provided the conditions for a large-scale second-hand market in Japanese-style clothing that operated as a means to transmit fashion geographically and through the income range. As Lemire (1991, pp. 61–64) shows in the British case, the existence of a second-hand market lessens the risks involved in buying an expensive, fashionable item and acts to diffuse fashion to the less well-off. Tamura demonstrates the spread of clothing fashion into the provinces in the mid-nineteenth century through analysis of items pawned or stolen, which typically included both relatively expensive formal silk goods and fashionable cotton stripes and *kasuri* (Tamura, 2004, pp. 311–16). In Tokyo, dealers in second-hand clothes, specialising and carefully differentiating what they had to sell by type and region of origin, collected in the Kanda area, and specialist shippers bought up large orders of items for transportation from nearby Ueno and Akihabara stations to dealers in the Northeast (Asaoka, 2003, pp. 161–80). There and elsewhere, networks of second-hand clothes shops and itinerant sellers expanded the market for male and female clothing and accessories in the growing range of colours, designs and types that city fashions first demanded.

Furthermore, the ways in which kimono were worn meant that, despite their cost and durability, a consumer would ideally want to own and display several outfits. Japanese-style clothes are clearly differentiated, in terms of colour/pattern and type of material, according to season, age and status of wearer, and degree of formality. Although there were shifts and relaxations over time within this structure, it remained the case that those who desired and could afford to be properly kitted out needed fashionable garments appropriate to each season, and for each degree of formality.[9] In particular, the distinction between

[8] For some literary descriptions of village girls using brightly coloured *obi* and other accessories in non-traditional fabrics to dress up their ordinary cotton kimono, see Asaoka, 2003, pp. 66–67.

[9] The 289 upper middle-class readers of *Fujin Gakō* (Women's Illustrated) who took part in a survey in 1941 owned around 16–20 kimono each (Muraki, 2006, pp. 100–1).

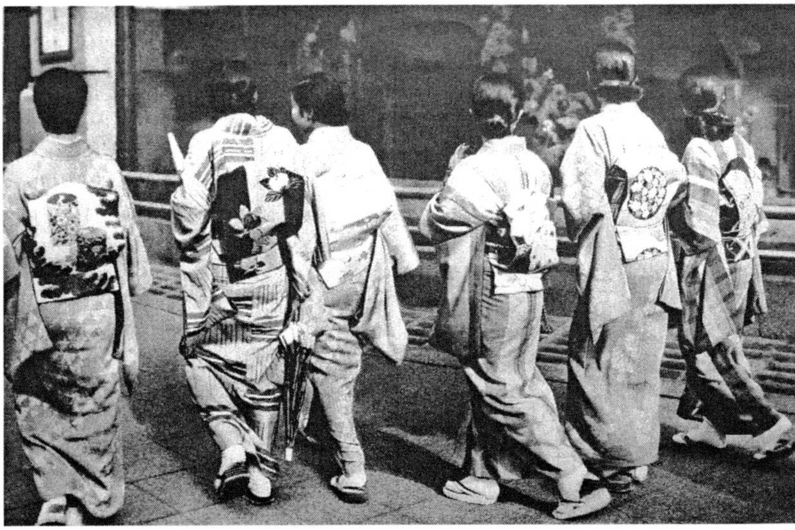

Figure 7.1 Young women displaying their finery on an inter-war high street
Source: Asahi Shimbun, 1933, p. 24.

everyday clothes and those that could be worn as 'best' remained strong. Moreover, 'best' was meant for display, and the custom of dressing up and going out to see and be seen in a relatively elaborate and fashionable outfit (*o-share*) can still be observed on Japanese streets. As soon as they could afford to do so, therefore, Japanese girls and women sought to acquire kimono, or at least accessories, which they could enjoy displaying on high days and holidays (Figure 7.1). By the inter-war period, the practice of *o-share* had spread well beyond the upper classes, as incomes had risen and new urban environments came to offer more opportunities for display (Fujiwara, 2006, pp. 38–40).

Hence, although 'traditional' Japanese dress never moved, as its Chinese counterpart did, from the draped to the fitted and tailored, this did not prove a barrier to the development of many of the same forces of fashion as can be observed driving the growth in demand for clothes in Europe. Commercially produced cotton fabrics offered a range of new, cheaper and more convenient possibilities for increasing numbers of clothing consumers; as their spending power grew, more and more women were able to acquire versions of urban high fashion, even if only in the form of accessories, and eventually to aspire to something in silk; the second-hand trade spread fashion more widely and reduced the cost of being up to date. While modernising Chinese women gradually shifted from flowing robes to more-and-more close-fitting and fashionably-cut *qipao*, just as European ones had earlier developed the fitted dress, Japanese women focused on new colours, textures and designs in cheaper and more convenient forms of cotton, silk and even wool fabric that could be incorporated into the basic structure of a kimono outfit. The implications of this path in kimono fashion for producers within the textile industry are the subject of the next section.

Demand and supply interact: fashion and the development of the textile industry

As a result of the processes described above, producers of textiles for the domestic market in Japan faced expanding and changing demand, in forms largely determined by the nature of fashion in Japanese-style clothing. Their responses involved the development of more widely available versions of the high-class kimono fabrics and accessories that had been urban fashion among the better-off, but this was intertwined with the influence of imported goods that opened up new possibilities in terms of colour, texture and design. What emerged was an industry made up of small-scale producers in regional concentrations, producing an ever widening range of products differentiated by colour and design, by texture and feel, by seasonal use and social function, as much as by price. As Itoh and Tanimoto recognise, 'quality', essentially involving the design and appeal of the fabric, was the key to success for small-scale producing regions in the competitive market that the growth of demand generated from the second half of the nineteenth century onwards (Itoh and Tanimoto, 1998, p. 58).

In broad terms, changes in demand were reflected in the fortunes of different fabrics in the domestic market. By the later decades of the nineteenth century, and before there were any significant exports of woven cloth, the domestic 'cotton revolution' had made cotton the dominant product, while silk remained something of a luxury.[10] Thereafter, however, the share of silk steadily rose, reflecting growing domestic demand, as consumers' incomes increased and producers took silk down-market in innovative, cheaper forms. The shares of cotton and silk (including silk mixes) in consumer expenditure on clothing

[10] In 1875, cotton accounted for 64 per cent of the value of total fabric output and silk 23 per cent. However, by the 1890s, cotton's share had fallen below 50 per cent. See LTES 10, 1972, p. 18.

were roughly equivalent at just over 40 per cent in 1910. By the 1930s, silk's share had risen to almost 50 per cent, while cotton's had fallen to little more than 25 per cent (LTES 6, 1967, table 78). Cotton's share in overall fabric production recovered somewhat after 1910, but on the basis of the significant growth in exports of cotton cloth.

Underneath these broad trends, however, lay a continually shifting and diversifying pattern of production, as the fabric industry responded to the growth in its market, under the influence of fashion. With the opening to trade in the 1850s, imported textiles became part of the picture, but the cotton broad-cloth that foreign producers mainly had to sell was not, for the most part, in direct competition with home-produced textiles for kimono and accessories. Nonetheless, newly available fabrics, such as wool and calico, dyed in bright colours and exciting patterns, suggested the directions in which textile producers had to go to meet the growing and widening demand for clothing materials. Increasingly, success in the domestic market depended on being able to offer populuxe textiles that combined the look and feel of the high-quality silk fashions of the Tokugawa cities with the colours, textures and design possibilities opened up by imported inputs and new techniques.

For cotton fabric producers, it thus became increasingly hard to rely on sales of the same basic stripes and *kasuri*. By the end of the nineteenth century, they faced growing competition in the domestic clothing market, not from imported or factory-made textiles, but from an expanding range of narrow-width kimono materials using new inputs, such as wool muslin or cotton flannel, but also lower-grade silk, on its own or in combination with cotton and later rayon. Such fabrics were not necessarily cheaper than standard cotton, but they were produced in more varied and colourful designs than the straightforward stripes and splash patterns, and they could be made to look and feel much more like luxury silk (Uchida, 1988, pp. 167–68). As a result, ordinary striped and *kasuri* cotton was gradually relegated to the role of rural work-wear, eventually to be transformed into the 'traditional' craft textile that it represents today. Meanwhile, consumers sought to choose from a wide and changing range of Japanese-style fabrics, available in quantities, consistent quality and innovative designs not known before.

The capacity to meet demand of this kind was determined by technical and organisational developments among the producers of Japanese-style clothing textiles. In cotton weaving, the shift to machine-made cotton yarn, produced from imported raw cotton, proved decisive for many production districts. Factory-produced yarn was not only cheaper and more uniform, but also finer and more even, creating a clearer and smoother effect when dyed, and making it possible to produce fabric of consistent quality in the colours and patterns that the growing market demanded (Tamura, 2004, pp. 9–12). In silk production, on the other hand, small-scale producers 'came to life' again in the 1910s (Matsumura, 2006, p. 94), in response to growth in domestic demand for kimono fabrics that were highly differentiated but made from less high-quality silk yarn than was required for the export market. In both sectors, synthetic dyes created opportunities for colours way beyond those traditionally used in ordinary woven fabrics, and inherited dyeing techniques were taken in complex new directions.

The use of new inputs was combined with technological improvements that enabled weavers to produce larger quantities of cloth in more complex patterns from cheaper raw materials, while maintaining quality and consistency (Tamura, 2004, pp. 381–82). These included improved looms and the Jacquard mechanism that revolutionised the design and production of complex woven patterns in silk. The electric motor was central to the survival of small-scale producers in many industries, but in none more so than weaving. Mechanisation of the production of Japanese-style textiles spread rapidly after the turn of the century, with electrification and the development of power-looms capable of producing cloth in kimono width (Minami, 1987, ch. 10).

Nonetheless, while the power-loom undoubtedly raised labour productivity, its attraction for small-scale weavers may also have lain in its ability to improve the quality of the product, in terms of the evenness and consistency of the weaving, and despite the greater use of powered machinery, techniques of production continued to require high levels of labour input and skill, especially given the differentiation and frequent design changes that a market driven by fashion increasingly demanded. Labour- and skill-intensive techniques of dyeing and weaving that only small-scale, 'traditional' producers could command remained the key to producing distinctive and differentiated colours and patterns in kimono fabric.[11] Hence, the relative cost reduction that the power loom offered was restricted by the frequent stops and changes necessary to achieve complex and differentiated woven designs and the consequent limitations to scale economies, while the share of the weaving element in overall cost of production was anyway lower than with simpler plain

[11] Dyeing, which was highly skilled and specialised but also crucial to the brand identity and appeal of the fabric, accounted for about a third of the cost of production in Japanese-style cotton fabrics (Uchida, 1988, pp. 162–63).

or printed fabrics that did not depend on skilled and costly dyeing (Uchida, 1988, p. 165).

The development of fashion in Japanese clothing thus continued to give advantages to small-scale producers, technologically and in terms of product differentiation. However, their incorporation into the fashion system did present new organisational challenges. A key factor in the capacity of *sanchi* textile producers to respond to the growth in clothing demand was the ability to manufacture fabric consistently in the identifiable colours and patterns that differentiation in kimono fashion involved.[12] Itoh and Tanimoto (1988, pp. 58–59) show how the dealers who sought to organise and market the production of small-scale contract weavers wrestled with the problem of ensuring that they produced to consistent and high-quality design standards. In their case-study region, local textile merchants adopted the putting-out system principally as a means of controlling what small-scale household weavers produced, supplying them with pre-dyed yarn and specifying colours and designs in the light of market trends.

putting out – to ↑ output but also to monitor output quality.

The solution in many cases lay in defining the qualities to which a local 'brand' label could be attached, and groups of small-scale weavers and dyers came together to create the institutions that could guarantee the identity and quality of their particular type of fabric.[13] These institutions also provided small-scale producers with a link to the market information necessary if they were to keep up with changing demands. Eventually, the congregation of small-scale producers into *sanchi* industrial districts made provision of market information and co-ordination of response easier and facilitated the regulation of location-specific brands. Local producer associations liaised with, for example, department-store buyers, in order to develop the product lines that the fashion market required. Electrification and the use of powered machinery also encouraged the concentration of textile producers within industrial districts, but the nature of the market for Japanese-style textiles continued to preclude large-scale mass production and to enable small-scale producers, suitably organised within their local *sanchi*, to survive and develop.

By the 1920s, therefore, while new fabrics were appearing in the market all the time, most continued to come from small-scale producers

---

[12] As Abe and Saitō (1988, p. 145) put it, it was necessary for a local area to produce 'traditional' textiles 'whose pattern or touch could easily be distinguished from (those produced) elsewhere'.

[13] For examples, see Itoh and Tanimoto, 1988, p. 61, as well as the *meisen* case-study below.

located in particular areas or industrial districts, using their local brand names. As Abe (1989, pp. 39–41) shows, for *sanchi* cotton weavers, for instance, it was no longer possible, by the inter-war period, just to go on producing more-or-less traditional Japanese-style cloth in stripes and splash patterns, but this did not mean that small-scale producers necessarily declined and disappeared. Some switched to larger-scale production of basic white cotton for export or the domestic market; others moved into new products for home or export markets, such as cotton flannel. But those who could respond, through product development and the adoption of new inputs and technology, to the diversifying fashion trends of the period, remained able to take advantage of the continuing growth in the market for Japanese-style clothing. This was even more the case for silk-fabric producers, and the case-study which follows describes the greatest success story among local, small-scale silk producers in the dynamic fashion market of inter-war Japan.

The *meisen* kimono

The emergence of a fashion system for Japanese-style clothing came to its apotheosis in the 1920s with a flowering of fashion in the form of what became known as the *meisen* kimono. The style icons of the period, including the famed and feared 'modern girls' and café waitresses who symbolised modern liberation, wore *meisen*, but surveys suggested that, in the inter-war years, more than half of all women walking on the Ginza were wearing it, and throughout the country girls desired the distinctive *meisen* look for their *o-share* outfits.[14] As growth in per capita expenditure on other textiles tailed off in the second half of the 1920s, that on silk continued to grow, driven by rapidly expanding purchases of *meisen*, which accounted for almost half of all sales of narrow-width silk cloth by 1930 (Yamauchi, 2009, tables 2 and 3). *Meisen* silk came in vivid and striking designs embodying the Japanese take on modernity,[15] but it was also relatively cheap and demonstrated many of the features of a mass-market fashion item. Nonetheless, it continued to be produced by small-scale weavers concentrated in a particular region, the name of which was used to brand the product.

---

[14] Such surveys recorded 50.5 per cent of women on the Ginza in 1925 and 84 per cent in 1928 as wearing *meisen* (Yamauchi, 2009, p. 9).

[15] Stuffy commentators complained that women were going out dressed in what looked like Western-style curtains (Nitta, Tanaka and Koyama, 2003, p. 54).

This region, known as Isesaki, was located in Gunma Prefecture, one of the main centres of silk production in Japan.[16] Weavers within farm households had been manufacturing silk textiles in the area since the Tokugawa period, using lower-grade silk to produce plain woven fabric that was nice to wear but relatively hard-wearing (Fujiwara, 2006, p. 49; Terada, 1979, pp. 215–20). As it developed into a specialist weaving district through the second half of the nineteenth century, production came to be organised by clothiers who sub-contracted work to weavers and dyers in farm households or small-scale workshops and sold the finished product on through locally based factors and wholesalers. In the 1890s, experiments began in the region with spun silk, which was produced from waste cocoons unsuitable for reeling into export-grade yarn. By the 1910s, power looms were being adopted and a new method of dyeing was developed that made possible the production of highly coloured and patterned, but relatively cheap, clothing fabric.

Traditionally, dyed pictorial designs on silk fabric could be produced only by means of the time-consuming and expensive method known as *yūzen*, which depends on painting and dyeing each kimono length individually by a highly skilled hand. The Isesaki method involved adaptations to traditional resist-dyeing techniques that enabled the desired pattern to be created through stencilling colours on to the individual threads to be woven. The subsequent weaving of the threads, combined with the use of spun silk, results in the distinctive fuzzy effect that defines *meisen*, but the technique could be used to produce dramatic and colourful designs consistently, on the repeated basis necessary for, relatively speaking, mass production.

Once the potential of Isesaki *meisen* techniques was recognised, an explosion of new, rapidly changing and increasingly radical designs was unleashed. *Meisen* kimono (and *haori*) are particularly famed for their use of art deco and art nouveau motifs, but surviving examples show them in everything from cubist-influenced abstract designs to dramatic re-workings of traditional flower patterns and geometrical repeats (Dees, 2009, pp. 78–101). As the popularity of this kind of kimono spread, new varieties were developed, involving both high- and low-quality silk, mixed with cotton or man-made fibres, and the *meisen* label could be attached to anything from cheap-and-cheerful mass-market silk kimono to the high-fashion outfit of the 'modern girl' (Fujiwara, 2006,

---

[16] See Matsuzaki, 2006 for the story of the region's development, together with the website of the Isesaki *meisen* producers' co-operative (http://www.kougei.or.jp/isesaki/) for illustrations.

p. 49). Production spread out from the Isesaki region and producers of other kinds of fabric were obliged to respond, so that the period from the Kantō earthquake of 1923 until the late 1930s was dominated by boldly patterned styles, quite different from the subdued and subtle fashions of earlier times (Fujiwara, 2006, pp. 64–65).[17]

However, *meisen* kimono were radical not just in how they looked and how they were made, but also in the ways in which they were marketed and consumed as fashion goods. For the big-city department stores, the *meisen* kimono provided the vehicle by means of which to introduce the techniques of the fashion system to the marketing of Japanese-style clothing. Yamauchi (2009, pp. 7–10) concludes that, by the end of the 1920s, almost all the output of Isesaki *meisen* was going to the big cities (Tokyo, Osaka, Kyoto and Nagoya), where it was sold in the department stores that were by then accounting for around half of urban clothes sales (see Figure 7.2).[18] New designs were produced every year and widely advertised in relevant media, such as women's magazines; *meisen* made a striking display to attract customers into stores and *meisen* kimono were commonly offered at bargain prices in sales. Although, by modern Western standards, *meisen* silk is of high quality and durable – plenty of pre-war examples have survived to go on sale on the internet today – it was cheap and disposable in comparison with more traditional kimono silks (Nitta, Tanaka and Koyama, 2003, pp. 66–71).[19] Hence, *meisen* kimono could be sold ready made-up, in the expectation that they would go out of fashion, rather than be taken apart, preserved and passed on as family heirlooms. Although by no means an everyday purchase for most women, the *meisen* kimono nonetheless brought the concept of the mass-market fashion item to a wide market of inter-war consumers.[20]

Meisen kimono - not an everyday purchase but brought the concept of mass market fashion to wide consumer market

[17] For example, those shown in Figure 13.1.

[18] Nakanishi and Futaya, in their chapter (Chapter 5), show how members of better-off rural households, such as Family X, also made shopping trips to big-city kimono shops and department stores in search of new clothes.

[19] It could also be washed at home and was easier to care for than other forms of silk so that, despite being smart and striking, it could be worn on a more everyday basis (Fujiwara, 2006, p. 51).

[20] In the later 1920s, Isesaki kimono lengths were being advertised in department store bargain sales in Osaka for between 5 and 8 yen, at a time when the average daily wage for a female worker in manufacturing was about 0.9 yen (Yamauchi, 2009, table 7 and Ohkawa and Shinohara, 1979, table A52). However, these were 'loss-leader' prices for ordinary patterns, intended to lure customers in to spot much more exciting and expensive possibilities.

Figure 7.2 Shopping for kimono textiles in an inter-war department store
Source: Asahi Shinbun, 1933, p. 233.

This depended, however, on the ability to produce *meisen* silk on the scale and in the rapidly changing designs demanded by the fashion market. With stencil-dyeing and power-looms, weavers could produce in relatively large quantities, but production remained in the hands of small factories and workshops. The Isesaki brand was regulated by a producers' association, founded in the 1880s, which sought to maintain quality as producer numbers and production volumes increased (Matsuzaki, 2006, pp. 249–52). As demand for the product grew, *meisen* techniques were copied by weavers outside the Isesaki area, but the skills involved in transferring design to fabric ruled out large-scale mass production and left the market to be supplied by relatively small-scale producers able to acquire and practise the still labour-intensive methods involved. Nonetheless, local institutions ensured that producers were in touch with fashion trends, and producers' organisations such as the Isesaki association liaised with the Tokyo and Osaka department stores that commissioned designs for their annual collections (Nitta, Tanaka and Koyama, 2003, pp. 66–67).

The *meisen* kimono thus displayed most of the characteristics of a modern fashion good: consciously designed to be visually striking but expected to date; advertised heavily in fast-changing designs; bought to be seen and enjoyed, rather than to last. Yet it continued to be produced by small-scale, regionally based businesses, capable of mechanised production on a relatively large scale, using factory-made inputs such as synthetic dyes and eventually yarns, but employing labour- and skill-intensive techniques derived from traditional textile-production methods. It reflected the growth in demand for up-to-date and distinctively new versions of the silk clothes the upper classes alone had once worn, as incomes rose and more and more young women, with wages of their own, found themselves in a position to buy and display clothes in the public spaces offered by modernising urban Japan. It cut out a path that might have led to the mass-market kimono, had war and Occupation not intervened to bring about a fundamental shift in the attitudes of Japanese people towards their clothing system,[21] and it demonstrated that, even in the modernising, industrialising world of inter-war Japan, 'traditional' clothing could become the subject of modern fashion.

Conclusion

The story of the growth of clothing demand and fashion in pre-war Japan, culminating in the phenomenon of the *meisen* kimono, undermines both the assumption that fashion does not operate in 'traditional' clothing systems and the argument that it has to be associated with the large-scale mass production of modern Western-style capitalism. As economic growth and industrialisation proceeded in Japan, increasing numbers of clothing consumers, like their European counterparts, switched to commercially produced items, at first in an expanding range of attractive and convenient cotton fabrics and later in 'modern' versions of once-luxury silk. However, the nature of Japanese-style clothing and the fashions that emerged within it meant that, although these materials were manufactured and marketed in ways that reflected the increasing absorption of new techniques and inputs, they continued to be produced in relatively small-scale establishments, concentrated in regional industrial districts. It was here that it was possible to develop and manage the skills required to create the kinds of fabric the market demanded, even if in new and fashionable designs.

It could of course be argued that the path followed by Japanese-style clothing and its production in the pre-war period represented a dead-end, cut off by the almost complete switch to Western style after the Second World War, which froze the kimono in a particular 'traditional' form suited only to the most formal of occasions (Dalby, 2001, pp. 125–36). However, the producers that it had fostered and allowed

[21] See Gordon's chapter (Chapter 3) for discussion of this shift.

to develop did not disappear with their pre-war product. Many were able to switch into production of fabric for Western-style garments, utilising the skills they had developed pre-war. Itoh and Tanimoto (1998, pp. 63–66) provide examples of the survival and development of putting-out systems in textile production in the post-Second World War period, with small-scale weavers in regions formerly specialising in silk and cotton entering into sub-contracting relationships with the large-scale suppliers of man-made fibres and wool yarn for the flexible production of a wide range of differentiated textile products. Ronald Dore, studying the weaving industry in the 1970s, found it still the domain of small-scale, family-based producers, congregating in industrial districts (Dore, 1986, pp. 153–78). Although most were by then producing Western-style cloth, their attention to detail, quality and differentiation reflected a market formed in the context of pre-war clothing and its fashions. Japanese people continued to spend a higher proportion of their income on clothing and to exhibit a higher turnover in clothes than their Western counterparts, while the ability of the domestic textile industry – still dominated, in crucial sectors, by small-scale, flexible businesses – to meet their exacting and changing demands was reflected in continued low levels of imports of textiles and clothing (Dore 1986, p. 193 and table 7.4). In the absence of a tradition of ready-made clothes production, home-sewing of purchased fabric, aided now by the sewing machine, remained the route to accessible women's fashion, even if now in Western style, well into the post-war period (see Chapter 3).

It is now coming to be accepted that, rather than simply 'catching up' with the West, Japan followed its own distinctive path of industrialisation, involving a continued role for small-scale, labour- and skill-intensive forms of production, market-oriented but organised within institutional structures rather different from those that characterised capital-intensive industrialisation of the Anglo-American variety (Sugihara, 2003; Saitō, 2008). If this is so, the story of pre-war clothing demonstrates both the part played by the 'modernisation' of 'indigenous', 'traditional' goods, such as the kimono, and the need to recognise the influence of the consumers of these goods in determining, through a process of fashion creation, the direction of technical and economic change in their production. The pre-war consumer in her art deco *meisen* kimono, bought from a department store for its striking design and fashionable appearance, stepping out in her city, cannot be ignored, if we are to understand how history formed the industrial economy of modern Japan.

References

Abe, T. (1989) *Nihon ni Okeru Sanchi Men'orimonogyō no Hatten* (The Development of the *Sanchi* Cotton-Weaving Industry in Japan), Tokyo: Tōkyō Daigaku Shuppan Kai.

Abe, T. (1990) 'Menkōgyō' (The Cotton Industry), in Abe, T. & Nishikawa, S. (eds) *Sangyōka no Jidai (1), Nihon Keizai Shi*, vol. 4 (The Age of Industrialisation 1, History of the Japanese Economy vol. 4), Tokyo: Iwanami Shoten, pp. 163–212.

Abe, T. & Saitō, O. (1988) 'From Putting-out to the Factory: A Cotton-weaving District in Late-Meiji Japan', *Textile History* 19(2): 143–58.

Asahi Shimbun (1933) *Changing Japan Seen through the Camera*, Tokyo: Asahi Shimbun.

Asaoka, K. (2003) *Furugi* (Second-hand Clothes), Tokyo: Hōsei Daigaku Shuppankyoku.

Bank of Japan Statistics Department (1966) *Hundred-Year Statistics of the Japanese Economy*, Tokyo: Bank of Japan.

Braudel, F. (1981), *The Structures of Everyday Life*, trans. Reynolds, S., London: Collins.

Dalby, L. (2001) *Kimono: Fashioning Culture*, London: Vintage.

Dees, J. (2009) *Taishō Kimono*, Milan: Skira.

Dore, Ronald (1986) *Flexible Rigidities: Industrial Policy and Structural Adjustment in the Japanese Economy 1970–80*, London: Athlone.

Finnane, Antonia (2008) *Changing Clothes in China: Fashion, History, Nation*, New York: Columbia University Press.

Fujita, Kayoko (2009) 'Japan Indianized: The Material Culture of Imported Textiles, 1550–1850', in Riello, G. & Parthasarathati, P. (eds), *The Spinning World: A Global History of Cotton Textiles*, Oxford: Oxford University Press, pp. 181–203.

Fujiwara Rika (2006) 'Yosoyuki to Fudangi' (Best Dress and Normal Dress), in Koizumi, K. (ed.), *Shōwa no Kimono*, Tokyo: Kawade Shoten, pp. 38–59.

Itoh, M. & Tanimoto. M, (1998) 'Rural Entrepreneurs in the Cotton-weaving Industry of Japan', in Hayami, Y. (ed.), *Toward the Rural-Based Development of Commerce and Industry*, Washington: The World Bank, pp. 47–68.

Jō, K. (2007) *Nihon no Fasshon* (Japanese Fashion), Kyoto: Seigensha.

Kiyoshi, F. (2006) 'Hyakkaten no Yakuwari' (The Role of Department Stores), in Koizumi, K. (ed.), *Shōwa no Kimono*, Tokyo: Kawade Shoten, pp. 68–70.

Lemire, B. (1991) *Fashion's Favourite: the Cotton Trade and the Consumer in Britain, 1660–1800*, Oxford: Oxford University Press.

Lemire, B. (1997) *Dress, Culture and Commerce: The English Clothing Trade before the Factory*. Basingstoke: Macmillan.

Lemire, B. (2005) *The Business of Everyday Life: Gender, Practice and Social Politics in England, c. 1600–1900*, Manchester: Manchester University Press.

Lemire, B. (2009) 'Revising the Historical Narrative: India, Europe and the Cotton Trade, c.1300–1800', in Riello, G. & Parthasarathati, P. (eds) *The Spinning World: A Global History of Cotton Textiles*, Oxford: Oxford University Press, pp. 205–26.

LTES 6 = Shinohara, M. (1967) *Kojin Shōhi Shishutsu, Chōki Keizai Tōkei Vol. 6* (Long Term Economic Statistics, Personal Consumption Expenditure), Tokyo: Tōyō Keizai Shinpōsha.

LTES 10 = Shinohara, M. (1972) *Kōgyōka, Chōki Keizai Tōkei, Vol. 10,* (Long Term Economic Statistics, Mining and Manufacturing) Tokyo: Tōyō Keizai Shinpōsha.

Matsumura, S. (2006) 'Dualism in the Silk-Reeling Industry in Suwa from the 1910s to the 1930s', in Tanimoto, M. (ed.), *The Role of Tradition in Japan's Industrialization,* Oxford: Oxford University Press, pp. 93–120.

Matsuzaki, H. (2006) 'The Development of a Rural Weaving Industry and Its Social Capital', in Tanimoto, M. (ed.), *The Role of Tradition in Japan's Industrialization,* Oxford: Oxford University Press, pp. 243–72.

McKendrick, N. (1982) 'The Consumer Revolution of Eighteenth-century England', in McKendrick, N., Brewer, J. & Plumb, J. H. (eds), *The Birth of a Consumer Society,* London: Europa Publications, pp. 9–33.

Minami, R. (1987) *Power Revolution in the Industrialization of Japan, 1885–1940,* Tokyo: Kinokuniya.

Muraki, K. (2006) 'Kimono no Kazu' (Numbers of Kimono), in Koizumi, K. (ed.), *Shōwa no Kimono,* Tokyo: Kawade Shoten, pp. 100–6.

Nakamura, K. (2005) *Shōwa Modan Kimono* (Modern Kimono of the Shōwa Era), Tokyo: Kawade Shobō.

Nitta, T., Tanaka, Y. & Koyama, S. (2003) *Tōkyō Ryūkō Seikatsu* (Tokyo Fashionable Lifestyle), Tokyo: Kawade Shobō.

Ohkawa, K. & Shinohara, M. (eds) (1979) *Patterns of Japanese Economic Development,* New Haven and London: Yale University Press.

Ozeki, M. (2003) 'Furō to Sutokku no Hifuku Shōhi' (Clothing Consumption and the Concepts of Flow and Stock), *Shakai Keizai Shigaku* 69(2): 93–107.

Rosovsky, H. & Nakagawa, K. (1963) 'The Case of the Dying Kimono: the Influence of Changing Fashions on the Development of the Japanese Woollen Industry', *Business History Review* 37(1/2): 59–80.

Saitō, O. (2008) *Hikaku Keizai Hatten Ron* (On Comparative Economic Development), Tokyo: Iwanami Shoten.

Saitō O, & Tanimoto, M. (2004) 'The Transformation of Traditional Industries', in Hayami, A., Saitō, O. & Toby, R. (eds), *Emergence of Economic Society in Japan,* Oxford: Oxford University Press, pp. 268–300.

Slade, T. (2009) *Japanese Fashion: A Cultural History,* Oxford: Berg.

Styles, J. (2009) 'What were Cottons for in the Early Industrial Revolution?' in Riello, G. & Parthasarathati, P. (eds), *The Spinning World: a Global History of Cotton Textiles,* Oxford: Oxford University Press, pp. 307–26.

Sugihara, K. (2003) 'The East Asian path of Development', in Arrighi, G., Hamashita, T. & Seldon, M. (eds) *The Resurgence of East Asia,* London: Routledge, pp. 78–123.

Sugiyama, S. (1988) 'Textile Marketing in East Asia, 1860–1914', *Textile History* 19(2): 279–98.

Tamura, H. (2001) 'Zairai Orimongyō no Gijutsu Kakushin to Ryūkō Shijō' (The Technological Development of Textile Production Centres in early Meiji Japan), *Shakai Keizai Shigaku* 67(4): 23–48.

Tamura, H. (2004) *Fasshon no Shakai Keizai Shi* (A Socio-economic History of Fashion), Tokyo: Nihon Keizai Hyōronsha.

Tanimoto, M. (1987) 'Bakumatsu Meiji ki Menpu Kokunaishijō no Hatten' (The Development of the Domestic Market for Cotton Cloth in the Meiji and Bakumatsu Eras) *Tochi Seido Shigaku* 115(April): 54–67.
Tanimoto, M. (2006) 'The Role of Tradition in Japan's Industrialization: Another Path to Industrialization', in Tanimoto, M., *The Role of Tradition in Japan's Industrialization*, Oxford: Oxford University Press, pp. 3–44.
Tanimoto, M. (ed.) (2006) *The Role of Tradition in Japan's Industrialization*, Oxford: Oxford University Press.
Terada, S. (1979) *Orimono no Kaisetsu* (A Manual on Textiles), Tokyo: Sen-i Kenkyūsha.
Uchida, H. (1988) 'Narrow Cotton Stripes and their Substitutes: Fashion, Technical Progress and Manufacturing Organisation in Japanese Popular Clothing', *Textile History* 19(2): 159–70.
Wilson, E. (2007 revised ed.) *Adorned in Dreams*, London: Tauris.
Yamauchi, Y. (2009) '1920-nendai no Meisen Shijō no Kakudai to Ryūkō Dentatsu no Shikumi' (Market Growth of the Silk Textile Meisen in the 1920s and the Fashion Creation System), *Keiei Shigaku* 44(1): 3–30.

8

Reviving Tradition: Patients and the Shaping of Japan's Traditional Medicines Industry

Maki Umemura

Introduction

In November 2009, Japan's newly elected government proposed to end the coverage of traditional medicines under universal health insurance. This move was driven by escalating health care costs and doubts over the cost-effectiveness of these therapies. In opposition, consumers of traditional medicine, together with producers, successfully petitioned the government to shelve its plan.

Government scepticism towards traditional medicines in Japan is more than a century old. When the country opened to the West in the late nineteenth century after more than two-and-a half centuries of seclusion, the government endorsed the practice of Western-style medicine at the expense of traditional medicine. This was part of Japan's elite-driven modernisation programme. Despite the government's efforts to stamp out a medical tradition regarded as 'backward', patients have continued to consume traditional medicines, alongside and despite their growing access to Western medical treatments. Consumers have played a vital role in ensuring the survival of traditional medicines in Japan. This chapter examines the decline and re-emergence of traditional medicine in Japanese society, as it evolved into a 'modern' product. My aim is to examine the reasons why traditional medicine made this comeback, and to highlight the role of consumers in its resurgence.

Historians of consumption in Western countries have debated a range of issues, from when consumer society emerged, what it constituted, and why it occurred, to how it should be studied (Brewer and Porter, 1994). In contrast to the availability of works on the history of consumption in the West, only now are historians beginning to explore the history of consumption in Japan. Economic historians of Japan have focussed on supply-side economic history, despite the country's flourishing consumer society. In one of the few works on Japanese consumption history, Penelope Francks has argued that Japanese consumer society emerged in the Tokugawa period, prior to industrialisation, and manifested itself predominantly through everyday, 'traditional' goods (Francks, 2009a). Osamu Saitō and Masayuki Tanimoto have also examined the growth of consumption in rural Japan in the nineteenth century (Saitō and Tanimoto, 2004). My study contributes to these discussions on the consumption of traditional products, arguing that they were indeed part of Japan's flourishing consumer society in the twentieth century. It also offers insight into why and how the popularity of consumer products changes, and what accounts for their resilience over time.

My use of the terms 'traditional' and 'modern' requires elaboration. Use of a simplistic traditional/modern dichotomy can often be criticised for oversimplifying what may be a very fluid and vague boundary of definition (Tipps, 1973). After all, even in the supposedly more 'modern' West, the idea that medicine should be 'scientific' was adopted very gradually and only achieved the status of orthodoxy in the inter-war period, following the widespread acceptance of the germ theory of disease (Bivins, 2007, p. 34).[1] Popular conceptions of orthodox medicine have been fluid over time, regardless of location (Ikai, 2010).

Despite these shortcomings, the term 'traditional medicine' in particular offers a useful distinction from modern biomedicine. This chapter adopts the World Health Organisation's definition of traditional medicine. This refers to,

> a diversity of health practices, knowledge and beliefs incorporating plant, animal, and/or mineral-based medicines...applied singly or in combination to maintain well-being, as well as to treat, diagnose, or prevent illness...A medical system is called 'traditional' when it is practised within the country of origin [It is referred to as 'alternative' when practised beyond the borders of origin]. (WHO, 2001, pp. 1–2)

Traditional medicine in Japan

Traditional medicine in Japan refers to a range of herbal medicines and physical therapies. These herbal medicines include folk medicines, pat-

[1] Scientific medicine refers to the idea that medicine should be universal, absolute, and objective, rather than individual, contingent, and subjective.

ent medicines, and the Japanese versions of Chinese medicines known as Kanpō, while the physical remedies include, among others, acupuncture and moxibustion (WHO, 2005, p. 193). These different types of traditional medicine have survived over the decades through different means and to different extents. In order to examine traditional medicine as a consumer product, this chapter will focus on herbal medicines. It will look particularly closely at Kanpō medicine, the main form of herbal medicine in Japan.

Among herbal medicines, folk medicines represent healing methods long-practised and preserved as accepted knowledge among the general population. Often, a particular herb is used to treat a specific ailment. Examples of commonly used folk medicines in Japan include aloe, *hatomugi* (Job's tears), and *dokudami* (chameleon plant). These have often been consumed as teas or food supplements.

Although the term 'patent medicines' is somewhat of a misnomer, it generally refers to secret and non-secret remedies that are trademarked.[2] These medicines have been available without a physician's prescription, through pharmacies or itinerant merchants. By the seventeenth century, medicine pedlars, particularly those from Toyama prefecture, were developing a sophisticated business supplying patent medicines across Japan. The dealers would deliver a medicine box filled with these medicines to each household and collect payment for whatever had been used at a later date – somewhat akin to the way the use of a hotel minibar is charged today. While no longer so common, this means of distribution was intended to compete with those of existing sellers of patent medicines by offering cash-poor commoners the option to purchase a few necessary items from a chest full of medicines kept at home (Tamagawa, 2005).

Kanpō is different from folk and patent medicines in that it belongs to a coherent, long-established system of medical thought. Kanpō medicine is a localised version of Chinese medicine, which arrived in Japan around the sixth century. Over the centuries, Kanpō medicine developed two streams of specialisation: one dedicated to herbal remedies, and another dedicated to acupuncture, moxibustion, and massage (Otsuka, 1976; Otsuka, 2001; Shinmura, 2006). Today, Kanpō medicines are used as complements to or substitutes for Western medicine.

Historically, Kanpō practitioners considered illness as a manifestation of imbalances in the body. To treat illness, they aimed to restore bodily balance in their patients. Kanpō medicine refers to a combination of medicinal herbs known to treat certain conditions according to a theory

[2] For the most part, 'patent medicines' are not patented. Medicines in Japan were not actually granted product patents until 1976.

of diagnosis and therapy. Its practitioners generally use several types of Kanpō medicines tailored to individual patients in order to treat a given ailment (Higashi, 1981; Matsumoto, Inoue and Kaji, 1999, pp. 254–55). Since the 1960s, most Kanpō medicines have been prescribed alongside Western medicines, by physicians trained in Western medicine (Takahashi, 1971, pp. 154–96). This use of Kanpō medicines differs from the use of traditional medicines covered under other national health insurance regimes, where the product is prescribed as part of a different medical approach to treating illness. In Britain, for example, homoeopathic treatments are prescribed by physicians who specialise in homeopathic medicine, rather than those who practise conventional Western medicine (WHO, 2001, p. 124–28). Kanpō medicine has seen a remarkable resurgence in popularity since the 1970s, particularly through the mediating role of physicians as 'proxy consumers'.

Whether in folk, patent, or Kanpō form, traditional medicines in contemporary Japan are generally used to treat chronic rather than acute conditions. For the most part, they are used to treat ailments such as allergies, arthritis, and hypertension, rather than infections or cancer. In terms of their safety and efficacy, traditional Japanese medicines are considered to have fewer side-effects and to be milder in operation than modern Western biomedicine (Ohnuki-Tierney, 1984, pp. 91–122; Yakuji Nippōsha, 1950–2006). They are also lower-priced compared to newer, innovative therapies such as cardiovascular or anticancer drugs (Shin Nihon Hōki Shuppan, 2008).

Traditional medicine and the study of consumption

There are several reasons why traditional medicine is an important subject of study in the context of consumption. First, as a widely consumed product, pharmaceuticals offer a valuable case-study through which to investigate Japanese consumer society. After all, Japan has consistently had one of the highest per capita expenditures on pharmaceuticals, including traditional medicines (OECD, 2010; WHO, 1996). Second, this subject demonstrates how a traditional, indigenous product survived amidst modernisation and Westernisation. My research shows how a 'traditional' product 'modernised' over the decades and explores how advances in technology and increased regulation, along with growing affluence and changing consumer expectations, influenced this process. Third, looking at traditional medicines offers a unique opportunity to examine not only how institutions shape consumer behaviour, but also the extent to which consumers have agency in highly regulated sectors where we might expect regulators and producers to dictate industrial development. Fourth, it highlights the role of proxy consumers – those who make the decision to consume on behalf of the end-user – in mediating and shaping consumption.

Medicines were part of Japanese consumer society long before Japan opened to the West and industrialised. Japanese traditional pharmaceutical firms were concentrated in the Doshōmachi district of Osaka, which had long been a centre for distributors of herbal medicines. Japan's leading Western-style pharmaceutical firms today, such as Takeda, Tanabe, and Shionogi, originated as importers and distributors of Chinese and domestic herbal medicines. Since the early eighteenth century, wholesalers had gathered in Doshōmachi to examine the medicines and bargain over prices. They were part of a merchant guild (*kabunakama*) that was given monopoly rights for nationwide distribution in exchange for inspection of the quality of medicines. From Osaka, the goods were distributed to markets nation-wide (Nihon Yakushi Gakkai, 1995).

The leaders of the Meiji regime delegitimised this market for traditional medicines, as officials ceased to recognise practitioners of traditional medicine as physicians. It is true that certain forms of traditional medicine were still consumed through markets, itinerant merchants, or the gathering of certain medicinal plants. Despite the call by practitioners of traditional medicine for a reappraisal of these medicines, however, official sanction remained limited to Western-style medicines. As Japan entered its years of militarisation and anti-Westernism, traditional medicines came to be consumed as less desirable remedies by those who were not able to buy Western-style medicines.

What makes traditional medicine particularly significant for consumption history, however, is that its decline in consumer society in the first half of the twentieth century was to be followed by what seemed a paradoxical resurgence in the second half of the century. The re-emergence of traditional medicines in the post-Second World War period was led by a number of factors, including the realisation of the limitations of Western medicine and the development of technologies to mass-produce standardised versions of traditional medicines that enabled physicians to prescribe them alongside Western medicines.

Consumers also drove this process. Without their willingness to buy traditional medicines, there would have been no resurgence. There were several developments in the post-war period that empowered consumers. For example, a greater number of people were wealthier, health-conscious, and better informed; various remedies created for chronic ailments did not quite 'cure' the diseases, and physicians emerged as powerful proxy consumers.

In what follows, I trace the evolution of traditional medicines in Japanese consumer society from the late nineteenth century to 2000, looking particularly closely at the post-Second World War period, both to illustrate how traditional medicines in Japan changed into modern products and to examine why they became popular again. Based on sources ranging from historical market research reports to the popular press, this chapter shows how even in a highly regulated industry – such as medicines – consumers had agency and played an important role in shaping what was produced and used.

Japan's opening to the West and the decline of Kanpō medicine, 1868–1912

As mentioned earlier, while Kanpō had been the country's mainstream medicine for more than a millennium, Japanese authorities discouraged its use following the country's opening to the West in the late nineteenth century. As part of Japan's programme of modernisation and Westernisation, the government suppressed the growth of traditional medicines as it endorsed Western medicine. After 1874, only physicians trained in Western-style medicine were permitted to practise in Japan. The new legislation sought to eliminate the popularity of traditional medicines that had flourished in Japanese consumer society since the eighteenth century (Sugaya, 1976, pp. 38–50).[3]

Predictably, existing practitioners of traditional Japanese medicine opposed the changes introduced by the Meiji regime. Their fight to maintain the legitimacy of their profession and resist the legislation took on three forms. First, they argued that Kanpō medicine was just as much based on theory as Western medicine was. They were responding to the criticism, made by the proponents of Western medicine, that Japan's traditional medicine lacked transparency or a systematic approach to treating illness that was based on scientific evidence (Kawakami, 1965, pp. 155–56).

Second, proponents of Kanpō tried to demonstrate that their treatments were more effective than Western medicine. Kanpō practitioners participated in government-sponsored trials that attempted to gauge the efficacy of Western and traditional Japanese medicine. For example, the government established a beriberi hospital in 1878 to evaluate whether Western medicine or traditional medicine would be more effective in treating this disease (caused by the lack of vitamin B in white rice) (Dajōkan, 1878; Carpenter, 2000). While the test results actually

[3] This legislation is known as the *Isei* (Medical system) of 1874.

came out in favour of Kanpō medicines, the practitioners' reluctance to reveal the reasons for their efficacy further undermined the legitimacy of these traditional medicines in an age that valued scientific empiricism (Dajōkan, 1879, 1881, 1882; University of Tokyo Medical Department Commemoration Committee, 1967, p. 138; Oberländer, 2005, pp. 11–36).

Third, practitioners of Kanpō medicine such as Asai Kokkan formed political organisations, for example Onchisha, set up in 1879 to lobby against the exclusion of Kanpō medicine from mainstream medical practice (*Yomiuri Shinbun*, 13 January 1891, p. 2; *Yomiuri Shinbun*, 29 November 1891, p. 2; *Yomiuri Shinbun*, 22 January 1893, p. 2). Their beliefs and political arguments are recorded in publications such as *Onchi Idan* and *Keikō Ihō* – periodicals designed to legitimise and promote Kanpō medicine (*Onchi Idan*, 1879–1889; *Keikō Ihōsha*, *Keikō Ihō*, 1893–1897). This political movement appears to have reached its height in the 1890s, but was quelled when a bill to reform regulations and extend medical licences to traditional practitioners was defeated in parliament in 1895 (House of Representatives, 6 February 1895).

By the early 1910s, Western medicine had triumphed – at least officially – over traditional Japanese medicines. In 1874, there were 23,015 physicians recorded as practising Kanpō, as compared with 5,274 practising Western medicine (Ministry of Health and Welfare, 1976, p. 45). While later national figures are not readily available, in Tokyo at least, by 1910, the number of Kanpō practitioners had dwindled to just eight (*Yomiuri Shinbun*, 21 July 1910, p. 3).

It is important to remember, however, that the majority of Japanese physicians were happy to embrace Western medicine. After all, in the 1890s fewer than 2,000 Kanpō practitioners had actually participated in overt resistance to the state's policy of promoting Western medicine (Sugaya, 1976, p. 49). Moreover, the licensing regulations of 1874 did not forbid the practice of traditional Japanese medicine, but only required physicians to understand and be able to practise Western medicine as well. Certainly, at a time when Japan was engaged in a war with China and was striving to catch up with the West, medicines of Chinese origin did not enjoy much official support.[4] Yet the demise of Kanpō medicines in the Meiji period also had much to do with the Kanpō activists' hostility to learning Western medicine. They were adamant that Kanpō medicines should be considered as alternatives rather than as complements

[4] These issues were discussed in the proceedings of the Imperial Diet mentioned above.

to Western medicines. Disagreement within the medical profession over whether to offer licences to Kanpō practitioners also undermined lobbying efforts (*Yomiuri Shinbun*, 5 December 1892, p. 1).

Yet articles from the popular press suggest that consumers were ambivalent towards Western-style medicines and continued to take traditional medicines in the early twentieth century. Newspapers, for example, repeatedly reported on the use of traditional remedies (e.g. *Yomiuri Shinbun*, 2 April 1930, p. 2; *Yomiuri Shinbun*, 7 September 1932, p. 9). Consumers effectively undermined the government's attempts to eradicate Kanpō medicines. Medical historians of Japan have referred to the plurality of medical practices and types of medicines consumed in Japan, from Western medicines to Japanese folk remedies (Lock, 1984, p. 63). Suzuki Akihito has argued that these reflected prevailing ambivalence towards any specific type of medicine (Suzuki, 2008, pp. 129–61). After all, this was a pre-antibiotics era; advances in Western medicine were still far from impressive, and the superiority of Western techniques remained questionable compared to their achievements in industry. Whether via a physician's prescription or direct purchase from a pharmacist or other seller, Japanese patients continued to consume a variety of medicines and, in so doing, supported the existence of traditional medicines.

Existing statistics do not allow us to make accurate estimates of the consumption of traditional medicines during the Meiji period. Even if credible data did exist, they would still not capture the many patients who visited 'physicians' with questionable qualifications or consumed a variety of folk medicines (Nagao, 1928, pp. 40–41). Between 1879 and 1912, annual per capita expenditures on medical and personal care increased from 0.6 yen to 2.1 yen, while total living expenditures rose from 18.7 yen to 81.3 yen (calculated from Ohkawa, Shinohara, and Meissner, 1979, pp. 338–39). Japanese people spent less than five per cent of their total living expenditures on their combined medical and personal care costs, a figure that remained constant for half a century. For most ordinary citizens, spending on medical services or medicines was a considerable expense.[5] As Margaret Lock notes, this was particularly true of Western doctors and their medicines – often of doubtful quality (Lock, 1984, p. 62). Most Japanese people continued to consume traditional medicine because the alternative product, Western medicine, was expensive and not much better (Fujikawa, (1932) 1980,

[5] For real examples, see the chapter by Nakanishi and Futaya (Chapter 5) in this volume.

p. 174). Before the Second World War, the main contribution of the germ theory of disease was in public health, rather than in medicine.

Refashioning traditional medicines: the Taishō and early Shōwa periods

In the minds of government officials and medical professionals, at least, the contest between Kanpō and Western-style medicines appeared to have been resolved by the end of the Meiji period. Yet there was one change in Kanpō medicines in the early twentieth century: this was an intellectual shift among Kanpō practitioners towards acceptance of Kanpō medicines as complements to Western medicines rather than substitutes for them. This shift in thinking among intellectuals reflected the reality among consumers, who were taking both types of medicine. As coverage by the popular press reveals, this discourse developed against a backdrop of growing militarism and nationalism in the interwar period.

Two publications at the time well reflected Kanpō's shifting relation to Western medicine. In 1910, Wada Keijūrō published *Ikai no Tettsui* (The Iron Hammer of the Medical World) (Wada, 1910). A physician trained in Western-style medicine, Wada argued that traditional Japanese medicine could be suitable for certain types of ailments, and argued against Kanpō's outright dismissal. Intriguingly, Wada drew upon the concept of holistic medicine, introduced by René Allendy in *Les Orientations des Idées Médicales,* to enhance Kanpō's popular appeal (Allendy, 1929; Oberländer, 1995, pp. 242–53). The journalist Nakayama Tadanao adopted a nationalistic rhetoric, claiming that Japanese medicine simply could not be inferior to Western medicine, and, if revived through Kanpō, would prove superior to Western medicine. His publication *Kanpō Igaku no Shinkenkyū* (New Research on Kanpō Medicine) was particularly well received, perhaps because it played to the nationalistic and militaristic tenor of the times (Nakayama, 1927; *Yomiuri Shinbun,* 5 June 1934, p. 4). Ironically, these authors' re-assertion of a Japanese traditional product over a Western one depended upon the borrowing of, or comparison with, Western concepts – whether it be holistic medicines or the superiority of Eastern over Western medicine. At any rate, interest in Kanpō medicines continued to endure, as evidenced in the recurrent petitions made to government (Ministry of Internal Affairs, 1920, 1923, 1939).

To most Japanese people, this debate amongst elites was irrelevant. The vast majority of Japanese commoners in the first half of the twentieth century continued to consume a combination of folk and patent medicines. We can estimate the growth in the consumption of traditional patent medicines from the growth of this industry in the early twentieth century. In 1928, for example, Toyama prefecture produced patent medicines worth 24.5 million yen at 1,021 production facilities. The leading remedies at this time included tonics, cold medicines, and treatments for female complaints (Toyama Prefecture, 1983, p. 533; 1987, pp. 658–62). Examples of popular products included *Hangontan,* used to treat stomach ailments, *Yūtan,* used for digestive ailments, or *Kyūmeigan,* a pediatric drug.

Despite the economic hardship experienced by many Japanese in the early twentieth century, between 1920 and 1939, annual per capita consumption of personal and medical products grew steadily, averaging 9.7 yen, with such expenditure representing an average of 3.6 per cent of gross national expenditure (Ohkawa, Shinohara, and Meissner, 1979, pp. 339–40). Besides the medicines from Toyama, Japanese people also purchased a variety of patent medicines from the market. Some of these were based on traditional remedies, such as *Ōta Isan,* a stomach remedy, or *Chūjotō,* a remedy for female complaints (Ōhta's Isan Co., 1979; Tsumura Juntendo Co., 1964). A few people were also able to afford Western-style medicines, such as salvarsan, produced by the leading Japanese pharmaceutical firms including Takeda, Ono, and Shionogi. These firms had switched from dealing in traditional Japanese medicine to dealing in Western-style medicines after the Meiji Restoration.

The war years and the fading market for medicines, 1930s–1940s

The outbreak of the Sino-Japanese War in 1937 cut off medicinal supplies for Kanpō medicines from China, as the war with the United States and its European allies was to do for Western medicines from 1941. As a result, medicines became increasingly less accessible to ordinary people. In terms of the medical products they did consume, a study in 1938 indicated that folk and patent medicines accounted for over half of the total (Suzuki, 2008, p. 143).

At any rate, the market for medicines all but disappeared in a wartime economy where people were near starvation. The limited amounts of essential medicines available were subject to price controls from 1939, and distributed via rations from 1941 (Yakugyō Keizai Kenkyūjo, 1951,pp. 245–46). As the war progressed, medicines of any type became increasingly scarce. Newspapers encouraged people to 'plant herbal medicines to substitute for the lack of available medicine', or to 'opt for herbal medicines in times of scarcity' (*Yomiuri Shinbun*, 21 March 1940, p. 4). Others suggested ways in which people could use ordinary plants or everyday foods for medical purposes. These included using sweet flag as an antiseptic, or baking soda for hangovers (*Yomiuri Shinbun*, 5 May 1942, p. 4; *Yomiuri Shimbun*, 30 December 1940, p. 4). While a black market did exist, records indicate that what thrived in it were Western, not traditional medicines (Hōshi, 1946).

Tamagawa Nobuaki notes that, for the first six years after the war, traditional patent medicines proved very popular (Tamagawa, 2005, pp. 268–69). Between 1946 and 1952, for example, the production value of patent medicines in Toyama prefecture increased in real terms from 7.5 billion yen to 43.9 billion yen (Toyama Prefecture, 1958). This was due to the widespread incidence of infectious disease, lack of essential Western medicines, the high prices of medicines on the black market, and the ready availability of traditional patent medicines. In an inflationary environment, the fact that the Toyama medicine pedlars collected their dues several months after prices were set meant that in real terms consumers also got a better deal for their purchases.

Yet as inflation in the late 1940s subsided and Western 'miracle' medicines such as penicillin and streptomycin became both available and affordable, the demand for traditional medicines subsided. Western medicines proved decisively more effective in combating the infectious diseases such as syphilis and tuberculosis prevalent in the immediate post-war period (Ministry of Health and Welfare, 1876–1999). Yet as morbidity and mortality trends began to change in the 1950s, patients demanded new types of medicines.

The post-war resurgence of traditional medicines, 1950s–1980s

In the early twentieth century, traditional Japanese medicines were generally consumed when Western alternatives were not available. Yet in the decades after the Second World War, a growing number of patients began to consume Kanpō by choice, after Western medicines had become readily available. Signs of popular resurgence were appearing in the press in the 1950s, and by the 1960s, there were recurrent references to a 'Kanpō boom' (*Yomiuri Shinbun*, 15 October 1962, p. 9; 20 April 1964, p. 15; 18 April 1967, p. 9; 12 June 1967, p. 7).

This revival of Kanpō medicines could be observed in several ways. First, a number of academic and professional organisations dedicated to Kanpō were established in the 1950s. In addition to the various regional

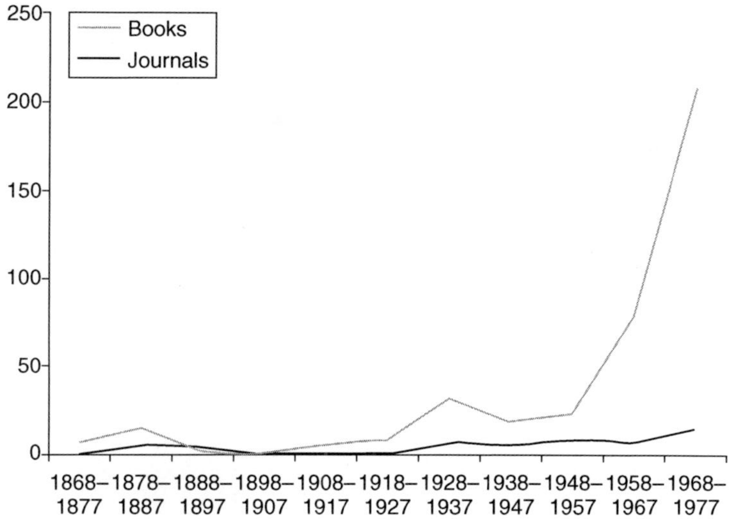

Figure 8.1 Number of Kanpō publications, 1868–1977
Source: Yakazu, 1979, p. 26.

organisations, the Japan Society for Oriental Medicine was established in 1950 and the All Japan Kanpō Physicians Federation in 1953 (Japan Society for Oriental Medicine, 2010, pp. 159–64). Including the Association of East Asian Medicine established in 1938, there were now three national Kanpō organisations. As indicated in Figure 8.1, there was also a marked increase in the number of published books and journals dedicated to Kanpō. In addition, articles in newspapers and magazines about Kanpō became more positive than they previously had been (*Yomiuri Shinbun*, 2 May 1962, p. 3; *Yomiuri Shinbun*, 9 December 1965, p. 9).

Perhaps more importantly, the market for Kanpō medicines expanded rapidly, particularly after the mid-1970s. As Figure 8.2 indicates, between 1976 and 1980, the combined production value of prescription and over-the-counter Kanpō medicines increased more than 11 fold in real terms, from 15.2 billion yen to 169.2 billion yen (Ministry of Health and Welfare, 1953–2000; Ministry of Health, Labour and Welfare, 2001–2006). An increasing number of people also consumed Kanpō medicines on prescription. While prescription medicines accounted for 27.8 per cent of the Kanpō medicines produced in 1976, within a decade they had come to account for more than 76 per cent. Although the actual value of over-the-counter drugs declined, they still accounted for

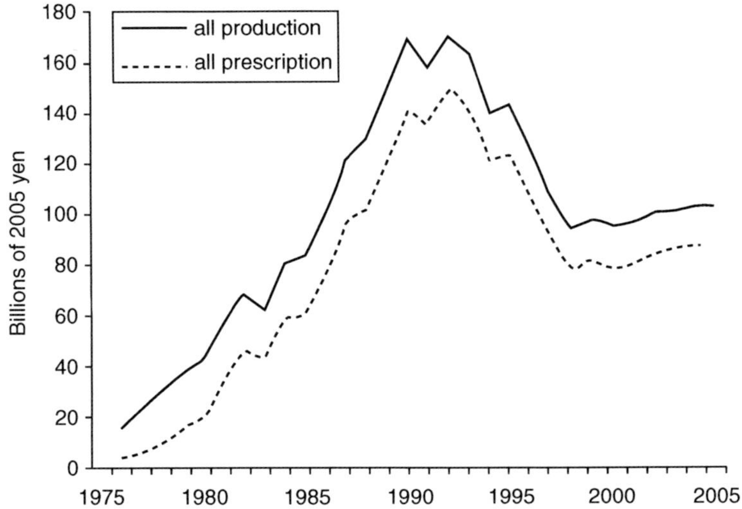

Figure 8.2 Value of Kanpō medicine production, 1976–2005

Source: Ministry of Health and Welfare, 1953–2000; Ministry of Health, Labour and Welfare, 2001–2006.

well over 10 billion yen annually for the next two decades. Even after a series of drug tragedies and corruption scandals caused a sudden fall in the Kanpō market in the 1990s, demand for Kanpō remedies proved resilient beyond the millennium.

This revival of Kanpō medicines in the second half of the twentieth century was due to a number of factors. First was the development of technologies to mass-produce standardised versions of Kanpō medicines. A key turning point that fundamentally changed the nature of Kanpō medicines as products occurred in 1957, when Kotarō Pharmaceutical succeeded in developing a method to mass-produce granulated extracts of Kanpō medicines (Kotarō Pharmaceutical Co., 2002). Previously, the consumption of Kanpō medicines had involved a cumbersome process of decocting the medicinal herbs in hot water. The new process was revolutionary because it offered Kanpō in standardised packages as powders or pills – without the hassle or the odours. As Figure 8.3 shows, Kanpō medicines became much more convenient and accessible to the modern consumer. The introduction of quality standards further instilled a sense among consumers that Kanpō was a reliable form of medicine.[6]

[6] For example, the *Iryōyō Kanpō Ekisuseizai GMP* (GMP Requirements for Kanpō Extract Products), Yakkan 72, 5 August 1987.

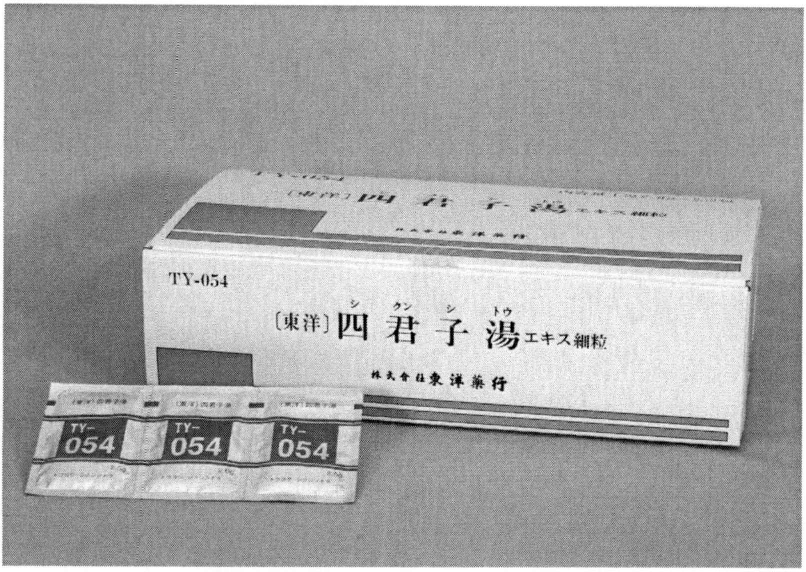

Figure 8.3 Mass produced, granulated extracts of a prescription Kanpō medicine, Shikunshitō

Source: Courtesy of Tōyō-yakukō Corp.

This transformation of Kanpō medicines was similar to that which occurred in American food products in the late nineteenth century, when pre-packaged and branded convenience foods such as Campbell's Soup or Heinz Ketchup emerged (Chandler, 1977, p. 295). As in the late nineteenth-century American food industry, the revolution in Kanpō production and packaging was made possible by the use of capital-intensive machinery, multidivisional forms of corporate organisation and the emergence of a new breed of consumers. Whether it was in form, production, quality or distribution, after 1957 Kanpō medicines were reinvented – and consumed as very different products.

Another factor behind the resurgence in Kanpō was the change in diplomatic relations with China in the 1970s. For centuries, China had been the source of Japan's medicinal herbs. In the first decade of the twenty-first century approximately 80 per cent of the raw ingredients for Kanpō were imports; among these, 80 per cent were still sourced from China (*Bio Industry*, 1999, p. 49; Ministry of Health and Welfare, 1953–2000; Ministry of Health, Labour and Welfare, 2001–2006). While informal Sino-Japanese trade had continued since the 1950s, the normalisation of relations in 1972, followed by the Treaty of Peace and Friendship between Japan and the People's Republic of China in 1978, made it easier for Japanese firms to secure stable supplies of quality medicinal herbs to produce Kanpō medicines. For example, improved bilateral relations facilitated regular talks between Japanese and Chinese industry officials regarding yearly fluctuations in the price and quality of medicinal plants. While some attempts have been made to expand domestic production by taking advantage of government subsidies or by establishing networks of contract farms within Japan, the volume of medicinal herbs sourced domestically has remained limited (Kondō, 1981; *Chūō Kōron*, 1995).

Demand-side factors also played an important role in this revival of Kanpō medicines. One significant change among consumers was the realisation of the limitations of Western medicine. The faith placed in Western medicine following the discoveries of 'miracle' drugs such as antibiotics had been subsequently undermined by drug tragedies such as those involving thalidomide in 1961 or cold ampoules in 1965 (*Yomiuri Shinbun*, 1967b). Popular anxiety over the safety of Western medicines lingered over the following decades as Japan experienced other widely publicised drug scandals, such as those involving chinoform in 1970 and chloroquine in 1971 (Takano, 1979; Katahira, 1995). Western medicine was also increasingly viewed as overly analytical and symptom based, lacking the holistic approach taken in traditional medicine. The government was still ideologically wedded to the view that Western-style medicines were better than traditional ones. But in a period of growing affluence, Japanese people consumed more Kanpō medicines, undermining the government's goal to eradicate these medicines.

In addition, there was a change in common patterns of disease from acute, infectious illnesses to chronic, lifestyle related ones that were more conducive to traditional treatments. In 1947, tuberculosis was the leading cause of death. By 1951, cerebrovascular diseases had taken the lead, followed by cancer in 1981 (Ministry of Health, Labour and Welfare, 1899–2004). Unlike the medicines that treated infectious diseases, those Western medicines that treated cerebrovascular conditions or cancer tended to offer symptomatic relief, rather than an immediate 'cure'. These medications also had to be taken for a much longer period of time – months and years, rather than days and weeks. They were rather similar to Kanpō medicines in being expected to deliver mild curative effects after being taken for a prolonged period of time.

Furthermore, in 1976, the government included numerous Kanpō medicines on the official drug list. While a handful of Kanpō medicines had been approved for prescription use in 1967, this recognition of Kanpō medicines as a new category of prescription drugs to be covered under

Japan's national health insurance system further fostered the growth of the sector. Japanese patients could now purchase Kanpō treatments on prescription at a fraction of what they had previously cost, and at lower prices than over-the-counter Kanpō medicines. In addition, physicians who were trained in and practised Western medicine emerged as powerful proxy consumers.

The 'new' traditional medicines had also made it easier for physicians to prescribe them alongside Western medicines. Japanese physicians both prescribe and dispense medicines (Reich, 1990, p. 135), and they were able to bargain down the price at which they purchased their drugs from wholesalers, profiting from the difference between this and the government-set, official prices at which they resold their drugs to patients. Japanese physicians were particularly incentivised to recommend drugs like Kanpō, which could be prescribed to a large patient population, as they could negotiate a steeper discount on wholesale prices. In an age of chronic ailments for which there were no magic bullets, physicians were incentivised to prescribe drugs that might alleviate some symptoms, cause few side-effects, and have high pharmaceutical price differentials.

Until the mid 1970s, the vast majority of Kanpō medicines were sold as over-the-counter drugs rather than by prescription. Since the legislation that turned numerous Kanpō medicines into prescription drugs, however, most of these medicines have been sold under prescription. This legislation changed physicians' position as proxy consumers; they now played a major role in shaping the traditional medicines market.

While physicians are prominent mediators in the consumption of prescription drugs, the mediation of consumption in fact occurs across various sectors of the economy. However, unlike the proxy consumers described in Mitsuzono's chapter (Chapter 11) in this book – the department-store clerks who mediated the purchase of mail-order goods for a small group of affluent consumers – Japanese physicians had far greater leverage in determining what drugs a large number of patients might consume.

As Figure 8.4 indicates, the use of Kanpō medicines by physicians increased substantially over the 1970s and 1980s. While Kanpō medicines were not widely prescribed immediately after their inclusion on the official drug list, a survey in 1981 found that among physicians who prescribed Kanpō medicines nearly 75 per cent had begun to use them in the past four years. Remarkably, by the end of the 1980s, nearly 70 per cent of physicians used Kanpō medicines alongside regular practice.

It is important to remember that Kanpō medicines were used more as a complement to Western medicines than as a substitute. As Table 8.1 suggests, they were selectively used for chronic ailments with relatively mild

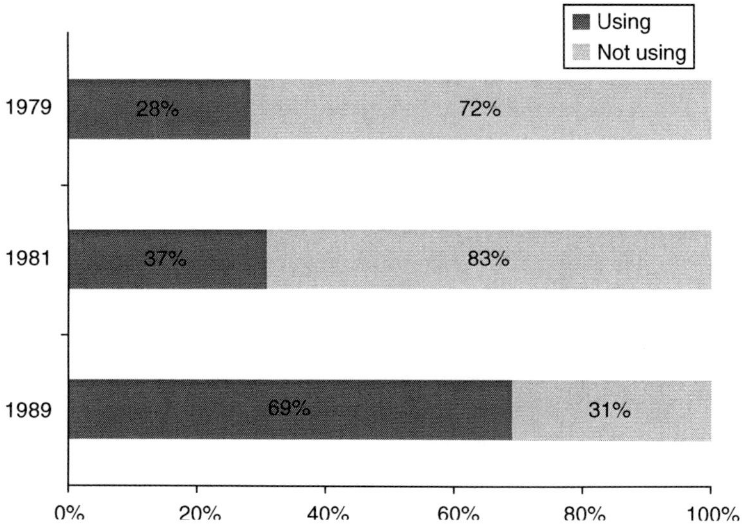

Figure 8.4 Physicians using Kanpō medicines, 1979–1989

Source: *Nikkei Medical*, October 1979, pp. 26–28; October 1983, pp. 28–31; October 1989, pp. 31–34.

Table 8.1 Popular uses of Kanpō medicine

	1979	**1983**	**1989**
1	Cold	Chronic liver disease	Chronic liver disease
2	Menopause	Anxiety	Cold
3	Constipation	Menopausal symptoms	Menopausal symptoms
4	Stomach ailments	Cold	Liver complaints
5	Cough/asthma	Autonomic imbalance	Asthma

Source: *Nikkei Medical*, October 1979, pp. 26–28; October 1983, pp. 28–31; October 1989, pp. 31–34.

symptoms that had no 'immediate' cure. Most physicians used Kanpō medicines only as a second-line treatment to Western medicine. They used the drugs when Western medicines had been found ineffective in treating the patient, or when the Western drug had undesirably strong side effects. As Julia Yongue has noted, Japanese medical practice has generally preferred drug safety over efficacy (Yongue, 2008, pp. 172–73). Kanpō medicines catered to this preference. Throughout the 1970s and 1980s, physicians trained in Western medicine prescribed Kanpō medicines alongside other,

Table 8.2 Most commonly prescribed Kanpō medicines

	1979	1983	1989
1	Kakkontō	Hachimijiōgan	Shōsaiikotō
2	Hachimijiōgan	Shōsaiikotō	Hachimijiōgan
3	Shōsaiikotō	Kakkontō	Kakkontō
4	Tōkishakuyakusan	Tōkishakuyakusan	Shōseiryūtō
5	Kamishōyōsan	Keishifukuryōgan	Kamishōyōsan

Source: *Nikkei Medical*, October 1979, pp. 26–28; October 1983, pp. 28–31; October 1989, pp. 31–34.

Western drugs, according to Western approaches to medicine. Kanpō medicines came to be consumed as another type of modern medicine.

As Table 8.2 indicates, there was very little change in the leading Kanpō medicines prescribed in the 1970s and 1980s. The commonly prescribed Kanpō medicines also differed little from the leading over-the-counter Kanpō medicines, where the market also expanded during this period. These trends suggest that the strength of demand increased among patients as well as physicians (Ministry of Health and Welfare, 1953–2000). In his 1988 study, Kyoichi Sonoda also found that Kanpō patients of the 1980s were increasingly urban and highly educated (Sonoda, 1988, pp. 77–101). Unlike consumers of the pre-war period, they consumed Kanpō medicines out of choice, not because they were poor, ignorant, or lacked alternatives.

At any rate, the commonly consumed Kanpō medicines treated a wide variety of mild conditions. For example, Kakkontō treats headaches, fever, chills and shoulder pain, Hachimijiōgan treats fatigue, back pain, hot flushes, and dry mouth, while Shōsaikotō treats lack of appetite, nausea, asthma, and digestive complaints (*Nikkei Medical*, October 1979, pp. 12–19). The uses of Kanpō medicines were specific to non-acute, non-life threatening conditions.

The rise of Kanpō medicines in the second half of the twentieth century seems in some ways slightly anachronistic. After all, following the introduction of universal health care in 1961 and the introduction of free elderly health care in 1973, many Japanese citizens could for the first time access Western medicines just as the citizens of most other developed countries did. They did not need to rely on herbal medicines for treating diseases, as previous generations had done. Yet what was notable during this period was the re-acceptance of Kanpō medicines among physicians trained in Western medicine. While some may attribute the resurgence of Kanpō largely to the 1976 change in regulation, it could not have occurred without considerable demand-side support from both patients and physicians.

Overcoming delisting attempts and institutionalising Kanpō medicines, 1990s–2000s

As Japan's population became older and the numbers of those afflicted with milder and chronic ailments grew, the government began to introduce measures to curtail the escalating costs of universal health care. Early proposals to delist Kanpō medicines began in the early 1980s. Delisting would have meant that the government no longer underwrote demand by subsidising payments for Kanpō prescriptions. Discussions evolved over rising health care costs, the efficacy of Kanpō medicines, and significant differences in prescription and over-the-counter prices for the same drug (*Yomiuri Shinbun*, 3 May 1983, 1; House of Councillors, 29 September, 1983; House of Representatives, 29 September, 1983; House of Representatives, 7 August, 1984).

As much as the government appeared to want to delist Kanpō medicines, petitions launched by physicians, patients, and Kanpō producers appeared to defeat these initiatives (*Nikkan Yakugyō*, 22 November 1993, 2; *Pharmaweek*, 6 December 1993, 6). The recurrent delisting initiatives proposed in the early 1990s should have been more successful (*Mediapex*, 15 September 1993, 5). After all, this was a time when Kanpō fell into some disrepute. In 1991, for example, the Ministry of Health and Welfare called for a re-evaluation of eight Kanpō preparations and issued a safety warning regarding the strong side-effects of the best-selling Kanpō drug. At the time, it was estimated that a million Japanese consumed Shōsaiikotō, which accounted for almost a third of total Kanpō sales (*Yomiuri Shinbun*, 28 March 1991, 30). Over the 1990s, deaths caused by the drug were reported in the popular press, and the government subjected several other drugs to re-evaluation (*Yomiuri Shinbun*, 2 March 1993, 39; *Yomiuri Shinbun*, 5 March 1998, 38). The publication of problems with Kanpō medicines undermined the popular belief that they were a safe alternative to Western medicines – one of the major reasons why many physicians and patients had opted to consume them in an age when Western drugs were available (*Yomiuri Shinbun*, 3 March 1996, 29).

Moreoever, in the 1990s, Tsumura, the leading Kanpō producer holding more than 80 per cent of the market, was caught in a series of highly publicised scandals. A corruption scandal revealed that it had made significant political 'contributions' to members of the Liberal Democratic Party's health policy 'tribe', previous ministers of health, and other senior Health Ministry officials (*Mainichi Shinbun* 25 October 1996, 1, 10, 31). The family firm was also accused of poor management, which had resulted in massive losses following rampant diversification strategies pursued during the bubble years of the 1980s (*Nihon Keizai Shinbun*, 14 September 1994, 19; *Nihon Keizai Shinbun*, 28 October 2000, 19).

As Figure 8.2 showed, the market for Kanpō medicines did tumble following these scandals, from a peak of 170.3 billion yen in 1992, to around 100 billion in the late 1990s (Ministry of Health and Welfare, 1953–2000; Ministry of Health, Labour and Welfare, 2001–2006).[7] Despite the drug tragedies and the notoriety surrounding Tsumura, however, Japanese people continued to consume Kanpō medicines. These events had limited impact on the popularity of Kanpō. As Figure 8.5 indicates, by the 1990s, over three quarters of Japanese physicians prescribed Kanpō medicines. As in the 1970s and 1980s, they were used to treat the mild symptoms of long-term ailments such as chronic liver disease, constipation or menopause, as second-line treatments after Western medicines proved unsatisfactory (*Nikkei Medical*, October 1993, pp. 30–35; October 1997, pp. 30–36; October 2003, pp. 32–38; October 2007, pp. 41–47). The leading Kanpō drugs had also changed little from the previous decades. In 1998, for example, the top five Kanpō drugs consisted mostly of familiar names such as Shōsaiikotō, Kakkontō, and Hachimijiōgan. While the proportion of physicians who used Kanpō medicines dipped slightly over the 1990s and 2000s, well over 70 per cent of physicians continued to use these medicines.

In fact, none of the government's recurrent initiatives to delist Kanpō medicines came to fruition. Intriguingly, popular attitudes appeared much less sceptical of these medicines compared to earlier decades, even after the scandals. When articles in the popular press reported on the government's recurrent proposals to delist Kanpō medicines, they highlighted the voices of opposition from physicians, patients, and firms, rather than the voices of support for delisting (*Pharmaweek*, 13 October 1997, 2; 8 December 1997, 2; *Mainichi Shimbun*, 28 November 2009, 29). Two factors in particular appeared to contribute to the popular acceptance of Kanpō medicines during this period: the spread of Kanpō curricula in Japanese medical schools and the scientific evaluations carried out on Kanpō medicines.

---

[7] In terms of real production value.

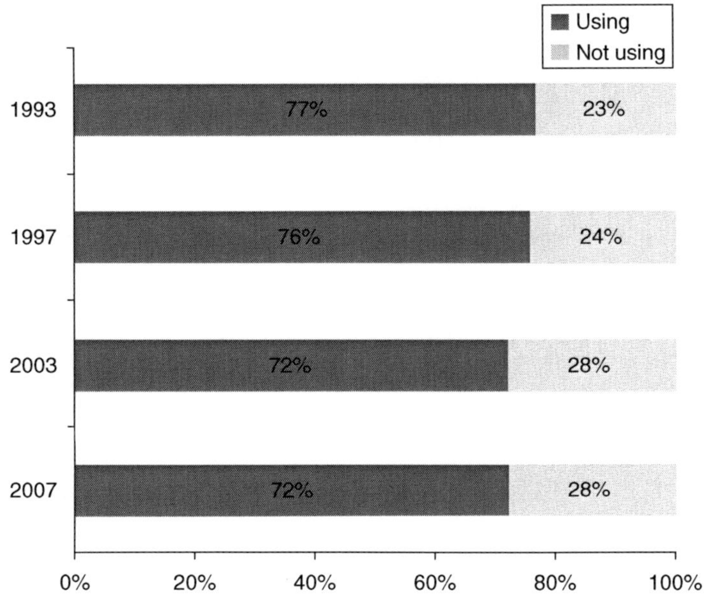

Figure 8.5 Physicians using Kanpō medicines, 1993–2007

Source: *Nikkei Medical*, October 1993, pp. 30–35; October 1997, pp. 30–36; October 2003, pp. 32–38; October 2007, pp. 41–47.

The spread of Kanpō curricula in Japanese medical schools over the 1990s and 2000s was quite remarkable. In 1986, there were only five medical schools offering Kanpō education (Yakazu et al., 1987, p. 92). By 1995, there were 20 (*Nikkei Medical*, 15 October 1995, 8–9). In 2001, the Ministry of Education included Kanpō modules as part of the 'Model Core Curriculum' to be used in Japanese medical schools (Ministry of Education, Culture, Sports, Science and Technology, 2007). After 2004, all 80 medical schools incorporated Kanpō education into their teaching (*Asahi Shimbun*, 17 January 2005, p. 2) The standardisation of Kanpō education in Japanese medical schools legitimised Kanpō treatments and effectively created a new generation of powerful proxy consumers more knowledgeable and accepting of Kanpō medicines (*Doraggu Magajin*, June 2006, 45–48).

Another change that occurred during this period was an increasing emphasis on evidence-based medicine in Kanpō, leading to more rigorous testing for safety and efficacy (*Nikkei Medical*, July 2001, 42–53). Unlike Western-style medicines, Kanpō medicines had not been approved under rigorous scientific criteria when they were accepted as prescription medicines (*Asahi Shimbun*, 15 January 2005, p. 2). Regulators approved these medicines on the basis of the idea that Kanpō could not be evaluated according to Western scientific standards and that their value was evident from centuries of practice (Japan Kampo Medicines Manufacturers Association, 2003, p. 119). From the 1990s, however, a growing number of Kanpō medicines were evaluated according to the same standards as Western-style medicines at leading institutes such as the Kitasato University Oriental Medicine Research Center and the Institute of Natural Medicine at the University of Toyama (*Nihon Keizai Shinbun*, 12 June 2005, p. 11; *Nikkei Medical*, July 2001, pp. 42–53). These studies have lent greater credibility to the tested medicines and have helped translate Kanpō medicines into more acceptable, legitimate products that can be credibly used as scientifically and medically advanced therapies in contemporary Japan.

Conclusion

This chapter has followed the transformation of traditional medicines in Japanese consumer society from the late nineteenth century to the millennium. It has focussed on Kanpō medicines in particular and on the post-1945 period, when there was a prominent resurgence in the popularity of these medicines. The aim was to identify the reasons for this revival and to emphasise the role of consumers in this process.

The existing literature on consumer history might suggest that the re-integration of traditional medicines into Japanese consumer society in the second half of the twentieth century would be the result of a desire for a higher standard of living or because consumers were manipulated by excessive promotion on the part of producers. These explanations alone, however, are incomplete. This chapter offers additional reasons for this phenomenon.

The revival of traditional medicines in the second half of the twentieth century was due to a number of reasons. First was consumers' realisation of the limitations of Western medicine. The faith placed in Western medicine following the discoveries of 'miracle' drugs such as antibiotics had been subsequently undermined by drug tragedies such as that of thalidomide. In addition, people increasingly viewed Western medicine as excessively rational and symptom based, lacking the holistic approach taken in traditional medicine. Second, common patterns of disease shifted from acute, infectious illnesses to chronic, lifestyle-related illnesses that were more conducive to Kanpō treatments. Third, the development of technologies to mass-produce standardised versions of Kanpō medicines enabled physicians to prescribe traditional medicines alongside Western medicines. Fourth, the change in diplomatic relations with China allowed Japanese firms to secure the supplies of medicinal herbs necessary to produce Kanpō medicines. Fifth, the development of evaluation technologies provided scientific evidence regarding the safety and efficacy of Kanpō medicines, lending greater credibility to the tested medicines.

Consumers played a vital role in the resurgence of traditional medicines in the post-war period. They were empowered by several factors. First, Japanese consumers became wealthier, more health conscious, and better informed about the different medicines available on the market – particularly as they experienced the information technology revolution that enabled them to access information on the Internet. Second, consumers faced a growing number of Western medicines that treated but did not necessarily 'cure' chronic ailments. Third, the government's inclusion of numerous Kanpō medicines on the official drug list not only made traditional medicines more affordable for patients, but also established physicians as powerful proxy consumers who played an integral role in mediating, shaping, and altering consumption. Physicians' prescription of Kanpō medicines gave greater legitimacy to Japanese traditional medicines. In addition, physician activism against the government's recurrent proposals to delist Kanpō medicines proved powerfully effective in sustaining a viable market for traditional medicines in Japan.

Of course, not all Kanpō medicines were consumed on prescription. A minority of consumers bought traditional medicines over the counter – particularly after many Kanpō medicines were recognised as prescription drugs. But both the volume and value of Kanpō medicines purchased over the counter continued to grow after the 1970s. Some may question whether it has been appropriate to consider medicines prescribed by physicians as consumer products, given that their consumption is heavily regulated and mediated. It is true that, for example, regulations may condition the ways in which certain goods, such as pharmaceuticals, are consumed. However, that does not mean that consumers do not have a choice; they are not powerless in what they buy. In the case of traditional medicines, both physicians and patients chose to consume these particular products and played a crucial role in their revival.

Traditional medicines have transformed into a modern product, accompanied by fascinating changes in who purchases them, in what way and for what end. In the early twentieth century, traditional medicines were still largely considered backward products, second-rate therapies for the unenlightened masses. By the end of the century, however, they had become a progressive alternative for more selective consumers who opted for a more holistic approach to health and well-being.

It is worth noting that the increase in the enduring popularity of traditional medicines in step with advances in biomedicine has parallels in other countries; it is not a phenomenon unique to Japan. In India and China, for example, progress in and improved access to Western medicine have been accompanied by the growth of the traditional medicines sector, which has 'modernised' through the expansion of education in traditional medicines and the introduction of more rigorous quality and efficacy standards (WHO, 2005, pp. 89–95, 187–92). Complementary therapies in Europe have also shown a rapid increase in popularity since the 1980s (Fisher and Ward, 1994, p. 107). The medical historian Matthew Ramsey has argued that the recent resurgence of alternative medicine, particularly homeopathy, in France comes from a sort of weariness with scientific medicine, resulting from its inability to conquer old or new infectious diseases, its association with over-consumption, and its sheer expense. He argues that consumers' desire for a medicine less bound by existing paradigms has led to the rising popularity of non-orthodox medicines (Ramsey, 1999, p. 321).

Changes in the demand-side environment help explain the greater roles played by consumers in shaping the traditional medicines industry in the second half of the twentieth century. Yet what I have also hoped to show is that consumer agency is a fuzzy concept, not only because there may be different types and layers of consumers, but also because – where interests coincide – consumers can act in collaboration with supply-side actors in shaping a particular sector. In the case of traditional medicines, physicians, patients, and firms sustained the vitality of Japan's traditional medicines sector.

While they might seem unlikely collaborators, the cooperation of supply-side and demand-side actors can act as a powerful force in shaping the history of consumer society. In the traditional medicines industry, multiple consumers and supply-side actors bolstered consumer agency. In the late nineteenth century, physicians alone could not reverse the declining popularity of traditional medicines in Japanese consumer society. More than half a century later, patients helped to breathe life into traditional medicines once again.

References

Allendy, R. (1929) *Les Orientations des Idées Médicales*, Paris: Au Sans Pareil.

Bivins, R. (2010) *Alternative Medicine? A History*, Oxford: Oxford University Press.

Brewer, J. & Porter, R. (1994) *Consumption and the World of Goods*, London: Routledge.

Carpenter, K. J. (2000) *Beriberi, White Rice and Vitamin B: A Disease, a Cause, and a Cure*, Berkeley: University of California Press.

Chandler, A. (1977) *The Visible Hand: The Managerial Revolution in American Business*, Cambridge, MA: Harvard University Press.

Chūō Kōron (1995) 'Kanpōyaku no Genryō wa Chūgoku Zendo kara Chōtatsu' (Raw Materials for Kanpō Medicines Sourced from All Regions of China)', vol. 110, no. 14, pp. 451–55.

Dajōkan (1878) *Kakkebyōin Kaiin Todoke* (Beriberi Hospital Opening Notification), [Microfilm] Tokyo: Dajōkan.

Dajōkan (1879) 'Tōkyōfu Kakkebyōin Daiichi Hōkoku Shintatsu no Ken' (On the First Report of the Tokyo Beriberi Hospital)' [Microfilm] Tokyo: Dajōkan.

Dajōkan (1881) *Tōkyōfu Kakkebyōin Daini Hōkoku Dōjō* (On the Second Report of the Tokyo Beriberi Hospital) [Microfilm] Tokyo: Dajōkan.

Dajōkan (1882) *Kakkebyōin Daisan Hōkoku Shintatsu no Ken* (On the Third Report of the Beriberi Hospital) [Microfilm] Tokyo: Dajōkan.

Fisher, P. & Ward, A. (1994) 'Complementary Medicine in Europe', *British Medical Journal* vol. 309, no. 9 (July), pp. 107–11.

Francks, P. (2009) *The Japanese Consumer: An Alternative Economic History of Modern Japan*, Cambridge: Cambridge University Press.

Fujikawa, Y. (1980) *Fujikawa Yū Chosakushū 3* (Collected Works of Fujikawa Yū), Kyoto: Shibunkaku.

Higashi, J. (1981) 'Kanpō ni Kagaku no Mesu o' (Applying Science to Kanpō), *Ekonomisto* vol. 60 no.6, pp. 56–57.

Hōshi, M. (1946) 'Yakuhin no Yamine to Kōteika' (Black Market Prices and Official Prices of Medicines), *Sōgō Igaku* vol. 3, no. 8, pp. 18–19.

Ikai, S. (2010) *Byōin no Seiki no Riron* (A Theory on the Hospital Century), Tokyo: Yūhikaku.

Japan Kampo Medicines Manufacturers Association (2003) *Nikkankyō 20 nenshi* (A 20 Year History of the Japan Kanpō Medicines Manufacturers Association), Tokyo: Japan Kampo Medicines Manufacturers Association.

Japan Society for Oriental Medicine (2010) *About JSOM* [Online] Available from http://www.jsom.or.jp/english/index.html [accessed 30 June 2010].

Katahira, K. (1995) *Nō Moa Yakugai* (No More Drug Tragedies), Tokyo: Kiri Shobō.

Kawakami, T. (1965) *Gendai Nihon Iryōshi: Kaigyōisei no Hensen* (History of Medical Supplies in Contemporary Japan), Tokyo: Keisō Shobō.

Keikō Ihōsha (1893–1897) *Keikō Ihō* (Tokyo: Keikō Ihōsha).

Kondō, K. (1981) 'Kanpōyaku Būmu no Shakai Keizaigaku' (A Socioeconomic Study of the Kanpō Boom)', *Ekonomisto*, 1 December, pp. 81–83.

Kotaro Pharmaceutical Co. (2002) *Kotarō Kanpō 50 nenshi* (A 50 year History of Kotaro Pharmaceutical), Osaka: Kotaro Pharmaceutical Co.

Lock, M. (1984) *East Asian Medicine in Urban Japan*, Berkeley: University of California Press.

Matsumoto, M., Inoue, K. & Kaji, E. (1999) 'Integrating Traditional Medicine in Japan: The Case of Kampo Medicines', *Complementary Therapies in Medicine* vol. 7, no. 4, pp. 254–55.

Ministry of Education, Culture, Sports, Science and Technology (2007) *Igaku Kyōiku Moderu Koa Karikyuramu* (Medical Education Model Core Curriculum) [Online] Available from http://www.mext.go.jp/b_menu/shingi/chousa/koutou/033/toushin/1217987_1703.html [acessed 30 June 2010].

Ministry of Health and Welfare (1953–2000) *Yakuji Kōgyō Seisan Dōtai Chōsa Tōkei* (Annual Survey on Production in the Pharmaceutical Industry), Tokyo: Yakugyō Keizai Kenkyūjo.

Ministry of Health and Welfare, *Patients and Deaths of Infectious Diseases and Food Poisoning, 1876–1999* [Online]. Available from: http://www.stat.go.jp/data/chouki/24.htm [accessed 30 June 2010].

Ministry of Health and Welfare (1976) *Isei Hyakunenshi – Shiryōhen* (Hundred Year History of the Medical System – Materials), Tokyo: Gyōsei.

Ministry of Health, Labour and Welfare (2001–2006) *Yakuji Kōgyō Seisan Dōtai Chōsa Tōkei* (Annual Survey on Production in the Pharmaceutical Industry), Tokyo: Jihō.

Ministry of Health, Labour and Welfare, *Death by Leading Cause of Death 1899–2004* [Online]. Available from: http://www.stat.go.jp/english/data/chouki/02.htm [accessed 21 June 2010].

Ministry of Internal Affairs (1920, 1923, 1939) *Kanpō Iyaku Kenkyū Hozon n Kansuru Seigan no Ken* (On the Request to Continue Support of Research in Kanpō Medicines), Tokyo: Ministry of Internal Affairs.

Nagao, S. (1928) *Ā Ihei* (Oh Bad Medicine), Tokyo: Tohōdō.

Nakayama, T. (1927) *Kanpō Igaku no Shinkenkyū* (New Research into Kanpō Medicine), Tokyo: Hobunkan.

Nihon Yakushi Gakkai (1995) *Nihon Iyakuhin Sangyōshi* (The History of the Japanese Pharmaceutical Industry), Tokyo: Yakuji Nippōsha.

Oberländer, C. (1995) *Zwischen Tradition und Moderne: Die Bewegung für den Fortbestand der Kampō-Medizin in Japan,* Stuttgart: Franz Steiner Verlag.

Oberländer, C. (2005) 'The Rise of Western '"Scientific Medicine'" in Japan: Bacteriology and Beriberi', in Low, M. (ed.) *Building a Modern Japan*, New York: Palgrave Macmillan, pp. 11–36.

Ohkawa, K., Shinohara, M. & Meissner, L. (1979) *Patterns of Japanese Economic Development: A Quantitative Appraisal*, New Haven: Yale University Press.

Ohnuki-Tierney, E. (1984) *Illness and Culture in Contemporary Japan: An Anthropological View,* Cambridge: Cambridge University Press.

Ohta's Isan, Co. (1979) *Ōta Isan Hyakunen no Kaisō* (Ohta's Isan, Reflections on 100 Years), Tokyo: Ohta's Isan Co.

Organisation for Economic Co-operation and Development (2010) *OECD Health Data* [Online]. Available from: http://www.sourceoecd.org/database/health-data [accessed 29 June 2010].

Otsuka, K. (2001) 'Kanpō Igaku no Hensen' (Changes in Kanpō Medicine), in *Shinpan Kanpō Igaku* (Kanpō Medicine, New Edition), Osaka: Sōgensha, pp. 38–74.

Otsuka, Y. (1976) 'Chinese Medicine in Japan', in Leslie, C. (ed.) *Asian Medical Systems, A Comparative Study*, Berkeley: University of California Press, pp. 322–40.

Ramsey, M. (1999) 'Alternative Medicine in Modern France', *Medical History* vol. 43, no. 3, pp. 286–322.

Reich, M. (1990) 'Why the Japanese Don't Export More Pharmaceuticals: Health Policy as Industrial Policy', *California Management Review* vol. 32, no. 2, pp. 124–50.

Shin Nihon Hōki Shuppan (2008) *Yakka Kijun* (Official Drug List), Tokyo: Shin Nihon Hōki Shuppan.

Saitō, O. & Tanimoto, M. (2004) 'The Transformation of Traditional Industries', in Hayami, A., Saitō, O. & Toby, R. (eds) *Emergence of Economic Society in Japan, 1600–1859, Volume 1*, Oxford: Oxford University Press, pp. 268–330.

Shinmura, T. (2006) *Nihon Iryōshi* (History of Medical Care in Japan), Tokyo: Yoshikawa Kōbunkan.

Sonoda, K. (1988) *Health and Illness in Changing Japanese Society*, Tokyo: University of Tokyo Press.

Sugaya, A. (1976) 'Kindai Ishi Seido no Kakuritsu to Kōkan'i no Suitai' (The Establishment of a Modern Medical System and the Decline of Kanpō Physicians)', in *Nihon Iryō Seidoshi* (History of the System of Medical Care in Japan), Tokyo: Hara Shobō, pp. 38–50.

Suzuki, A. (2008) 'Chiryō no Shakaishiteki Kōsatsu' (Considering Medical Treatment from the Perspective of Social History)', in Kawagoe, O. & Suzuki, A. (eds) *Bunbetsu Sareru Seimei: Nijūisseiki Shakai no Iryō Senryaku* (Selections in Life: Medical Strategies for the 21st Century), Tokyo: Hōsei University Press, pp. 129–61.

Takahashi, K. (1971) 'Chūgoku Igaku no Saihakken' (The Rediscovery of Chinese Medicine)', *Chūō Kōron* vol. 86, no. 16, pp. 154–96.

Tamagawa, N. (2005) *Hangontan no Bunkashi; Etchū Toyama no Kusuri Uri* (A Cultural History of the Hangontan; The Medicine Peddlers of Toyama), Tokyo: Shakai Hyōronsha, pp. 268–69.

Takano, T. (1979) *Nihon no Yakugai* (Medicine Tragedies in Japan), Tokyo: Ōtsuki Shoten.

Tipps, D. C. (1973) 'Modernization Theory and the Comparative Study of National Societies: A Critical Perspective', *Comparative Studies in Society and History* vol. 15, pp. 199–226.

Toyama Prefecture (1958) *Toyama-ken Ruinen Tōkei Yōran: Meiji 16 nen - Shōwa 30 nen* (Toyama Prefecture Statistical Handbook: 1883–1955), Toyama: Toyama Prefecture Statistical Division.

Toyama Prefecture (1983) *Toyama-ken Yakugyōshi, Shiryō Shūsei* (History of the Pharmaceutical Industry in Toyama Prefecture, Resource Collection), Toyama: Toyama Prefecture.

Toyama Prefecture (1987) *Toyama-ken Yakugyōshi, Tsūshi* (History of the Pharmaceutical Industry in Toyama Prefecture, Overall History), Toyama: Toyama Prefecture.

Tsumura Juntendo Co. (1964) *Tsumura Juntendō 70 nenshi* (A 70 Year History of Tsumura Juntendo Co.), Tokyo: Tsumura Juntendo Co.

University of Tokyo Medical Department Commemoration Committee (ed.) (1967) *Tokyo Daigaku Igakubu Hyakunenshi* (A 100 Year History of the University of Tokyo Medical Department), Tokyo: University of Tokyo Medical Department Commemoration Committee.

Wada, K. (1910) *Ikai no Tettsui* (The Iron Hammer of the Medical World), Tokyo: Nankōdō.

World Health Organization (1996) *Fact Sheet N134: Traditional Medicines*, Geneva: WHO.

World Health Organisation (2001) *Legal Status of Traditional Medicine and Complementary/Alternative Medicine: A Worldwide Review*, Geneva: WHO.

World Health Organisation (2005) *WHO Global Atlas of Traditional, Complementary and Alternative Medicine, Volume 1*, Geneva: WHO.

Yakazu, D. (1979) *Meiji 100 nen Kanpō Igaku no Hensen to Shōrai: Kanpō Ryakushi Nenpyō* (The Changing Face of Kanpō Medicine in the Century since Meiji, and its Future), Tokyo: Shunyōdō.

Yakazu, D., Muroga, S., Mayanagi, M., Kosoto, H., Cyong, J. & Ōtsuka, Y. (1987) 'Igaku, Yakugaku Kyōiku ni okeru Dentō Igaku 1: I, Shi, Yakka Daigaku Karikuramu no Genkyō (Education for Traditional Medicine in Japan 1: The Present Status of Curricula for Medical, Dental and Pharmaceutical Courses)', *Nihon Tōyō Igaku Zasshi* vol. 38, no. 2, pp. 91–101.

Yakugyō Keizai Kenkyūjo (1951) *Yakuji Nenkan* (Pharmaceutical Affairs Annual), Tokyo: Nihon Yakugyō Shimbunsha.

Yakuji Nippōsha (1950–2000) *Saikin no Shinyaku* (New Drugs in Japan), Tokyo: Yakuji Nippōsha.

Yongue, J. (2008) 'Shinyaku Kaihatsu o Meguru Kigyō to Gyōsei: Chiken o Chūshin ni' (Firms and Government in Drug Development: An Examination of Clinical Trials)', in Kudō, A. & Ihara, M. (eds) *Kigyō Bunseki to Gendai Shihon Shugi* (Corporate Analysis and Contemporary Capitalism), Kyoto: Minerva, pp. 166–91.

Part III

Spaces and Pathways of Consumption

9

Getting on a Train: Railway Passengers and the Growth of Train Travel in Meiji Japan

Naofumi Nakamura

Introduction

In early Meiji Japan, the railway was one of the icons of civilisation and progress. The positive image of the railway and rail travel, both as a symbol and as a 'convenience of civilisation', was clearly widely held in those days (Ericson, 1996, pp. 53–55). Passengers who used the railways for special and occasional purposes, such as tourism, predominated, because railway travel was expensive at that time (as will be discussed further later), and in the 1870s, when the railways were being established, most passengers belonged to the upper and middle classes. Figure 9.1, which reproduces a print by one of the most well-known *ukiyo-e* artists of the period, shows the waiting room at Shinbashi Station in Tokyo in 1873, full of apparently richly dressed men and women.

Around 1900, when the railway expanded and fares began to fall (see Table 9.1), enthusiasts who used the railways for business trips, and to expand their field of activities, also emerged as among the first to experience the convenience of train travel for special purposes. For them, the railway was not only a symbol, but also a key element in a civilisation based on industrialisation. For Natsume Sōseki, in his 1906 novel *Kusa Makura* (*The Three-Cornered World*), the train has become a tool of a twentieth-century civilisation characterised by mass transport, standardisation, and loss of individuality (Takemura, 2002, p. 43).

> Anywhere that you can find a railway train must be classed as the world of reality, for there is nothing more typical of twentieth-century civilisation. It is an unsympathetic and heartless contraption which

> rumbles along carrying hundreds of people crammed together in one box. It takes them all at a uniform speed to the same station, and then proceeds to lavish the benefits of steam upon every one of them without exception. People are said to board and travel by train, but I call it being loaded and transported. Nothing shows a greater contempt for individuality than the train. (Natsume, 1965, p. 181)

By this time, for 'ordinary people' – by the mid-Meiji era, implying the middle classes such as merchants and businessmen – rail travel was no longer a special event but part of daily life.[1] In Akamatsu Rinsaku's 1901 painting *Yo-gisha* (Night Train), shown in Figure 9.2, men and women passengers no longer appear as tourists, but rather as merchants wearing *waraji* (straw sandals) and carrying big packs. By the 1900s, the 'convenience of civilisation' had become an efficient means whereby traders and business-people could expand their range of activity.

This chapter seeks to analyse these developments in the usage patterns and social effects of rail travel, with a special focus on what shaped the demand for it and how its use fitted into and changed the everyday lives of passengers in Meiji Japan. Up to now, most work on the development of the railways in Japan has tended to concentrate on the supply-side growth of the rail network and its use in the transport of freight (Nakamura, 1995).[2] However, it was in fact passenger travel that offered the greatest profit to railway companies, and this chapter breaks new ground in considering who early railway passengers were, why they travelled and what impact train travel had on their lives. The geographer Miki Masafumi has published a notable study of passenger railway transport in the pre-war period. In this study, Miki uses the development of the phenomenon of commuting to work from the Osaka suburbs as a case study to consider changes in the railway usage patterns of passengers in modern Japan. His findings indicate that railway commuting on the Osaka suburban railway network truly became a fixture in society when students began commuting, in the period after the Sino-Japanese War, and when salaried workers increasingly started to commute to work, in the period after the First World War (Miki, 2005).

Miki additionally hypothesised that the change in railway travel patterns could be explained by the fact that students who had become used

---

1 By the end of the Meiji period, rail travel had also spread to the lower classes (Gluck, 1985, pp. 162–63).

2 In contrast to Japan, there has been considerable research on railway travel in the US and Europe. See Schivelbush, 1979.

Figure 9.1 The waiting room at Tokyo-Shiodome (Shinbashi) station, 1873
Tōkyō Shiodome Tetsudō-ka Jōkisha Machiai no Zu, by Utagawa Hiroshige (3rd), by kind permission of the Modern Transportation Museum, Japan.

Figure 9.2 'The Night Train' *(Yo-gisha)*, by Akamatsu Rinsaku, 1901
(By kind permission of the University Art Museum, Tokyo University of Art).

to commuting to college by railway then moved to the suburbs, after becoming salaried workers, and began commuting to work (Miki, 2010, pp. 148–56). This provides a persuasive explanation of how rail travel became an everyday part of life during the inter-war period, on the basis of salaried workers' usage of railways. However, it is important not to forget that during the Meiji period, when the Japanese railway industry achieved remarkable development, railway companies engaged in marketing activities, such as special discount tickets and newspaper advertisements, designed to attract a different kind of regular railway traveller.

In the Meiji period, merchants, businessmen and politicians were representative of this group of people. In those days, they belonged to the middle class and were the main consumers of 'civilising goods', including newspapers, trains and electricity (Francks, 2009, pp. 74–79). For them, as early as the middle of the Meiji era the railways became an essential tool and a fixture of everyday life. Before the First World War, in the Osaka suburbs, merchants accounted for 20–30 per cent of third-class season-ticket and discount ticket-book users. Miki indicates that this is how the merchants' inter-city business-travel 'commute' was established (Miki, 2010, pp. 131–32). Railway travel opened up new possibilities and facilitated engagement with new goods, services and social practices more widely. Using the railways, people could travel speedily and punctually and construct inter-regional social networks that were built on face-to-face relationships. Merchants, businessmen and politicians were early pioneers, discovering the uses to which railway travel could be put and the possibilities that it opened up.

It is in this context that this chapter aims to explain the development of rail travel in the Meiji era from the viewpoint of the railway passenger. In order to do this, we will mainly use the case of the Kyūshū Railway Company and its users, who were from Fukuoka Prefecture (see Map 9.1).[3] These passengers included Nakahara Kazuo, a coal merchant from the town of Kokura in Kiku County; Nagae Junichi and Noda Utarō, two businessmen and politicians from Miike County; and Yasukawa Keiichirō, a coal-mine owner from the Chikuhō region. These individuals were important figures in the industrial development and political activity of the region (Nakamura, 2010, chs 4 and 6). Furthermore,

[3] The Kyūshū Railway Company was established in June 1888 to operate the Moji-Yatsushiro, Tosu-Nagasaki, Kokura-Yukuhashi, and Uto-Misumi lines. It continued to hold its position among the largest railway companies of the time, alongside Nippon Railway Company, for 20 years, until its incorporation into the nationalised railway system in 1907.

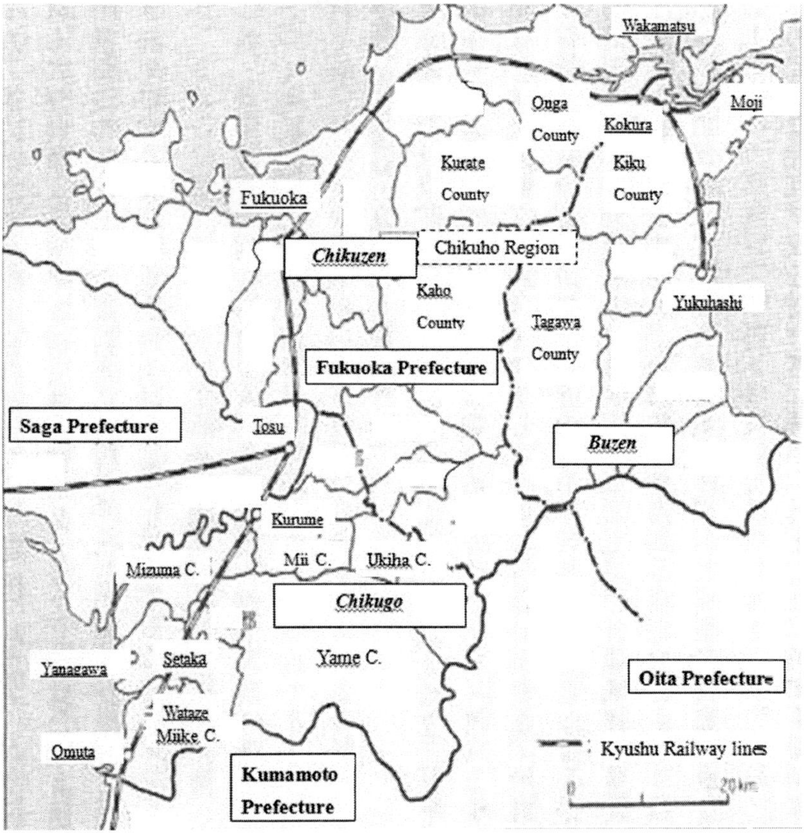

Map 9.1 Fukuoka prefecture in 1890
Source: Nakamura, 2010, p. 103.

they all left detailed diaries, and through clues about their movements recorded there, it is possible to deduce the frequency, purpose and range of their railway usage. Hence, using these diaries, we can investigate how rail travel enabled provincial integration with the metropolis, and the emergence of local- and national-level business networks.

The structure of this chapter is as follows. The first section considers general statistical trends in passenger transport for the whole country, together with the background to the case studies. Subsequently, in the second section, the business activities of service-providing railway companies will be explained, using annual reports and company in-house journals. In the third section, through analysis of the diaries of industrialists and politicians who regularly used Meiji-era railways, the question of whether railway usage influenced their business and social activities will be addressed.

The growth of train travel: an overview

From 1872, when Japan's first railway line between Shinbashi and Yokohama was opened, up until the First World War, passengers were the main source of railways' income. Figure 9.3 shows the change in relative importance of income from passengers in the total income of railway companies, between the establishment of the railway industry and its nationalisation (1906–7). Although the share of income from passenger traffic, which had exceeded 90 per cent at the start of operations, decreased continuously, due to the growth in freight transport that accompanied industrial development, it still maintained a level of around 60 per cent until the mid-1900s.

Figure 9.4, which charts the trend in railway passenger numbers, reveals a sharp increase around the Sino-Japanese War period (1894–95) when private railways were developing quickly, with the first peak appearing around 1900. Subsequently, during the first half of the decade after 1900, the number of passengers tended towards stagnation, in part influenced by the confusion after the war. However thereafter, with the unification of the national trunk-line network as a result of

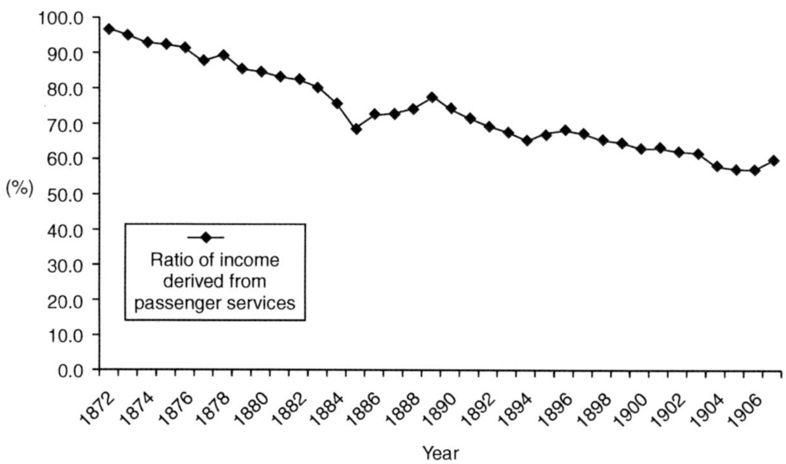

Figure 9.3 Share of revenue from passenger traffic in total railway revenue
Source: Nakamura, 1998b & Annual Report of the Railway Bureau 1907.

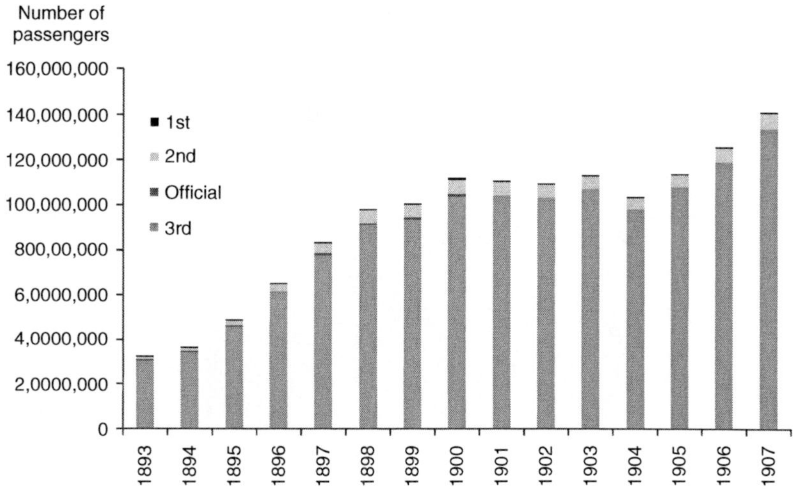

Figure 9.4 Total passengers of Japanese railways, by class
Source: Annual Reports of the Railway Bureau.

the nationalisation of the railways, the number of railway passengers started to increase again. In addition, Figure 9.4 categorises Meiji-period railway passengers by the class in which they travelled, and shows that regardless of whether the railway was government-owned or private, third-class passengers accounted for about 95 per cent of all passengers.[4] When the standard third-class fares for both government and privately owned lines are analysed, the result is as shown in Table 9.1.

At the time of Japan's first railway, even the third-class fare was 20 *rin* per mile, and the fare between Shinbashi in Tokyo and Yokohama (37 *sen* 5 *rin*) was more expensive than the steamboat (31 *sen* 25 *rin*).[5] Afterwards, with the growth of competition between various modes of transport including the steamboat, the Imperial Government Railways' passenger fare was gradually reduced, so that in 1889 it was, at 10 *rin* per mile, half the cost at the start of operations. At that time, however, the fare between Shinbashi and Yokohama (20 *sen*) was one-and-a-half times as much as the average daily wage of manufacturing workers (13 *sen*).

After the first enterprise boom period (1886–90), the Imperial Government Railways' fare levels continued to exert a strong influence

[4] In the case of the Imperial Government Railways, the second-class fare was double, and first-class fare triple that of the third class.
[5] 1000 *rin* = 100 *sen* = 1 yen.

Table 9.1 Fare tables of Japanese railways

	Imperial Government Railways					
Year	**~50 miles**	**50–100**	**100–200**	**200–300**	**300~**	**Notes**
(per mile, 3rd class, *sen/rin*)						
1872	20					Shinbashi-Yokohama: 37sen 5rin (steamboat: 31 *sen* 25 *rin*)
1874	15	15				S-Y: 30 *sen*
1887	13	13	13	13		S-Y: 25 *sen* (average daily wage: 13 *sen*)
1889	10	10	10	10	10	S-Y: 20 *sen*(average daily wage: 13 *sen*)
1899	15	13	11	9	8	Introduction of Tapering Fare Rate to Distance System (TFRDS); S-Y: 27 *sen* (average daily wage: 27 *sen*)
1902	16.5	14	11	9	8	Introduction of season tickets and ticket books
1907	16.5	13	10	8	7	Standardisation of fares due to nationalisation; S-Y: 29.7 *sen* (average daily wage: 38 *sen*)

	Sanyō Railway					
Year	**~70 miles**	**70–120**	**120–170**	**170–220**	**220~**	**Notes**
1889	10	10				
1892	10	–	6.7			
1896	15	14	13	12	11	Introduction of TFRDS
1905	16.5	13	10	8	7	

	Kyushū Railway									
Year	**~10 miles**	**10–20**	**20–40**	**40–60**	**60–80**	**80–100**	**100–120**	**120–140**	**140~**	
1889	12	12	12	12						
1892	14	14	14	14	14	14	14	14		
1899	15	14	13	12	11	10	9	8	7	Introduction of TFRDS

Note: one *sen* = 0.01 yen; one *rin* = 0.1 sen; average daily wages are those for manufacturing workers.

Sources: Annual Reports of the Railway Bureau; Business Records of the Kyūshū Railway Co.; Business Records of Sanyō Railway Co; all as collected in Tetsudō-in, 1916, pp. 113–123; Ohkawa et al., 1967, p. 243.

on the established private railways.[6] For example, when the Sanyō Railway was opened in 1889, its cost was 10 *rin* per mile, and the Kyūshū Railway fare was set at 12 *rin*. However this fare level was rather high compared to equivalent fares for steamboats. For example, immediately after the Kyūshū Railway started operations in mid-April 1891, the coal merchant Nakahara Kazuo, travelling between Kokura and Shimonoseki and making his outward journey by railway and ferry, and his return journey by steamboat, paid the following fares (Yonezu, 1976, pp. 309–11):

Outward journey: Kokura-Moji railway fare: 10 *sen*, plus Moji-Shimonoseki ferry fare: 2 *sen*; total: 12 *sen*

Return journey: Shimonoseki-Kokura steamboat fare: 8 *sen*; total: 8 *sen*

Although travel by railway was somewhat more expensive than the steamboat, Nakahara was on this occasion travelling for the purpose of sightseeing, and so ventured to use the railway. Subsequently, he and others associated with him started using the railway when making business trips to the prefectural government offices in Fukuoka City to apply for judgements, permits and so on (Yonezu, 1976, pp. 311–422; Yonezu, 1977, pp. 1–231). He utilised the particularly speedy characteristics of the railways for the purposes of urgent business trips.

On the other hand, the railway was cheaper than other forms of land transport. For example, the businessman and politician Nagae Junichi, commuting between Enoura (his home village) in Miike County and Ōmuta (his workplace) in 1891 and 1892, paid the following fares (Nagae, 1891 and 1892).

19 January 1891: Enoura-Ōmuta, *jinriki-sha* (rickshaw) fare: 30 *sen*

9 January 1892: Ōmuta-Wataze (nearest station), 3rd class railway fare: 6 *sen*

Thus the rickshaw fare was five times the railway fare. As a result, Nagae's usage of the railway increased rapidly after Wataze Station was opened (see Table 9.2), and railway travel became a regular feature of his life.

[6] The reason that the standard fares of the Imperial Government Railways determined the level of fares for the whole railway industry, including private railways, was that railway fares at the time had to be approved by the government (Railway Bureau). Each time any railway changed its fares, it had to apply to the Railway Bureau for permission.

Table 9.2 Use of transport facilities by Nagae Junichi in 1891, 1892 and 1894

Place of departure	Place of arrival	Mode of transport	Apr–May 1891		Jan–Feb 1892		Jan–Mar 1894	
			times	purpose	times	purpose	times	purpose
Enoura	Ōmuta	Rickshaw	7	commuting	1	commuting		
Setaka	Ōmuta	Railway	4	commuting	1	commuting		
Setaka	Fukuoka	Railway	2	business	1	political		
Enoura	Nagasaki	Steamship	2	political				
Ōmuta	Fukuoka	Railway	2	business	1	political	2	political
Ōmuta	Moji	Railway	2	sightseeing				
Ōmuta	Yanagawa	Railway & rickshaw	2	political	4	political	4	political
Nagasu	Ōmuta	Railway	1	business				
Wataze	Ōmuta	Railway			6	commuting	23	commuting
Enoura	Futsukaichi	Railway			2	sightseeing		
Ōmuta	Tamana	Railway			2	business		
Ōmuta	Setaka	Railway			4	political	2	political
Ōmuta	Kurume	Railway					8	business
Ōmuta	Kumamoto	Railway					6	business
Total			22		22		45	
Total days in the period			40		40		90	

Note: A round trip counts twice.
Source: Nagae *Diary* 1891, 1892 and 1894.

Attracting passengers: the case of the Kyūshū Railway Co.

This section investigates attempts to attract passengers by the railway companies in the Meiji period, mainly using the case of the Kyūshū Railway. The Kyūshū Railway Company started operations on the Hakata (Fukuoka)-Chitosegawa (Kurume) line in December 1889. Subsequently, its lines were steadily extended, and transport began in earnest with the start of operations on the Moji-Kumamoto line in July 1891, and the Tosu-Saga line in August of the same year. However, after this, the extension of lines was halted for a short period, when recession made it difficult to raise capital. Eventually, by December 1899, all planned lines had been completed (Nakamura, 1998b, pt 2).

Against this background, and with the help of the data presented in Figure 9.5, we can now look at transport trends on the Kyūshū Railway from its beginnings until its nationalisation in 1907. First, if we consider the real volume of traffic, along with the extension of the railway lines, it appears at first glance that passenger and freight traffic both increased steadily. However, if we look at the average value per mile of operation, it is clear that, in contrast to freight traffic, which is shown to have increased relatively steadily, passenger traffic was strongly affected by the financial crises first in 1890 and then in 1901 in the wake of the Sino-Japanese War. Hence it is possible to say that a particular characteristic of

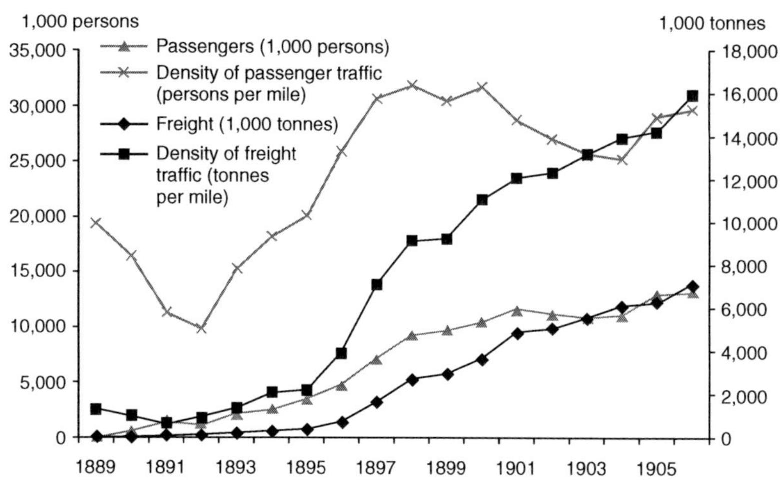

Figure 9.5 Trends in traffic on the Kyūshū Railway

Source: Business Records of the Kyūshū Railway Co.

this period was that passenger traffic volumes reacted more sensitively to adverse economic conditions than freight traffic.

Turning next to analysis of the seasonal character of railway transport, Figure 9.6 shows the monthly total of income from fares for the Kyūshū Railway from September 1891 to April 1894, a period when the number of lines operating was stable due to a suspension of construction work on line extensions. If we look first at the trend in income from passengers, we find that during the peak farming seasons from the end of May until June, when planting was carried out, and at the end of the year, when rice was harvested, there is a sudden drop in income, while from February to May (the agricultural off-season) and in October, income increases. For railway companies at that time, passenger numbers increased most at the times when religious festivals were held near the line, in February (the lunar new year) and October (the autumn festival period), as well as in April, when the best spring weather for excursions could be experienced. If we take the year 1892 as an example, the number of passengers at the peak time in February (125,787) was 1.4 times the number of passengers in June (87,210). On the other hand, freight traffic income, despite a peak during the December to March period due to transport of rice and coal, was not as seasonal as passenger traffic.

Hence, in order to keep a steady flow of customers on the railways in the quiet periods of June, when farmers were busy planting their crops,

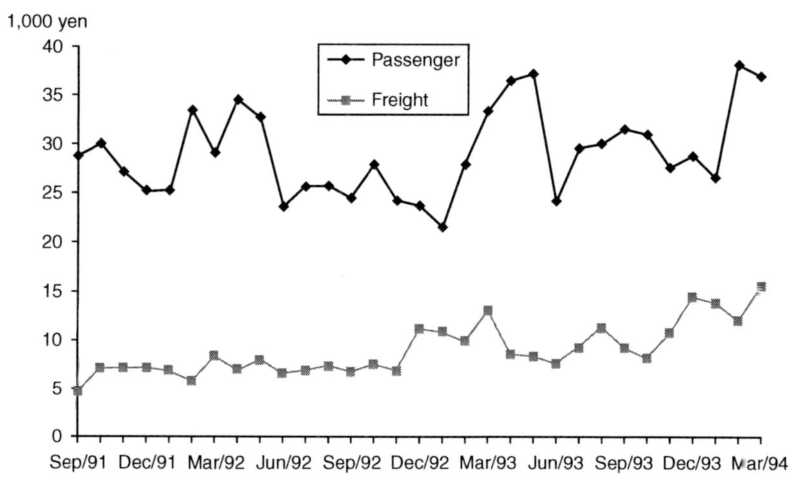

Figure 9.6 Seasonal changes in passenger and freight revenue of the Kyūshū Railway

Source: Business Records of the Kyūshū Railway Co.

and July to August, when the weather was too hot for tourists, Kyūshū Railway Company offered discounted fares to students, who were on holiday at those times. For example, from June to September 1898, the company decided to give a 20 per cent discount to students of imperial universities, teachers' colleges, high schools and vocational schools, in line with their summer vacation periods (Kyūshū Railway Company, 1898, pp. 54–55). For the railway companies, students who were travelling home or on study trips during their summer vacations provided a small though stable source of demand in the summer season.

Additionally, after 1901, when the Sanyō Railway's Kōbe-Shimonoseki line was fully opened, and traffic using the Kanmon transfer ferry to get to the mainland of Honshū became substantial, Kyūshū Railway developed promotions to attract passengers from all over the country. Specifically, after June 1901 it placed half-page advertisements in every issue of the specialist railway magazine *Japan Railway Times*, giving transfer timetables for Shinbashi to Nagasaki and Yatsushiro (via Kōbe, Shimonoseki and Moji) and information about tourist spots and large factories along the line, such as the Yawata Steel Works and Mitsubishi Nagasaki Shipyard (*Japan Railway Times*, 29 June, 1901).[7] At the same time, in collaboration with the Sanyō Railway and Imperial Government Railways, a 'transfer and return discount ticket' was sold for all classes (first to third class) in order to attract passengers from the Kansai and Kantō regions.[8] Later, after the Russo-Japanese War, an official guidebook (Kyūshū Railway Company, 1905) containing information about timetables, fares, route maps and details of tourist and business spots along the lines was published.

With this series of promotions to attract passengers, the number and density of passengers on the Kyūshū Railway increased sharply through the 1890s (Figure 9.5). Figure 9.7 compares the income from passengers (average per mile per day) in 1893 and 1899 and shows that, while there is still a peak around April and a fall in January and June as previously, there is an across-the-board increase in overall income in 1899 compared

[7] In the *Japan Railway Times*, although there is plentiful information about places along the lines of the Kantō and Kansai private railway companies from the first edition in April 1894, there is no information other than timetables and route maps about the Kyūshū Railway until June 1901.

[8] Sanyō-Kyūshū Railway transfer return tickets gave discounts of 10–20 per cent off on standard fares, if the return journey was made from within the Sanyō Railway network to within the Kyūshū network. The Sanyō Railway also gave a similar discount on tickets for travel between the Sanyō and the Imperial Government Railways networks (*Japan Railway Times* 1901, Sanyō Railways Report).

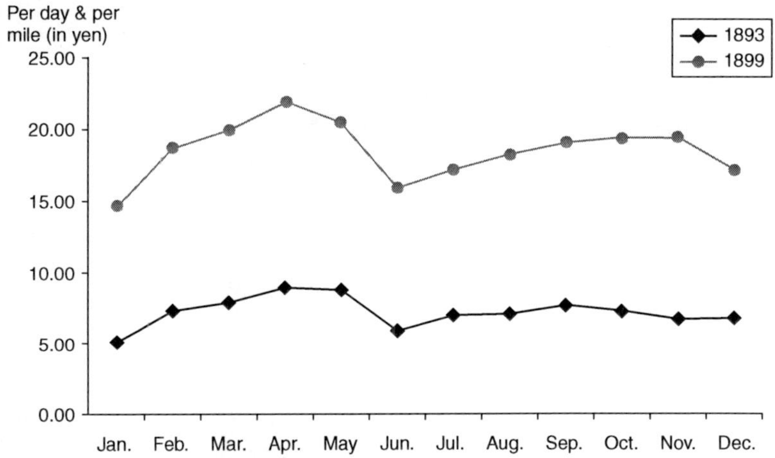

Figure 9.7 Seasonal change in passenger revenue of the Kyūshū Railway
Source: Business Records of the Kyūshū Railway Co.

with 1893. If we focus on the January and June periods, which reveal the fundamentals of rail travel not related to leisure,[9] the density of passengers rose threefold between 1893 and 1899.

As a result of this invigoration of passenger use, not only did people begin to use the railways regularly for special purposes such as tourism, but also as part of their everyday lives and business activities.

Getting on a train: cases of local businessmen and politicians

In this section, the cases of two businessmen and politicians, Nagae Junichi and Noda Utarō, as well as the case of a coal-mine owner from the Chikuhō region called Yasukawa Keiichirō, will be used to consider some aspects of the nature of passenger use of the railways in the Meiji period.

(1) The railway usage of Nagae Junichi and Noda Utarō

1. Nagae Junichi's business activities

Nagae Junichi was born to the household of a landlord in Enoura village in Miike County, Fukuoka Prefecture. His experience as a businessman

[9] In those days, January was an off-peak travel period due to New Year and June was the rice-planting season (see Takemura, 2002, p. 40).

started when he became the president of Miike Bank, which he established by bringing together a group of wealthy investors in the region. Subsequently, while engaged in activities to establish the Kyūshū Railway Company, he also set up several local companies, such as Miike Civil Engineering Company (1887) and Miike Cotton Spinning Company (1889), becoming a board member in each case.[10] Especially in the first half of the 1890s, he was absorbed in the management of Miike Cotton Spinning Company, as a board member and managing director. Nagae's *Diary* enables us now to investigate his travel activities during this busy period of his involvement in the Miike Cotton Spinning Company.

The first railway to pass through Miike County was Kyūshū Railway's Kurume-Ōmuta-Takase line, which opened for business on 1 April 1891. On this day, as a guest at the opening ceremony, Nagae tried riding the train between Ōmuta and Takase, as well as between Takase, Ōmuta and Yabegawa (Setaka) (Nagae, *Diary*, 1891, April). Later, from 4–6 April, he travelled to Shimonoseki using the express line between Ōmuta and Moji. Immediately afterwards he also began to use the railway enthusiastically for work purposes. Table 9.2 sets out Nagae's movements over 40 days between 7 April and 16 May 1891, and shows that he used the railway 13 times (counting a return trip as 2 uses). However, as the nearest station, Yabegawa (Setaka), was far from his home in Enoura village, he only used the railway 4 times out of a total of 11 trips to his workplaces in Ōmuta, the Miike Cotton Spinning Company and the Miike Civil Engineering Company. The remaining seven times he used a rickshaw. At that time, his main use of the railway was to travel to Fukuoka for business activities related to his companies, as well as to travel between Yanagawa and Ōmuta to carry out political activities (Nagae, 1891, April and May).

With the opening, on 7 June 1891, of the new Wataze station which was near Nagae's house, he was able to use the railway much more easily. As can be seen from his railway use between 1 January and 9 February 1892 shown in Table 9.2, Nagae used the railway 21 times in 40 days. During this period, he only used alternative transport on days when he went to Wakatsu port (on the way back to his house from Miike Cotton Spinning Company in Ōmuta), as there were no railway lines going there. His most common purpose in using the railway (8 times out of 21)[11] was to go to work at Ōmuta (Miike Cotton Spinning) from

[10] For details of Nagae's business activities see Nakamura 2010, ch. 4.

[11] Including one trip directly from Futsukaichi to Miike Cotton Spinning in Ōmuta.

his house in Enoura. On the other hand, the only time he used the railway for tourism was when he travelled on one occasion to Futsukaichi hot springs. In other words, he quickly began to use the railway for everyday commuting.

Getting on the train also meant saving money. Table 9.3 shows the transport fares from Nagae's home, Enoura (Wataze), to Ōmuta; the rickshaw fare (around 30 *sen*) was five times the railway fare (6 *sen*). In addition, the table shows that Nagae always travelled third class on the train, indicating that he was typical of ordinary railway passengers in those days.

Furthermore, Nagae's business activities as managing director were not limited to travelling between his house and the company. For example, if we look at his movements from January to March 1894, shown in Table 9.2, out of 45 trips by railway in 90 days, he used the train for commuting between Enoura and Ōmuta 23 times, went six times on business trips to one of Miike Cotton Spinning's most important markets, Kumamoto, and also travelled on business to Kurume eight times for various negotiations and discussions regarding a merger with Kurume Cotton Spinning. In particular, he used the railway frequently between March 7 and 11, going from work in Miike Cotton Spinning in Ōmuta to Kumamoto and Kurume for business trips as follows: Ōmuta→Kumamoto (7th, 8th)→Ōmuta→home (Enoura, 9th)→Ōmuta→Kurume (10th)→Ōmuta (11th) (Nagae, *Diary* 1894, March). As managing director, he made enthusiastic use of the railway, with the aim of opening up business opportunities by investigating markets, negotiating with customers, and making agreements with other companies in the same industry. The range of Nagae's regular

Table 9.3 Transport fares paid by Nagae Junichi in 1891 and 1892

Mode of transport	From	To	Fare (*sen*)		class	Date
Rickshaw	Enoura (home)	Ōmuta	27	single	–	1891/1/12
Rickshaw	Enoura (home)	Ōmuta	30	single	–	1891/1/19
Railway	Ōmuta	Setaka (home)	12	single	3rd	1891/4/13
Railway	Setaka (home)	Hakata	47	single	3rd	1891/4/25
Railway	Hakata	Ōmuta	52	single	3rd	1891/4/26
Railway	Wataze (home)	Ōmuta	6	single	3rd	1892/1/9
Railway	Ōmuta	Kurume	26	single	3rd	1892/1/22

Source: Nagae *Diary* 1891and 1892.

activities as head of commerce at Miike Cotton Spinning Company thus extended from Ōmuta to as far as Kurume and Kumamoto. In the light of his activities, we can conclude that he used the railway frequently to create a business area that extended beyond prefectural borders.

2. Nagae Junichi's political activities

Meanwhile, Nagae Junichi was also launching his career as a politician with the development of his participation in the Freedom and People's Rights Movement in Fukuoka Prefecture from 1878. Having served as mayor of Enoura Village, he was first elected to the Fukuoka Prefectural Assembly in 1886, and remained a member until 1897. Subsequently, he was finally elevated on to the national stage, being elected as a member of the House of Representatives in the fifth general election in 1898. He was re-elected in the sixth, tenth, eleventh, and twelfth general elections, and in 1908 and 1913 he also held the post of secretary-general of the Seiyūkai political party. Following initial participation in the Freedom and People's Rights Movement, Nagae journeyed in political terms from the Kyūshū Kaishintō (Kyūshū Progressive Party) to the Jiyūtō (Liberal Party) to the Seiyūkai (Ejima, 1995).

When considering the relationship between political activities and the railway in Fukuoka Prefecture, the first event which comes to attention is the second House of Representatives election (February 1892), which was famous for the government's interference in the electoral process. At the time, Fukuoka Prefecture was a strong base for the Jiyūtō, which was opposing the government. For this reason, the prefectural government, led by the prefectural governor, sought to obstruct the Jiyūtō's election campaigning, and supported candidates standing against it. The Kyūshū Railway, which had just been opened, was heavily used as part of these tactics to move the *sōshi* (stalwart activists) who had been mobilised to intervene in the election.

What kinds of action did Nagae Junichi, at the time a Jiyūtō party member of the House of Representatives, undertake against the governor's moves? From Table 9.2, we can observe that his railway usage coincided with his political activities before the second general election (January to February 1892). During this time, Nagae covered a wide area in 40 days of political activity, using the railway ten times to travel to Yanagawa, Setaka, Fukuoka, and Tamana (in Kumamoto prefecture). In particular, from January 16–18, he had to cope with his duties as a businessman (taking part in board meetings) and his political activities (meetings with Jiyūtō party colleagues, attendance at candidates' meetings and so on), as shown by his extensive travel between his home (in

Enoura), Fukuoka, Ōmuta and Setaka (Nagae, *Diary*, 1892, January). The situation was similar after the election in 1894, when, between January and March, he carried out the political activities required of an elected candidate, travelling eight times over a period of 90 days, from Ōmuta to Yanagawa, Setaka and Fukuoka among other places (Table 9.2). This therefore suggests that, as early as the first half of the 1890s, the railway was emerging as an important mode of transport for politicians. This becomes particularly evident if we look at the usage of railway services of another businessman and politician, Noda Utarō.

3. Elections and the railway: the political activities of Noda Utarō

Prefectures were important geographical units in political terms; when politicians started actively moving around in a large prefecture such as Fukuoka, the railway became an indispensable factor in political activities. In particular, after counties were combined into large electoral constituencies following the 1900 election law reform, which separated cities (*shi*) and counties (*gun*), and adjustment of constituency boundaries was carried out by political parties at the prefectural level (the establishment of 'agreed constituencies' – *kyōtei senkyoku*), the importance of the railway as a mode of transport increased. Hence, we will now consider the relationship between House of Representatives elections under the 'large constituency system' and railway usage, by analysing the movement pattern of Noda Utarō in the seventh election of August 1902.

Noda Utarō, born into a merchant family in Iwazu (later Iwata) Village in Miike County, Fukuoka Prefecture, was a close friend of Nagae Junichi from the time of his participation in the Freedom and People's Rights Movement. Both men had similar careers spanning politics and business, and were first elected at the same time in the fifth election (March 1898) as members of the House of Representatives. In the fifth election, in order to avoid competing with Nagae, who was standing in constituency No. 6 (Yamato and Miike Counties) where Noda's hometown was situated, Noda stood in constituency No. 5 (Mizuma and Yame Counties). Later, in the sixth election, he stood in constituency No. 4 (Mii and Ukiha Counties), again outside his hometown, and was re-elected (Sakaguchi, 1929).

In this manner, Noda became a representative, even though he was 'imported' into constituencies with which he had no links. Nevertheless, in the fifth and sixth elections, his constituencies (Mizuma and Yame Counties, and Mii and Ukiha Counties respectively) were all in the Chikugo region, the same region as his hometown in Miike County; even if there had been no railway, it can be imagined that he could somehow have used rickshaws to move around. However, in the seventh election, the 'agreed constituency' to which Noda was assigned included areas of both Chikugo (Ukiha County) and Chikuzen (Onga and Kurate Counties) which were separated by long distances. Despite this, Noda came top of the list of elected candidates in the election (Fukuoka Daily News 4–13 August 1902) and continued to be elected for the same constituency until the eleventh election of 1912 (Arima and Suetake, 1996, 568–71). At a time when it was normal election practice to try to prevent other candidates from gaining a foothold, by opening election offices in important locations and then gathering regional votes by travelling around those locations, it is worth considering what kind of election activities he was actually carrying out.

A key factor behind Noda's election in places where he had no links, such as Onga and Kurate Counties, was certainly the support of Chikuhō coal-mining investors (Arima and Suetake, 1996). Nevertheless, however strong his backup support was, he could never have been elected without diligently travelling around the election constituency, securing votes as mentioned previously. Hence, using Fukuoka as a base, he frequently used the railway to move between Onga, Kurate and Ukiha, his workplace in Ōmuta and his home (in Iwazu Village, Miike County).[12] In each location he held 'discussion meetings' and 'political seminars', working to secure votes in the region. In particular, the seminars he held from 23 to 27 July in various locations in Onga County and Kurate County were all accomplished in day trips from Fukuoka (using return railway trips), and were akin to forced marches which could not have been achieved without the rapid transport provided by the railways (Noda, 1902, July).

Table 9.4, showing Noda Utarō's movements from June to August 1902, reveals that in the space of three months he travelled on no fewer than 50 days, using the railway 62 times. Although this was an unusual time, during the election period, he constantly moved not only between his home and Ōmuta (6 return trips, 12 railway journeys), but also to Fukuoka (9 return trips, 17 railway journeys); one day after another, he travelled all around the expanse of the three old *kuni* (provinces), Buzen, Chikuzen and Chikugo, which form Fukuoka Prefecture. In this 92-day period, Noda used the railway as much as 48 times for political activities. This high frequency of use demonstrates how the railway was an essential mode of transport during national elections at that time.

---

[12] At the time, Noda acted as a special director at Kyūshū Cotton Spinning (previously Miike Cotton Spinning, merged with Kanebō Cotton Spinning in July 1902).

Table 9.4 Modes of transport used by Noda Utarō in 1902

				Jun–Aug 1902	
Place of departure	**via**	**Place of arrival**	**Mode of transport**	**No. of journeys**	**Purpose**
Iwata		Fukuoka	Railway	11	political
Iwata	Kurume	Fukuoka	Railway	1	political
Iwata		Ōmuta	Railway	13	commuting
Iwata	Yame	Ōmuta		1	commuting
Iwata	Yame	Funagoya		1	sightseeing
Ōmuta		Fukuoka	Railway	4	political
Ōmuta	Kurume	Yoshii	Railway	1	political
Funagoya		Fukuoka	Railway	1	political
Fukuoka		Orio	Railway	2	political
Fukuoka	Orio	Nōgata	Railway	6	political
Fukuoka		Ueki	Railway	2	political
Fukuoka	Nōgata	Kurate	Railway	2	political
Fukuoka	Orio	Kurosaki	Railway	2	political
Fukuoka		Wakamatsu	Railway	2	political
Fukuoka		Takeo	Railway	2	political
Fukuoka		Saga	Railway	2	political
Fukuoka		Yabegawa	Railway	2	political
Fukuoka		Setaka	Railway	1	political
Fukuoka	Kurume	Yoshii	Railway	1	political
Fukuoka		Yukuhashi	Railway	1	political
Yukuhashi	Unoshima	Shiida	Railway& rickshaw	2	political
Yukuhashi	Gotōji	Nōgata	Railway	1	political
Total				62	
Total days during the period				92	

Note: A round trip counts as two journeys.
Source: Noda *Diary*, 1902.

(2) Yasukawa Keiichirō's business activities and railway use

The business activities of Yasukawa Keiichirō, who was one of the major coal-mining capitalists in the Chikuhō region, offer further insights into railway usage.[13] Yasukawa Keiichirō was born into a samurai family in Kuroda (Fukuoka) domain, and in 1874 began to be involved in the coal mine started by his brother Matsumoto Hisomu. He established a coal sales business, the Yasukawa Co., in 1877 in order to sell his company's coal; in 1885 he opened a branch in Kōbe, and in 1886 another in Osaka, thereby firmly establishing his business activities in the Hanshin region. Building on these foundations, Yasukawa gained control of the Daijo Coal Mining and Akaike Coal Mining operations, which were among the best mines opened up during the coal-mining boom (part of the first enterprise boom, 1886–1889), and expanded his business with determination. Later, in 1896, in collaboration with Osaka investors, he established the Meiji Coal Mining Company (headquartered in Osaka), to exploit the Daijo Mine and other mines in the same vicinity. By merging Daijo Coal Mining into Meiji Coal Mining, Yasukawa became a major shareholder as well as a director of the company, and after 1896 he started making frequent trips to Osaka in order to attend board meetings. In addition, he used the overnight train to travel to Tokyo (in coordination with his trips to Osaka), in order to conduct business talks and to lobby the government. According to research carried out by Hibino Toshinobu, the number of overnight stays made by Yasukawa each year from 1899 to 1902 is as shown in Table 9. 5. From this, we can see that, over this four-year period, he spent on average 160 days per year in Osaka or Tokyo, or on the train while travelling. This was clearly more than his average time in Chikuhō (Wakamatsu, Moji, and Chikuhō Coal Mining, average 137 days), showing how he had divided his base of business activities between three places, Chikuhō, Osaka and Tokyo.

Table 9.6 enables us to compare Yasukawa Keiichirō's transport methods in the periods January to April 1899 and January to April 1906. We can first recognise from this table that Yasukawa's mode of transport to Osaka changed between 1899 and 1906. In 1899 he used the following two different methods to move between Wakamatsu and Osaka: (1) Wakamatsu-Moji (railway), Moji-Kōbe (steamboat), Kōbe-Osaka (railway), and (2) Wakamatsu-Moji (railway), Moji-Tokuyama (steamboat), Tokuyama-Kōbe-Osaka (railway). The first method involved using the

[13] For Yasukawa's business activities, see Nakamura, 2010, ch. 6.

Table 9.5 Yasukawa Keiichirō's places of lodging, 1899–1902 (nights)

	1899	1900	1901	1902	1899–1902 (average)
Home (Wakamatsu)	155	118	97	79	112
Chikuhō coal mines	12	4	8	17	10
Fukuoka	14	18	69	60	40
Moji and Shimonoseki	28	19	7	7	15
Osaka	65	64	53	59	60
Tokyo	62	89	66	82	75
Traveling etc.	3	32	41	32	27
Aboard a train	26	21	24	29	25
Total	365	365	365	365	365

Source: Hibino, 2009, p. 16.

Kyūshū Railway from Wakamatsu to Moji, then taking the steamboat for a day and night through the Seto Inland Sea, arriving at Kōbe the next day, and finally taking the Imperial Government Railways from Kōbe to Osaka. When he travelled in April 1899, for example, he boarded the steamboat from Moji at 10.00 on 4 April; on the afternoon of the next day he arrived in Kōbe and took the Imperial Government Railways, arriving at Osaka Station at 15:00 on 5th April (KMH, 2007, p. 32). On the other hand, the second method involved travelling from Moji on the Sanyō Railway transfer ferry to Tokuyama, then using the partly opened Sanyō Railway from Tokuyama.

If we look at his journey in February 1899, we find that at 14:30 hrs on 23 February he took the transfer ferry from Moji, and arrived at Tokuyama at 20:00. There, he transferred on to the 21:00 Sanyō Railway train, arrived in Kōbe the next day at 11:00, changed to the Imperial Government Railways and arrived at Osaka station on 24 February at 12:00 (Yasukawa, *Diary* 1899, 23–24 February). It can be estimated from the above examples that the travelling time between Moji and Osaka via the Seto Inland Sea was 29 hours, and via the Sanyō Railway was 22 hours; hence using the railway saved seven hours. Despite this, out of seven trips between January and April 1899, Yasukawa used the Seto Inland Sea route five times, and the Sanyō Railway route only twice. This is likely to have been because using the Sanyō Railway route meant changing from the

Table 9.6 Modes of transport used by Yasukawa Keiichirō, 1899 and 1906

Place of departure	via	Place of arrival	Mode of transport	Jan–Apr 1899		Jan–Apr 1906	
				times	purpose	times	purpose
Wakamatsu	Moji, Kobe	Osaka	Railway & steamship	5	commuting	1	business
Wakamatsu	Moji, Tokuyama	Osaka	Railway & steamship	2	commuting		
Wakamatsu	Moji, Shimonoseki	Osaka	Railway & steamboat			4	business
Wakamatsu		Moji	Railway	9	commuting	2	commuting
Wakamatsu		Moji	Steamboat	1	commuting		
Wakamatsu	Tōbata	Moji	Railway & ship			3	commuting
Wakamatsu	Moji	Shimonoseki	Railway & steamboat	1	business	1	business
Wakamatsu		Shimonoseki	Steamboat	5	business		
Wakamatsu		Chikuhō Coal Mining	Railway	6	commuting	5	commuting
Wakamatsu		Fukuoka	Railway	1	private	4	private
Wakamatsu		Tōbata	Ship			4	sightseeing
Osaka		Tokyo	Railway	4	business	4	business
Shimonoseki	Moji	Fukuoka	Railway & ship	1	private		
Shimonoseki		Moji	Steamboat	1	business		
Total				36		28	
Total days during the period				120		120	

Note: A round trip counts twice.

Source: KMH, 2007, pp. 16–31, and 2010, pp. 171–197.

steamboat to the railway in the middle of the night, making this route inconvenient.

In 1901, when the Sanyō Railway between Kōbe and Shimonoseki was fully opened, the railway route changed from Moji-Shimonoseki (using the transfer ferry) to Shimonoseki-Kōbe-Osaka (by railway). As a result, it became more convenient and reliable to transfer from the Kyūshū Railway to the Sanyō Railway; it became possible to take the 15:10 ferry from Moji to Shimonoseki, then ride on the 15:45 night train from Shimonoseki and arrive in Osaka at 12:30 the next day (Yasukawa, 1906, 9–10 January). The inconvenient night transfer was eliminated, and the usefulness of the Sanyō Railway route increased greatly. For this reason, on business trips to Osaka between January and April 1906, Yasukawa used the Sanyō Railway route four times out of five, and only used the Seto Inland Sea route once when it was necessary to make a visit to Yasukawa Matsumoto Co. in Kōbe on the way back from Osaka.[14]

Next, we consider the transport methods used for inspection tours of the Chikuhō region's coal mines. In 1906 Yasukawa owned three coal mines, the Akaike Coal Mine, Meiji Coal Mine No. 1, and Meiji Coal Mine No. 2. He regularly visited the offices of these coal mines to inspect their results and to give directions on matters relating to their management decisions; on these occasions he often used the railway. For example, on an inspection tour in April 1906, Yasukawa went from Wakamatsu to Kotake, using the Kyūshū Railway Chikuhō line on the twelfth, and inspected the management results of Meiji No.1 Coal Mine. The next day, he went to Meiji No. 2 Coal Mine to perform a similar inspection, and to conduct the opening ceremony for a new pit. He then left from the nearest station, and travelled by railway to Kanda, where he stayed over at the Akaike Coal Mine. On the morning of 14 April, after carrying out an inspection of Akaike Coal Mine's business results, he boarded the train and returned from Kanda to Wakamatsu via Nōgata (Yasukawa, *Diary*, 1906, 12–14 April). He made the same coal-mine inspection tour twice between January and April in both 1899 and 1906, using the railway six times and five times respectively (Table 9.6). In this way, Yasukawa was able to make use of the railway to direct efficiently the operations of several coal-mines in dispersed locations.

In addition, Yasukawa commuted to the head office of the Kyūshū Railway Company in Moji. As can be seen from his rail use between 1 January and 30 April 1906 (Table 9.6), he travelled to Moji five times

---

[14] The Yasukawa Matsumoto Co. was established in 1899 after Yasukawa Co. was restructured (Nakamura, 2010, ch. 6).

to attend board meetings as a director of the company. At that time, he frequently got on the train from his home (Wakamatsu) to Moji (9 times out of 10). Using the railways, Yasukawa was well able to cope with both his own business and his additional posts in other companies.

From the above analysis it can be seen that in the Meiji period Yasukawa Keiichirō was able to travel regularly between his three places of business in Chikuhō (including Wakamatsu and Moji), Osaka and Tokyo, using the railway, and thereby to form a cross-regional business information network, as he sought to achieve the expansion of his business.[15] At a time when the market was still undeveloped, travelling speedily in person between regions for face-to-face negotiations, so as to seize and hold on to business opportunities, proved crucial to entrepreneurial success. In this way, it can be said that the railway was an essential tool for Yasukawa to rise to become one of the major coal-mining capitalists.

Concluding remarks

This chapter has considered train travel in Meiji Japan, using the case of the Kyūshū Railway and its users in the area of Fukuoka Prefecture. It has looked at both quantitative data on the growth of passenger numbers and qualitative evidence derived from sources such as train company journals and the advertising by means of which companies sought to attract more travellers. Finally, it has used diary evidence to probe the demand-side impact of train travel on a key group – businessmen and politicians – among early train travellers.

During the Meiji period, passenger transport was the greatest source of profits for railway companies, and they concentrated their business efforts on thinking about how to increase the number of passengers. Their activities were aimed at enabling people to experience first-hand the convenience of the railways, thereby promoting their everyday use. Thereafter, businessmen and politicians emerged as the pioneers who started using the railways as part of their everyday lives, dramatically expanding their range of activity. The multi-layered sales areas and political constituencies they created exceeded the scope of existing geographical spaces, such as the counties, old 'provinces' and prefectures, and sometimes even extended as far as the nation as a whole.

In the Meiji era, when markets in finance, capital and human resources were all underdeveloped, building face-to-face relationships with

[15] On the formation of Yasukawa's network and its business expansion in the Meiji era, see Nakamura, 2010, ch. 6.

negotiating partners avoided problems of adverse selection, reduced transaction costs and brought great benefits to business activities (Nakamura, 2010, Introduction). For these reasons, dense inter-regional social networks, which were constructed through the enthusiastic use of the railways, played an important role when local politicians and businessmen such as Nagae Junichi, Noda Utarō and Yasukawa Keiichirō extended their activities beyond the local to the national level (Nakamura, 2010, chs 4, 6). Making full use of the railways was the first step for Meiji-era local businessmen and politicians to advance their activities on to the national stage.

References

Arima, M. & Suetake, Y. (1996) 'Sengen-ki ni okeru Iwayuru Daisenkyoku-sei to Seitō Shibu' (So-called Large Electoral Constituency System and Local Political Party Branches in Pre-war Japan), in *Fukuoka-kenshi: Kindai Kenkyū-hen, Kakuron 2* (History of Fukuoka Prefecture: Source-Book of Modern History, vol. 2) Fukuoka: Fukuoka Prefecture, pp. 557–648.

Ericson, S. (1996) *The Sound of the Whistle: Railroads and the State in Meiji Japan*, Cambridge MA: Harvard University Press.

Ejima, K. (1995) 'Kaidai Dai 1 bu' (Bibliographical Introduction, Part 1), *Fukuoka-kenshi: Kindai Shiryō-hen, Jiyūminken-undō* (History of Fukuoka Prefecture: Source-Book of Modern History: the Freedom and People's Rights Movement) Fukuoka: Fukuoka Prefecture, pp. 56–78.

Francks, P. (2009) *The Japanese Consumer: An Alternative Economic History of Modern Japan*, Cambridge: Cambridge University Press.

Gluck, C. (1985) *Japan's Modern Myths: Ideology in the Late Meiji Period*, Princeton: Princeton University Press.

Hibino, T. (2009) 'Nisshin-Nichiro-Senkanki ni okeru Yasukawa Keiichirō' (Yasukawa Keiichirō between the Sino-Japanese and Russo-Japanese Wars), in Arima, M. (ed.) *Kindai Nihon ni okeru Kigyōka to Seiji; Yasukawa Keiichirō to sono Jidai* (An Entrepreneur and Politics in Modern Japan: Keiichirō Yasukawa and his Age), Tokyo: Yoshikawa Kōbunkan, pp. 12–39.

Japan Railway Times (1901) no. 93, 29 June, Kyūshū Railway report.

Kita-Kyūshū Museum of Natural History and Human History (KMH) (2007) *Yasukawa Keiichirō Nikki; Dai 1 kan* (Diary of Yasukawa Keiichirō, vol.1), Kita-Kyūshū; Kita-Kyūshū Museum of Natural History and Human History.

Kita-Kyūshū Museum of Natural History and Human History (KMH) (2009) *Yasukawa Keiichirō Nikki; Dai 2 kan* (Diary of Yasukawa Keiichirō, vol. 2), Kita-Kyūshū: Kita-Kyūshū Museum of Natural History and Human History.

Kyūshū Railway Company (1898), 'Monthly Report' No. 8 (July).

Kyūshū Railway Company (ed.) (1905) *Kyūshū Tetsudō Annai* (A Guide to the Kyūshū Railway).

Miki, M. (2005) 'The Origins of Commutation in Japan', *Geographical Review of Japan*, vol.78 no.5, pp. 1–18.

Miki, M. (2010) *Toshi-kōtsu no Seiritsu* (The Formation of Urban Traffic in Japan), Tokyo: Nippon Keizai Hyōronsha.

Nagae, J. (1891) *Tōyo Nikki Meiji 24 Nen* (Diary 1891).
Nagae, J. (1892) *Tōyo Nikki Meiji 25 Ne'* (Diary 1892).
Nagae, J. (1894) *Tōyo Nikki Meiji 27 Nen* (Diary 1894).
Nakamura, N. (1995) 'Meiji-ki ni okeru Tetsudō no Hattatsu to Sekitan Yusō' (Railways and Coal Freight in Meiji Japan), *History and Geography*, no. 475, pp. 1–20.
Nakamura, N. (1998a) 'Tetsudō ga tsukutta Chiiki' (Regions made by Railways), in Matsumoto, N. & Yamada, K. (eds) *Idō no Chiikishi* (Regional Histories of Mobility), Tokyo: Yamakawa Shuppan-sha, pp. 367–99.
Nakamura, N. (1998b) *Nihon Tetsudō-gyō no keisei: 1869–1894* (Formation of the Japanese Railway Industry, 1869–1894), Tokyo: Nippon Keizai Hyōronsha.
Nakamura, N. (2010) *Chihō kara no Sangyō Kakumei* (The Industrial Revolution from the Provinces), Nagoya: Nagoya University Press.
Natsume, S. (trans. Turney, A.) (1965, original in Japanese 1906) *The Three-Cornered World* (*Kusa makura*), Washington DC: Regnery Gateway Inc.
Noda, U. (1902) *Tōyo Nikki Meiji 35 Nen* (Diary 1902).
Ohkawa, K., Noda, T., Takamatsu, K., Yamada, S., Kumazaki, M., Shionoya, Y. & Minami, Y. (1967) *Estimates of Long-Term Economic Statistics of Japan*, Vol.8, *Prices*, Tokyo: Tōyō Keizai Shinpōsha.
Sakaguchi, J. (1929) *Noda Taikai Den* (Biography of Noda Taikai), Tokyo: Noda Taikai Den Kankōkai.
Schivelbush, W. (1979) *The Railway Journey: Trains and Travel in the 19th Century*, New York: Urizen Books.
Takemura, T. (2002) 'The Time Revolution of the Railway in the 1920s: The Impact of the Changeover to Automatic Couplers', *Nichibunken Japan Review* no.14, pp. 39–62.
Tetsudōin (Railway Board) (ed.) (1916) *Honpō Tetsudō no Shakai oyobi Keizai ni oyoboseru Eikyō* (Social and Economic Influence of Railways in Japan), Tokyo: Tetsudōin.
Yasukawa, K. (1899 & 1906) *Nikki Meiji 32 Nen* & *39 Nen* (Diary 1899 & 1906).
Yasukawa, K. (1935) *Bushō Yoin* (The Soughing of the Wind among the Pines), private edition.
Yonezu, S. (ed.) (1976) *Nakahara Kazuo Nikki; Dai 10 kan* (Diary of Kazuo Nakahara, No.10), Fukuoka: Nishi-Nihon Cultural Association.
Yonezu, S. (ed.) (1977) *Nakahara Kazuo Nikki: Dai 11 kan* (Diary of Kazuo Nakahara, No.11) Fukuoka: Nishi-Nihon Cultural Association.

10
People and Post Offices: Consumption and Postal Services in Japan from the 1870s to the 1970s

Janet Hunter

Introduction

Although the importance of transport infrastructure in the process of industrialisation has long been recognised, 'for economic historians, postal systems are a neglected topic; many economic history textbooks ignore them altogether' (John, 2003, p. 315). And yet postal services have long enabled the movement of physical items and money, and played a key role in the transmission of information. In the nineteenth century new state-run systems transformed the scale and speed of postal communication, and other related activities, dramatically widening accessibility across classes and populations. As one observer of the British Post Office remarked in 1938, it was not just a question of running a vast and intricate postal service, a telegraph service, a telephone service and the remittance of money to anywhere in the country and almost anywhere in the world. The Postmaster-General was also 'a banker with whom one in every four of the population has an account... sells £98 million worth of health and unemployment insurance stamps during the year, pays 220 millions of old age and widows' and orphans' pensions, and dispenses licences of many kinds... He is the largest employer of labour in the country and last but not least, he is a tax gatherer' (Crutchley, 1938, p. 23). This wide remit was far from atypical (for example, Fuller, 1972, p. 238 for the US).

A similarly comprehensive remit underpins the importance of postal services for the history of consumption in modern Japan. This importance falls into two main categories. The first is the increasing consumption of postal services. The period from the mid-nineteenth century was characterised by the continuation and growth of consumption of goods, and by increasing consumption of a whole range of services. Users of services such as railways and the post may not necessarily have regarded such usage as part of their consumption,[1] but services accounted for an increasing amount of expenditure by individuals, families and organisations. If we accept recent findings on the significant contribution of services to growth in industrialised economies (for example, Broadberry, 2006), it becomes all the more necessary to understand the demand for those services. The second is the role of the post office as an intermediary institution for consumer decision making. Post offices were integral to the process of consumption, serving as pathways to consumer activity. Their national physical presence helped to embed consumption-related activities into the social, economic and political lives of towns and villages across Japan. Post offices were sites for information exchange and social interaction. They engineered the transfer of information, goods and money integral to the consumption process, and helped integrate localities and consumers into the wider market and commercial world. In the process they helped to extend consumer choice, and reinforce local tastes and niche markets, while creating the national consumer market that was a major driver of Japan's growth in the nineteenth-twentieth centuries. Post offices therefore played a crucial role in facilitating and validating consumption and the growth of a consuming society.

The purpose of this chapter is to explore these two consumption aspects of the development of postal services in modern Japan. The first section will outline the main trends in the take-up of postal services in Japan from the 1870s. We know a considerable amount about the supply of postal services from the nineteenth century, but far less has been written about the demand side. Yet understanding how and why people and organisations used postal services is important, because the new postal systems were associated with socio-economic transformation on an unprecedented scale. The second will focus on the physical location and organisation of the post office, and what that meant for the broader growth of consumption.

Consumption of postal services

Understanding postal usage is important to our analysis of Japan's consumption history because it represents a final service that customers

[1] Problems in defining consumption are discussed in the introduction to this volume.

can decide whether to purchase, based on considerations of price and utility. In Japan and elsewhere postal services have increasingly become a consumer item, with customers facing ever-expanding choice backed up by aggressive marketing and competing providers, and having to choose which of those services to consume. When Japan's Western-style postal system was established in 1871, its architects recognised its individual, social, governmental and economic implications. The preamble to the Postal Regulations of 1872 stated that the new service would 'deepen friendship, spread civilisation', and also constitute 'the basis for an increase in trade and production' (Maejima, 1952, p. 6). By the time of the First World War regular use of postal services was a fact of life for all Japanese. Despite this, our knowledge of how individuals and organisations used the modern postal service remains limited. The objective of this section is to offer some insight into the nature and extent of use of the service by individuals, families and businesses from the 1870s through to the end of the high-growth period a century later. A state monopoly initiated in 1873 operated throughout these years Particular attention will be paid to the period up to the 1930s, during which modern postal consumption was initiated and then consolidated. While the complete range of services offered by Japan's postal system will be acknowledged, analysis of consumption will for reasons of practicality focus on mail and related services.[2]

Consumption of postal services was a function of four main factors. The first was access to the services provided by the state. The second was the cost of services; to have a realistic chance of growth, prices had to be set at an affordable level. Thirdly, the consumer, or potential consumer, had to have sufficient knowledge to understand how to engage in that consumption, and hence to perceive and maximise its benefits. Where something is very new, consumers are likely to have to be persuaded of the advantages that can be derived from its consumption. Finally there are what might be called contingent circumstances. Consumption was shaped by a whole host of contextual factors, including alternative options to making use of postal services, and historically specific economic and social conditions. These contingent circumstances changed over time, and the state as service provider had to respond to them proactively to maintain or increase take-up.

[2] It is not possible within the constraints of a single chapter to consider all services physically delivered through post offices. For telegraph and telephone see, for example, Fujii, 1998, and for savings Horioka, 2006. All these services are important for the saving-spending-consumption cycle supported by post offices.

The Meiji government was committed to universal access to the new mail service. Every effort was made to provide the poorest farmer in the most remote village with a service equivalent to that available to the citizens of Tokyo or Osaka, and at a price that all were likely to be able to afford. By 1920 land and sea routes amounted to 76,600 kilometres (Teishinshō, 1940, vol. 2, pp. 599–601).[3] On local routes horse-drawn carts gradually replaced handcarts, in turn to be replaced by bicycles and motor vehicles. From the 1880s railways increased provision on trunk routes, complementing the existing use of shipping (Tahara, 2003). In Tokyo motor vehicles were used to carry post from 1908. The first scheduled air service for post items was in 1925. By the turn of the twentieth century most domestic mail reached its destination in 2–3 days at most (Teishinshō, 1921, p. 96). The number of deliveries varied according to volume of mail, but by the late 1880s some offices were making as many as 12 deliveries per day (Tahara, 2003, p. 52). The number of post offices rose consistently for over a century (Yūseishō Yūmukyoku, 1991, pp. 215–17), and the number of postboxes and places selling stamps also increased rapidly, except during the Pacific War years. Mailboxes with automatic stamp dispensers appeared in Tokyo in 1938, and spread rapidly in the post-Pacific War period. All the evidence suggests that accessibility rapidly ceased to be a barrier to consumption.

As expansion took place, postal activities became increasingly diversified.[4] Diversification within mail services consisted of more provisions for specially designated categories of mail, and the introduction of new mail products. Provision for the carriage of letters containing money was made in 1871, and a cheap rate for newspapers and printed matter introduced the same year. Postcards were first issued in December 1873, followed by the prepaid return postcard in 1884. Registered mail for the carriage of valuable items was introduced in 1872 (Teishinshō, 1940, vol. 2, pp. 155–56). Postal money orders (*yūbin kawase*) started in 1875, as a preferred substitute to money enclosures. From 1885 there were three separate categories of postal orders: standard postal orders, telegraphic money orders, and small postal money orders (Teishin Daijin Kanbō, 1898, pp. 59–60, 107, 110–11). Other new categories of mail provided for reduced rates for items of cultural, political and economic importance. Special low rates were applied to agricultural inputs

---

[3] This total had declined from a peak in 1900, as the logistics of carrying mail were rationalised.

[4] Except where indicated, information on the timing of the diversification relies on Yūseishō Yūmukyoku, 1991.

and products, commercial samples, patterns and models, and items and information relating to domestic industrial exhibitions (Teishin Daijin Kanbō, 1898, pp. 93–96; Teishinshō, 1940, vol. 2, pp. 139–41, 278–85). In 1899 special provision was made for the carriage of silkworm egg cards (Teishinshō, 1921, pp. 79–80). A domestic parcel post service was established in 1892, and this was followed by cash-on-delivery, which was introduced right at the end of the Meiji period (Teishinshō, 1940, vol. 2, pp. 146–49). Special provision for New Year's mail started from 1905, and for unaddressed advertisements and leaflets (*hikifuda*) in 1907. Other innovations included a designated military post service (1894) and airmail letters (1929). International mail services were initiated in the early 1870s, and Japan became a member of the Universal Postal Union in 1877.

The second form of diversification was the provision of additional non-mail services. Most conspicuous were postal savings and postal insurance. The postal savings system was initiated in 1875 with the objective of encouraging a habit of saving among the population (see, for example, Garon, 1998; Garon, 2006; Horioka, 1993; Horioka, 2006). The postal insurance system (*kan'i hoken*) was started in 1916 to provide accessible and cheap life insurance, and later pensions, and it was closely associated with the first radio exercise programmes (*rajio taisō*) in 1928.

Pricing the new services was initially problematic. When the postal service was first extended north from Tokyo the cost of sending a letter from the city of Sendai to the capital (a distance of around 300 km) was 8 *sen*, at the time estimated to be equivalent to the cost of purchasing nearly 5.5 litres of white rice in the city (Teishinshō, 1940, vol. 2, pp. 218–19). The cost of sending mail decreased considerably with the introduction of a uniform rate in 1873, and from 1882 all domestic letters were charged at 2 *sen* (Teishinshō, 1940, vol. 2, pp. 221–22). While letter rates remained relatively low, postal rates for some mail categories were revised with some frequency during the Meiji period, and cost remained a significant concern for the business community. The fact that from the 1890s the system consistently ran a healthy profit inevitably led to complaints about its charges, but the government does seem to have sought to keep the basic cost of communication down. A number of mail categories, including newspapers, printed matter, business documents, commercial samples, and items related to the growth of manufacturing, commerce and agriculture, continued to receive preferential or reduced rates. The aggregate rate of increase in postal charges from the late 1870s through to the mid-1930s was comparable to the rise in the consumer

Figure 10.1 Cost of sending mail
Note: Cost is measured in *sen*. 100 *sen* = 1 *yen*.
Source: Yūseishō Yūmukyoku, 1991, pp. 222–24.

price index over the same period, but, as Figure 10.1 shows, basic letter and postcard rates remained unchanged from 1899 through to 1939. This meant a gradual decline in the real cost to the consumer across those four decades.[5] During these decades nominal wages for most workers rose considerably; the cost of sending a letter became proportionately far less significant in terms of a worker's total disposable income (see for example Ohkawa, 1974, tables A50, A52). For most Japanese consumers, making use of the post became more affordable.

The data that we do have suggest that expenditure on postal services was for most households a very small part of total spending. From an estimated 0.1 per cent of personal consumption expenditure in the early Meiji years, expenditure on 'communications' rose to a peak of 0.7 per cent in the 1930s; in real terms this represented an increase of over 800 per cent, but a disproportionate part of this growth can be attributed to expenditure on telegraph and telephone (Shinohara, 1967, pp. 138–39, 248). Post-war household expenditure surveys suggest that in 1963 the average household spent 688 yen on postage, 238 yen of this on postcards, but through the 1960s postage expenditure remained a minute proportion (barely 0.001 per cent) of total household expenditure, compared with expenditure on, for example, food, which accounted for up

[5] Using retail price data from Miwa and Hara, 2007, pp. 4–5 and postal price data from Yūseishō Yūmukyoku, 1991, pp. 222–24.

to 40 per cent (based on data from Ministry of Internal Affairs and Communications, 2010). This low percentage underplays the extent of overall use of the service, because it was business expenditure on mail services that accounted for the largest share of all postal usage. It underlines the fact, though, that in real terms the cost of sending mail remained extremely low, including by comparison with other means of communication such as the telephone. More importantly, such statistics tell us nothing about the wider range of services for which Japanese citizens visited post offices, or what they used this low-cost service for. This role of the postal system as a pathway for consumption will be considered later in this chapter.

Statistical data collected by the postal authorities provide some indication of the overall volume of mail, as well as of changes over time in consumption of postal services (basic data available in Yūseishō, 1971b). The growth in usage was initially slow, and the total number of domestic items increased only gradually for much of the Meiji period. Growth then accelerated, particularly around the time of the First World War. The volume of basic mail (letters and postcards) declined during the Great Depression but recovered somewhat in the late 1930s, before dropping very significantly in the late 1930s–early 1940s. Post-war growth was rapid, with the pre-war level recovered by the mid-1950s. Growth in parcel post was steady from the 1890s, was slowed but not reversed in the early 1930s, and then peaked in 1940 prior to almost complete collapse during the early 1940s. By the early 1960s the pre-war peak had been surpassed, but this was followed by a marked decline during 1970–75. International mail was characterised by generally slow growth until the late 1930s, a remarkable peak in use in 1940, then total collapse. The data show clearly the impact of the Pacific War years, in which postal provision declined, with restrictions imposed on consumers, and problems with manpower and transport shortages. They also demonstrate how postal consumption responded to the business cycle, slowing during the period after the Russo-Japanese War, recovering in the context of the First World War and then suffering again from the Shōwa Depression. The falls in both parcel post and foreign mail consumption in 1975 were closely associated with the aftermath of the Oil Shock.

Take-up of the new service was initially sluggish, but by around 1895 individual Japanese were on average sending or receiving ten mail items a year. Usage remained considerably lower than in higher-income industrialised countries, such as Britain, though the gap with other European countries such as Sweden and Italy was narrower (Teishinshō Tsūshinkyoku, 1910). By the late 1920s Japanese annual per capita usage had risen to nearly 80 items (Teishinshō, 1940, vol. 2, pp. 604–6). By 1975 it had recovered to over 120.[6] It is clear that postal usage grew as incomes increased. Over the period before the First World War, when postal usage was increasing from a very low base, the rate of postal growth exceeded the growth rate in production and national income. Thereafter the two rose broadly in parallel. Increased postal usage was part of an overall expansion in private consumption that was facilitated by rising wealth, but it was also a function of consumers being able and willing to use the post more, and for more things.

Analysis of the composition of Japan's mail shows an unusual dependence on the postcard, with postcards overtaking letters by 1887. By 1895 the head postmaster of Kōbe could claim that postcard use in Japan was the highest in the world (cited in Yūseishō Yūmukyoku, 1991, p. 7). Postcards continued to account for 60 per cent or more of all Japanese mail throughout the pre-war years (Yūseishō Yūmukyoku, 1991, p. 47). Price clearly played a role here, with postcards consistently costing around half the price of a letter throughout the pre-war period, putting them more within the reach of low-income consumers. They were also convenient. With no stamp or envelope, pre-printed postcards were an easy way to send short messages (Tahara, 2003, pp. 37–38). Postcards appear to have been used extensively both by the lower-income groups at whom they had been aimed, and by those in higher-income groups who felt that their communication did not require privacy (Ishii, 1994, pp. 70–73). Enthusiasm for the picture postcard was initiated when the authorities allowed the use of commercial and privately printed postcards from 1899. Clearly identifiable as consumer items, some of these picture postcards were said by Basil Hall Chamberlain to 'follow the vulgarest European precedents' (Chamberlain, 1905, p. 395). Picture postcards also facilitated other forms of consumption, being used for advertising or to promote tourism. The private sector joined the state in issuing commemorative postcards to celebrate important events, and these were purchased enthusiastically by postal users. When official commemorative postcards for the Russo-Japanese War went on sale there was a near riot in front of the Tokyo Post Office, and the police had to be called to keep order (Yūseishō Yūmukyoku, 1991, p. 58). Postcards were increasingly used for New Year and other seasonal greetings. By the end of the First World War 220 million items of New Year mail were being handled,

[6] Calculated from total domestic and foreign mail and population census figure for 1975. This compares with 415 items per head of population handled by the US mail in 1970 (Fuller, 1972, p. 334).

and in 1936 the figure was nearly 850 million. New Year mail bounced back from wartime constraints to reach over 2,580 million items in 1975, over 23 items for every member of the population. The addition of lottery numbers to printed New Year cards from 1948 strongly appealed to consumers in a war-torn and occupied country (Teishinshō, 1921, pp. 138–39; Yūseishō Yūmukyoku, 1991, pp. 62, 218–19).

The number of newspapers carried by mail rose from over four million in 1877 to over 200 million annually by the end of the Meiji period, and 260 million in 1919 (Teishinshō, 1921, pp. 61–62, 64–66, 128), and increased further thereafter. Greater circulation was associated with increasing literacy, price reductions and a newspaper war, as well as a growing interest in the political and economic affairs that newspapers reported. By the early twentieth century newspapers were becoming increasingly important for the diffusion of advertisements for a wide range of consumer products, helping to involve consumers in mail-order purchases and cash-on-delivery. The expansion of magazines after the First World War, especially those targeted at women (Satō, 2003), disseminated further information on consumption, and these, too, were carried by post. The implications for consumption of some other mail categories are more difficult to pin down. Officials took recurrent steps to try to ensure that the category of commercial samples and models could not be used for the covert sale of consumer goods, but the extensive use of this mail category to support the development of agriculture and industry had an indirect effect on the availability and diffusion of goods (Teishinshō, 1940, vol. 2, pp. 139–41 Teishinshō, 1921, pp. 86–87; Yūseishō, 1971a, p. 246).

Provision for the transmission of money was a prerequisite for the greater circulation of goods, but postal arrangements for carrying money, effectively just putting money into envelopes, were initially restrictive and unsafe. In the 1870s postmen were often armed with pistols, and postal wagons accompanied by guards riding shotgun to discourage potential theft. Customers frequently failed to pay the additional fee required (Teishinshō, 1940, vol. 2, pp. 158–59; Teishin Rokujūnen Shi Kankōkai, 1931, p. 105). The postal money-order was explicitly aimed at providing a better substitute for letters containing money, and such was its success that money-letters had virtually ceased to exist by the 1890s. The value of postal money orders handled by the post office rose from something over 2 million yen in its first year of operation to reach 92 million yen by the turn of the century, and close to 800 million yen by 1921. In 1940 over 62 million postal orders were issued, with a total value of around 1,920 million yen (Teishinshō, 1921, p. 163; Maejima, 1956, p. 368). In most years the value of cashed orders was relatively close to that of purchased orders, suggesting that they were facilitating spending as well as saving. The introduction of telegraphic postal orders and the 'small postal order' in 1885 allowed businesses to make transactions more quickly and those on low incomes to remit very small amounts of money relatively cheaply. The small money-order remained a vital element in popular consumption, as the less affluent had more limited access to the growing financial sector, for reasons of cost, location and knowledge. The ability to transfer very small amounts of money through postal orders opened the way for many longer-distance transactions, while migrant workers, even those abroad, could send small remittances home to their families. The system was simple, with no specified payee or payment office; the bearer merely had to take the postal order (usually received through the mail) to the post office to get paid. It was also cheap. When small postal orders were started they cost 2 *sen*, later increased to 3 *sen*, equivalent to the cost of a letter (Teishin Daijin Kanbō, 1898, pp. 117, 119–24). By the early 1920s small money-orders accounted for around two-thirds of all money orders. Their average value was by this time 20 yen, compared with 500 yen for telegraphic orders and 300 yen for ordinary money-orders (Teishinshō, 1921, pp. 271–72). Being able to transmit money in this way played a significant part in expanding purchases of goods, particularly within Japan itself. Postal money orders were just one of the services by means of which the postal system acted as an interface between producer, retailer and consumer.

Services of this kind served to blur any distinction between business and personal use, but what does seem clear is that business-related mail constituted a high proportion of all mail from the start, and that proportion is likely to have increased over time. Postal orders, for example, were a crucial way in which commerce and consumption were facilitated. One businessman from Kanda ward in Tokyo wrote to the *Yomiuri* newspaper in 1885 complaining about delays in cashing postal orders, on which he was dependent for his income since most of his business was with the provinces (reproduced in Yūseishō, 1971b, vol. 21, pp. 59–61). The introduction of the parcel post and cash-on-delivery opened the way to mail-order use (Osaka Mainichi, 1928, p. 26; Mitsuzono, 2009).[7] Writing to the *Tōkyō Nichi Nichi* paper in the early 1890s, a Wakayama-born businessman, Shimomura Fusajirō, noted the significance of the proposed parcel post for provincial economic activity, and hence its particular importance for a Japanese economy in which small landlords, producers

[7] See also Mitsuzono's chapter (Chapter 11) in this volume.

and merchants were still by far the most important group (reproduced in Yūseishō, 1971b, vol. 21, pp. 101–4). Taking advantage of postmen's visits to private homes on a daily basis to deliver unaddressed handbills and flyers set Japan on the path to 'junk' mail and postal advertising at a very early stage. In 1919 37 million items were distributed under this category (Teishinshō, 1921, p. 135).

It is much more difficult to draw any conclusions regarding the implications for consumption of the largest categories of mail, namely letters and postcards. We know that the category of 'letters' from the start included a large number of items that were technically not letters at all, including contracts, accounts, financial estimates, receipts and other business-related documents (Teishin Rokujūnen Shi Kankōkai, 1931, p. 81). All the evidence that we have suggests that the number of letters received and sent by businesses and other economic organisations was very considerable indeed, and estimates in the *LTES* work on the assumption that only 30 per cent of total expenditure on communications in the pre-war years was accounted for by households (Shinohara, 1967, p. 248). It seems not unreasonable to assume that through most of its history the postal service user was more likely than not to be a person or an organisation using it for business or economic purposes. Knowing how far this use may have related to the consumption decisions of individuals and groups, however, is almost impossible. We do have one estimate suggesting that in 1973, at the end of the high-growth years, 41.1 per cent of all postal usage was business to business, 39.4 per cent business to individuals, and only 17.1 per cent person to person (cited in Yūseishō Yūmukyoku, 1991, pp. 47–48), but we have no breakdown of the all-important 'business to individuals' category.

Postal usage, particularly of the specifically commercial mail categories, was highly concentrated in the main urban and economic centres.[8] Sugiyama's study of Gunma Prefecture, for example, shows that increasing postal use was closely aligned with the growth of production and consumption of silk and other textiles (Sugiyama, 1992, pp. 237–41). As early as 1883–84 residents of the Tokyo urban area averaged over 13 letters per year, and those of Osaka over eight per year, while Okinawa residents averaged barely a letter for every four persons (Yūseishō, 1971b, vol. 30, pp. 266–68). By 1904 Tokyo residents, at over 90 items a year, averaged over nine times as much mail as residents in many rural areas,

[8] Regional breakdown of use by prefecture and city shows this to have been consistently the case at least after the 1880s (eg. Nagoya Yūbinkyoku 1905, pp. 108–63, 261–305; Ōsaka Yūseikyoku, 1971, p. 710).

and 50 times as much as Okinawans (Teishinshō Tsūshinkyoku, 1904, pp. 11–14). Throughout the period under consideration highest per capita usage of mail was in Tokyo, followed by Osaka, and then other leading commercial areas such as Kyoto, Nagasaki, Hyōgo and Kanagawa. Concentration of use also existed at the local level. By the early 1880s residents of Akita City were sending on average up to eight times as many letters as their fellow citizens in the remainder of this largely rural prefecture (Akita Ekitei Shutchōkyoku, 1885, pp. 3–4). Local and national time series data also suggest that high per capita postal usage was consistently associated with a net outflow of mail. By 1895 only six prefectures (out of a total of 47) were sending more mail items than were delivered in the area, but those six prefectures were the same centres of urbanisation and commercial importance that made the most use of the system. In the case of Tokyo the number of mail items sent was almost twice the number received (Sugiyama, 1992, pp. 237–41; Teishin Daijin Kanbō, 1897, pp. 258–61). Tahara has shown that Tokyo in particular had a distinctive mail profile at this time, being the only place in which newspapers and printed matter took second place after postcards. Many of these publications were sent to readers in the northern regions of Tōhoku and Hokkaidō (Tahara, 2003, pp. 40–41). A high level of 'one-way' communications in the largest commercial centres supports the claim that the postal system acted as an important agent for the diffusion of information, impacting on consumer decision making as well as the actual provision of consumer goods.

Analysis of the extensive use of postal money-orders that allowed consumers across the archipelago to conduct the transactions involved in acquiring the goods that they demanded shows the other side of this picture. Use of postal money-orders was concentrated in specific regions, with some prefectures experiencing a net outflow of funds through the system, and others enjoying a net inflow. Large conurbations and commercial centres were most likely to enjoy a net inflow. In 1895 Tokyo cashed over three times the value of the orders that were purchased in the city. In 1921 Osaka and Kyoto together enjoyed a net inflow of 18 million yen in postal order transactions (Ōsaka Yūseikyoku, 1971, p. 701). The greatest net outflow of postal-order money was from Yamaguchi, Okinawa and Akita prefectures, suggesting that postal orders could be a means of channeling funds out of rural areas into the growing urban centres. The picture is not consistent, as some rural areas of Toyama and Tokushima had a net inflow of funds, while Gunma and Yamanashi (centres of the silk industry) had a net outflow (Teishin Daijin Kanbō, 1897, pp. 279–93), but there seems little doubt that the postal money-order system was a key link in producer–consumer transactions, allowing rural consumers to access goods from other parts of Japan, and particularly from the growing metropolitan areas.

The growth of postal services therefore played a crucial role in the flow of information, goods and capital, enabling the growth of choice and transactions that we associate with the emergence of consumer society. It was a critical intermediary institution for the consumption-production cycle. But the physical location through which this role was discharged, the post office, was also of major importance in embedding the use of the service – socially, politically and economically – in localities across Japan. It is to the post office as the public face of the postal system, and the space where consumers interacted with it, that we now turn.

People and post offices

Figure 10.2 shows the growth in the number of post offices in Japan from the 1870s. The number of offices had reached nearly 5,000 in just 15 years, by the mid-1880s. Regulations of 1903 allowing local governments to apply for some kind of post office to be established in their locality set the number of post offices on an ever-rising trajectory. Post offices spread across the empire, and the flags denoting military post offices on the battle-front during the wars against China and Russia were branded 'beacons of hope amidst the hardship', allowing soldiers and

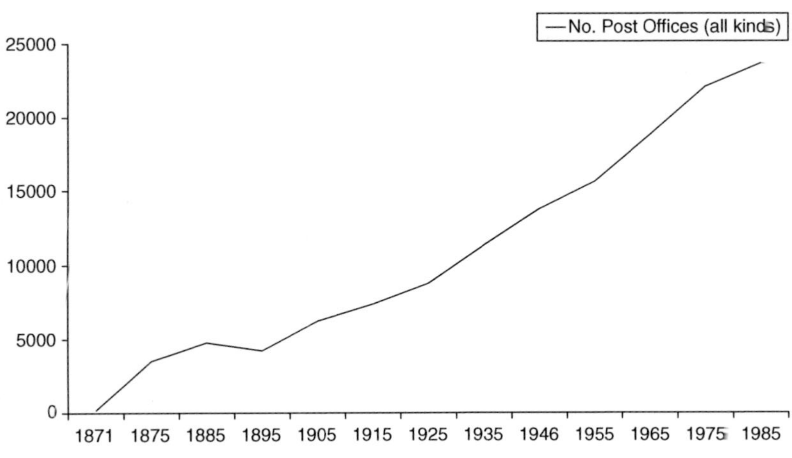

Figure 10.2 Number of post offices (all kinds)
Source: Yūseishō Yūmukyoku, 1991, pp. 215–17.

sailors to remain in touch with their friends and relatives (Teishinshō, 1921, p. 90). By the eve of the Pacific War there were over 12,000 post offices in the Japanese islands for a population of around 72 million. By the time of the Oil Shock in 1973 close to 22,000 post offices served a population of around 109 million (Ministry of Internal Affairs and Communications, 2010; Yūseishō Yūmukyoku, 1991, p. 217).[9] Post boxes were to be found on almost every corner in urban areas, and early legislation specified the maximum distance that people should have to travel to a post-box. As the number of post offices grew, the average area covered by each office diminished; officials claimed that by 1919 the average catchment area of each post office was 7,300 residents (Teishinshō, 1921, p. 94).[10] Throughout the pre-war years most urban and large post offices accepted mail from 6.00 in the morning through to 10.00 at night, with slightly shorter hours in the winter months. During the high-growth years post offices still tended to be open at least 10 hours a day (Yūseishō Yūmukyoku, 1991, pp. 117, 194). The spread of facilities and access to them for the full working day made for universal accessibility. It was at these local post offices that Japanese consumers bought their stamps, posted their parcels, sent their telegrams, deposited their savings, cashed their money orders and purchased other postal services. The ubiquity of the post office made it, for most Japanese, the face of the state, but it was much more than that. It was a physical presence whose very embeddedness in the local community helped to confirm the role of postal services in relation to consumption.

Not all post offices were able to discharge the full range of tasks; some functions were restricted to the large regional post offices. Initially, for example, only a limited number of offices offered access to telegraph services, but by the inter-war period such access was near 100 per cent. For the customer any distinction between post office functions diminished over time, although it never disappeared, even in the high-growth years. Moreover, who actually handled the logistics of carrying and delivering the mail was largely a matter for the provider; what mattered to the consumer was that mail was collected and delivered, and other necessary services made available. The impressive record of the authorities in achieving this across the nation should not, however, blind us to the extent of the challenge that they faced.

---

[9] This compares with a UK figure of about 24,500 post offices for a population of around 46 million in the late 1930s (Crutchley, 1938, p. 2).

[10] These figures are deceptive in that they take no account of the many Japanese citizens outside a formal post office catchment area.

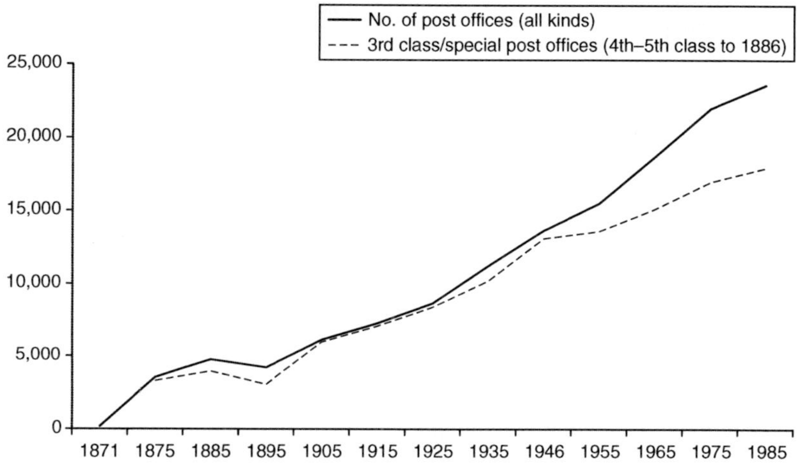

Figure 10.3 Number of third-class/special post offices, 1871–1985
Source: Yūseishō Yūmukyoku, 1991, pp. 215–17.

Creating a nationwide network of post offices was difficult and costly for a cash-constrained Meiji government. The solution was in effect a sub-contracting system, building a Western-style institution on pre-existing Japanese foundations. The main urban and provincial post offices were staffed by paid government officials, but the remainder were operated by local residents who effectively volunteered their time and premises for work in return for a very small stipend and the cachet of a nominal government appointment. These post offices were from 1886 referred to as third-class post offices (*santō yūbinkyoku*), and were rebranded as special post offices (*tokutei yūbinkyoku*) in 1940. Figure 10.3 shows the consistent importance of these post offices. From over 89 per cent of all post offices in 1875, they grew to account for nearly 97 per cent of the total number of offices throughout the pre-war years. Their declining share in the post-Second World War period was due to the development of the so-called simple post offices (*kan'i yūbinkyoku*), whereby the Ministry of Posts and Telecommunications commissioned local bodies such as cooperatives and consumer groups to open a post office counter service.[11] These simple post offices increased from around 1,000 in the early 1950s to nearly 4,000 by 1975; their consumer orientation was clear. They followed closely in

[11] The pre-war Communications Ministry (*Teishinshō*) was after the Second World War replaced by the Ministry of Posts and Telecommunications (*Yūseishō*).

the subcontracting tradition of the special offices, and together the two groups still accounted for nearly 95 per cent of all post offices at the end of the high-growth era.

One non-Japanese writer on world postal history in the 1920s regarded the Japanese system as highly anomalous, and was sceptical of postmasters who 'deemed it honourable to perform such duties as tend to benefit and promote the welfare of the public' (Harlow, 1928, p. 55), but by this time the subcontracting system was firmly fixed in Japanese life. In the early years it was not always easy to commission individuals to run the subcontracted post offices. Candidates were expected to have received some education and be literate, and to possess a certain amount of capital, but local respect often seemed scarce reward for what could be a considerable amount of work. Many found that formally appointed local government officials looked down upon them, and sought to emphasise their official commissioned status, often by publicly displaying their appointment letter from the government's Director of Communications (*Ekiteinokami*). The payment of only a small fixed allowance, insufficient to cover building and other costs, and no pension, did not help. A number of postmasters got discouraged, and resigned their office (Maejima, 1986, p. 107; Maejima, 1956, p. 72).[12] From the late Meiji period some began to be paid a salary in recognition of the very large volume of business they handled, but reports suggest that the income of most third-class postmasters was inadequate for the survival of a couple, let alone a family. High turnover and supplementary income-earning activities were the norm. Not until the 1930s were the most serious attempts made to improve the position of this crucial group of employees (Yūseishō Yūmukyoku, 1991, pp. 38–39).

These constraints inevitably limited the pool of potential applicants to those with existing social and economic capital. Being a local postmaster allowed an individual to confirm or establish for himself a leading position in the local community; postmasters constituted a major group of so-called local notables (*meibōka*). Of course, the tasks were undertaken with varying degrees of competence, but there were clearly many who regarded what they were doing as important, and were prepared to throw themselves into it. It was these postmasters who were the key to the importance of the post office in the local community. They played a significant role in encouraging postal consumption, and worked

---

[12] More information on the local postmasters and other aspects of the service will be available in Maclachlan, forthcoming, which is not yet available at the time of writing.

to embed postal services in the life of most Japanese.[13] The authorities saw them not only as the interface between people and officials in the provinces, and employees who over time acquired a strong knowledge of the business, but as local figures who could use their key position to promote state objectives, whether it was encouraging postal savings or recommending more use of insurance (Teishinshō, 1921, p. 38). Many of the improvements in local services that occurred over time were in fact dependent on postmasters and other local worthies making use of privately owned facilities, effectively co-opting the local community into the expansion of postal consumption (Tahara, 2003, p. 59). Partner's biography of the mayor of Hashimoto village, Aizawa Kikutarō, suggests how this worked in practice well into the twentieth century. The mayor and the local postmaster, who was also his brother, together organised funding for a telegraph connection at the post office in 1911. The family continued to act as officials in the post office, which was attached to the main family residence and became the location of the village's first public telephone in 1921. It was reported that 'an arch was constructed in front of the post office and festooned with the flags of the world, symbolizing Hashimoto's connection to the rest of the world through communications technology' (Partner, 2009, pp. 144, 162). Some local postmasters instituted innovations that were then enshrined in national practice. Post office savings deposits, for example, conventionally had to be made in cash at the post office window, but from 1899 an official could be sent out to collect such deposits where the volume was very great or they were being made by a government office. Soon after, it became possible for depositors who lived a long way away from a post office to have their deposits collected by the postman (Teishinshō, 1921, p. 287).

For customers and consumers, therefore, going to the post office meant dealing with the existing village hierarchy. Postmasters who were former village headmen or from well-known local families could draw on a tradition of expecting respect and trust. The cachet of government appointment added to this authority, which was important in the early years of the service, when postmasters had to persuade their customers that what was offered was worth having. Despite this, business was initially very slow. When the Kōbe Post Office was opened in the summer of 1871, the nine staff initially collected fewer than 150 items per day, and delivered under a hundred. Residents of the busy

[13] Tahara (2004) focuses on the attempts made by one local postmaster to deliver a better service in line with the demands of his customers. There are a number of such studies of local post offices.

open port averaged only one letter per 500 persons in this first year, and it took several years for the volume of mail to rise to the level where it not only fully employed the existing staff, but necessitated the construction of a new postal building to cope with the pressure of business (Yokota, 1974, pp. 13–19). Customers had to be persuaded to think of post offices as places of government business, rather than as business premises like those of the old courier system. The service was derogatively referred to as the 'post company' (*yūbin kaisha*), and it was in an attempt to counteract this image that post offices were initially called just that (*yūbin yakusho*), using as the suffix the word applied to government offices (Maejima, 1986, pp. 104–6).

Consumers' initial perceptions of how to interact with the new service were characterised by an understandable mistrust attaching to the new and unfamiliar. Early customers would try to negotiate over the price, arguing that what they wanted to send was particularly light, or was not going very far. They might request a receipt. In some cases they would demand tea or tobacco, and when this was not forthcoming they would complain vociferously about the 'company's' incompetence (Maejima, 1986, p. 104; Maejima, 1956, p. 72). While, as Sugiyama has noted, the postal service was sold to the public as part of a new 'civilised' image, and lack of take-up was frequently blamed on the service being in its infancy (Sugiyama, 1992, pp. 232–33, 236), local post offices were regarded as having a key role to play in increasing consumption. As late as 1905 local postmasters in the Tōtōmi region southwest of Tokyo were meeting to discuss the establishment of a discussion group, whose specific function would be to spread a better knowledge of the postal communications business to the public (Tōtōmi no Kuni, 1905, pp. 13–15).

Many post office premises did little to enhance the image of the service. The first headquarters was reportedly a miserable set of rooms, cramped, vulnerable to fire and plagued by market smells (Maejima, 1986, pp. 105–6). The subcontracted post offices by definition did not at first have their own premises. Customers conducted their business at the window of a private residence, or in a corner of existing commercial premises, invariably of old-style *minka* construction. Many smaller offices long continued to be little more than windows facing on to the street. Some of the earliest Western-style post offices built of brick had a relatively short life, being brought down by major earthquakes (Yūseishō Yūmukyoku, 1991, pp. 27–29); they were few in number, in strong contrast to the vast majority of very small-scale operations in which the presence of the state was hardly visible. In the larger early purpose-built post offices the service lobby and the office area were

Figure 10.4 Tokyo post office window lobby, 1885

Source: *Yūbin Toriatsukai no Zu*, in possession of the Communications Museum in Tokyo (*Teishin Sōgō Hakubutsukan*).

separated by walls, and cashiers dealt with customers through small windows (see Figure 10.4). This design emphasised the official nature of the service, setting it apart from conventional 'shopping' architecture and modes of customer service. The new Tokyo office of the early 1890s instituted glass barriers with a small window opening up at the bottom to serve customers. Glass or lattice-work separated customers and officials, and screens continued to be used to deter theft, but the aspect became more open. It was not until the 1970s that post offices in Japan began to make a major shift towards a more open-plan design of the kind that might be associated with consumer choice (Yūseishō Yūmukyoku, 1991, p. 33).

As services expanded and diversified, the willingness of consumers to use them became closely associated with the whole package that was offered. A consumer going to post mail could be more easily persuaded to save or take out life insurance, while a failure of the authorities to tailor one service to a consumer could prevent him or her from using another. For example, unfamiliarity, low incomes and the level and methods of interest payment deterred early consumers of savings provision. When post office savings opened in Niigata in the late 1870s there were complaints that the interest rate was well below the average 10 per cent paid by the private sector, no interest was payable if total deposits were under 1 yen (a considerable amount for a low-income individual), and the procedures were said to be 'very troublesome', including requiring the consent of the household head for all savings transactions by family members (Ishiguro, 1986, pp. 133, 166–70). As efforts were made to adapt the original English model to the far lower incomes of potential Japanese consumers, business began to grow, and by 1940 there were close to 100 million accounts totaling almost 8,000 million yen (Maejima, 1986, p. 122; figures from Maejima, 1956, p. 368). Evidence on the composition of savers in the Meiji period suggests that some groups in the population were more likely to be represented than others (Den, 1910, p. 417), but the number of accounts held by individuals and organisations by the 1930s suggests that a very high proportion of the total Japanese population participated in the total package of services offered by the Post Office. Savers, however small, were potential mail customers, and *vice versa*. Savers were also consumers, who purchased by mail-order and paid by postal order. As the number of customers and usage grew, of course, so did consumers' expectations and requirements. It was the ability of the providers to cater to those changing needs that drove the overall trajectory of postal consumption. In the process the government-sponsored postal system became an agent for the validation of consumption more broadly.

Conclusion

Take-up of postal services was conditioned by a number of factors. Access was extended rapidly and efficiently, and the extensive use of postcards and small money orders is evidence that the price to the consumer was as far as possible set at a level appropriate for a low-income economy. Initial problems in persuading potential consumers of the advantages of that consumption were tackled by emphasising the official status of the services and by using local postmasters, mostly in third class/special offices, to help overcome the knowledge gap. Changing income levels, the growth of the economy, the business cycle, faster transport networks and urbanisation were all crucial parts of the environment within which postal usage increased. Rising levels of literacy drove consumption of written communication of all kinds. Moreover the post faced only to a limited extent an environment of competing institutions. The carriage of mail was a government monopoly, and well into the twentieth century there were few financial institutions to compete with the service offered by the postal money order or the postal savings bank. Where there were competitors, the postal services managed to find and build on a niche that the private sector was unable or willing to take-up. The monopoly position of the postal service went unchallenged in Japan until the late twentieth century. Whereas in the United States many saw government control of the telegraph and telephone, and even government-run postal savings and parcel post, as exceeding the traditional limits of government activity (Kielbowicz, 2007, pp. 88–93), no such worries were raised in Japan.

As Garon (2006, p. 91) has noted, the term 'consumption' (*shōhi*) was not widely used in Japan until the 1920s, and Trentmann argues persuasively that while consumption had always happened, the idea of a 'consumer' was a product of the Western industrialised economies of the nineteenth–twentieth centuries (Trentmann, 2006, p. 2). Particularly in advance of the inter-war growth of mass consumption in some of Japan's urban areas, those who made use of the government-run postal service saw themselves as 'users' rather than 'consumers'. Because they were engaging in market transactions, though, they also saw themselves as 'customers', a self-perception indicated by early users' demands for tea and tobacco. The potential tensions between the government's objectives for the service and those of its consumers were held at bay through to the high-growth period by the ability of the service to respond proactively to a constantly changing environment, the control exercised by government at central and local level, and the successful embedding of the postal system in local lives and communities. Unlike in the United States, being a consumer was not regarded as a central part of national identity.[14]

By the 1970s the evolution into consumers had begun to constitute a new and major challenge for the postal authorities, but long before this the services that they offered had made a significant contribution to embedding consumption in the lives of most Japanese people. The impact of increased usage of postal services on Japan's economy and society was enormous, going way beyond the improved and ongoing personal contact with family members, friends and other contacts experienced by individuals and households. People came to know more about events outside their own localities, and were able to engage in the transfer of money and new forms of market transaction, for example through mail-order firms. More people were provided with more written information. Postal services also provided businesses with improved information on production, prices, consumers and risks, and

---

[14] The central thesis of McGovern, 2006 is that mass consumption came to be articulated as a specifically American social practice, and an important element in nationality and kinship. See also Cohen, 2006.

enhanced the provision for circulation of commodities and capital. Local post offices were increasingly focal points for local information and activities: they enabled one locality to link into another through the provision of a uniform set of services, in the process bringing them together as part of a more integrated whole. They promoted the concept of choice for consumers. As a vehicle of market integration, postal services helped to spread the consumption of both traditional and new products, enhancing and developing existing distribution and retail systems. As part of a new infrastructure associated with the growth of consumption, and places that, because they were government run, indicated official approval of such activities, post offices changed the behaviour of Japan's citizens in multiple ways that affected their overall consumption patterns.

References

Akita Ekitei Shutchōkyoku (March 1885) *Akita Ekitei Shutchōkyoku Daiichiji Nenpō* (Akita Communications Office First Yearbook).

Broadberry, S. (2006) *Market Services and the Productivity Race, 1850–2000: Britain in International Perspective*, Cambridge: Cambridge University Press.

Cohen, L. (2006) 'The Consumers' Republic: An American Model for the World?' in Garon, S. & Maclachlan, P. L. (eds) *The Ambivalent Consumer: Questioning Consumption in East Asia and the West*, Ithaca, NY & London: Cornell University Press, pp. 45–62.

Chamberlain, B. H. (1905) *Things Japanese* (5th edn), London: John Murray.

Crutchley, E. T. (1938) *GPO*, Oxford: Oxford University Press.

Den, K. (1910) 'Japanese Communications: the Post, Telegraph and Telephone', in vol.1 of Ōkuma, S. (ed.) *Fifty Years of New Japan*, 2 vols, London: Smith, Elder, & Co, pp. 408–23.

Fujii, N. (1998) *Terekomu no Keizai Shi* (Economic History of Telecommunications), Tokyo: Keisō Shobō.

Fuller, W. E. (1972) *The American Mail: Enlarger of the Common Life*, Chicago & London: University of Chicago Press.

Garon, S. (1998) *Moulding Japanese Minds*, Princeton NJ: Princeton University Press.

Garon, S. (2006) 'Japan's Post-War "Consumer Revolution", or Striking a "Balance" between Consumption and Saving', in Brewer, J. & Trentmann, F. (eds) *Consuming Cultures, Global Perspectives: Historical Trajectories, Transnational Exchanges*, Oxford, New York: Berg.

Harlow, A. F. (1928) *Old Post Bags: The Story of the Sending of a Letter in Ancient and Modern Times*, New York & London: D. Appleton & Company.

Horioka, C. Y. (1993) 'Consuming and Saving', in Gordon, A. (ed.) *Postwar Japan as History*, Berkeley, California: University of California Press, pp. 259–92.

Horioka, C. Y. (2006) 'Are the Japanese Unique? An Analysis of Consumption and Saving Behavior in Japan', in Garon, S. & Maclachlan, P. L. (eds) *The*

Ambivalent Consumer: Questioning Consumption in East Asia and the West, Ithaca, NY & London: Cornell University Press, pp. 113–36.
Ishiguro, M. (1986) *Niigata Yūbinkyoku Shi* (History of Niigata Post Office), Niigata: Niigata Yūbinkyoku Shi Hensankai.
Ishii, K. (1994) *Jōhō Tsūshin no Shakaishi* (Social History of Information and Communication), Tokyo: Yūhikaku.
John, R. R. (2003) 'Postal Systems', in Mokyr, J. (ed.) *Oxford Encyclopaedia of Economic History Vol. 4*, Oxford: Oxford University Press, pp. 315–18.
Kielbowicz, R. (2007) 'Testing the Boundaries of Postal Enterprise in the U.S. Free-Market Economy, 1880–1920', Willis, J. (ed.) (2007) *More than Words: Readings in Transport, Communications and the History of Postal Communication*, Quebec: Canadian Museum of Civilization, pp. 85–100.
Maclachlan, P. L. (forthcoming) *The Postal Services in Modern Japanese Politics and Society, 1871–2009*, Cambridge, MA: Harvard University Centre for East Asian Studies.
Maejima, H. (1986) 'Teikoku Yūbin Shōgyō Jimu Yodan' (Observations on the Commercial Business of the Imperial Post), in Hashimoto, T. (ed.) *Yukimichi no Shirushi*, Tokyo: Nihon Yūshū Shuppan, pp. 71–188.
Maejima, H. (1951) *Yūbin Sōgyō Dan* (On the Founding of the Mail), Tokyo: Teishin Kyōkai Yūbin Bunkabu.
Maejima, H. (1956) *Yūbin Sōgyō Dan* (On the Founding of the Mail), Tokyo: Maejima Hisoka Denki Kankōkai.
McGovern, C. F. (2006) *Sold America: Consumption and Citizenship, 1890–1945*, Chapel Hill, NC: University of North Carolina Press.
Ministry of Internal Affairs and Communications of Japan (Statistics Bureau) 2010 website, Historical Statistics section, http://www.stat.go.jp/data/chouki/zuhyou/02–01.xls
Mitsuzono, I. (2009) 'Senzenki Nihon ni okeru Daitoshi Gofukukei Hyakkaten no Tsūshin Hanbai' (Mail Order Selling of the Large City Department Stores in Pre-War Japan), *Keiei Shigaku* 44, 1, June, pp. 31–57.
Miwa, R. & Hara, A. (eds.) (2007) *Kingendai Nihon Keizaishi Yōran* (Survey of the Economic History of Early Modern and Modern Japan) Tokyo: Tokyo University Press.
Nagoya Yūbinkyoku (1905) *Nagoya Yūbinkyoku Daiyokkai Nenpō* (Nagoya Post Office Fourth Yearbook), Nagoya: Nagoya Yūbinkyoku.
Ohkawa, K. *et.al.* (eds.) (1974), *Kokumin Shotoku (National Income)*, vol.1 of *Long Term Economic Statistics of Japan*, Tokyo: Tōyō Keizai Shinpōsha.
Ōsaka Mainichi (1928) *Development of Postal Enterprise in Japan* (bilingual), Ōsaka: Ōsaka Mainichi.
Ōsaka Yūseikyoku (1971) *Shiryō Ōsaka Yūsei no Hyakunen* (Historical Materials relating to a Century of the Osaka Postal System), Ōsaka: Yūsei Kōsaikai Ōsaka Chihō Honbu.
Partner, S. (2009) *The Mayor of Aihara: A Japanese Villager and His Community*, Berkeley CA: University of California Press.
Sato, B. H. (2003) *The New Japanese Woman: Modernity, Media and Women in Interwar Japan*, Durham, NC: Duke University Press.
Shinohara, M. (1967) *Personal Consumption Expenditures*, vol. 6 of *Estimates of Long Term Economic Statistics of Japan since 1868 (LTES)*, Tokyo: Tōyō Keizai Shinpōsha.

Sugiyama, S. (1992) 'Jōhō Nettowaaku no Keisei to Chihō Keizai' (The Formation of Information Networks and Regional Economies), *Nenpō Kindai Nihon Kenkyū* 14, *Meiji Ishin no Kakushin to Renzoku*, Tokyo: Yamakawa Shuppansha, pp. 228–49.

Tahara, K. (2003) 'Meiji Kōki ni okeru Yūbin Jigyō no Seichō to Tetsudō Teisō' (Growth of the Postal Business in the Late Meiji Period and its Carriage by Railway), *Nihonshi Kenkyū* 490, June, pp. 193–215.

Tahara, K. (2004) 'Meiji Zenki Shōgyō Hattatsuchi ni okeru Yūbin Jigyō no Jittai' (The Actual Situation of the Postal Business in Centres of Commerce in the Early Meiji Period), *Keizaigaku Zasshi (Ōsaka Shiritsu Daigaku Keizai Gakkai)* 1, 105, June, pp. 34–65.

Teishin Daijin Kanbō (1897) *Teishinshō Daijū Nenpō* (Ministry of Communications Tenth Yearbook), Tokyo: TeishinDaijinKanbō, March.

Teishin Daijin Kanbō (1898) *Teishin Shiyō* (Overview of Communications), Tokyo: Teishin Daijin Kanbō.

Teishinshō (ed.) (1940) *Teishin Jigyō Shi* (History of the Communications Business, 5 vols), Teishin Kyōkai.

Teishinshō (1921) *Tsūshin Jigyō Gojūnen Shi* (Fifty Years of Communications), Tokyo: Teishin Kyōkai.

Teishinshō Rokujūnen Shi Kankōkai (1931) *Teishin Rokujūnen Shi* (Sixty Years of Communications), Tokyo: Teishin Rokujūnen Shi Kankōkai.

Teishinshō Tsūshinkyoku (1904) *Tsūshin Tōkei Yōran* (Statistical Overview of Communications), Tokyo: Teishinshō.

Teishinshō Tsūshinkyoku (1910) *Teishin Tōkei Yōran* (Statistical Overview of Communications), Tokyo: Teishinshō.

Tōtōmi no Kuni (1905) *Tōtōmi no Kuni Santōkyokuchō Kyōgikai* (Meeting of Third Class Postmasters of Tōtōmi Province) (report of meeting).

Trentmann, F. (2006) 'Knowing Consumers – Histories, Identities, Practices: an Introduction', in Trentmann, F. (ed.) *The Making of the Consumer*, Oxford & New York: Berg, pp. 1–27.

Yokota, T. (1974) *Hyakunen Shi: Kōbe Yūbin no Dōjun* (Hundred Years of the Post in Kōbe), Kōbe: Kōbe Yūbin Shiki no Kai.

Yūseishō (1971a) *Yūsei Hyakunen Shi* (A Hundred Years of the Postal System), Tokyo: Yūseishō.

Yūseishō (1971b) *Yūsei Hyakunen Shi Shiryō* (Historical Materials relating to a Hundred Years of the Postal System 28 vols), Tokyo: Yūseishō.

Yūseishō Yūmukyoku (1991) *Yūbin Jigyō 120-nen no Rekishi* (120 Year History of the Postal Business), Tokyo: Kyōsei.

11

Mail-Order Retailing in Pre-War Japan: A Pathway of Consumption Before the Emergence of the Mass Market

Isamu Mitsuzono

Introduction

As is generally known, by the end of the nineteenth century the remarkable development of mail-order retailing in the United States had given birth to two retailing giants, Sears, Roebuck & Co. and Montgomery Ward. Given the lack of highly developed distribution systems in the United States at the time, they supplied a large quantity of standardised goods at low prices to rural people, for the most part meeting the demand for basic everyday goods in the expanding frontier market. In Chandler's historical study of big business, these two companies represented typical mass distribution corporations in the United States (Chandler, 1977). That is, they provided one of the main pathways of consumption over the course of the expansion of the mass market.

Little is known, however, about Japan's mail-order history. Needless to say, mail-order retailing in pre-war Japan did not give birth to giant traders, as happened in the United States. Since, by the Tokugawa period, Japanese distribution systems were already highly developed, and consumer tastes complicated and diversified, we might assume that there was little room for growth in mail-order retailing (Nakagawa, 1981, pp. 214–15). Moreover, although the inflow of new Western consumer goods, following the opening of ports to foreign trade in 1854, provided commercial opportunities, the growth in the number of rural retail stores that dealt in such goods was sufficient to limit the size of the mail-order market in the years up to the introduction of the parcel-post service in 1892 (Nakanishi, 2000).

Nonetheless, the development of mail-order retailing in pre-war Japan is to some extent comparable to that in European countries, as will be shown below. Although general retailers who sold goods exclusively by mail order could not develop their business, store-based retailers in big cities, as well as producers (or wholesalers) in local industrial districts, began to supply their goods by mail order to the upper classes. The former sold fashionable items, such as Japanese- or Western-style clothes, ornaments, and watches, while the latter sold regional products, such as green tea, kimono, and glass-ware. This chapter uses the examples of department stores, representing the former, and the tea producers of the Uji district, representing the latter, to show how mail-order traders in pre-war Japan provided a new pathway of consumption before the emergence of the mass market. At the same time, within the context of the history of consumption in Japan, the cases demonstrate that the distinction between 'traditional' and 'modern' goods was far from static, and reveal how 'traditional' goods could take on 'modern' values. This dynamic process created new forms of consumption and promoted the expansion of the mass market, while also ultimately decreasing the presence of mail-order retailing in the distribution and information system.

Mail-order retailing in Japan in comparative context

The beginning of the parcel-post service in 1892 and the cash-on-delivery (COD) postal service in 1896 provided the opportunity for mail-order retailing to develop in Japan. Above all, the COD service played a vital role in helping to reduce the business costs incurred as a result of time lags between settlement and the delivery of goods. In addition, the fact that this service was provided as part of the governmental postal system and sustained by local postmasters – who were respected within the community – was significant in three ways. First, a nationwide postal network was made available to users, including those in rural areas. Second, both settlement and delivery occurred effortlessly. Third, suppliers who dispatched goods on a COD basis were considered reliable dealers (Mitsuzono, 2009b).[1]

Figure 11.1 shows the number of COD postal parcels delivered in pre-war Japan, by financial year (Teishinshō, 1899–1936, 1942). Even allowing for some limitations of these data, this graph can be regarded as

[1] See also Hunter's chapter (Chapter 10) in this volume for the role of the postal system.

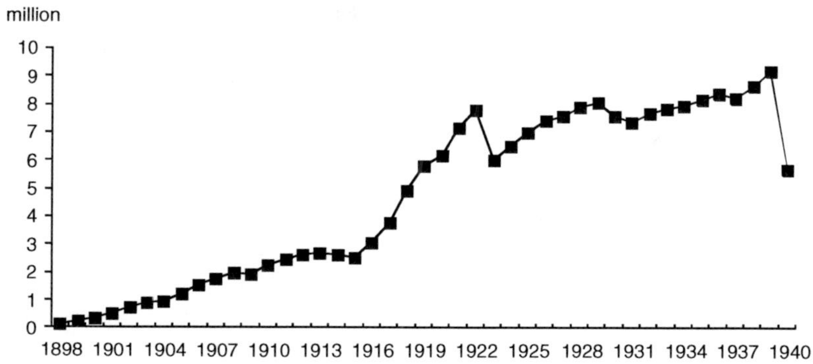

Figure 11.1 Number of C.O.D. parcels, 1898–1940
Source: Teishinshō, 1899–1936, 1942.

giving an index of the development of mail-order retailing. Although it would be preferable to have data on total sales or full monetary values related to mail-order retailing, no such information exists for pre-war Japan. It is possible that COD delivery was also used to sell wholesale goods, as well as mail-order retailing; however, this is unlikely to have been significant, because COD terms were not suitable for large continuous transactions at the wholesale level. Payment was made not on credit, but with cash, and COD delivery imposed more severe restrictions *vis-à-vis* the maximum permissible volume than did rail.

As Figure 11.1 indicates, the number of COD parcels increased rapidly up to 1922, but by 1923 had reached a plateau.[2] The later, sluggish phase was the result not only of the effects of the Great Kantō Earthquake of 1923 and the Shōwa panic of 1930, but also of the progress of urbanisation and the increased presence of store-based retailers. For example, the percentage of the population who lived in a town or village of 10,000 people or fewer fell from 81.6 in 1898 to 59.4 in 1925 (Nakamura, 1971, pp. 17–18). Meanwhile, according to Japan's national census, the number of workers engaged in the wholesale and retail trade increased from 2,180,000 (37.7 per 1000 people) in 1920 to 5,554,000 (77.8 per 1000 people) in 1939 and this trend was not restricted exclusively to big cities.[3]

[2] The drop in 1940 (financial year) was caused by the discontinuation of the COD postal service in November.

[3] Unfortunately, data pertaining to numbers of retail stores are unavailable except for the year 1939.

Table 11.1 Number of COD parcels: various countries

	1892	1922	
	thousands	thousands	per 1000 population
Germany	8,213	18,792	297
Japan		5,595	100
France	1,136	4,333	112
Switzerland	915	3,867	997
Italy	347	2,132	56
Hungary	1,801	2,073	259
Austria	3,725	698	107
Denmark	205	610	187
Holland	98	596	87

Sources: Miyamoto, 1896, pp. 6–7; Bureau Internationale de L'Union Postale Universelle, 1924; Mitchell, 1998.

Table 11.1 shows the number of COD postal parcels sent in two years, 1892 and 1922, for a selection of countries. Unfortunately, data are not available for the United States and Britain, but in terms of the number of parcels, we see that by 1922 Japan was second only to Germany. Of course, the large gap between Germany and Japan cannot be ignored. However, the scope for mail-order retailing in Germany appears to have been strongly connected to the limited development of the distribution system, which placed mail-order retailers there in an environment more like that of the United States than that of Japan (Amemiya, 2000, pp. 142–45, pp. 168–69). Meanwhile, the number in Japan is at least comparable to the figures for other European countries.[4] Although we should not overestimate the degree of development in Japan, particularly in the light of the 'per 1000 population' column in Table 11.1, the fact remains that we do not have to consider it as extremely undeveloped. This suggests the potential for growth and change, as well as the limitations, of mail-order retailing in pre-war Japan.

It is also possible to make a rough estimate of mail-order sales in the pre-war period as a share of total retail sales by extrapolating on the

[4] If we accept the number of 7.79 million for 1922 shown in Figure 11.1 (but not in Table 11.1), Japan's position would be somewhat higher.

Table 11.2 Ratio of mail-order sales to total retail sales (by value; per cent)

	1962	1971
West Germany	3.5	4.7
Great Britain	2.5	3.8
France	0.7	1.1
Holland	0.6	0.9
Belgium	0.5	0.8
Denmark	0.1	0.2
Italy	0.1	0.2

Note: Figures refer to general mail order houses only.
Source: Ryūtsū Sangyō Kenkyūjo (1977), p. 36.

basis of post-war figures. In Japan in 1974, mail-order sales represented 0.6 per cent of total retail sales (Ryūtsū Sangyō Kenkyūjo, 1977, p. 36). In the same year, the number of COD postal parcels was 1,360,000 (Yūseishō, 1980, pp. 204, 209), less than one-fifth the number in the 1930s.[5] This almost certainly implies a contraction in the mail-order market compared with the pre-war period, but we do not have the evidence to make a final judgement on this. If we assume, therefore, as a conservative estimate, that the value of mail-order sales remained the same, given that total retail sales, which had increased as a result of high economic growth, were four times larger in 1974 than in 1939 in real terms, it would follow that the estimated proportion of mail-order sales as a percentage of total retail sales in the 1930s would be more than 2.4 per cent (= 0.6% × 4).[6]

It should be noted that this estimated percentage is higher than that of Britain in the 1930s, which was 1 per cent (Jefferys, 1950, pp. 151–52), and lower than that of the United States in 1928, which was 4 per cent (Tokunaga, 1992, p. 37). For reference, Table 11.2 presents the proportion of mail-order sales to total retail sales in 1962 and 1971, across a selection of countries. In relation to the figures for 1971, Japan's percentage around the same period – 0.6 per cent in 1974 – was much lower than those of West Germany and Great Britain, but only slightly

[5] This number had reached a post-war peak of 2,130,000 in 1958.

[6] Based on data in Naikaku Tōkeikyoku, 1939.; Tsūsan Tōkei Kyōkai, 1983; Shinohara, 1967, pp. 21, 30; Statistics Bureau Home Page (*http://www.stat.go.jp/data/chouki/zuhyou/22–13.xls*).

below those of France, Holland and Belgium. Assuming that the estimated percentage for pre-war Japan is accurate, this would be consistent with the fact that Japan had lost its high position evident in Table 11.1. For the United States, incidentally, mail-order sales represented 2.9 per cent of total retail sales in 1978 (Kiwata and Miura, 1985, p. 233), and it is clear that both its mail-order share and its international position had dropped below the levels of 1928.

Although further quantitative research needs to be conducted, it seems reasonable to conclude, on the basis of the data above, that the development of mail-order retailing in pre-war Japan bears comparison with that of European countries, with the exception of Germany, even if it differs distinctly from the model case of the United States.

Mail-order retailers

In the period up to the early twentieth century, Sears, Roebuck & Co. and Montgomery Ward, the two retailing giants that emerged out of the rapid growth of mail-order retailing in the United States, expanded their line of goods to include watches, bicycles, sewing machines, agricultural implements, clothes, shoes, jewellery, furniture, crockery, musical instruments and many other goods, as they supplied the rural market for standardised, low-priced, daily goods. The absence of complicated and diversified tastes in rural areas allowed them to promote standardised mass-selling and enjoy scale economies. Their respective catalogues became increasingly thick and the numbers distributed steadily grew. In the case of Sears, the number of pages in the general catalogue – published twice yearly – grew from 527 in 1895 to 1,615 in 1914. The number distributed increased from 605,000 for the spring edition and 987,000 for the autumn edition in 1902, to 4,839,000 and 5,088,000 respectively in 1920 (Tsunematsu, 2005, p. 73; Toba, 1969, pp. 88, 144). In 1908, Sears received up to 100,000 letters per day (Toba, 1969, p. 104).

While a very large number of customers were gained in this way, the development of mail-order retailing in the United States nonetheless reached a ceiling in the 1920s, due to the effects of urbanisation and motorisation. The companies started store-based retailing in the mid-1920s, and by the early 1930s were shifting their resources from mail-order business to their multiple stores.

Meanwhile, mail-order retailing in Britain had begun to grow in the latter half of the nineteenth century. Department stores, which targeted upper middle-class people, and mail-order firms, which targeted working-class people, took a lead role in the development of mail-order retailing. Unlike the two giants in the United States, both department stores and mail-order firms in Britain mainly sold to customers in urban, rather than rural, areas. Although the British mail-order market was initially very small – largely because many consumers had easy access to retail shops, owing to the high level of urbanisation in Britain – mail-order retailers offered competitive goods or services in the urban retail market.

In Britain, the competitive advantage of the mail-order departments of department stores lay in the selling of sophisticated, high-quality goods. In fact, sales from mail-order departments accounted for approximately 25 per cent of all sales by London department stores between 1880 and 1914 (Pasdermadjian, 1954, p. 32), and there is considerable evidence of the prevalence of mail-order retailing in Britain. The mail order department of Marshall and Snelgrove, for example, received 1,000 letters per day in 1888 (Benson and Shaw, 1999, p. 136). In 1913 Lewis's produced 50,000 catalogues per issue (Benson and Shaw, 1999, p. 136), and Whiteleys dispatched 2,500,000 circulars each year (Coopey, O'Connell and Porter, 2005, p. 16). Moreover, the mail-order catalogue published by Harrods in 1912 contained a formidable 1,525 pages (Harrods, 1912).

On the other hand, there were between five and seven specialist mail-order firms in Britain, selling goods such as watches, jewellery, clothes and shoes, on instalment-payment plans.[7] They were dependent on neighbourhood-based agents or club organisers, who had been selected from members of working-class communities with a view both to promoting sales and collecting accounts due. For example, Kays, which started mail-order retailing in this way in 1886, dispatched 1,200 parcels per day in 1918. In 1919, it had 500,000 customers and received 1,000 letters per day. During the 1920s and 1930s, the mail-order firms developed further lines of business based on the instalment-payment system, including new lines such as furniture and home electrical goods, at a time when the mail-order departments of department stores remained on a sales plateau.

By contrast, in Japan general retailers who supplied goods exclusively by mail order proved unable to establish themselves. This was partly the result of the fact that they could not promote standardised mass selling because people in Japan, unlike those in the United States, had complicated and diversified tastes derived from their traditional culture.

[7] This paragraph is based on Coopey, O'Connell and Porter (2005).

In addition, unlike in Britain, mail-order firms selling goods on instalment-payment plans did not appear in pre-war Japan. However, this type of mail-order firm is in general unusual, outside Britain, because of the difficulties involved in collecting payments associated with long-distance trade such as mail-order retailing. Consequently, in pre-war Japan, it was store-based retailers in the large cities, as well as producers (or wholesalers) in local industrial districts, that emerged as the pioneers of mail-order retailing, supplying goods to upper-class customers on the basis of 'traditional' consumption patterns. We will now take a closer look at department stores on the one hand, and the Uji tea industry on the other, as examples of the two forms of mail-order retailing that did succeed in pre-war Japan.

The mail-order business of department stores[8]

The beginning of the department store in Japan is generally dated to the 'Declaration of the Department Store', released by Mitsukoshi in 1904. In fact, even prior to this, some very large kimono retailers in the big cities, including Mitsukoshi (then called Mitsui Gofukuten), had launched management reforms, and introduced not only the display of goods for sale, but also mail order, as new ways of marketing. Periodicals that doubled as both PR magazines and mail-order catalogues began to appear at around the same time. For example, Mitsukoshi started its mail-order business around 1894, and in 1898 set up a new section dealing with mail order as part of the Large Customer Department, reorganising it in 1900 as the Rural Customer Department. Its periodical, entitled *Jikō,* was launched in 1903.

Unfortunately, little is known from that time about the volume of trade carried out by department stores through mail order; such quantitative data as we can obtain are only fragmentary. At Mitsukoshi, sales fulfilled by the Rural Customer Department accounted for about 20–25 per cent of the store's total sales of 100 million yen around 1910 (Kurozumi, 1993, p. 193). Although it must be noted that the Rural Customer Department was in charge of door-to-door sales in rural areas as well as the handling of mail orders, it is likely that mail-order sales had surpassed those from door-to-door selling by the early 1920s (Mitsuzono, 2009a, p. 53). We know, for example, that more than 160,000 postal parcels were delivered in fulfilment of mail orders in 1910; 80 per cent were COD posts, and these accounted for 14.6 per cent of all COD postal

[8] This subsection is based on Mitsuzono, 2009a.

Figure 11.2 Cover of the Mitsukoshi mail-order catalogue *Mitsukoshi Times*, September 1912. The catalogue contains 52 pages in total and 148 photos of items.

parcels dispatched from Tokyo City (*Teishin Kyōkai Zasshi* 23, June 1910, pp. 48–50; Tokyo Teishin Kanri Kyoku, 1912, p. 6). At the same time, Mitsukoshi received 1,000 letters per day, and sent out 30,000–50,000 copies of its catalogue each month and 200,000–300,000 pamphlets per year in support of its mail-order business (Kurozumi, 1993, p. 193). In terms of employment, the mail-order department included nearly 100 clerks – a number that consistently made the department one of the top two or three largest employee contingents in Mitsukoshi's main store in Tokyo throughout the 1910s.[9] On the other hand, Shirokiya, the second-largest department store in Tokyo after Mitsukoshi, employed 35 clerks in charge of mail-order business; in 1911, it received 300 letters per day and issued 15,000–18,000 monthly catalogues (entitled *Ryūkō*) per month (*Teishin Kyōkai Zasshi* 128, February 1919, p. 24). Although no further information is available on the mail-order departments of other

[9] This figure is culled from the Mitsukoshi staff list, which is in the possession of Mitsui Bunko.

stores, Mitsukoshi was considered the largest mail-order trader among not just department stores but also all retailers at that time (Mitsuzono, 2009b, p. 68).

It is likely that these companies' customer bases comprised mainly upper-class individuals, as evidenced by reported cases such as those of a large landowner in Genna Village in Saitama Prefecture, a wealthy merchant from the town of Suzaka in Nagano Prefecture, and the president of Tōhoku Imperial University in Sendai City. From these town and city cases, it can be presumed that the department stores' mail-order customers also had easy access to retail stores in the city, and that the mail-order companies were therefore competing head-to-head with local shops. In fact, while the list of Mitsukoshi's sales in 1910 included a wide range of goods – such as kimono, Western-style clothes, shoes, Japanese footwear, bags, jewellery, cosmetics, furniture, eating utensils and toys – local retailers would also have sold these kinds of goods, albeit perhaps not of the same quality. Rather as their catalogues emphasised, what the department stores were able to supply by mail order were sophisticated, differentiated goods in the forefront of trends in the big city.

From the 1900s through to the 1910s, the catalogues of department stores not only served as trade catalogues but also contained articles on the latest city fashions, reports about new in-store facilities and events, and literary works such as novels (Tsuchiya, 1999). In particular, the stores repeatedly sought to educate readers so as to promote a fashion-based consumption culture. For example, *Jikō,* the catalogue of Mitsukoshi, described one item in the October 1905 issue as 'the latest fashion this winter – those who would not like to miss the wave must read about it' (see Figure 11.2). In such ways department stores consciously embraced the strategy of emphasising fashion in the mail-order business, and it is widely recognised that stores such as Mitsukoshi spent considerable resources on themselves creating fashion trends (Jinno, 1994). For instance, according to a clerk in the Rural Customer Department of Mitsukoshi, 'it is very important [for Mitsukoshi] to be at the centre of fashion, because customers will place orders for goods only with a store that is at the centre of fashion in Tokyo' (*Shōgyō Kai* 9, 6, May 1908, p. 30). In fact, department stores succeeded in stimulating the desire among people in rural areas to follow the latest big-city fashions. The following inquiry to Mitsukoshi from a rural customer is an apt example of this point:

> They say 'in Mitsukoshi, the goods sold to rural people are different from the ones sold in the store and are behind the fashion trends. I

> don't want to place an order, because the name of the department, "Rural Customer", has a derisive sound suggesting an obvious hick'. I think this is a misunderstanding, but let me know if it is true or not, just in case (*Mitsukoshi Times* 11, 6, May 1913, p. 14).

Although Mitsukoshi replied that there was no rural–urban difference in product offering as a matter of course, the Rural Customer Department was a short time later renamed as the Mail-Order Department, probably in response to such inquiries. We can assume that this renaming was performed as part of the reorganisation of departments in 1914.

Moreover, there was in fact a genuine impetus for this inquiry related to a form of transaction unique to the mail-order business of department stores. In practice, department-store catalogues were ill equipped to fulfil their function as a tool in promoting catalogue sales in a satisfactory way. The average catalogue typically contained only 30 pages and could show in detail only a very small portion of the whole range of goods (Figure 11.3). Customers were informed about most other items in the catalogue only in terms of category and price range. In the case of Mitsukoshi, while a copy of a 1906 catalogue showed no more than 100 items in detail, it listed 488 categories, complete with price ranges; that latter number grew to 1,425 categories in the 1913 catalogue. Much the same was true for other department stores. In this respect, Japanese practice was quite distinctive by comparison with that of the mail-order retailers in Britain (including the London department stores), and the mail-order giants of the United States.

This reflected the fact that the mail-order business of department stores in pre-war Japan was mainly based not on catalogue sales, but on a different and peculiar form of transaction. For instance, with respect to kimono (one of their main goods), customers would mail in their order sheets, recording their age, physical size, facial shape, skin colour and the intended kimono usage; a clerk would then choose and dispatch the kimono considered most suitable, on the basis of the order sheet information. That is to say, customers did not choose the item they wanted *per se*. Several studies (e.g. Tsuchiya, 1999, p. 237; Kurozumi, 1993, p. 195) point to the existence of such a kimono trade, but what is noteworthy is that the same practice was also used in the mail-order purchase of non-kimono goods. This sort of transaction can be observed in real-life orders received by Matsuya, one of the major department stores in Tokyo (*Shōten Kai* 9, 12, October1929, pp. 37–39). For example, in a typical form of kimono order, a customer mailed in an order sheet requesting 'a smart kimono for a geisha aged 28–29'. In another case,

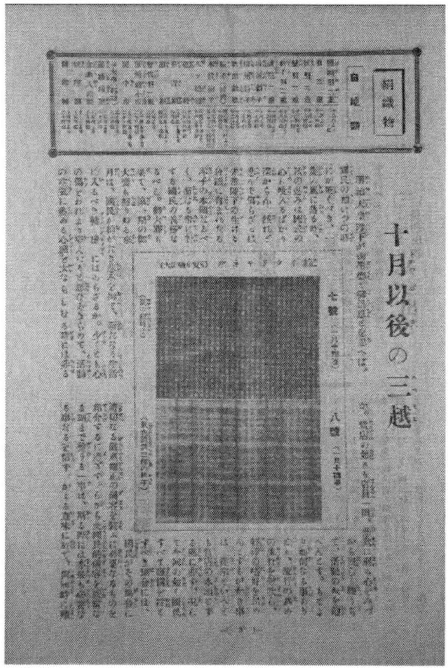
十月以後の三越

Figure 11.3 A page from the Mitsukoshi catalogue of September 1912 (as in Figure 11.2).

More than half of the pages in this volume are built up mainly from text in this way. At the top of the page is the list of items and price ranges. Customers ordered in reference to this list and entrusted choice of goods to a clerk if they wanted goods which were not on the photo pages.

a customer in Hokkaidō wrote that she wanted 'an article of Western-style clothing with a skirt for someone aged 17–18, which is ahead of the trend this summer', signing her name as 'TOSITAKE HANAYO', in Roman characters. The Mail Order Department in Matsuya then chose and dispatched a luxury, high-priced good, because it was presumed from her signature that the customer was a 'modern girl'. Another customer wrote about wanting 'a flower ornament made with imitation flowers, costing around 1.5 yen', while another ordered 'a patterned toy made from wood, costing around 1 yen, for a girl aged two'. The Mail Order Department in Matsuya would choose and dispatch a suitable item on the basis of the order sheet, whether it was clothing or sundry goods, and sales based on this type of transaction accounted for two-thirds of all mail-order sales by Matsuya around 1929 (*Shōten Kai* 9: 13, November 1929, p. 90). In the light of the appearance of their catalogues between the 1890s and the 1930s, it is natural to assume that other department stores, including Mitsukoshi and Shirokiya, followed similar practices during the pre-war period.

I will refer to this type of transaction as one based on 'entrusted choice'. Such 'entrusted choice' is exercised by a clerk from the mail-order department, who chooses goods on behalf of a customer after due consideration of both the suggested price and the taste of the customer. In general terms, it is clear that transactions based on 'entrusted choice' have no economic rationality, given that there is an increased risk of goods being returned. Therefore, it is important to consider why such transactions became a staple of the mail-order trade of department stores in pre-war Japan. In any case, we need to demonstrate why the mail-order business of department stores grew and came to supersede that of specialist mail-order retailers.

First of all, it would be erroneous to assume that mail-order department clerks in pre-war Japan did not possess the business expertise needed to sell goods effectively via catalogue; we know, for example, that Hamada Shirō, head of the Mail-Order Department in Mitsukoshi, observed the catalogue sales of the American mail-order giants with his own eyes (Tsuchiya, 1999, p. 237). He believed that mail-order retailers in Japan could not adopt the same method of catalogue selling as used in the United States, for three reasons: (1) Japan had more complex and diverse consumer tastes (especially in clothes); (2) the Japanese market featured a smaller retail margin (i.e., less than 20 per cent in Japan, compared to as much as, or more than, 30 per cent in the United States); and (3) there was a shortage of buying power among the Japanese lower classes. He concluded that these factors would complicate inventory control and prohibitively increase the ratio of sales/administrative expenses to price (Hamada, 1948, pp. 183–84). Hence, in his view, the 'break-even point' was too high for a full-scale adoption of catalogue-sale methodologies in pre-war Japan.

In particular, Japan's complex and diverse consumer tastes prevented department stores from creating comprehensive mail-order sales catalogues. In fact, according to one representative of the Mail-Order Department in Mitsukoshi, 'it is impossible to contain all kimono patterns [within a catalogue], because fashion varies by season and taste depends on age and preference' (*Mitsukoshi Times* 7, 12 October 1909, p. 16). A chief of that Department also remarked that, in general, people in Kyūshū prefer flashy clothes because they live in a warm area, while people in Hokkaidō prefer quiet clothes because they live in a cold area' (*Jitsugyō Kai* 24: 4, April 1922, pp. 328–29). Meanwhile, in local government social circles, one lady is quoted as saying to another, 'Oh, no! You don't have a black ceremonial kimono? In this prefecture, you must wear a black kimono when you visit the governor to give New Year's greetings!' Such anecdotes provide good examples of how consumer choice in Japan was influenced by local customs, and Francks's chapter (Chapter 7) in this volume also suggests that the nature of the market for kimono made it unsuitable for mass production. Hamada's account (Hamada, 1915) shows that in fact many kinds of goods were far from standardised.

Because the department stores in pre-war Japan could not create comprehensive catalogues of all the goods they offered, it was necessary to adopt the 'entrusted choice' method of fulfilling customer requests. As far as I can tell, such a method of mail-order retailing cannot be found in the United States, Britain, or other European countries, and could be considered a limitation of mail-order retailing in pre-war Japan.[10] Furthermore, it is important to note that the fashion trends created by the department stores had little impact on consumer tastes, and therefore did not 'standardise' consumer culture, so that in practice the mail-order business of the department stores provided a pathway of consumption based mainly on 'traditional' rather than 'modern' consumer practices. However, we should also note that 'entrusted choice' had the operational advantage of making it easier for the department stores to manage their stock. The inquiry to Mitsukoshi from a rural customer mentioned above was based on a fear of being forced to buy clearance goods. The department stores tried to quell customers' anxiety in this respect and developed managerial responses that enabled them to become the leading mail-order traders. These tended to assume one of four forms: (1) taking advantage of the acquired skills of kimono experts, among others; (2) accepting returned goods; (3) establishing and enhancing their store's image as a leader in fashion trends; and (4) preparing themselves to handle the various consumer tastes of different regions.

In terms of point (4), Mail-Order Department clerks recognised that they had to consider regional differences in taste, and not simply

---

[10] For example, Bon Marché, the French department store, issued 'bulky mail-order catalogues which contained illustrations of all goods' (Kashima, 1991, pp. 148–50). Merlo and Polese (2007) emphasise that mail-order catalogues issued by department stores in Italy (particularly in Milan) played an important role in diffusing fashion goods.

choose whatever was fashionable in the big city. For instance, the clerk in Mitsukoshi who pointed out the importance of fashion, as quoted above, noted that 'fashion is created in Tokyo, but the mode of life is different for different regions, owing to the diversity of climate. So, it is absolutely necessary for us to take such differences into account in choosing goods' (*Shōgyō Kai* 9: 6, May 1908, p. 32). The Mail-Order Department in Mitsukoshi consisted of five sections, each dedicated to a different geographical area, in order to achieve effective customer management (*Kinjitō* 215, Autumn 1987, p. 8). Moreover, Mail-Order Department clerks were also assigned to door-to-door sales and were involved in advertising for the mail-order business, so that they obtained information on the local market directly (Mitsuzono, 2009a, p. 43). These facts suggest that the mail-order business of the department stores of that time should to some extent be seen as an embodiment of Japanese consumer-market adaptation.

Let us now shift the emphasis from the supply side to the demand side. It can be presumed from the media environment in rural areas that transactions based on 'entrusted choice' were both rational and convenient for customers. Since the Japanese media was still in its nascent stage prior to the launch of women's magazines such as *Shufu no Tomo*, which emerged as an informational magazine in the 1920s, information seeking among rural individuals exacted an excessively high cost, and information about goods from the big city was in any case insufficient. Of course, there were plenty of advertisements in newspapers at that time, but it was difficult for rural people to determine which items advertised in the newspaper were the best or the most suitable for their needs. We can presume, given the business undertaken by other general mail-order retailers, that this supposition is not too far from the truth.

This is demonstrated by the fact that mail-order retailers not only sold a wide range of goods by catalogue, but also complied with special requests from customers, such as 'I would like you to determine whether the item advertised in the newspaper is a good one or not', or 'please search for the right shop and buy a suitable one on my behalf' (Hayashi, 2006, pp. 573, 651). These requests clearly suggest that people in rural areas could not collect sufficient information by themselves, even with regard to big-city retail stores. In this light, it appears that rural people were perfectly willing to entrust the choice of goods to the clerk of a department store that offered a wide range of items and had a positive image as a centre of fashion. In all, as far as ordering modes are concerned, we can say that customers in certain circumstances did not consider choosing goods on their own as the highest priority. Hence specialist mail-order companies that modelled themselves after the two American mail-order giants and issued 'American-style' general catalogues twice per year had disappeared by around 1910, largely because they had been squeezed out in competition with the mail-order business of department stores (Ōtani, 1927, p. 4).[11]

At the same time, an understanding of traditional shopping methods offers another key to explaining transactions based on 'entrusted choice'. As is well known, the method of display-based selling, which was introduced in the giant kimono stores (later department stores) in the 1890s, brought about revolutionary changes in the Japanese purchasing style (Fujioka, 2004, pp. 175–78). Before that time, customers were not able to compare goods freely or to pick up goods on their own; rather, sales assistants chose suitable goods and brought them from the warehouse. Since most stores in the towns and villages did not introduce display-based selling until the 1920s, rural people rarely chose goods by themselves before that. Therefore, it is natural to suggest that transactions based on 'entrusted choice' were comfortably accepted by rural customers as an extension of the traditional purchasing style.

Although the mail-order business of the department stores continued to develop until the early 1920s on the basis of 'entrusted choice', it stagnated after that time and lost its prominence within such stores' activities. In the case of Mitsukoshi, in 1935 its mail-order sales were worth 1,170,000 yen and 910,000 catalogues were dispatched (*Kinjitō* 215, Autumn 1987, p. 8). However, mail-order sales accounted for only 1.1 per cent of all Mitsukoshi sales in that year. Compared with data from around 1910, mail-order sales had actually *decreased* in real terms, while the number of catalogues remained at the same level. This suggests that the Mail-Order Department had been left behind while other departments, especially the store-based ones, flourished. However, the department stores eagerly continued to exploit the market in rural areas by means of both door-to-door sales and the opening of branch stores, instead of mail order.

This change was caused by the development of the information and distribution system associated with the emergence of the mass market. Women's magazines such as *Shufu no Tomo,* which showed the middle classes how to engage in 'modern' consumption through 'modern' goods,

---

11 Although there is little historical record of them, the 1901 catalogue from one of these firms had about 150 pages (Hayashi, 2006). Therefore, it also appears to have been the case that their catalogues did not compare well with 'American-style' ones.

achieved circulations in the hundreds of thousands of copies in the 1920s, and some of them sold over a million copies in the 1930s. This is more than ten times the number of mail-order catalogues issued by the department stores. In addition, rural-area retailers succeeded in modernising in terms of merchandise and operation. Therefore, rural people could easily acquire enough information to choose goods by themselves, and they could purchase the same articles sold in big cities even from local stores which introduced the method of display-based selling. It seems reasonable to assume that the conditions which had fostered the development of the mail-order business of the department stores, especially transactions based on 'entrusted choice', had by then ceased to exist.

Mail order in the Uji tea industry[12]

As mentioned previously, mail-order retailing in pre-war Japan also involved another type of trader: producers (or wholesalers) in local industrial districts, such as those specialising in green tea, kimono (in Kyoto) and glass-ware (in Yamanashi Prefecture). In this subsection, we will examine in detail the case of green tea, particularly the Uji green tea produced in the Kyoto region, as an example of the most developed use of mail order in this kind of industry.

At the end of the Tokugawa period, the green-tea industry was second only to silk-reeling as a source of exports in Japan. However, exports reached a ceiling in the 1880s, and the green-tea industry had no choice but to transform itself from an export industry into one led by domestic demand. In terms of volume, the share of exports in total green-tea production decreased from around 80 per cent in the 1880s to around 50 per cent before the First World War. It fell further, to around 30 per cent, after 1919. Export volumes decreased by half, from around 20,000 tonnes in the late 1880s to around 10,000 tonnes in 1920s (Teramoto, 1999, pp. 16–17).

As a result, after the 1890s the Uji tea industry was largely shut out of the export market, in which price competition was very severe, mainly because Uji tea was a high-quality and high-price product. Although it was necessary for the Uji tea district (comprising Uji-*gun*, Kuse-*gun*, Tsuzuki-*gun* and Sōraku-*gun*, all in Kyoto Prefecture) to develop its domestic market, the brand value of Uji tea was at a crisis point, due to the fact that wholesalers at the distributing centres or in the consuming regions had without permission been mixing it with cheap tea. Around

[12] This subsection is based on Mitsuzono, 2008.

that time, postal services were developing as the infrastructure for the mail-order system, opening up the possibility not only of expansion of the domestic market, but also of the removal of such unscrupulous wholesalers from the supply chain.

This was because the development of mail-order retailing had a direct influence on the wholesale and distribution system, which had to reorganise to comply with the system implemented by the producing districts. Once there were customers who purchased tea by mail order directly from the producers, wholesalers throughout the country were no longer able to defraud consumers. Thus, mail-order retailing in the Uji tea industry contributed to the reconstruction of the brand's value as a high-quality tea.

We can confirm that the first trader to sell Uji tea by mail order did so in 1894. There were also several traders dealing in the product in this way in the 1900s. According to *Nihon Zenkoku Shōkō Jinmei Roku,* the national listing of individuals involved in agriculture and commerce, the number of traders who were specified as mail-order retailers – including wholesalers who sold tea by mail order as a subsidiary business – increased from 10 in the 1914 edition to 39 in the 1925 edition. (As a point of comparison, the total number of traders in the district was 51 in the 1914 edition and 79 in the 1925 edition.) We can assume that there were actually more mail-order retailers than this, on the grounds that this listing included only traders of a certain size. Other historical materials state that around 1923 there were 48 mail-order retailers – or one-third of all dealers – in Tahara Village and Ujidawara Village alone, and nearly 200 mail-order retailers in all the districts at the end of the 1920s (Kyōtofu Nōson Kenkyūjo, 1962, p. 806).

Meanwhile, mail-order sales of green tea in Kyoto Prefecture, at 1,600,000 yen (*Kyōto Chagyō Kai* 2: 2, April 1920), accounted for 69 per cent of the total value of production of primary processed tea (2,310,000 yen) in 1919 (Kyōto Furitsu Sōgō Shiryōkan, 1970). On the basis of these data, we can estimate that mail-order sales represented 36 per cent of all shipments of finished tea products from Kyoto Prefecture (Mitsuzono, 2008, p. 47).[13] According to another data source, the number of mail-order parcels dispatched from Tahara Village increased from 33,453 (worth 167,256 yen) in 1919 to 86,850 (434,745 yen) in 1923 (*Kyōto Chagyō Kai* 6: 3, October 1924, p. 29). Mail-order sales figures for Kyoto Prefecture in 1919 indicate that

[13] Finished tea products were made by adding primary processed tea from other districts to primary processed tea from Kyoto.

traders in the Uji tea industry district dispatched more than 330,000 parcels that year in the course of their mail-order business. This represents twice the annual number of parcels dispatched by Mitsukoshi's Mail-Order Department around 1910.

It is useful to examine the Uji tea industry's customer segmentation in greater detail. According to historical materials from 1909, Uji tea, especially *gyokuro* (refined green tea), was often consumed by aristocrats and others in Tokyo pursuing a particular form of tea ceremonial (Ujidawara Chō Kyōiku Iinkai, 1979). The increasing pursuit of this refined practice in rural areas enabled mail-order retailers in the Uji tea-industry district to develop an expanding new market; for example, since tea culture is closely linked to Buddhism in Japan, they ran a considerable number of advertisements in Buddhist magazines in the 1900s (Ōtsuki, 2004).

However, the customer segment of interest to mail-order retailers in the Uji tea district changed over time. For example, a representative of the Yamashiro Seicha Company, a leading producer of Uji tea, wrote in 1926:

> From 1916, the domestic consumption of Uji green tea grew at a dramatic rate because the practice of enjoying the drinking of tea had spread among ordinary people, and the population had also increased. Growth was led by the strong demand for middle- or low-grade tea and roasted tea, while the consumption of high-grade tea did not grow much due to a lack of leisure time for the genuine tea culture. (Katō, p. 336)

This description implies that the mass market for green tea was appearing, creating new opportunities not directly related to the tea culture of the wealthy classes.

Within this historical context, the discovery that green tea is rich in vitamin C was highly significant. As soon as this discovery was made in 1924, the green-tea industry districts excitedly planned to exploit it as a means of increasing green-tea consumption. Of course, the Uji tea-industry district was no exception, and the industry magazine *Kyōto Chagyō* reported this discovery as a great opportunity to advertise Uji tea, proclaiming, for example, 'this discovery amazed the middle class!' and 'we must do an extensive advertising campaign and not miss this opportunity!' (*Kyōto Chagyō* 6: 4, October 1924, pp. 7–8). Uji tea was thereafter increasingly sold as a nutritious and necessary everyday beverage, rather than as a luxury item associated with a particular tea culture.

The mail-order retailers in the Uji tea-industry district also undertook an advertising campaign and contributed to extending this new market. For example, advertising copy in the mail-order catalogue of Nakagawa Jōryoku En, an Uji tea trader engaged in both wholesaling and mail-order selling, went from using words associated with tea culture, such as 'elegant' and 'sophisticated' (1910s), to words associated with everyday life, such as 'hygienic', 'vitamin-rich', 'nutritious' and 'healthy' (1930s) (*Jōryoku En Chahō* December 1917, July 1934, July 1935, July 1937).

However, we should not overlook the fact that mail-order sales of Uji tea declined after the Shōwa panic of 1930. In fact, around 1933, the volume of Uji tea sales by mail order was only 563–600 tonnes per year (Kyōto Shōkō Kaigi Sho, 1934, p. 75). This represented 32–34 per cent of the total output of primary processed tea and less than 20 per cent of total shipments of finished tea products from Kyoto Prefecture (Kyōto Furitsu Sōgō Shiryōkan 1970; *Chagyō Ihō* 29, 1935). These percentages were almost half those of 1919. In the case of Nakagawa Jōryoku, the proportion of mail-order sales, as a percentage of total sales, decreased from 87.7 per cent (22,944 yen/26,148 yen) in 1924 to 49.0 per cent (8,964 yen/18,301 yen) in 1935. It can be assumed that the absolute value of mail-order sales also decreased significantly, since the volume

Table 11.3 Kyoto's share of the domestic market for green tea

	Domestic consumption (m. t.)	Per capita consumption (kg)	Volume shipped from Kyoto Prefecture (m. t.)	Kyoto's Market Share (%)
1919	25,434	0.458	3,394	13.3
1922	22,508	0.391	4,665	20.7
1929	28,877	0.454	3,397	11.8
1930	29,674	0.460	3,306	11.1
1931	27,051	0.415	3,088	11.4
1932	27,421	0.416	3,071	11.2
1933	30,870	0.464	3,145	10.2
1938	33,507	0.464	4,266	12.7

Note: Domestic consumption = production + imports – exports (outside the empire).

Sources: Tetsudō Shō Unyu Kyoku (1919); *Chagyō Ihō* 14 (1926), 25 (1932), 27 (1933), 28 (1934), 29 (1935); Nōrinshō (1939); Kyōto Shōkō Kaigi Sho (1940); Zenkoku Nōgyōkai Chagyō Bu (1948).

of finished tea products shipped from Kyoto had severely decreased between 1919 and 1933, as shown in Table 11.3.

At the same time, we must note that Kyoto's share of the domestic green tea market remained stagnant after the 1920s, as indicated in Table 11.3. This stagnation reflected severe competition from other districts, such as Shizuoka and Sayama. The domestic market gradually expanded due to comparatively low prices after the 1920s, as the export market for green tea shrank. Since other regions' comparatively low-priced goods suited the new mass market for green tea, the Uji tea-industry district sensed a crisis. Hence *Kyōto Chagyō* wrote in 1923,

> According to the results of a survey, Shizuoka's share of regional markets, in which people used to drink Uji tea by preference, accounts for 70 per cent (Uji's share is only 15 per cent). Following this trend, we are sure to lose our share of the domestic market in the near future. (5, 2, April 1923, p. 5)

Similarly, in 1931 it reported 'we are losing market share, unlike other industry districts, because they are expanding their markets by investing huge expenditures in advertising' (13, 3, July 1931, pp. 50–51).

The Uji tea district then launched extensive advertising campaigns in an organised fashion, involving posters, promotional films and advertising in a number of newspapers and magazines, among other media (Kyōto-fu Chagyō Hyakunenshi Henshū Iinkai, 1994, pp. 519–22). The same key words seen previously, such as 'hygienic', 'vitamin-rich', 'nutritious', 'healthy' and the like, were emphasised again. As it turned out, those Uji tea traders in the district specialising in wholesaling enjoyed lower operational costs than those in mail-order retailing. In Nakagawa Jōryoku En the respective shares of advertising and operating costs in total costs decreased from 22.5 per cent (1,015 yen) and 14.6 per cent (663 yen) in 1934, to 16.4 per cent (714 yen) and 8.4 per cent (364 yen) in 1938. During this period, mail-order sales as a proportion of all sales fell from roughly 50 per cent to 40 per cent, while the value of total sales increased from 15,780 yen to 22,964 yen (Mitsuzono, 2008, pp. 48–52). On this basis, it can be said that mail-order retailing in the Uji tea industry did not reap benefits commensurate with its expenditure on advertising.

In conclusion, although mail-order retailing in the Uji tea industry contributed to the reconstruction of the brand's value as a high-quality tea that was associated with tea culture in the upper-class market, it lost its edge in the phase during which the mass market for tea developed after the 1920s. In this context, it should be noted that since the

Tokugawa period the majority of ordinary people had been consuming a large variety of the coarse teas known as *bancha*. *Bancha* was harvested as a subsistence crop or distributed only through small local markets, and its process of manufacture and taste varied widely by region (Nakamura, 1998, pp. 156–69). After the 1920s, green tea industrial districts, such as Uji, Shizuoka and Sayama, indeed faced a challenge. They had to drive out 'traditional' and diverse local preferences in order to sell their products throughout Japan. Hence, it was necessary for them to undertake extensive advertising campaigns that could sufficiently influence the lifestyle choices of ordinary people. At the same time, given the association between industrialisation and consumption in pre-war Japan, it was the values of modernity – as embodied in terms such as 'hygienic', 'vitamin-rich', 'nutritious', 'healthy' and so on – that they emphasised in this process.

Conclusion

Mail-order retailing in pre-war Japan did not give birth to large traders, as had been the case in the United States, since distribution systems were already highly developed and consumer tastes more complicated and diverse, as early as the Tokugawa period. However, its development bears comparison with that in European countries, with the exception of Germany. In fact, the store-based retailers in the large cities and traders in the local industrial districts supplied their goods to the upper class by mail order. It should be stressed that we can consider the mail-order business of department stores that was based on 'entrusted choice' an act of adaptation to the Japanese consumer market. Additionally, it can be pointed out that several Uji tea traders, including small ones, introduced their own mail-order systems without hesitation as a new method of retailing. However, the growth of mail-order retailing in Japan was based on 'traditional' consumption patterns and could not entirely overcome them. Therefore, it ceased to play a historical role as a pathway of consumption for rural people, when the mass market, which was dominated by many kinds of 'modern' value, began to develop on the basis of other types of information and distribution systems in the inter-war period.

References

Amemiya, A. (2000) *Teisei-ki Doitsu no Shin Chūkan-sō* (The New Middle Class in Imperial Germany), Tokyo: Tokyo University Press.

Benson, J. & Shaw, G. (eds) (1999) *The Evolution of Retail Systems, c1800–1914*, Leicester and New York: Leicester University Press.

Bureau Internationale de l'Union Postale Universelle (1924) *Statistique Générale du Service Postal Année 1922*, Communications Museum in Japan: YS-A2.
Chandler, A. D. J. (1977) *The Visible Hand: The Managerial Revolution in American Business*, Cambridge, M A: Belknap Press.
Coopey, R., O'Connell, S. & Porter, D. (2005) *Mail Order Retailing in Britain: A Business and Social History*, Oxford and New York: Oxford University Press.
Fujioka, R. (2004) 'Hyakkaten' (Department Stores), in Ishihara, T. & Yahagi, T. (eds) *Nihon no Ryūtsū 100 Nen* (A Century of Circulation in Japan), Tokyo: Yūhikaku.
Hamada, S. (1915) *Gendai Shiki Shōten no Keiei* (Management of Modern Shops), Tokyo: Satō Shuppanbu.
Hamada, S. (1948) *Hyakkaten Isseki Banashi* (Talking about Department Stores), Tokyo: Nihon Denpō Tsūshin Sha.
Harrods (1912) Reprinted as *English Department Store and Mail Order Catalogues, 1900–1940; Pt 1*, Tokyo: Athena Press, 2008.
Hayashi, J. (2006) *Meiji Jidai no Tsūhan Katarogu: Hayashi Joji Korekushon Fukkoku Ban* (Sales Catalogues of the Meiji Period), Tokyo: Katarogu Hausu.
Jefferys, J. B. (1950) *The Distribution of Consumer Goods: A Factual Study of Methods and Costs in the United Kingdom*, Cambridge: Cambridge University Press.
Jinno, Y. (1994) *Shumi no Tanjō: Hyakkaten no Tsukutta Teisuto* (The Birth of Hobbies), Tokyo: Keisō Shobō.
Kashima, S. (1991) Depāto wo Hatsumei Shita Fūfu (The Couple who Discovered the Department Store) Tokyo: Kōdansha.
Katō, T. (ed.) (1926) *Nihon Naichi ni okeru Seicha Jijō* (The Situation of Tea Manufacturing within Japan), Tokyo: Chagyō Kumiai Chūō Kaigi Sho.
Kinjitō (1987), 215, Autumn
Kiwata, Y. & Miura, I. (eds) (1985) *Tsūhan Māketingu Senryaku* (Mail Order Marketing Strategy), Tokyo: Nihon Keizai Shinbunsha.
Kurozumi, B. (1993) *Nihon Tsūshin Hanbai Hattatsu Shi* (Development of Mail Order Selling in Japan), Tokyo: Dōyūkan.
Kyōto-fu Chagyō Hyakunenshi Henshū Iinkai (ed.) (1994) *Kyōto-fu Chagyō Hyakunen Shi* (Hundred-year History of the Tea Industry in Kyoto Prefecture), Kyoto: Kyōto-fu Chagyō Kaigisho.
Kyōtofu Nōson Kenkyūjo (ed.) (1962) *Kyōtofu Nōgyō Hattatsu Shi* (Development of Farming in Kyoto Prefecture), Kyōto: Kyōtofu Nōson Kenkyūjo.
Kyōto Furitsu Sōgō Shiryōkan (ed.) (1970) *Kyōtofu Tōkei Shiryōshū* (Kyoto Prefecture Statistical Materials) *2*, Kyōto: Kyōto-fu.
Kyōto Shōkō Kaigi Sho (ed.) (1934) *Uji Cha no Kenkyū* [Research on Uji Tea] (Kyōto: Kyōto Shōkō Kaigi Sho).
Kyōto Shōkō Kaigi Sho (ed.) (1940) *Uji Cha no Chōsa* [Survey of Uji Tea] (Kyōto: Kyōto Shōkō Kaigi Sho).
Merlo, E. & Polese, F. (2007) 'Accessorizing, Italian Style: Creating a Market for Milan's Fashion Merchandise', in Blaszczyk, R. L. (ed.), *Producing Fashion: Commerce, Culture, and Consumers*, Philadelphia: University of Pennsylvania Press.
Mitchell, B. (ed.) (1998) *International Historical Statistics: Europe 1750–1993*, London: Macmillan.
Mitsuzono, I. (2008) 'Senzenki Uji Cha Sanchi ni okeru Kokunai Shijō e no Tenkai' (Switch to the Domestic Market in the Uji Tea Production Area before the War), *Shakai Keizai Shigaku*, 74, 1.

Mitsuzono, I. (2009a) 'Senzenki Nihon ni okeru Daitoshi Gofukukei Hyakkaten no Tsūshin Hanbai' (Mail Order Selling by Large City Department Stores in Pre-war Japan), *Keiei Shigaku* 44, 1.

Mitsuzono, I. (2009b) 'Senzenki Nihon ni okeru Tsūshin Hanbai no Seidoteki Kiban: Daikin Hikikae Yūbin no Igi to Genkai' (Institutional Foundations of Mail Order Selling in Pre-war Japan), *Shigaku Zashi* 118, 9.

Miyamoto, M. (1896) 'Sekai Yūbin Tōkei Ron' (On Global Postal Statistics), *Kōtsū*, 127, April.

Naikaku Tōkei Kyoku (ed.) (1939) *Rinji Kokusei Chōsa Kekka Hyō* (Result of the Provisional Census) *1*, Tokyo: Naikaku Tōkei Kyoku.

Nakagawa, K. (1981) *Hikaku Keieishi Josetsu* (Introduction to Comparative Business History), Tokyo: Tokyo Daigaku Shuppankai.

Nakamura, T. (1971) *Senzenki Nihon Keizai Seichō no Bunseki* (A Study of Economic Growth in Pre-war Japan), Tokyo: Iwanami Shoten.

Nakamura, Y. (1998) *Bancha to Nihonjin* (*Bancha* and the Japanese), Tokyo: Yoshikawa Kōbun Kan.

Nakanishi, S. (2000) 'Bunmei Kaika to Minshū Seikatsu' (Civilisation and Englightenment and People's Daily Lives), in Ishii, K., Hara, A. & Takeda, H. (eds) *Nihon Keizaishi 1 Bakumatsu Ishinki*, Tokyo: Tokyo Daigaku Shuppankai.

Nōrinshō (1939) *Chagyō Yōran* (Outline of the Tea Industry), Tokyo: Nōrinshō

Ōtani, H. (1927) *Tsūshin Hanbai no Hiketsu* (Secret of Mail Order Selling) Tokyo: Shiire Annai Sha.

Ōtsuki, M. (2004) *Sencha Bunka Kō* (Green Tea Culture), Kyoto: Shibunkaku Shuppan.

Pasdermadjian, H. (1954) *The Department Store: Its Origins, Evolution and Economics*, London: Newman Books.

Ryūtsū Sangyō Kenkyūjo (ed.) (1977) *Nihon no Tsūshin Katarogu Hanbai* (Mail Order Catalogue Selling in Japan), Tokyo: Ryūtsū Sangyō Kenkyūjo.

Shinohara, M. (1967) *Chōki Keizai Tōkei 6: Kojin Shōhi Shishutsu* (Long Term Economic Statistics of Japan vol.6: Personal Consumption Expenditures) Tokyo: Tōyō Keizai Shinpō Sha.

Teishinshō (ed.) (1899–1936) *Tsūshin Tōkei Yōran* (Handbook of Communication Statistics), Tokyo: Teishinshō.

Teishinshō (ed.) (1942) *Yūbin Tōkei Yōran* (Handbook of Postal Statistics), Tokyo: Teishinshō.

Teramoto, M. (1999) *Senzenki Nihon Chagyō Shi Kenkyū* (Research on the Pre-war History of Japan's Tea Industry), Tokyo: Yūhikaku.

Tetsudōshō Unyu Kyoku (ed.) (1919) *Tetsudō Shuyō Kamotsu Sūryō Hyō* (Statistical Tables on Major Goods Carried by Rail), Tokyo: Tetsudōshō Unyu Kyoku.

Toba, K. (1969) *Shiāzu Rōbakku* (Sears Roebuck), Tokyo: Tōyō Keizai Shinpō Sha.

Tokunaga, Y. (1992) *Amerika no Ryūtsūgyō no Rekishi ni Manabu* (Introduction to the History of Circulation of Goods in America), 2nd edn, Tokyo: Chūō Keizai Sha.

Tokyo Teishin Kanri Kyoku (1912) *Tokyo Shi Tsūshin Jigyō no Hensen* (Changing Face of Communications in Tokyo City), Tokyo: Tokyo Teishin Kanri Kyoku.

Tsuchiya, R. (1999) 'Hyakkaten Hakkō no Kikan Zasshi' (Department Store Magazines), in Yamamoto, T. & Nishizawa, T. (eds) *Hyakkaten no Bunka Shi* (A Cultural History of Department Stores), Kyoto: Sekai Shisō Sha.

Tsunematsu, Y. (2005) 'Tsūshin Hanbai to Amerika Shakai: Chūseibu Nōmin no Shōhi Kōdō' (Mail Order Sales and American Society), in Tsunematsu, Y.

& Matsumoto, Y. (eds) *Shōhi to Amerika Shakai: Shōhi Taikoku no Shakai Shi* (Consumption and American Society: A Social History of the Great Consumer Power), Tokyo: Yamakawa Shuppansha.

Tsūsan Tōkei Kyōkai (ed.) (1983) *Sengo no Shōgyō Tokei Hyō* (Statistical Tables of Post-war Commerce), 1, Tokyo: Ōkura Shō Insatsu Kyoku.

Ujidawara Chō Kyōiku Iinkai (ed.) (1979) *Ujidawara Chōshi Sankō Shiryō* (Reference Materials on the History of Ujidawara-chō), 13, Kyōto: Ujidawara Chō Kyōiku Iinkai.

Yūseishō (1980) *Yūsei Tōkei Nempō: Yūbin Denki Tsūshin Gyōmu Hen* (Yearbook of Postal Statistics), Tokyo: Yūsei Shō.

Zenkoku Nōgyōkai Chagyō Bu (1948) *Nihon Chagyō Shi* (History of the Tea Industry in Japan), 3, Tokyo: Zenkoku Nōgyōkai Chagyō Bu.

12 From Corporate Playground to Family Resort: Golf as Commodity in Post-War Japan

Angus Lockyer

Introduction

From a distance, say on Google Earth, the mountainous landscape of the archipelago would seem to make Japan an inhospitable place for golf. The familiar statistic of the uncultivable 80 per cent of the land mass suggests that real estate might be better turned to other, less profligate uses. Closer up, however, many cities are ringed with the tell-tale worm castings of fairways, bunkers and greens. In the countryside, the bucolic vista of paddies climbing into the hills, abutting the woods that, if not primeval, are still reassuring as to the Japanese ability to coexist with nature, is rudely interrupted. Decapitated hills and shaven slopes announce the presence of a course which is more often than not brown, despite the chemicals required to maintain the pretence of the green carpet (*midori no jūtan*) that is thought to be the object of desire. At ground level, suburban landscapes are punctuated by the tall nets of driving ranges, city centres by equipment emporia, membership exchanges and even golf bars, while bookshops and station kiosks are festooned with the tell-tale green, and now pink, of golf-related publications.

Similarly, the waves of demand for discretionary golf goods – courses, ranges and equipment – that have swept through post-war Japan might seem to be at odds with the producer-oriented GNP-ism that provides the *basso ostinato* of many historical accounts of the period. We know, of course, that the latter is a little too simple. Urbanisation in the early-modern period and industrialisation in the early twentieth century had long established habits of consumption, albeit hedged about with ecological, geo-political and other constraints, which placed a premium on discrimination and refinement, producing the cultivation of a somewhat obsessive practice well-suited to the frustrations of golf. Panning in beyond the iron triangle that has been seen to structure the post-war political economy, we can see the myriad of local actors, whose individual decisions to invest in ventures not sanctioned by the Ministry of International Trade and Industry, to spend rather than save, may have provided the wherewithal for the creation of a middle-mass habit.

Might golf, then, also provide a counter-point to the corporatist line that underpins our standard accounts of post-war growth? To cut to the chase, probably not. In terms of both supply and demand, the drivers of the explosion in golf-course development, practice and play in post-war Japan seem to have been corporate. In contrast to the pre-war period, when golf was sustained by private membership clubs, post-war golf was provided and consumed for the most part by companies, who built the courses, bought the memberships and mandated that executives and aspiring middle managers should learn to play the game. Together with an interesting set of external factors (financial speculation, yakuza involvement, membership scandals, labour disputes and environmentalist critiques), this produced a strange kind of pastime: at the end of a 60-hour week, a salaryman might leave the house at six on a Sunday morning to trek out to the countryside, where he would spend the day wining and dining, as much as hitting, establishing and re-establishing the corporate hierarchies and business networks through which the work of the week might be facilitated. Entertaining in any society has its protocols, which raises problems for an account of consumption premised on the individual choices of free agents; but Japanese *settai gorufu* – golf as a means of oiling the wheels of corporate business – seems to have generated an extremely prescribed kind of demand, resting on a rather productivist, if highly conspicuous kind of consumerism. That is, if you built it, you could almost guarantee that they would come, either because they already worked for the company that owned it and paid for their membership, or because the proximity of the club to a major population centre and/or the prestige of its designer and members could ensure that it would become an object for speculation on the relevant, sky-rocketing membership exchange.

This kind of golf, however, had its limits. Investment continued into the early 1990s; the majority of the clubs have survived, and it is still common to break after the first nine holes for a long, carb-heavy, alcohol-enabled lunch. But the model for golf has begun to change. Both the commercial case for course development and the social demand for golf à la Japonaise were unsustainable. In the wake of the bursting of the economic 'bubble' of the 1980s, business practice has had to evolve, with a new regard for the bottom line, if not yet for quarterly results, and a gradual retreat from the provision of all things to all employees. As companies pulled back from the table, so the distressed asset of Japanese golf became a prime target for new players; Goldman Sachs and others swept in during the fire sale, creating portfolios designed to cultivate a new kind of demand. Together with the industry more broadly (equipment manufacturers, designers, publishers and the rest), the new owners and brokers are targeting a new consumer and creating a new golf, one that is family friendly, young at heart and often female. The individuality that is the stock in trade of the virtual memberships and leisure advertising directed towards this audience might suggest that Japan too is finally acknowledging the economic potential of consumer demand, but this is true only up to a point. It would be easy enough to assume that American ownership and, at last, a consumer orientation might mean convergence with golf as it is played elsewhere. But as is clear to anyone who spends an hour or so navigating the baroque complexity of booking systems, the technophilic prose of a golf magazine or the glacial play of a Japanese foursome, golf, however changed, remains an unlikely place to find the free radical of liberal fantasy.

Or, perhaps, golf might be one place to rethink how and why consumers form and manage demand. As with much else in Japan, golf may trouble our easy distinction between production and consumption, with its faint echo of the battle between capital and labour and its clear preference for the consuming individual over the faceless corporation. Japanese golf, however, underlines the extent to which demand can be prompted by supply, desire canalised, and everyday life and leisure coordinated with the imperatives of development, company and work. In what follows, therefore, through a brief history of how golf has been consumed in and beyond the archipelago by Japanese people over the past century or so, I want to suggest not only why we need the Japanese consumer, if not necessarily Japanese golf, in our accounts of Japan's modern history, but also how Japanese golf can reveal the way in which consumption is always more complicated than our transparent language of, and clear distinctions between, demanding subjects and desired objects might suggest.

Prelude

Golf did not emerge *ex nihilo* from the ashes of defeat. While pre-war golf was a minority interest at best and its history is more often than not an occasion for antiquarian debates about who came first (see, for example, Kubota, 2004, p. 35 ff.), it is nonetheless significant for the story of golf as consumer good, in as much as pre-war clubs and golfers established both the local rules by which golf was played in Japan and the hierarchy of value that continues to determine the golfing economy today. At this point, it is not clear exactly when and where the former were first put in place, but it is still pre-war courses – Hirono, Hodogaya and others – that are the most celebrated (the *meimon*) among golf cognoscenti, and that have retained their value in the past two decades, even as bubble-era late comers have seen their value and reputation collapse. Koganei Country Club, established in 1937, has notoriously long been the most expensive club in Japan, able to demand a joining fee equivalent to more than a million US dollars (Interview, September 2007).

The first golf in Japan, however, was expatriate, a by-product of the trading profits and lifestyle aspirations of the foreigner communities in Kōbe, Yokohama and beyond. Kōbe Golf Club was formed in 1903 on top of Mt Rokkō, using land purchased as a means to create the facilities for summering away from the muggy port below. Negishi followed three years later, making do with the land in the middle of the Yokohama race course, thereby adding another dimension to the inter-port rivalry. Unzen, in 1912, was an initiative on the part of the local government rather than foreigners, but again targeted at the latter as a summer resort, not least for those seeking to escape the heat of Shanghai (Mowa, 1977, pp. 8–28; Kubota, 2004, pp. 18–34). These early courses allowed space for the development of a particular kind of sociality, which did not exclude Japanese members. There were seven Japanese among the founders of the Kōbe Golf Club, including two members of the Matsukata family (sons of the former Finance Minister, who had stabilised the economy – and devastated many smallholders – in the 1880s), a Sumitomo (a scion of the local industrial aristocracy) and the head of the Kōbe tax office. None of them played, however: the club was useful as a place to network with locally prominent foreigners (Kubota, 2004, p. 20; Lockyer, 2010, p. 600). This function of the club, absent the foreigners, would remain at the core of the demand for golf in Japan, although in the first decade of the twentieth century, there was still little such demand.

It was not until 1914 that the first indigenous sprouts were visible, with the creation of the Tokyo Golf Club. The nature of its cultivators was telling. Inoue Junnosuke, then President of the Yokohama Specie Bank and soon to be head of the Bank of Japan, had played a bit of golf while studying in England, like many of those who found themselves sent to America and Europe during the Meiji period. He was not a golfing enthusiast, but understood its value for rest, recreation and networking. Together with the 30 founding members, who included representatives of both the old court aristocracy (a Saionji) and the new industrial elite (Iwasaki Koyata), he was able to raise the capital to lease a site in Setagaya, then on the western outskirts of the imperial capital, newly accessible through the Tamagawa railway. The characteristic combination of public figures, private capital and informal networks inaugurated the playing of golf in Japan. The importance of the last was evident in the number of non-playing members, which prompted the introduction of green fees for those among the membership who chose to use the course itself, in addition to their joining fee and annual dues. Soon enough, the practice had spread. Karuizawa, located in the mountains to the northwest of Tokyo and so away from the summer heat, had been developed in the 1880s and saw its first nine holes established in 1921. At the same time, a tussle with the landlords at the Tokyo club had produced a search for an alternative site, which resulted in a move to Komazawa, and also the creation of a second club, Hodogaya, in 1922. One year later, golf went imperial. Crown Prince Hirohito had watched golf during his visit to the UK in 1921, and played a couple of times at Komazawa later in the year. He then took on the Prince of Wales when Edward visited Japan the following year, albeit not with much success. In 1923, a nine-hole course was opened in the imperial gardens of Shinjuku Gyōen for the exclusive use of the imperial family (Mowa, 1977, pp. 31–70; Tanaka, 1992, pp. 75–76).

Following its most venerated chronicler, the pre-war history of Japanese golf falls easily into a number of periods (Mowa, 1977). The first expatriate and the second inaugural were followed by a third, which took the story up to 1929, and a fourth, which carried the enthusiasm for golf past the depression and the invasion of Manchuria. The third was marked officially by the creation of the Japan Golf Association in 1924, acknowledging a certain critical mass of courses and golfers. This demanded, and could sustain, a coordinating infrastructure, nation-wide competitions and such like, but was also able to exploit an increasing media interest in the sport. The latter was catalysed by Akaboshi Rokurō, a young, well-connected tyro, who was then in the United States, but would quickly become the leading celebrity of the pre-war golf scene. Having attended prep school and Princeton, in the spring of 1924, Akaboshi won a tournament at Pinehurst. The potential of golf as a media event was soon evident. The *Osaka Mainichi* newspaper was quick to take on the organisation of the Japanese professional championship from its second year in 1927, although it might have preferred to sponsor the first Japanese

Open, in the same year at Hodogaya, where Akaboshi triumphed, beating a number of pros in the field (Mowa, 1977, pp. 47–48; Tanaka, 1992, pp. 76–80). Nor did the enthusiasm ebb in the wake of the economic crisis or the invasion of Manchuria in 1931. For decorum's sake, presumably, the now reigning Emperor Hirohito had to keep his swinging in-house, on a practice course inside the palace grounds, but golf, like much of life, continued to thrive during the 1930s. The year 1933 saw the beginning of the domination of the Japanese Amateur Championship by the newly married Marquis Nabeshima Naoyasu and the first golf exhibition at Mitsukoshi in Nihonbashi, 1935 the inauguration of the All-Japan Student Championship and 1937 the establishment of the Koganei Country Club with a lay-out by Walter Hagan. The well-publicised visit to Japan, in October that year, by Gene Sarazen, meant that two of the three dominant US players of the time were involved in Japanese golf, and Hagan went on to play an exhibition match at Koganei the following April (Tanaka, 1992, p. 80; Koganei Kantorī Kurabu, 1990, pp. 77–93).

There was interest in and demand for golf, therefore, throughout the pre-war period, but the interest seems to have been limited, and golf remained something played almost exclusively by the elite. Golf occasionally appears in the visual culture of the day: a panel depicting an iridescent course and elegantly attired golfers by Yamaguchi Hōshun in a 1928 hand-scroll illustrating contemporary customs and mores (*Gendai fūzoku emaki*) might be evidence that golf was one element of the modern life to which one was meant to aspire (Yamaguchi, 1997). However the strange placement of the golfers suggests that the painter did not himself play the game and, as Kubota Seiichi has noted, the absence of golf in pre-war books about sport indicates that it was at least seen as a different kind of pastime (Kubota, 2004, p. 15). The statistics bear this out: in 1940, there were only 71 courses and some 110,000 golfers in Japan, comprising 0.8 per cent of the population (Tanaka, 1992, p. 82). The extent to which golf remained an aristocratic monopoly is suggested by a recent genealogy published by *Choice*, the most up-market of the many golf magazines, which sketches a network, centered on the aristocratic politician Prince Konoe and incorporating most of the golfing great and good from the pre-war years (*Choice*, 2008, pp. 116–17). By the same token, golf was an object of desire for a newer elite, the club a place where alliances might be forged and support assured. Golf was therefore a private affair, not yet a consumer good.

For the same reason, perhaps, golf was vulnerable during the wartime and post-war recovery periods, making it ripe for investment and reinvention in the second half of the century. Golf was a particular target as the country was mobilised for war in the late 1930s and early 1940s, given its elite status and foreign origins, evident not least in the English terms (converted into Japanese using the katakana script) with which the game had to be played. The authorities made various attempts to indigenise things, renaming balls, clubs and the sport itself using Chinese characters, in an effort to disguise what was clearly a 'foreign' activity with a veneer of East Asian respectability. Golf enthusiasm persisted and golf was played throughout the war. However golfers were targeted and had to resort to subterfuge, sending clubs ahead and dressing down in an attempt to reach the course unmolested. Golf courses, too, proved tempting for the Japanese government simply as land, while the resources needed to maintain them as such were seen to be better deployed for other uses (Kubota, 2004, p. 135 ff.). By the last years of the war, even golf magazines were beyond the pale. The oldest such publication, which had started life in 1922 as *Hanshin Gorufu,* had prophylactically changed its name to *Nippon Gorufudomu* in 1933 and had been re-christened again under military pressure at the beginning of the Pacific War as *Nippon Dakyū,* was forced to cease publication in February 1944.

The problems continued during the Occupation. Americans were eager to play golf during their sojourn, commandeering the remaining courses and demanding that their Japanese staff provide the material wherewithal to play the game (Kubota, 2004, p. 155 ff.). Their enthusiasm suggested one possible use for golf as the Occupation came to an end. In 1951, a Mr. Hirayama, writing in *Kankō* (Tourism) magazine, pointed out that there had been some 50 courses before the war, but that there were only 12 left, with another three under construction, and only four could be used by Japanese players. His statistics may not have been entirely accurate. The United States Golf Association (USGA) in 1957 suggested that 18 had survived of 62, while more recent accounts have revised both figures upwards. In any case, as Hirayama argued, the current supply was inadequate to meet even the existing domestic demand. But his purpose in writing was to suggest how golf might also comprise a key ingredient in the development of a tourist industry with which to resuscitate the Japanese economy. It was not enough simply to give foreigners something to look at; one also needed to provide things to do: hunting, shooting, golf. Twenty years ago, Hirayama noted, when golf was booming in the US, there were 13 golfers born every minute (Hirayama, 1951; Anon., 1957). Hirayama was looking in the wrong direction, however. As in the US, the demand, when it came, would be home-grown. And while it may not have outpaced the American miracle simply in quantitative terms, given the respective populations of continent and archipelago, its effects, despite the constraints of the landscape, were striking.

Boom

As in the pre-war period, so the post-war enthusiasm for golf in Japan can be seen to have come in several waves, the first of which appeared in the late 1950s. Already by 1957, there had been some improvement over the dire situation at the end of the Occupation, with some 118 courses and 300,000 golfers (increases of 66 per cent and 172 per cent respectively over the figures for 1940) combining to produce a total of 1.8 million rounds of golf during the year. The USGA, commenting on the nascent Japanese scene, emphasised the pent-up demand visible in the rapid increase in the number of golfers, with some 5,000 taking up the sport every month. Nearly every club, it noted, had a membership of at least 1,000, with some topping 2,000, and most had barred visitors at weekends. Five years later, it might have been encouraged to observe, the landscape had been transformed, with some 295 courses hosting nearly 7.4 million rounds (see Table 12.1). The year 1961 alone had seen an additional 68 courses and 1.4 million rounds (Anon., 1957; Tanaka, 1992, pp. 98–99).

The usual reason given for this first boom is the staging of the Canada Cup international tournament in Japan for the first time in 1957. The competition was televised and saw Nakamura Torakichi win in both the individual and team competitions. Nakamura became the first post-war golf celebrity, his rivalry with Hayashi Yoshirō providing fodder for the media, before passing the baton to the first of a number of 'big

Table 12.1 Golf courses and rounds played, 1957–1992

Year	Golf courses	Rounds (thousands)	Rounds per course
1957	116	1,823	15,715
1962	295	7,357	24,939
1967	496	14,686	29,608
1972	669	28,619	39,789
1977	1,322	44,823	33,905
1982	1,425	64,392	45,187
1987	1,588	77,630	48,885

Source: Tanaka, 1992, pp. 98–99.

threes' (Tanaka, 1992, pp. 101–4). The Canada Cup may indeed have provided inspiration for some, not least Miki Tokuchika, then building up an organisation called Perfect Liberty Kyōdan; the gospel of this body included the power of golf as a medium of self-expression, and it was busy in 1957 building what would become Seikyo Country Club next to its headquarters in Tondabayashi, Osaka (McFarland, 1960, p. 33). Despite the media coverage, however, as well as the clear potential, not least for spiritual growth, and the astonishing numbers, golf in the 1950s and 1960s still seems to have been a pastime for a privileged class. By the middle of the latter decade, it was clear to ambitious salarymen that they needed to work on their swing if they were to aspire to the executive suite. In 1964, *Life* captured the serried ranks of white-singleted office workers practising at a floodlit three-storey driving

Figure 12.1 A three-storey driving range, presumably in Tokyo

The Tokyo Olympics provided an opportunity for the West to take stock of Japan and to discover the ways in which it diverged from Western norms. Although the white shirts had been discarded, the trousers of the golfers suggest that they are predominantly salarymen, practising for the day when they might make it to the executive suite.

Source: *Life Magazine*, August 1964. Photograph courtesy of Getty Images.

range, presumably somewhere in the Tokyo suburbs (Figure 12.1). But there would be an enduring distinction between using a range and playing a course. At least anecdotally, the latter privilege seems to have been restricted to the top three in most companies (Interview, November 2007). While the numbers suggest that there must have been a few rounds played by people other than executives, the fact that golf had not yet been taken up as grist to the mill of the emerging manga industry might support the impression that it remained a minority, if no longer entirely elite interest.

Change was in the air, however. The year 1964 saw the Tokyo Olympics and the widespread adoption of colour TV, and 1967 the broadcasting of the 'Big Three in Japan' by the TV station TBS, showing Arnold Palmer, Jack Nicklaus and Gary Player as they demonstrated just how good one could look on the green carpet of the golf course (Tanaka, 1992, p. 107). The following year, the inauguration of the Japan Women's Open introduced a new factor into the media equation. Women remained the main attraction of golf on TV for the next few years, until the emergence of the out-sized figure of Jumbo Ozaki in the early 1970s (Tanaka, 1992, pp. 124–25), and were a useful source of revenue for much longer, though not yet as consumers themselves. Golf Digest's World Ladies Golf Calendar was produced for the first time in 1975. The photographs of foreign female pros in mini-skirts seem to have excited enough interest for the proceeds to have paid for a new building for the company, and they remain in demand today (Interview, June 2009). The previous year had also seen the publication of the first golf-themed manga in a general-interest magazine (Fujiko, 1975–79), but there remained a gap between the various aspirations of viewers and readers, as encouraged and reflected on screen and page, and the material world of building courses and swinging clubs.

By the end of the 1960s, however, opportunities for bridging the gap were expanding. The accumulating profits of Japanese companies required investment outlets; the shift away from older industries demanded that land be turned to new uses. Reminiscing in 2008 with Shima Kōsaku, the manga phenomenon whose own 25-year ascent to company president was at least smoothed, if not enabled, by his golf prowess, Asō Tarō recalled his own experience as head of Asō Cement converting mines to golf courses (Asō, 2008). (Neither the conversation nor the company history published at the time mentioned the wartime forced labour that continues to haunt what is now the Asō Iizuka Golf Club.) By the 1970s, a tipping point had been reached. For one interviewee who worked in Osaka, the 1970 Expo saw the beginning of a shift from golf as a monopoly of company executives to something played by middle management (Interview, December 2007). The statistics support the contention of a rapid expansion in both the playing population and the number of courses. The steady growth of the first boom had continued through the 1960s, with an increase of some 1.5 million rounds per year, but the early 1970s saw a sudden spike, taking the total rounds from 20.5 million in 1970 to 41.7 million in 1975. New courses soon followed, with over 100 being built every year from 1973 to 1976, taking the total number from 773 to 1,228 (Tanaka, 1992, pp. 98–99; see also Table 12.1).

Not all the increase in demand for golf can have been corporate. There was a general shift in the 1970s away from older uses for the countryside, such as hunting, to the newer hobby of golf (Interview, May 2008). But the supply was calibrated to meet a corporate demand, producing a particular kind of course and a particular kind of golf. As for the former, courses were not designed to challenge the pro, but to flatter the executive hacker with a 24 handicap. This meant crafting holes that were difficult to par, but easy to birdie, so raising the possibility that even the company president might play to his potential, if not beyond; putting bunkers within driving distance, for instance, was a no-go, whatever the club professional might have wanted (Interview, December 2007). The golf itself, after all, was only one part of a complete package. Everyone arrived at the same time, played at the same time and had lunch together. Coordinating the whole operation took some doing, in as much as only four golfers could tee off on the first or the tenth at any one time. But the day was facilitated by female company, carrying the bags around the course and bringing the food and drink in the restaurant. The impression was only intensified by the grandeur of the clubhouse, designed by a famous architect if possible, so that the amount of time spent on the day was made worthwhile by the exclusivity of the surroundings. In other words, this was *settai gorufu*, golf as corporate entertainment, where membership at a club, more often than not owned by one's company and not too far from one's work, was part of the remuneration package, and where playing the game was subsidiary to the corporate bonds and business relationships that were thereby strengthened (Interview, November 2007). Golf was perhaps the counterpart of the company training long ago identified by Tom Rohlen and others as central to the creation of the white-collar class; work and play were both disciplined, corporate concerns, annexing what might look as if it should have been consumption to the interests of capital (Rohlen, 1979).

The boom in the 1970s, however, was only a small indication of what was to come. The history of the period is sometimes caricatured as a shift from the high growth of the 1960s, driven by industry and exports, to what would become a boom in the 1980s, catalysed by consumerism. As the above may suggest, the contrast is overdone; domestic, somewhat captive, demand had always been an important part of the post-war equation, although its visibility certainly increased as the objects of its desire became more conspicuous. Rather, the boom perhaps revealed how hard it was to rein in those desires, to redirect the channels of investment and construction, habit and presentation, given the mounting surpluses of savings and foreign exchange and the absence of any effective constraint. In golf, the numbers of courses and users continued to tick upwards in the late 1970s and early 1980s. By 1983 there were just under 1,500 courses in Japan, seeing some 63 million rounds a year (Tanaka, 1992, pp. 98–99). Then things got out of hand. In part what followed was simply a story of surplus capital seeking decent returns. The supply was such that much of it washed up overseas, flooding prestige golf properties such as Turnberry and Pebble Beach, but perhaps nowhere more strikingly than in Hawaii, where at one point every course on Maui was Japanese-owned (Interview, February 2008). In Japan itself, however, irrational investment became outright speculation. This was fostered by Prime Minister Nakasone's attempts to prop up the economy in the wake of the upward valuation of the yen under the Plaza Accords of 1985, most significantly in the form of the notorious Resort Law. Low interest rates, government funds, land privatisation and weakened regulations prompted a flood of investment into shady ventures, not least by local governments and criminal syndicates. The subsequent attempt, under Prime Minister Takeshita, to revive the rural economy with a 100 million yen grant to all local authorities only exacerbated the lemming-like stampede. By 1989, there were over 1,700 courses in Japan, with another 325 under construction and 983 in their planning stages, together with a total of 4,790 ranges, which would increase to nearly 6,000 the following year. Golf courses alone became a trillion-dollar industry in 1988. One year later, courses and ranges generated a market worth some 1.663 trillion yen, to which the golf equipment industry added another 237 billion (Tanaka, 1992, pp. 98–99, 144–45, 184–92). It was no surprise that by this point golf was also a prime target for an environmentalist critique that accused the courses of destroying the archipelago (Yamada, 1989).

Supply was part of the story, therefore, but it was overwhelmed by demand. Throughout the 1980s, apart from 1983 and 1985, Japan's courses saw an increase of over 5 per cent per annum in the total of rounds played. In 1989, this amounted to almost 90 million rounds, added to which were the 135 million individual uses of driving ranges. Practising on the range was the seventh most popular leisure activity in the country, playing on a course the fifteenth. Nearly 26 per cent of men were habitués of the range (23 per cent of a course), including over 30 per cent of those in their 30s and 40s, and golf still led all others as the sport which men wanted to take up (Tanaka, 1992, pp. 92, 98–99, 143). The ravening hordes enabled all kinds of excess. Just as golf course development had invited infusions of unaccountable capital, so golf club membership became a target for speculation (Figure 12.2). It was no surprise that the Nikkei stock exchange index should have created an index of membership prices, nor that this should have seen a nearly eight-fold increase between 1982 and 1990. The aggregate concealed all kinds of variation, of course. At the top end, a club like Aqualine, an hour southeast of Tokyo, could charge the equivalent of almost $135,000 as a joining fee, while still under construction. The objective was to have as few members and to be as luxurious as possible. It was no wonder that memberships and even rounds soon became a useful bait with which to tempt politicians and bureaucrats, and so a leitmotif of political scandals from the Recruit scandal of 1989 to the present. The pre-sale tactic was a general one, but elsewhere, the strategy was to maximise the return by selling as many memberships as possible. The problems that arose from such a system had been evident from the 1960s, but by the late 1980s the situation was out of hand. In some places, clubs had over 20,000 members, meaning that it was almost impossible for most to play the course. At Gatsubi Golf Club in Shizuoka things got so bad that the disgruntled members formed an association to protect their rights (Tanaka, 1992, pp. 194–205).

Much evidence suggests that, by the end of the 1980s, golf had spread beyond the corporation to become an object of desire more generally. Golf manga became commonplace, holding out the possibility that even an overweight junior high school student from the wrong side of the tracks might end up beating Nicklaus in the Open at St Andrews, albeit this did not happen until volume 58 (Chiba, [1981–92] 1995–96). Meanwhile, the late Chūsonji Yutsuko created the *oyaji gyāru*, the ball-busting, take-no-prisoners office lady, whose resistance to office norms was signaled by her free-wheeling adoption of the obsessive habits of her male superiors, including smoking, drinking and, not least, golf (Chūsonji, 1989–92). Despite the dreams of popular culture, however,

Figure 12.2 A golf club membership trader in downtown Kyoto

Business was not good by 2007, when this photograph was taken. The continuing existence of such exchanges, however, suggests the extent to which golf in the post-war period became not only an experience to be consumed, but an asset to be exploited. The purchase of a good, here, becomes not the final stage in a product's life, but a moment in an ongoing cycle.

Source: Photograph by author.

the average consumer remained a salaryman of 39 years old, with an income of 6.1 million yen, a wife and a child, and an allowance of 50,000 yen per month, almost all of which went on the 1.5 rounds and 4 practices at the range that he allowed himself (Tanaka, 1992, p. 208). More generally, the extent to which demand outpaced supply meant that even if golf could be consumed at various price points (none of them reasonable by international comparison), there was little incentive to change the product itself – or indeed to provide a public alternative. There were only 27 public courses out of the 1,722 total in 1990 (Tanaka, 1992, p. 140). Golf remained the privatised, corporatised product that had emerged over the previous eight decades, a very prescribed kind of consumption, with female caddies, mandatory lunches and largely male patrons.

Bust

And then the wheels came off. The broad narrative is a familiar one, given what we know of the past two 'lost' decades. Already in 1990, there was a slight downturn, with 400,000 fewer rounds and 1.1 million fewer practices than the year before (Tanaka, 1992, p. 142). The following year saw perhaps the most notorious revelation of the shifting sands on which the whole edifice had been constructed. The company behind Ibaraki Country Club had pre-sold memberships, promising to limit the total to 2,830 (still a bloated roll by the standards of many clubs elsewhere in the world). In fact, however, the developer sold over 52,000 memberships, channeling the 100 billion yen thus acquired to associated companies. The course was never completed, the company went bankrupt and the main defendant was given 11 years and fined 700 million yen for his troubles, a fair exchange, perhaps, for a take of nearly 15 billion and tax avoidance of nearly 6 billion (Tanaka, 1992, pp. 193–95). Despite the warning signs, it took some time for the house of cards to collapse fully. The Nikkei membership index had halved by 1992, as the slump in the property market brought the speculative trade in memberships to a grinding halt, but for most of the 1990s, golf club bankruptcies hovered in the single figures, with total liabilities running under 5 billion yen. Then, at the end of the decade, the problem exploded, with 27 bankruptcies in 1999, 25 in 2000, 57 in 2001 and 98 (with liabilities of over 30 billion yen) in 2002. The problems continued through the rest of the decade. In 2005, there were 71 bankruptcies, with over 14 billion yen in liabilities, while even in 2009, there were 26 bankruptcies, so that, although total liabilities had again subsided to under 5 billion yen, fully 33.6 per cent of the then 2,356 courses in Japan were in administration (Tsubaki Gorufu, 2010a and 2010b). Given the over-supply, it was no surprise that construction too came to a halt. The year 2007 saw the opening of the first new golf course in Japan in nearly a decade (Interview, September 2007).

The trail of destruction, however, proved fertile ground both for new players and for new ways of playing the game. It was American vultures that were the first to take the initiative, Ripplewood Holdings swooping early in the new millennium to buy out the hubristic Seagaia resort in Kyūshū, over extended after acquiring a bank and a record label known for its catalogue of sentimental Japanese songs (Cullen, 2002; *The Economist* 2002). However, it was soon overtaken by slightly more established, though no less ravenous beasts. By the end of the decade, the two largest portfolios were held by Goldman Sachs, operating as Accordia, and Lone Star, a Texas-based investment firm, operating as Pacific Golf Management. Both saw past the highly leveraged position of many bubble-era courses to the positive cash flow, averaging the equivalent of US$1 million a year, which most were generating. Buying the debt at a nominal price put them in a position to negotiate with the various stakeholders, repaying the banks some 20 to 30 per cent of their holdings and the long-suffering members only 2.5 per cent of their investment. Not everyone was happy and many chose to walk away. The Nikkei began to creep upwards again from the middle of the decade, but remained at less than 10 per cent of its 1990 peak towards the end of the decade (Harden, 2008; Hyūga, 2006). Nonetheless, for those who chose to remain, the new owners also began to provide a new kind of product.

At Aqualine, even in the mid-1990s, when the writing should have been on the wall, having paid one's massive joining fee, one was expected to submit to the familiar rigmarole of corporate golf. 'We didn't realise that there is an alternative to everyone arriving at the same time, playing at the same time and having lunch together.' Following Goldman's purchase of the club in 2005, course maintenance and food have both improved, while the cost of a round for non-members has halved. Most important, perhaps, you can start to play more-or-less when you want, you don't have to stop for lunch and you don't have to hire a caddy. You can even drive a cart on to the fairway. It has become conceivable, if not always achievable, for a round of golf to take less than an entire day (Harden, 2008). It is not only the Americans, however, who have understood the potential for changing the game. Golf Digest Online (GDO), an offshoot of Japan's largest golf-related publisher, has also gone into the business of making golf accessible to a larger audience, by acting as an intermediary between a huge number of clubs and an increasing number of customers (Figure 12.3). Its rationale for doing so points to older scruples that may still govern the consumption of golf: for the club, to admit their eagerness to cater to visitors would be to damage their special relationship with the existing membership; for the visitor, to call a club directly and to be asked whether one is a member is to risk awkwardness. For both sides, the use of an intermediary provides a solution, as well as a nice source of earnings for GDO itself (Interview, March 2008). The technology through which it operates, the number of courses to which it can provide access, and the range of other goods available online also suggest a new consumer orientation in the world of Japanese golf.

Figure 12.3 The website of *Golf Digest Online*

As the textual density, particularly the number of tabs near the top of the page, suggests, the company makes it possible to consume almost anything connected to golf. The top-level blue tabs, from left to right, take one to the home page; a golf shop (for equipment); a golf course reservation service; golf news; advice on the latest golf fashions; a travel service; 'MY GDO', which provides access to the members' part of the website; lessons and tips on technique; 'community', which provides a place to write a diary, create a golf 'circle', and exchange information and 'memories'; a place to keep track of and analyse your scores; and finally, information from, and an opportunity to subscribe to, the various Golf Digest magazines.

Source: Photograph courtesy of *Golf Digest Online*.

Such an orientation is essential for the golf industry, no less than for any other sector, if it is to sustain the demand for its various products in the face of falling discretionary incomes and ongoing demographic decline. It is not enough to cater to the traditional male market, particularly given the well-documented cost cutting by most companies and the anecdotal unwillingness of many younger employees to give up their weekends to play interminable rounds alongside the colleagues with whom they spend the rest of the week. Courses, manufacturers and publishers are searching for new markets, promoting younger role models like the internationally successful young golfer and 'bashful Prince' Ishikawa Ryō, emphasising the family-friendly fun to be had at made-over resorts, and above all targeting women. While 23.6 per cent of men already played golf in 1996, only 5.8 per cent of women had picked up a club. Declining participation rates over the following decade further suggest the urgent need to explore new markets (Amano Keizai Kenkyūjo, 2008, pp. 445–46). And so the past few years have seen a wave of initiatives and publications inviting women to play the game. The serried ranks of green-jacketed course guides and technical manuals that distinguish the well-populated golf section in most bookstores are now complemented by a small but growing number of introductory guides, more often than not bound in pink. Many golf magazines have a 'ladies' corner' (*redisu senyō kōnā*) and most fashion magazines carry regular golf-related features, while *Regina* leads the pack of golf magazines targeted explicitly at women. Some of these include at least some emphasis on playing the game. Elsewhere, performance and turnout are emphasised as elements in the requisite repertoire of a professional young woman on the golf course. More often than not, however, golf is merely an excuse for other kinds of consumption, above all of fashion but also of food, travel and perhaps even love. Equipment as accessory course as backdrop, golf becomes another stage on which to craft the cute quasi-cosmopolitan self at home in the commodified world. As *Regina* memorably put it, when describing the joys of 'romantic golf in Hawaii', 'no love, no golf, no life' (*Regina*, 2008, p. 14).

In conclusion

What does all this say about consumption and everyday life? Golf of course cannot be perceived as a staple, like sugar or rice, however much the needs for these might have been manufactured during the process of modernisation. Golf is not a necessity, like clothing or medicine, although the transformation of the former into fashion and the commodification of the latter suggest a common mechanism that also worked to promote the practice of golf. Nor is golf part of the material infrastructure – of rail, mail, and long-distance retail – through which the modern consumer came into being. Golf is discretionary at best, more likely marginal to the grand narrative of Japanese consumption.

Figure 12.4 The front cover of *Regina*, a ‘golf fashion magazine in which ♥ blossoms’, Spring 2008

That the emphasis is on fashion rather than on playing is clear from the wooden club being used as a prop by the model on the right. (The pink-orange ball is functional, but, more importantly, coordinated with both sets of earrings.) The first three headlines in order of size read, ‘turbulent brand fever 72 [topics] for spring 2008’; ‘spring accessories are [all about] colour, colour, colour’; and ‘golf can’t begin if there’s no love’.

Source: Photograph courtesy of Alba.

But golf is also telling, albeit of a story that may already be quite familiar. At the macro level, golf reminds us that consumption was always part of the economic equation in modern Japan, even as its objects became more prominent – golf courses replacing heavy industry – as production moved offshore and spending became more discretionary following the first two decades of high economic growth. At the micro level, however, golf cautions us against an over-hasty celebration of the liberated consumer, suggesting the extent to which even seeming luxuries could be prescribed and made to serve a corporate, if not quite corporatist, agenda. Golf in Japan seems to have been consumed not so much for the joy of playing the game, although an extensive literature on the epiphanic experience of a well-struck long iron might argue otherwise; rather, playing the game provided and provides access to a particular kind of space – for speculation, interaction and performance – through which to fashion an appropriate self, equal to the demands of company, career, even love. (The latter is, of course, no less rigorous in its requirements of conformity, discipline and practice.) This space for much of the past century was of course the club rather than the course, the pantomime exertions on the course counterbalanced by the well-heeled ease of the nineteenth hole to provide a convincing stage for the sophisticated man of leisure. As such, golf in Japan underpins Daniel Miller's argument for a turn away from the liberal emphasis on individual choice to a Hegelian acknowledgment of the interaction between consuming subject and consumed object subsequent to the moment of choosing (Miller, 1987). What is striking in Japan, perhaps, is the limited nature of the choices that were available for much of the twentieth century. If you wanted to play golf, you had to be a member, you had to pay a lot, you had to stop for lunch and you had to use a caddy. That model proved unsustainable, and more recently the choices have appeared to multiply, but it still seems hard to claim that golf is any less prescribed. The complexities of online booking, the necessity for the latest clubs and kit, the re-iteration of rules and etiquette and the torrent of technical advice (about everything from swing to slope, stretching to diet) make it quite clear that there is a right way to play the game. Meanwhile the female caddies who continue to help and applaud customers, as they navigate the virtual fairways of golf bars in downtown Tokyo, are evidence that it will take some time for older habits to die (Tharkrar, 2008). To suggest that the Japanese consumer historically has had little say in how he or she might play golf is not necessarily to revert to a productivist account of political economy, much less to a familiar indictment of missing subjectivity, long the holy grail of post-war intellectuals, but it does point to the way in which a crowded island and corporatist growth have left little room for the awkwardness which some would say should characterise the game.

References

Amano Keizai Kenkyūjo (2008) *Gorufu Sangyō Hakusho* (White Paper on the Golf Industry), Tokyo: Amano Keizai Kenkyūjo.

Anon. (1957) 'Post-war Revival in Japanese Golf', *USGA Journal and Turf Management*, 10, 12–13.

Asō, T. (2008) 'Nihon yo Genki o Dase' (Japan Cheer up!), *Shūkan Asahi*, 113(26), pp. 26–29.

Chiba, T. ([1981–92] 1995–96) *Ashita Tenki ni na are* (Good Weather Tomorrow), 36 vols, Hōmusha.

Choice (2008) 'Konoe Fumitaka' (Konoe Fumitaka), 163, March, pp. 114–27.

Chūsonji, Y. (1989–92) *Suīto Supotto* (Sweet Spot), 8 vols, Fusōsha.

Cullen, L. T. (2002) 'Foreign Invaders', *Time*, March. Accessed 15 July 2010: http://www.time.com/time/magazine/article/0,9171,214144,00.html

Fujiko, F. (1975–1979), *Puro Gorufā Saru* (Pro Golfer Monkey), 19 vols, Tokyo: Shōgakkan.

Harden, B. (2008) 'US Firm's Deft Play Helps Japanese Golf Out of Rough', *Washington Post*, 15 June.

Hirayama, T. (1951) 'Gorufu' (Golf), *Kankō*, 38, pp. 17–18.

Hyuga, T. (2006) 'Goldman Plans IPO for Golf Unit in Japan', *Bloomberg News*, 25 September. Accessed 15 July 2010: http://www.bloomberg.com/apps/news?pid=newsarchive&sid=aqSGKlzB2yEc&refer=worldwide_news

Koganei Kantorī Kurabu (1990) *Koganei Kantorī Kurabu Gojūnenshi* (Fifty Year History of Koganei Country Club), Tokyo: Koganei Kantōrī Kurabu.

Kubota, S. (2004) *Nihon no Gorufu 100-nen* (Hundred Years of Golf in Japan), Nihon Keizai Shinbunsha.

Lockyer, A. (2010) 'Arthur Hesketh Groom (1846–1918): Emblematic Edwardian, Compulsive Clubman, Accidental Ancestor' in Cortazzi, H. (ed.) *Britain and Japan: Biographical Portraits, Volume VII*, Folkestone: Global Oriental.

McFarland, H. N. (1960), 'The New Religions of Japan', *Contemporary Religions in Japan*, 1(3), pp. 30–39.

Miller, D. (1987), *Material Culture and Mass Consumption*, Oxford: Blackwell.

Mowa, S. (1977) *Nihon Gorufu 60-Nen Shi* (Sixty Years of Golf in Japan), Tokyo: Bēsubōru Magajin-sha.

Regina (2008), 'LOVE o fukumeru rakuen GOLF ♥ dēto', Spring Edition.

Rohlen, T. P. (1979) *For Harmony and Strength: Japanese White-Collar Organization in Anthropological Perspective*, Berkeley, CA: University of California Press.

Tanaka, Y. (1992) *Gorufu to Nihonjin* (Golf and the Japanese), Tokyo: Iwanami Shoten.

Tharkrar, R. (2008) 'Get into Golf's Virtual Swing', *Japan Times*, 15 June.

The Economist (2002) 'Vulture's-eye view', 21 December, 105.

Tsubaki Gorufu (2010) 'Gorufujō no Hōteki Seiri, Fusai Sōkaku (Legal Restructuring of Golf Courses, Aggregate Debt) (1997–2009 nen). Accessed 15 July 2010: http://www.mmjp.or.jp/tubaki-golf/newsfail/1news.html.

Tsubaki Gorufu (2010b) 'Baburu Hōkai Ikō kara Kotoshi Sangatsu made Zenkoku Hōteki Seiri Gorufujō wa 800 Kōsu' (Following the Bursting of the Bubble until March this Year 800 Golf Courses Nationally under Legal Restructuring). Accessed 15 July 2010: http://www.mmjp.or.jp/tubaki-golf/newsfail/2010/0421-hoteki-zennkoku.html

Yamada, K. (1989) *Gorufujō Bōkokuron* (On a Nation without Golf Courses), Tokyo: Shinhyōron.

Yamaguchi, H. (1997) *Yamaguchi Hōshun: Shin Nihonga e no Kiseki* (Yamaguchi Hōshun: The Course to New Japanese Prints), Tokyo: Yamaguchi Hōshun Kinenkan.

13

History and the Study of Consumerism: A Historian of the West Looks to Japan

Beverly Lemire

Introduction

For generations, histories of the West were infused with assumptions of that region's exceptionalism – exceptionalism in culture, politics and economy. This powerful underlying narrative shaped analyses and directed research, while many unwarrantable claims remained untested for generations. As a hypothesis, it was a by-product of the unprecedented imperial expansion of Western powers in the nineteenth and twentieth centuries, along with exceptional industrial growth, both concurrent with the expansion of the Western academy. Disciplines such as history developed within this political milieu. And academics commonly echoed the dominant discourses of their age.

Thus the often-triumphal histories of Western nations or industries shaped the parameters of historical enquiries, even as the thematic foci evolved. For example, in 1835 Edward Baines claimed that 'the Cotton Manufacture of England presents a spectacle unparalleled in the annals of industry' (Baines, 1835). The histories of this subject that followed mirrored many of the precepts of this early writer, the cotton industry becoming emblematic of Western industrial prowess. Indeed, no systematic attempts were made at broad comparative assessments of the cotton trade from a global perspective for over a century and a half.[1] Thus historians focused intently on the seemingly unique features of Western industrial development, some identifying cultural or religious

[1] The first wide-ranging comparative work was Farnie, 2004, to be followed by Riello and Parthasarathi, 2009.

factors as key to industrial growth, others celebrating claims of unique local genius for the achievements of a nation or region (Goody, 2006).

This intellectual vantage point gradually lost its dominant position in the wake of the seismic transformations of the later twentieth and early twenty-first centuries that arose out of intellectual struggles for a more comprehensive view of the historical past. In the post-colonial world, inspiration came from the new comparative perspectives of world and global history, which placed regional histories within a wider analytical calculus, producing new interpretations of past events. The process of re-examination and revision is still underway, providing the opportunity to discern comparable and unique paths over the course of human history. Assumptions are being challenged and histories recast, although not without controversy. However, many more historians now subscribe to Steven Runciman's assertion, made decades ago, that 'our [Western] civilization has grown...out of the long sequence of interaction and fusion between Orient and Occident' (quoted in Dalrymple, 2005, p. x).

In this short commentary, I will consider the particular history of consumerism that began as a thematic focus within Western precincts and the changes now underway in the study of this subject. This marks the conclusion of a singular project on Japanese consumption that adds to the rethinking of historical categories and historical practice. The chapters presented here represent a contribution not simply to a specific national history of consumerism in nineteenth- and twentieth-century Japan, but to the wider alterations underway within contemporary history more generally.

Reconsidering historical traditions: from production to consumption

Jack Goody has been a long-time critic of the claims for Western exceptionalism, disputing the central thesis that 'Europe was (always?) at the centre of innovations'. He points to the presence of this hypothesis as an organising principle even in such magisterial works as Fernand Braudel's three-volume survey of the rise of capitalism *Civilization and Capitalism*, a work that inspired and informed generations (Goody, 2006, p. 184). Goody charges Braudel, among others, with 'the theft of history', noting that Braudel 'accepts an important number of Western propositions about East–West differences relating to its growth'. Goody notes that the past painted from this perspective was seen solely through a European lens, thereby producing profound distortions. In Goody's words, 'the past is conceptualized and presented according to what happened on the provincial scale of Europe, often Western Europe, and then imposed upon the rest of the world' (Goody, 2006, p. 182). Regional experiences within Europe were represented as the ideal against which all others were judged.

This account of the exceptional 'rise of the West' was likewise exemplified by many histories of British or Western industrialisation that equated the first trade in industrial products or the first industrial nation as necessarily the apogee of this phenomenon. Indeed it was typical that, in accounts of the history of the industrialisation of the cotton trade in Britain, India was mentioned, if at all, only in passing. On the contrary, no recognition was offered of India's technological achievements or its global role over millennia in developing and supplying markets for cotton textiles. The opportunity for enhanced material lives in the West was typically associated, in this context, with the factory production of the industrial era. There was too little recognition of the debt owed to Asia as the source of the plethora of manufactures that poured into Europe after 1500, or of the creative Asian technical and commercial systems that responded so deftly to world markets before 1800. Asia's commodities set the benchmark for popular consumer wares and were pivotal catalysts in Europe's development (Finlay, 1998; 2010). To the extent that India appeared at all in these histories, it was typically presented as a region in decline, one that had stood still in contrast to the technological developments in the West.[2] However, historians of Asia are uncovering a past that is at odds with the assumptions and precepts of earlier European scholarship, travel literature and colonial accounts. The results of these revisionist histories are transforming our understanding of both Asia and Europe (Parthasarathi, 1998, pp. 105–6).

The histories of international production, trade and consumption are more complex, and world regions are much less fixed in their relationships with each other, than some have supposed; nor has the balance always favoured Western Eurasia, as has often been assumed. As Jack Goody notes, 'what is clear is that the superior achievements of the West

[2] Prasannan Parthasarathi is one of the contemporary historians revising our understanding of the comparative standing of Britain and India, offering the first systematic assessment of the standard of living of textile workers in South India and Britain. His findings – that eighteenth-century textile workers in South India had a higher standard of living than English textile workers – challenge long-held assumptions and reflect the creative potential of comparative studies of this sort. See Parthasarathi, 1998; 2011.

can no longer be seen as permanent or even long-standing features of those cultures but as the result of one of the swings of the pendulum that has affected those societies over the millennia' (Goody, 1996, p. 7). Indeed, Kenneth Pomeranz argues that the 'Great Divergence' in economic fortunes between East and West occurred after 1800. Only in the early nineteenth century did levels of economic growth in Northwest Europe surpass those of other dynamic regions of Southeast China and Japan. As a number of contributors have noted above, Pomeranz offers an important new perspective on the question of Western growth, with comparative interpretations that point to comparable growth and material change in the most prominent of the world's regions up to 1800 (Pomeranz, 2000).

Pomeranz, like other agnostics, questions the existence of a 'consumer revolution' in Europe prior to 1850 (Pomeranz, 2000, p. 119). However he does acknowledge the value of assessing features of fashion that distinguish European and Asian societies. His speculations on the possible significance of fashion's appearance in China are worth repeating here, as fashion is such a generative and vital indication of societal change. Pomeranz writes of an 'important period' in the rise of fashion in the 'late sixteenth and early seventeenth centuries, in which the growing uncertainties and frustrations of official career paths seem to have encouraged a search among elites for other life activities ... that did not depend as directly on the state-sponsored examination system. This quest, plus growing private wealth, helped fuel ... the rise of fashion' (Pomeranz, 2000, p. 154). Augmented spending outside elite circles – spending on often ephemeral material goods charged with meaning – constitutes an ingredient of social change that some have termed the development of consumer society (Thirsk, 1978). Debates continue as to the precise chronology and nature of these changes, particularly given the regional variations in the timing and characteristics of these events, but positioning Asian experiences within this chronology is a vital element in this wider project.

The history of consumption is a subject that has had enormous influence in the past three decades, linking domestic and personal practice to larger issues of production, distribution, retailing and fashion. Scholars who first interrogated these issues were based in Atlantic-world universities and focused on those regions exclusively. As a consequence of their numbers and energies, findings quickly emerged within this new field focused on European or North American communities. Researchers approached the old question of the standard of living of non-elites from this new vantage point, considering the pre-industrial as well as the industrial period, and the rural as well as the urban population. Through the accumulation of data from probate inventories, it soon became clear that substantial changes in material life predated the industrial era, the effects evident for many regions of Western Europe and colonial North America.[3]

For example, Lorna Weatherill's ground-breaking work, based on a large database of probate inventories, traced the expanded ownership of key consumer goods, such as clocks, books, ceramics, mirrors, window curtains and various furnishings. Weatherill examined evidence from heterogeneous social communities in England and Scotland between 1660 and 1760. The data she amassed revealed the accelerating growth in ownership of these items over time, most notably among urban commercial populations, with telling regional differences reflected in, for instance, a far more austere material environment in Scotland than in Southern England. Weatherill's most significant finding was that the consumer hierarchy and the social hierarchy were not identical. There were some obvious commonalities between these two phenomena, and wealthier gentry had the means to own quantities of new goods sooner than other sectors, with many from this group indulging in that way. However, urban tradesmen likewise owned key commodities in significantly higher quantities than did rural dwellers of comparable wealth (Weatherill, 1988, p. 185). Joan Thirsk was another of the first generation of historians to address the genesis of consumer culture in England, focusing on the expansion of trade in consumer goods over the 1600s, which facilitated the spread of new commodities and the emergence of new customers among the common folk. The new industries she described not only produced a wider range of affordable niceties, such as lace, hosiery, pins and combs, but also augmented opportunities for employment, particularly among women and children. Thirsk uncovered the wealth of cheap goods being produced, inexpensive ephemeral wares that appealed to a seemingly boundless clientele. Importantly, she observed 'the magnificent range of choice available to the customer in seventeenth-century England ... and the influence different classes of customers exerted upon producers' (Thirsk, 1978, p. 107). Thirsk discerned in the aggregate of these modest trades and humble customers a powerful alliance of interests.

These developing social and economic practices opened up new sources of profit for investors, enhanced the income of plebeian families

---

[3] For the use of probate inventories to track transformations in consumption see, for example, Weatherill, 1988; Bauland, Schuurman and Servais, 1988; Shammas, 1990; Carson, Hoffman and Albert 1994; and especially Carr and Walsh, 1994.

and generated a growing inventory of affordable items for local and overseas markets. In combination, these factors unleashed what many accept as a consumer 'revolution', although the date and features of that phenomenon continue to be debated and refined for the various regions of Europe and the Atlantic world, as well as, now, for parts of Asia too.[4] Historians uncovered an expanding desire for goods among the peoples of the North Atlantic world and these findings informed histories of production and international trade, generating insights into the driving forces that sustained this enterprise.[5] Most recently, Jan de Vries has tracked 'the transformation of consumer desire' through the long eighteenth century, noting the composite structural changes underway in Northwest Europe and colonial North America (de Vries, 2008, pp. 1–39). Indeed, he posits that consumer demand was a key factor in what he terms an 'industrious revolution', a precursor to industrialisation. This is characterised by new behaviour among plebeian households, whereby they reorganised their time and priorities in order to increase their capacities to purchase more of the new goods becoming available through the seventeenth and eighteenth centuries. Women and children from such families redirected their energies to secure an improved material life (de Vries, 1993; 2008).[6] In sum, the focus on transformative consumer practices recast the narrative of Western development and cultural change from the early-modern to the modern era. Researchers continue to refine these findings.

However, this scholarship was not without its critics. In particular, some felt that the widely reviewed volume *Consumption and the World of Goods* (Brewer and Porter, 1993), which showcased some of the early research, made global claims for the nature of the 'world of goods' that sat uneasily on its scholarly base. Peter Burke offered one of the earliest and most cogent critiques of this volume, its title and underlying premise.

---

[4] McKendrick, Brewer and Plumb (1983) claimed the birth of consumer society for eighteenth-century England but in subsequent years alternative regions and time periods have been cited as reflecting commercialised fashions and consumerism. The claims for commercialisation in the 1700s remain among those most consistently critiqued elements of this work, along with McKendrick's emphasis on trickle-down fashions. See McKendrick, Brewer and Plumb, 1983; Shammas, 1990 and Welch, 2005. For new work on consumerism in Asia see, for example, Finnane, 1996 and 2008; Dwyer and Pinney, 2001; McGowan,2006; Haynes, McGowan, Roy and Yanagisawa, 2009.

[5] For works considering the colonial world see, for example, Breen, 1986 and 2004; Martin, 2008.

[6] For a new perspective on this topic involving both trade and social and cultural change in Britain see Berg, 2005.

Burke was a contributor to this collection and presented one of only two contributions from outside the Western sphere. A European specialist, Burke nonetheless looked outside that region and assessed the changing representations of conspicuous consumption among elites, as revealed in the literature of the age, comparing Italian and Japanese sources from the sixteenth to the eighteenth century. He insisted that 'historians of Europe will never be able to say what is specifically western unless they look outside the west' (Burke, 1993, p. 148). Burke sought to build on the work of Fernand Braudel, whose attempted comparative survey had relatively little extra-European research to hand. Importantly, Braudel championed the significance of fashion and consumerism as indicators of societal transformations. However, Braudel claimed that fashion and rising consumerism had an exclusively Western provenance, during the time in the early-modern world when, in his view, the material culture of other great societies like China, Japan, India and Ottoman Turkey 'stood still' (Braudel, 1985, pp. 312–13). Burke was sceptical of this untested claim, undertaking comparative research into Japanese sources the like of which Braudel had not attempted. Burke quickly found suggestive commonalities among European and Japanese elite practices, and he noted the importance of the fact that 'an increasing concern with material culture can be found in the literature of Europe and Asia, between the late sixteenth and the late eighteenth centuries' (Burke, 1993, p. 157). Burke's hope was that regional specialists would refine his generalised observations in the future and uncover those features of consumerism particular to Asia or extant in various forms in many societies. His wish is now being fulfilled.

However, in the interim, Western-oriented scholarship continued to dominate the field of consumer history numerically and theoretically. One result was the publication of surveys, such as that by Peter Stearns, who also assumed consumerism to be a Western creation, only later 'exported' to other regions of the world with the development of regional, modern economies and the 'export' of industrialisation.[7] The list of those who unthinkingly subscribed to the doctrine of Western exceptionalism in the rise of consumerism is long, and includes many who are otherwise thoughtful on points of analysis.

Equally troubling has been the continuing insistence that fashion, too, was an innovation of the West, with no attempt made to

[7] With slight caveats, this is pretty much the picture painted by Stearns in his introduction to the study of world consumerism (Stearns, 2001, p. i). The second edition of this book does not substantially change this perspective.

investigate or contextualise this assertion. For example, editors of a recently published academic reader on fashion state baldly at the outset that 'Fashion was born in Europe and it developed there' (Welters and Lillethun, 2007).[8] The French literary scholar Joan Dejean followed in this well-worn track with an even narrower claim, insisting that fashion was a uniquely French invention (Dejean, 2005). She made no effort to glance across Europe's borders for contrary evidence, never mind consider Asian innovations. Regional specialists confuse the robust expressions of consumerism or fashion in one society with a monopoly on its invention. Marco Belfanti continues the debate about fashion's origins in Europe, a topic that will animate research in the years to come.[9] Fashion systems generated new practices of consumption, new material priorities and new economic opportunities for both elite and plebeian populations. These systems typically flourished amidst dynamic urban commercial societies, and they are recognised as a critical adjunct of consumer culture by a range of historians (see for example Berg, 2005; Allman, 2004; Brekke, 2006; Lemire, 2010). More research is necessary to craft a full chronology of where and when fashion systems arose in various societies and the discrete or common features of their emergence, but to begin by precluding the very existence of fashion systems outside the West shuts a vital avenue of enquiry and distorts our potential understanding of comparative historical processes.[10] There is now a greater attention paid to the multiplicity of consumer practices playing out within many societies, along with recognition of the contingent forces of fashion as these evolved within discrete regions.

---

8 A similar assumption of Western exceptionalism also underpins the work of Lipovetsky, 1994, particularly chapter 1.

9 Belfanti's conclusion is that 'fashion was not a European invention, but it first fully developed as a social institution in Europe, while in India, China, and Japan it only evolved partially in pre-modern times, without being able to obtain full social recognition. In the nineteenth century, there was no other fashion than that established in Western society, which was then imposed on the rest of the world, relegating the other clothing traditions to particular niches' (Belfanti, 2008, p. 443).

10 For example, Finnane (2008, p. 8) observes that: 'recent work on Chinese dress in the sixteenth to nineteenth centuries, revisionist in intent, shows evidence of short-term changes in urban fashions, and a high degree of consciousness of their significance'.

The place of Japan in comparative histories of consumption

I was honoured to participate in the symposium that preceded this volume, learning more about Japan's important contributions to the history of consumerism. From my perspective, there are common and distinct features of the Japanese story that will engage generations of scholars in the future. Since Peter Burke's notable intervention, scholars pursuing various research agendas have uncovered more of the characteristics of early modern China, Japan and Europe, noting the economic, legal and cultural elements common (or distinct) to these regions. In 1996, Alan Hunt published a study of sumptuary legislation, seeing, in these attempts at legislated material constraint, important signals of societal change: cultural, material and economic. Hunt likewise pointed to the common features of sumptuary laws in China, Japan and Europe, all designed to restrain social change and inhibit insurgent consumerism among the urban merchant classes. As in the West, silk was a major focus of sumptuary legislation in Japan (Hunt, 1996, pp. 24–25). From my perspective, these regulations highlight the economic and social forces at work within society, and it is improbable that the laws themselves arrested material desires. The plurality of sumptuary regulations suggests active consumer processes, in defiance of tradition. Several years ago I heard Osamu Wakita speak about the recurring sumptuary regulations instituted in Tokugawa Japan.[11] From this and other suggestive comments, I wondered about the repeated iteration of such laws that suggested the failure of authorities to control behaviour, rather than their success. Were the material aspirations at work in early-modern Japan similar to those in Europe at the same time? Were financially successful professionals or distinct occupational groups developing group-specific fashions, contesting or complicating assumptions of hierarchy? Do these pieces of legislation reflect a new material culture and a new mentality among more defiant or ambitious people?

Eiko Ikegami addresses many of these questions, providing a rich depiction of a society in transition, where, as she contends, 'a series of developments in the Japanese economy and urban culture during the seventeenth century led to a remarkable and unexpected phenomenon: the

[11] Unpublished paper presented at the workshop 'Dressing Up Japanese History', 5 September 2007, Peter Wall Institute for Advanced Studies and the Institute for Asian Research, Centre for Japanese Research, University of British Columbia.

rise of popular fashion' (Ikegami, 2005, p. 245). There are important parallels between the Japanese and European experiences, most particularly in the practices of fashion and the manifestations of expanding consumer demand, within which strategic commodities performed similar roles in the articulation of aspirations. New items of clothing or accessories were employed to relay the shifting styles of social or cultural communities. Scholars of Japan, like Ikegami, echo factors similar to those identified by Pomeranz in explaining fashion's rise in sixteenth- and seventeenth-century China. Ikegami notes the importance of cultural alliances among urban groups officially proscribed from prominent positions. Outside the rigid 'status system', 'merchants and other commoners could aspire to the higher reaches of the aesthetic world without risking punishment' (Ikegami, 2005, p. 149). To help establish these 'aesthetic networks', they employed a growing assortment of material goods (imported or manufactured in Japan), purchased and deployed in ways designed to define and distinguish cultural alliances and aspirations. Consumer practices were policed with regulations outlining approved and forbidden material forms – for example, one sumptuary law insisted that '*sumo* wrestlers' loincloths should not be made of silk' (Ikegami 2005, p. 255). Thus, urban men and women manoeuvred through legal thickets, seeking to avoid penalties, while still crafting the appropriate appearance. The attempt to restrict luxuries to designated hierarchies replicated similar efforts throughout Europe; however, the group censured in this particular indictment was quintessentially Japanese, and the social dynamics mirror the distinctions within that society.

Historians of Tokugawa Japan observe the economic changes that spurred consumer experimentation and innovation. Catalyst commodities, like cotton, played critical roles in communities throughout Eurasia, and the fashion ethos animated more and more of the material engagements in parts of this great continent. It is important to recognise the features of popular commodities, like Indian cottons, and the impact they had in new markets for these goods, such as Japan. Dutch East India Company traders had successfully cultivated markets for Indian textiles in Japan since the 1630s, and these textiles poured into the port of Nagasaki in previously unequalled volumes in the later 1600s (Fujita, 2009, p. 184). The physical properties of cotton captivated Japanese people; in practical terms, it was more easily processed and dyed than alternative fibres like hemp and ramie, and physically, its texture and feel offered pleasures unmatched by other materials (Tanimoto, 2009, p. 369). Cotton epitomised what Jan de Vries terms

'New Luxury'. De Vries defines the 'Old Luxury' of jewels, furs and precious metals as marking hierarchies of 'exquisite refinement'. In contrast, 'New Luxury' emphasised 'comfort and pleasure, [and] lent itself to multiplication and diffusion' (De Vries, 2008, p. 44). He further notes the capacities of these new luxury products 'to communicate cultural meaning, permitting reciprocal relations – a kind of sociability – among participants in consumption' (De Vries, 2008, p. 45). De Vries addresses the early modern European context; but his analysis can also be applied to the case of cotton in Japan.

In the Japanese case, Ikegami argues for the importance of *iki*, a vibrant urban aesthetic that knitted together new social networks. Its adherents expressed this sensibility through apparel with a subtle tonal palate and occasional splashes of colour. The spirit of *iki* flourished in commercial centres, and the city of Edo was one of the largest cities in the world at this time, one of many metropolitan venues in Japan. *Iki*-inspired kimono assumed a growing importance for a widening social cohort, and Ikegami notes that the 'most creative and robust cultural innovations in Tokugawa fashion came largely from the "rule-breakers"' (Ikegami, 2005, p. 250). The spirit of *iki* swept city neighbourhoods and was expressed through plays, prints and dress in 'subtle and subversive ways' according to Jay Keister. He writes of the 'two sides of *iki* – refinement and resistance', conveyed in fashionable forms (Keister, 2009, p. 216).

Cotton textiles enabled a wider participation in this cultural performance, with profound economic and cultural consequences. Indian fabrics stimulated both new production and new consumer practices in Japan, in ways unique to that region. As Kayoko Fujita states, 'from the mid-sixteenth century, trade shaped "traditional" Japanese material culture' (Fujita, 2009, p. 181). Thus, as *iki*-inspired kimono grew in popularity, allegiances to what Ikegami calls 'aesthetic networks' were manifested in cotton garments and accessories of various sorts. Officially, cotton was approved for many ranks, although embroidery and 'unusual weaving and dyeing' were not (Shively, 1964, pp. 126–30). But a subtly subversive defiance, involving discrete counterpoints of stripes, checks and accents of floral patterns on kimono and their accoutrements, might escape notice (See Figure 13.1) More vibrant prints were forbidden common people, but were employed by them nonetheless in wallets, purses and the like (Fujita, 2009, pp. 194–95). These styles were captured in the many woodblock prints produced in this period featuring city scenes, as well as images of actors, courtesans, sumo wrestlers and other common city folk. (See Figure

Figure 13.1 Tokugawa-period traders wearing *iki*-inspired kimono

The spirit of *iki* flourished in commercial centres in Edo Japan. *Iki*-inspired kimono assumed a growing importance for a widening social cohort; both the men and woman reflect this style in their choice of apparel.

'Traders'. Woodblock colour print by Utagawa Toyokuni. Image taken from Yakusha Sangaikyo ('Amusements for Actors On The Third Floor'). Originally published in Edo, 1801. (c) All Rights Reserved. The British Library Board. License Number: UNIALB07.

13.2) It is intriguing to note the proliferation of printed books in Japan in this period, many portraying the styles of *iki* 'with detailed illustrations of how to look, dress, and act for both men and women' (Keister, 2009, p. 221).

These depictions further energised the fashion ethos tied to Indian fabrics, stimulating local production and consumption. Japan embraced the production of cotton cloth, much of it imitating Indian varieties and carrying Indianised names. As Ikegami writes, this 'allowed ordinary Japanese to enjoy wearing attractively colored kimono for the first time in the country's history' (Ikegami, 2005, p. 253). She further concludes that the 'increase in the supply of inexpensive but warm cotton fabric revolutionized the daily clothing of ordinary people and laid the social foundation of Tokugawa fashion.... The material and economic basis of popular kimono fashions as such was made possible only by the increase in domestic cotton production' (Ikegami, 2005, p. 253). The colours and fashionable patterns popular in Tokugawa Japan took somewhat different material forms to those preferred in Western

Figure 13.2 The sumo wrestler Musashino Monta wearing a fashionable kimono
This sumo wrestler's involvement in fashion is reflected in his kimono and accessories.
'The Sumo Wrestler Musashino Monta'. Utagawa Toyokuni, 1848–1854. FP 2 – JPD, no. 654. Library of Congress Prints and Photographs Division, Washington, D.C.

Europe at this time, although not entirely so. In both regions of the world communities of women and men negotiated their social positions through the purchases and disposition of goods, as opportunity and family budget allowed. More and more individuals strove to secure larger quantities of fashion-laden commodities. These 'New Luxuries' reshaped their public and private figures in keeping with practical and aspirational objectives.

Cotton was likewise the quintessential consumer textile in Europe, enabling a widening of popular fashion in ways quite comparable to those in Japan (Lemire, 1991a; 2006; 2011). However, in most of Europe legal constraints instituted around 1700 quashed the sales of Indian cottons. These enactments were framed outside the structure of sumptuary legislation, often for protectionist reasons. In this regard, as in others, Japan and Europe sometimes responded differently to the challenges of rising popular consumption, even as their citizens' wardrobes grew over this period.[12] In both Europe and Japan, however, sumptuary laws appear symptomatic of the expanding appetites for key commodities, linked to evolving fashionable practices of many sorts. Urban commercial locales provided the stage and the goods for expressions of this sort (see Figure 13.2).

Japan's interpretations of consumer processes offer important evidence of this region's history of material change. Antonia Finnane illustrates the ways in which articulations of nation, region and gender are manifest through the fashioning of dress in China (Finnane, 2008). The history of kimono stimulates a similarly broad research agenda. In the context of this volume, the question of the kimono and home-sewing raises issues I will pursue briefly. The physical profile of the Japanese kimono is visibly different from that of dress in the early-modern West. Nonetheless, although it shows Japanese features and sensibility, there were also elements in common with Western Europe. For example, in the early-modern era Western women's gowns, like kimono, were routinely unmade and remade – the value of the garment lay in the textile, not the stitchery. Textiles represented a vital element of domestic and personal investment in both cultures.[13] Indeed, one of the markers of rising consumer demand was the growth in the quantity and range of textiles acquired. In Japan and in Europe the variety of textiles changed dramatically from the 1600s onward, as Indian cottons transformed the marketplace and inspired imitations by local manufacturers. Facsimiles of Indian textiles likewise became an important new element of Japanese manufacture in the Edo period, with cheaper striped and checked fabrics, locally made, dominating kimono fashions (Fujita, 2009, pp. 189–91). Similar instances of manufacturing innovation took place throughout Europe, also based on Indian examples. The diffusion of cotton textiles from India and the imitation of these fabrics by local manufacturers stimulated economies and societies across the globe and this pattern of development is one followed on both sides of the Eurasian continent.

Another suggestive feature of rising consumer demand can be observed in the patterns of use, reuse and manipulation of clothing textiles. Francks' work, as well as that of Kayoko Fujita and others, points clearly in this direction. Fabric reuse is commonplace in many societies,

12 Daniel Roche (1989, pp. 118–50) charts the rising ownership of Indian cottons as part of the spread in popular fashions through eighteenth-century France.

13 Prasannan Parthasarathi notes that 'for centuries, cloth was the most important manufactured item in world trade' (Parthassarathi, 1998, p. 107).

and textiles represent an investment that can be enhanced through the creative remaking of garments or by the resale of used material in markets for second-hand wares. The circulation of second-hand textiles provided additional choice to a wide range of customers, augmenting the complexity of the market in important ways. Further research into the second-hand circulation of textiles in Japan would be of great value in revealing the features of popular consumption and the ways in which it was sustained or constrained. Extensive research in many parts of the world, for many periods, has shown how pivotal the second-hand trade was in facilitating demotic consumerism among a wide range of men and women of various social classes and ethnicities (for example Lemire, 1988; Lemire, 1991b; Allerston, 1999; Hansen, 2000; Fontaine, 2008).

The physical characteristics of the kimono, the routine stitching and re-stitching of the garment over the lifetime of the fabric, and the continued wearing of kimono through the twentieth century represent a unique confluence of factors that may also have shaped twentieth-century Japanese production and consumption patterns. The reuse of clothing textiles took place in all textile societies, but the manner of use and reuse could vary significantly across different time periods and could be a distinctive marker of an era. I am left to wonder at the singular pattern of home-sewing that developed in twentieth-century Japan, as also at the degree to which long-standing patterns of Japanese clothing culture and textile use shaped the modern development of domestic manufacturing. As Andrew Gordon suggests, Japan is surely unique in its modern interpretation of domestic needlework, and in the routes taken to this modern sewing culture. Women's domestic work or quasi-market work had traditionally involved the routine manipulation of textiles, including the cyclical sewing and re-sewing of kimono. It seems to me a small step to the adaptation of these embedded economic and cultural traditions into the home-based sewing of Western forms of dress in the mid-twentieth century. This example is one of many instances that illustrate the remodelling of traditional skills or traditional knowledge to fit evolving Japanese priorities.

Tradition and modernity in Japan thus took on different forms from the seemingly normative models of Europe. Japanese innovations assumed a variety of characteristics as the demands of the market were reconceived through Japanese practice. Maki Umemura presents another example of the ways in which tradition and modernity were navigated in her study of traditional medicine in Japan. This and other chapters in this volume emphasise the fact that there is not one route to the development of a consumer society, no more than there is a singular authentic path to industrial development. Kaoru Sugihara emphasises the multiple paths to industrialisation, including the 'labour-intensive' route arising from the unique characteristics of Asian societies (Sugihara, 2003; 2007). In the chapters collected in this volume, we see evidence of the Japanese path to consumerism and the unique histories that arise from that process. Topics such as kimono, sewing, traditional medicine, retailing and sugar consumption, for example, illustrate the distinctive Japanese features of consumption, shaped in large part by local 'ecosystems of knowledge'.[14]

Conclusion

The importance of comparative history is increasingly recognised among historians of Europe; more have taken to heart Peter Burke's injunction and looked to Asia to discover what is uniquely European or what may be a shared experience among many regions, albeit with subtle differences in timing and materiality. Ulinka Rublack, for instance, approaches her study of Renaissance Europe and its cultural identity with a close attention to the cultures of dress in other societies of that same era. She finds a common ethos between Renaissance Europe and Tokugawa Japan and takes the Japanese experience as her exemplar, noting the aesthetic inspiration found among its urban populations, wherein 'the importance of beauty in their personal attire [was] ... a necessity of life' (Rublack 2010, p. 4, quoting Ikegami, 2005, p. 285). This, too, could equally be found in the West. The generative power of comparative history is revising the agenda for historical research.

Issues remain to be resolved, including that of a clear comparative framework for the periodisation of consumerism, as material life was gradually transformed across societies. What is apparent is that consumerism was not 'imported' into Asia from an external birthplace, but emerged over the seventeenth and later centuries as an organic expression of regional forces. Asia did not depend on interventions from the West for the regional genesis of this phenomenon, even though later, in the modern era, Western industry exerted forces that affected expressions of consumerism in various ways. It remains to be seen how a closer study of consumer practice in Japan will inform wider histories in the years to come. The tasks yet to be accomplished include tying together features of consumerism within Japanese history and knitting

[14] A term used (and perhaps coined) by my colleague Michael Polushin.

these findings into broader historical narratives. Japan has a central place in the history of Asia and also stands in a unique position with respect to Asian/Western interactions. There is great scope to consider Japan's consumer influences more widely and to recognise as well the reciprocal effects of Japanese material culture within the wider world.

References

Allerston, P. (1999) 'Reconstructing the Second-hand Clothes Trade in Sixteenth and Seventeenth-century Venice', *Costume* 33, pp. 46–56.

Allman, J. (ed.) (2004) *Fashioning Africa: Power and the Politics of Dress*, Bloomington, Indiana: Indiana University Press.

Baines, E. (1835), *History of the Cotton Trade in Great Britain*, London: H. Fisher, R. Fisher, and P. Jackson.

Bauland, M., Schuurman, A. J. & Servais, P. (eds) (1988) *Inventaires Après-Decès et Ventes de Meubles: Apports à une Histoire de la Vie Economique et Quotidienne (XIVe–XIXe siècle)*, Louvain-la Veuve: Academia.

Belfanti, C. M. (2008) 'Was Fashion a European Invention?' *Journal of Global History* 3, pp. 419–43.

Berg, M. (2005) *Luxury and Pleasure in Eighteenth-Century Britain*, Oxford: Oxford University Press.

Braudel, F. (trans. Reynolds, S.) (1985) *Civilization & Capitalism 15th–18th Century: The Structure of Everyday Life*, New York: Harper & Row.

Breen, T. H. (1986), 'An Empire of Goods: the Anglicization of Colonial America, 1690–1776', *Journal of British Studies* 25, pp. 467–99.

Breen, T. H. (2004) *The Marketplace of Revolution: How Consumer Politics Shaped American Independence*, New York: Oxford University Press.

Brekke, L. (2006) 'To Make a Figure: Clothing and Gender Politics in Early National America', in Vickery, A & Styles, J. (eds) *Gender, Taste, and Material Culture in Britain and North America, 1700–1850*, New Haven, CT: Yale University Press.

Brewer, J. & Porter, R. (1993) *Consumption and the World of Goods*, London: Routledge.

Burke, P. (1993) 'Res et verba: Conspicuous Consumption in the Early Modern World', in Brewer, J. & Porter, R. (eds) *Consumption and the World of Goods*, London: Routledge.

Carr, L. G. & Walsh, L. S. (1994) 'Changing Lifestyles and Consumer Behavior in the Colonial Chesapeake', in Carson, C., Hoffman, R. & Albert, P. J. (eds) *Of Consuming Interests: the Style of Life in the Eighteenth Century*, Charlottesville: University Press of Virginia.

Carson, C., Hoffman, R. & Albert, P. J. (eds) (1994) *Of Consuming Interests: The Style of Life in the Eighteenth Century*, Charlottesville: University Press of Virginia.

Dalrymple, W. (2005) 'Foreword: The Porous Frontiers of Islam and Christendom: A Clash or Fusion of Civilizations?' in MacLean, G. (ed.) *Re-Orienting the Renaissance: Cultural Exchanges with the East*, Basingstoke and New York: Palgrave Macmillan.

Dejean, J. (2005) *The Essence of Style: How the French Invented High Fashion, Fine Food, Chic Cafés, Style, Sophistication, and Glamour*, New York: Simon & Schuster.

de Vries, J. (1993) 'Between Purchasing Power and the World of Goods: Understanding the Household Economy in Early Modern Europe', in Brewer, J & Porter, R. (eds), *Consumption and the World of Goods*, London: Routledge.
de Vries, J. (2008) *The Industrious Revolution: Consumer Behaviour and the Household Economy, 1650 to the Present*, Cambridge: Cambridge University Press.
Dwyer, R. & Pinney, C. (eds) (2001) *Pleasure and the Nation: the History, Politics and Consumption of Public Culture in India*, Oxford: Oxford University Press.
Farnie, D.A. (ed). (2004) *The Fibre that Changed the World: The Cotton Industry in International Perspective, 1600–1990s*, Oxford: Oxford University Press.
Finlay, R. (1998) 'The Pilgrim Art: the Culture of Porcelain in World History', *Journal of World History* 9(2), pp. 141–87.
Finlay, R. (2010) *The Pilgrim Art: Cultures of Porcelain in World History*, Berkeley, CA: University of California Press.
Finnane, A. (1996) 'What Should Chinese Women Wear? A National Problem' *Modern China* 22(2), pp. 99–131.
Finnane, A. (2008) *Changing Clothes in China*, New York: Columbia University Press.
Fontaine, L. (ed.) (2008) *Alternative Exchanges: Second-Hand Circulations from the Sixteenth Century to the Present*, New York & Oxford: Berghahn Books.
Fujita, K. (2009) 'Japan Indianized: The Material Culture of Imported Textiles in Japan, 1550–1850', in Riello, G. & Parthasarathi, P. (eds) *The Spinning World: A Global History of Cotton Textiles, 1200–1850*, Oxford: Oxford University Press.
Goody, J. (1996) *The East in the West*, Cambridge: Cambridge University Press.
Goody, J. (2006) *The Theft of History*, Cambridge: Cambridge University Press.
Hansen, K. T. (2000) *Salaula: The World of Secondhand Clothing and Zambia*, Chicago: University of Chicago Press.
Haynes, D. E., McGowan, A., Roy, T. & Yanagisawa, H. (eds) (2009), *Towards a History of Consumption in South Asia*, Oxford: Oxford University Press.
Hunt, A. (1996) *Governance of the Consuming Passions: A History of Sumptuary Law*, Basingstoke: Macmillan.
Ikegami, E. (2005) *Bonds of Civility: Aesthetic Networks and the Political Origins of Japanese Culture*, Cambridge: Cambridge University Press.
Keister, J. (2009) 'Urban Style, Sexuality, Resistance, and Refinement in the Japanese Dance Sukeroku', *Asian Theatre Journal* 26(2), pp. 215–249.
Lemire, B. (1988) 'Consumerism in Pre-industrial and Early Industrial England: the Trade in Secondhand Clothes', *Journal of British Studies* 27(1), pp. 1–24.
Lemire, B. (1991a) *Fashion's Favourite: The Cotton Trade and the Consumer in Britain, 1660–1800*, Oxford: Oxford University Press.
Lemire, B. (1991b) 'Peddling Fashion: Salesmen, Pawnbrokers, Taylors, Thieves and the Secondhand Clothes Trade in England, c. 1700–1800', *Textile History* 22(1), pp. 67–82.
Lemire, B. (2006) 'Shaping Demand, Making Fashion: Asia, Europe and the Trade in Indian Cottons – A Well-worn Tale Revisited', *Shakai Keizai Shigaku*, 72(3), pp. 41–61.
Lemire, B. (ed.) (2010) *The Force of Fashion in Politics and Society: Global Perspectives from Early Modern to Contemporary Times*, Aldershot: Ashgate.
Lemire, B. (2011) *Cotton: Textiles that Changed the World*, Oxford and New York: Berg Publishers.
Lipovetsky, G. (trans. Porter, C.) (1994) *The Empire of Fashion: Dressing Modern Democracy*, Princeton: Princeton University Press.

Martin, A. S. (2008) *Buying into the World of Goods: Early Consumers in Backcountry Virginia*, Baltimore: Johns Hopkins University Press.
McGowan, A. (2006) 'An All-consuming Subject? Women and Consumption in Late-Nineteenth- and Early-Twentieth-Century Western India', *Journal of Women's History* 18(4), pp. 31–54.
McKendrick, N., Brewer, J. & Plumb, J. H. (1983) *The Birth of a Consumer Society: The Commercialization of Eighteenth-Century England*, London: Hutchinson.
Parthasarathi, P. (1998) 'Rethinking Wages and Competitiveness in the Eighteenth Century: Britain and South India', *Past and Present*, pp. 79–109.
Parthasarathi, P. (2011) *Why Europe Grew Rich and Asia Did Not: Global Economic Divergence, 1600–1850*, Cambridge: Cambridge University Press
Pomeranz, K. (2000) *The Great Divergence: China, Europe and the Making of the Modern World Economy*, Princeton: Princeton University Press.
Riello, G. & Parthasarathi, P. (eds) (2009) *The Spinning World: A Global History of Cotton Textiles, 1200–1850*, Oxford: Oxford University Press.
Roche, D. (1989) *The Culture of Clothing: Dress and Fashion in the Ancien Régime*, Cambridge: Cambridge University Press.
Rublack, U. (2010) *Dressing Up: Cultural Identity in Renaissance Europe*, Oxford: Oxford University Press.
Shammas, C. (1990) *The Pre-Industrial Consumer in England and America*, New York and Oxford: Clarendon Press.
Shively, D. H. (1964–65) 'Sumptuary Regulation and Status in Early Tokugawa Japan', *Harvard Journal of Asiatic Studies* 25, pp. 123–64.
Stearns, P. N. (2001) *Consumerism in World History: The Global Transformation of Desire*, New York: Routledge.
Sugihara, K. (2003) 'The East Asian Path of Development: A Long-Term Perspective', in Arrighi, G., Hamashita, T. & Seldon, M. (eds) *The Resurgence of East Asia: 500, 150 and 50 Year Perspectives*, London: Routledge.
Sugihara, K. (2007) 'The Second Noel Butlin Lecture: Labour-Intensive Industrialisation in Global History', *Australian Economic History Review* 47(2), pp. 121–54.
Thirsk, J. (1978) *Economic Policy and Projects: The Development of a Consumer Society in Early Modern England*, Oxford: Clarendon Press.
Tanimoto, M. (2009) 'Cotton and the Peasant Economy: A Foreign Fibre in Early Modern Japan', in Riello, G. & Parthasarathi, P. (eds) *The Spinning World: A Global History of Cotton Textiles, 1200–1850*, Oxford: Oxford University Press.
Weatherill, L. (1988) *Consumer Behaviour and Material Culture in Britain 1660–1760*, London: Routledge.
Welch, E. (2005) *Shopping in the Renaissance: Consumer Cultures in Italy, 1400–1600*, New Haven, CT: Yale University Press.
Welters, L. & Lillethun, A. (eds) (2007) *The Fashion Reader*, Oxford and New York: Berg Publishers.

Index